Elm-shaded Main Road
Westerly across Winter Street

Some
Annals
of
Nahant
Massachusetts

By
Fred A. Wilson
Trustee of Nahant Public Library

HERITAGE BOOKS
2026

HERITAGE BOOKS
AN IMPRINT OF HERITAGE BOOKS, INC.

Books, CDs, and more—Worldwide

For our listing of thousands of titles see our website at
www.HeritageBooks.com

A Facsimile Reprint
Published 2026 by
HERITAGE BOOKS, INC.
Publishing Division
5810 Ruatan Street
Berwyn Heights, MD 20740

Copyright © 1928 Fred A. Wilson

Originally published: Boston
Old Corner Book Store
1928

Wright & Potter Printing Company
Boston

— Publisher's Notice —
In reprints such as this, it is often not possible to remove blemishes from the original. We feel the contents of this book warrant its reissue despite these blemishes and hope you will agree and read it with pleasure.

International Standard Book Number
Paperbound: 978-0-7884-2663-6

TO

MY WIFE

WITHOUT WHOSE ASSISTANCE

THIS BOOK

OR AUGHT ELSE BY ME

COULD NOT BE

AND TO

THOMAS ROLAND

WITHOUT WHOSE INSISTENCE

THIS BOOK

WOULD NOT BE

PREFACE

As I think over what I have done, or perpetrated, I am disturbed. I could do it better if I had more time, but I realize that one must stop somewhere, if results are to be useful. Even with the background of a generation of interest and familiarity with the matters considered, two years is a short time for such an undertaking, executed in the detail which I have attempted to give, and done in spare time taken from a busy life. Musing on all this, in front of an open fire one evening, watching expensive coal go to blazes, My Far Better Half offers comfort in this wise: "But surely so much work must have been productive and will prove a pleasure." To which I reply that "I have not even succeeded in pleasing myself."

Much ashes of past fires have been raked over. People will wonder why I mention one thing and not another, or why I thought "that" worth mentioning at all. I could be full of apologies, but they may be all summed up in the reminder that the sifting out process would never yield the same results at the hands of different operators. Very definite reasons for some of the material used or omitted are obvious. Where detailed record exists, with promise of permanency, brief reference is sometimes sufficient. Explanation of a troublesome period in the town records is given in one instance, where the bare official record does not tell the story. But above all, remember that time is the scarcest thing on earth, although the most wasted withal.

For the improvement of Nahant's historical record, I am anxious that people should write to me, correcting errors and offering additional material. This will be deposited in the Public Library, so that any future seeker may benefit by it. The moral obliquity, sometimes called by a ruder term, of the inanimate will, by itself, cause some blunders. Doubtless.

PREFACE

My many thanks are due to so many people who have assisted me, and have been interested and helpful, that it would be too long a list to name them all. The "Old Nahanters," to whom I naturally turned most frequently, were eager to help and have been uniformly kind. Very many have loaned pictures, but the extra line to each, to credit the courtesy, would take from the size of the illustration, and so is not given. Pictures of town officers are of those in office for eighteen or twenty years or more. There is also a long list of people who, by their financial assistance, made this publication possible. This was also a manifestation of a desire to see for Nahant a much-needed account of things historical and interesting. And so in one way or another very many folks have had a share in making this book a reality. The author may therefore only claim to be the correlator, the focal point, the slaving dissector and analyzer.

And then M. F. B. H. says: "To be wholly satisfied would end progress. If every one were suited with things as they are, nothing further would be done." This sounds specious, but may be partly true. The closing lines of a great novel, "Trilby," say we may as well leave off hankering after the moon. The final couplets are illuminating and soothing:

> A little work, a little play,
> To keep us going — and so, good day!
>
> A little warmth, a little light,
> Of love's bestowing — and so, good night!

I am now, like Lady Godiva, drawing near my close, and will only add further that these "Annals" are not called history, biography, memoirs, genealogy, or any such thing. They might be called a sort of travelogue, — a record of my impressions as I have travelled along for twenty-five or thirty years on either side of one of the century marks shown on things called calendars, with verifications and reminders numerously given by others, as said earlier.

FRED A. WILSON.

NAHANT, MASSACHUSETTS, March 1, 1928.

CONTENTS

	PAGE
CHAPTER I. THE EXODUS	3

Early visits and explorers; the Plymouth Colony; the Puritans; the Salem settlement.

CHAPTER II. THE INDIANS 11
The Indians around Boston and Lynn; Sagamore Hill; the name "Nahant;" old legend.

CHAPTER III. THE FIRST OF LYNN 20
Early settlers; William Wood; first settlers on Nahant; naming of Lynn; common land; planting lots on Nahant; division in 1706; ranges and old roads; Calf Spring; Lewis and Hammond map.

CHAPTER IV. EARLY NAHANT 35
Nahant titles; Hugh Alley; James Mills; the Breeds; Whitney's Hotel; the Hoods; the Johnsons.

CHAPTER V. EARLY EIGHTEEN HUNDREDS 50
"Old Castle;" the Johnsons; Thomas H. Perkins; Dr. E. H. Robbins; William Wood; Cornelius Coolidge; Frederic Tudor.

CHAPTER VI. HOTELS 72
Growth of town as a resort; various hotels; the great Nahant Hotel; Professor Agassiz's lecture; geological account.

CHAPTER VII. PROCESSION OF EVENTS 92
Comparisons with happenings elsewhere; the Revolution; smallpox; old customs; religion; "Shannon" and "Chesapeake;" horse racing; the boom of the 30's; the Johnsons; forty-niners; Civil War; Home Guards; veterans.

CHAPTER VIII. SUMMER RESIDENTS AND BOATING . . 106
Summer residents; the beginning of yachting around Boston; the first regatta around Boston; B. C. Clark; the "Alice" and her Atlantic crossing; small boat sailing and racing.

CHAPTER IX. INDUSTRIES 123
Present industries; list of houses with dates of construction; old village store; post office; postmasters; new Town Hall; fishing; winter lobstering; Johnson's "History of Nahant;" shoemaking; the residential town.

CONTENTS

CHAPTER X. MOSTLY NAUTICAL 140
Wrecks; storms; Long Beach and its road; steamboat service; early article on steam transportation.

CHAPTER XI. THE SEA SERPENT 160
Early mention; reports and letters; excitement in Boston.

CHAPTER XII. PUBLIC LIBRARY 168
Early public libraries; free public library; trustees; library rooms and buildings; Nahantiana.

CHAPTER XIII. THE MAOLIS GARDENS 180
An early amusement park; North Spring; Maolis Spring; the Witch House.

CHAPTER XIV. NATURE AND MAN 189
Description of beaches and general contour of Nahant; ownership of beaches; wharves.

CHAPTER XV. CHURCHES 213
Early ministers; the Nahant Church; the Independent Methodist Society; the St. Thomas Roman Catholic Church; the Irish; the Italians; the cemetery.

CHAPTER XVI. TRANSPORTATION 226
Early ways; barges; railroads, steam, horse and electric; the electric road; Johnson's Express.

CHAPTER XVII. SCHOOLS 240
The old schools; story of new buildings; list of teachers; exhibitions; lecture courses; expenditures; medals and prizes.

CHAPTER XVIII. THE NEW TOWN 254
Charter; first town meetings; first town officers; inhabitants in 1847; early expenses.

CHAPTER XIX. NAHANT OF THE FIFTIES 270
Description of conditions; summer residents; famous residents; Miss Cary's letter.

CHAPTER XX. TOWN DEPARTMENTS 292
Fire department; police department; local court; street lamps; electric lights and gas; highway department; forester's department; account of a fire.

CHAPTER XXI. THE SEVENTIES AND EIGHTIES . . . 306
Municipal methods and faults; the Wilsons; sundry items; streets and names in 1886; typhoid epidemic; sewer and water systems; the Cadets' encampment; first lawn tennis in America.

CONTENTS

	PAGE
CHAPTER XXII. BASS POINT	325

Early days; hotels; amusement district; the fire of 1925; government property; the trend of the town.

CHAPTER XXIII. THE NINETIES AND LATER 337
  Changing political conditions; municipal changes; fiftieth anniversary celebration.

CHAPTER XXIV. ORGANIZATIONS 350
  Brief account of clubs and other organizations on Nahant; first air-plane landing on Nahant.

CHAPTER XXV. LATER YEARS 365
  President Roosevelt's visit; sundry happenings; the Spanish American War; the World War.

CHAPTER XXVI. TAXATION, VALUATION AND EXPENDITURES 380
  Valuations; appraisals; problems of assessors; expenditures; comparisons with other towns; efficiency.

LIST OF TOWN OFFICERS 395

INDEX 405

LIST OF ILLUSTRATIONS

Title Page Vignette by Lucy H. Doane

Elm-shaded Main Road	*Frontispiece*

FACING PAGE

Poquanum selling Nahant	8
The Steamboat "Eagle"	8
Old Johnson Homestead	16
Joseph Johnson House	16
The "Nahant Hotel"	24
The "Nahant Hotel"	24
Ruins of "Nahant Hotel"	32
Farthest East	32
William Wood	40
Frederic Tudor	40
Alfred D. Johnson	40
Washington H. Johnson	40
Home of Frederic Tudor	48
The "Old Castle"	48
The "Witch House"	56
The "Maolis House" and "Witch House"	56
Bass Beach and the Mifflin House	64
The Mifflin House	64
The "Log Cabin"	72
The Steamer "Ulysses"	72
Hon. Henry Cabot Lodge	80
Joseph T. Wilson	80
Edmund B. Johnson	80
Walter Johnson	80
The Longfellow House	88
The Fremont Cottage	88
Tudor Peach Orchard	96
The Half Way Tree	96
Nahant Road from Summer Street	104
Nahant Road from Ocean Street	104
Old Stone Schoolhouse	112
Grammar Schoolhouse	112

LIST OF ILLUSTRATIONS

	FACING PAGE
Caleb Johnson	120
Joseph Johnson	120
Luther S. Johnson	120
C. Hervey Johnson	120
Old Village Store	128
Pleasant Street Schoolhouse	128
Old Railroad Station at Lynn	136
Ellingwood Chapel	136
Spouting Horn Cottage	144
Willow Road	144
Joseph's Beach	152
Nahant Road	152
Professor Louis Agassiz	160
Henry Wadsworth Longfellow	160
William Hickling Prescott	160
John Lothrop Motley	160
Entrance to Maolis Gardens	168
Barge at Lynn Station	168
Latest Type of Barge	176
Winter Barge	176
Nahant Road toward Whitney's	184
The Old North Spring	184
The Sea Serpent	192
The Old Wharf	192
John Q. Hammond	200
Welcome W. Johnson	200
William F. Waters	200
Fred A. Wilson	200
Tudor's "Ice King"	208
The "Nellie Baker"	208
The "Alice" in mid-ocean	216
Tudor's "Stone Barn" and "Brick House"	216
Lynn in 1838: Map	224
Nahant in 1855: Map	224
The Stone Lion	232
Tudor's High Orchard Fence	232
Thomas Handasyd Perkins	240
Amos A. Lawrence	240
James H. Beal	240
Frank Merriam	240

LIST OF ILLUSTRATIONS

	FACING PAGE
Amusement Park on Long Beach	248
Eastern Part of Nahant, 1856: Map	248
Joseph T. Wilson and Senator Lodge	256
George Abbot James and Joseph T. Wilson	256
The "Relay House"	264
The "Trimountain House"	264
Cartoon from "The Boston Post"	272
Dorothy's Cove	272
Hon. Curtis Guild	280
J. Colby Wilson	280
Albert G. Wilson	280
Charles W. Stacy	280
The Fire Engine "Eagle"	288
The Fire Engine "Dexter No. 1"	288
Site of Valley Road Schoolhouse	296
Ellerton James and Senator Lodge	296
Home of Senator Lodge	304
Town Meeting Cartoon, 1917	304
B. Frank Taylor and Captain William H. Kemp	312
President Roosevelt	312
Harry C. Wilson	320
Thomas Roland	320
Charles Cabot Johnson	320
Otis A. Johnson	320
The Old Town Hall	328
Town Meeting in the Old Town Hall	328
The Town Hall	336
The Public Library Building	336
The Nahant Church	344
The Village Church and the Catholic Church	344
Family of Caleb Johnson: Chart	352
Family of Joseph Johnson: Chart	360
Edward J. Johnson	368
Albert Whitney	368
A Piper Drawing of Trees	368
Town Expenditures: Chart	384

Some
ANNALS *of* NAHANT

TRANSLATION

By George Cabot Lodge

Sirmio, gem of Isles and of rock-bound peninsulas
Which on the clear lagoons or the infinite seas are
Borne up by Neptune — O with what longing and gladness
I, seeming scarce from the Thynian and the Bithynian
Meadows departed, stand here once more and behold thee!
Yea; when the mind from burdens reposes and, when the
Labors of travel ended, we come to our hearthstone
And on our bed so longed for we sink into slumber.
Here is the goal and gain for the labors accomplished!
Hail to thee, fruitful Sirmio, mayst thou rejoice, and
Also ye waves of the Libyan lake, be ye joyful;
Laugh, laugh loud, with whatever the house holds of laughter!

SOME ANNALS OF NAHANT

CHAPTER I

THE EXODUS

CENTURIES of history may be searched in tracing the beginnings of a place, the trend of events which culminated around it, and the political, social, industrial or religious movements which may have played a part in its establishment. John Fiske, in his "Beginnings of New England," tells in some detail, and delightfully, as always, of the early settlements and the motives behind them. Other sources of similar information are easily available, but the beginnings around Boston are too interesting to be passed with only references to other books or people, and they may well have a little space in any account of Nahant.

Soon after 1600 the colonization of the North American coast had become part of the avowed policy of the British Government. In 1606 a great joint stock company was formed, with two branches, for the establishment of two colonies in America. The branch which was to set up a southern colony had its headquarters in London, and that intrusted to place a colony farther north had headquarters at Plymouth. The two branches were thus naturally commonly known as the London and Plymouth Companies. The London Company had jurisdiction from 34 to 37 north latitude, and the Plymouth Company from 41 to 45 north latitude. The intermediate space, from 38 to 41, was, in effect, held up as a prize, to go to the company first planting a self-supporting colony. This area comprises about what is now from Washington up to New York. As a result of this organized effort came the settlement at Jamestown, Virginia, in 1607.

Before this time vessels had sailed our coasts, coming for fish, and probably hoping to discover other things of value to England's markets. In 1602 Bartholomew Gosnold landed on Cape Cod and named it for the abundance of fish thereabouts. This was the first English name given to any spot in this part of America. This expedition also named Marthas Vineyard and some other places, and built huts at Cuttyhunk, intending to stay awhile, but gave up and went back to England. Gosnold's story interested others, and in 1605 came George Weymouth, who found Cape Cod, and coasted as far north as the Kennebec River. He kidnapped five Indians and carried them back to England, and his stories probably had some influence in the formation of the great colonizing company, with its two branches, in the following year.

The leading spirit of the Plymouth Company was Sir John Popham, chief justice of England, and he made haste that the London Company should not get a colony established first. Within three months after the settlement at Jamestown, a party of one hundred and twenty, led by the judge's kinsman, George Popham, landed at the mouth of the Kennebec and built a village of fifty cabins, with storehouse, chapel and blockhouse. This was soon abandoned, and the failure spread the opinion that what we know as New England was uninhabitable because of the cold. No further attempts were made upon the coast until in 1614 it was visited by Captain John Smith, on an exploring voyage from the Virginia Colony at Jamestown. Of the region around Boston he told enthusiastically, calling it "the Paradise of all these parts, for here are many isles all planted with corn, groves, mulberries, salvage gardens, and good harbors." The Indians, who lived on all the most desirable spots, he calls a "goodly, strong and well proportioned people." He says they are kind but valiant. Smith explored the coast minutely from Cape Cod to the Penobscot River, and renamed it New England. He made a map, and introduced more English names; and Cape Ann, Cape Elizabeth, Charles River and Plymouth remain as Smith named them. In 1615 he came again, intending to set a colony for the Plymouth Company, but was captured by a French fleet and carried about on a long cruise. Although under forty, he voyaged little, if any, after this experience. He remained in England, stimulating interest in the New World; but as for the Plymouth Company, he had concluded that no other motive than riches would "ever erect there a commonwealth or draw a company from their ease and humours at home, to stay in New England."

Captain Smith was mistaken in this opinion. Of all migrations and settlements that in New England is pre-eminently the one in which the almighty dollar played the smallest part. By 1617 the Pilgrim Society at Leyden had decided to send vigorous members to found a Puritan state in America. The site was much discussed, and from Guiana north was considered. A tropical climate was finally discarded, partly because too near the Spaniards and Buccaneers around the Caribbean Sea. About half a century earlier a band of Huguenots were massacred in Florida. New England was considered too cold. In 1618 one Blackstone, a church elder at Amsterdam, arranged with the London Company to send a group to Virginia. About one hundred and eighty set sail, and the return of the vessel in 1619 reported the arrival of only fifty in Chesapeake Bay. Nothing daunted, these Puritans bargained with the London Company, and the King made no objection to these people going farther off than Leyden, for how could a handful of Puritans in America, so far away, pester him? Perhaps the farther they went the better he was suited.

Late in July, 1620, the "Speedwell" left Delft Haven and joined the "Mayflower" at Southampton. Soon the "Speedwell" proved unseaworthy, and the two vessels returned. A few voyagers were left behind, and the rest, about one hundred in number, crowded into the "Mayflower" which started out on September 6 to cross the Atlantic alone. Bad weather prevented any accurate sea bearings, and when land was sighted on November 9 it was Cape Cod of the Plymouth Company, and not any part of the London Company's domains. Without authority to settle there, they turned south, but were obliged to seek shelter in Cape Cod Bay. On November 11 they decided to find a place of abode in the vicinity, anticipating no trouble in getting a grant from the Plymouth Company, which was still anxious to obtain settlers. Probably it was only a coincidence that the place they chose had already been named Plymouth by Captain John Smith. When their first long winter ended, fifty-one had died, forty-nine were surviving. Thanksgiving Day was appointed, town meetings were held, and a few laws were passed. New England had begun.

After a year another ship arrived, the "Fortune," bringing fifty more settlers, but without much food, the burden of another winter was not lifted by her coming. She returned laden with beaver skins and choice wood, but was overhauled by a French cruiser and despoiled of everything worth taking. In 1621 this colony at Plymouth received its charter or grant from the Plymouth Company in England, and by 1624 its successful establishment seems to have become assured. In 1627 the settlers bought up all the stock and arranged to pay what they owed to the Plymouth Company, and by 1633 all debts were settled and they were undisputed owners of land they had occupied in the new country.

It is interesting to note that the hardships of the first few years compelled the colony to adopt autocratic methods of government, to which most people in all ages have reverted in time of stress however far from it they may have progressed under more ordinary conditions of living. The great struggles of our own country, which is a typical example of rule in ordinary times by more or less orderly democratic methods, have all seen one man, or a very small group, rise to almost autocratic powers. A singleness of purpose, needed in emergencies, is thereby achieved, which it would be difficult to get in other ways.

Another interesting factor of life is shown in these first years of the Plymouth Settlement. Undesirable citizens were sent back whence they came, and these undesirables may well have been very worthy people under other conditions. But with food scarce, such a person, even, as a botanist, an artist, or an astronomer was not wanted and was entirely out of place. This illustrates the fact that the fine arts, so important to any people, can only be cultivated after the useful arts have been carried to such an extent that there is a surplus which permits indulgence in those other things which are not primal needs of existence. Today what are called needs are an increasing list, and the surplus allowing a cultivation of the fine arts is more difficult to accumulate. Civilization in the light of modern tendencies has been called nothing but a means for increasing needs. The full dinner pail was a political issue thirty years ago; now it is the brimming gas tank. However involved are the economic and political processes of today, an instructive light may be cast upon them from the two features cited from these experiences of the settlement at Plymouth in the 1620's.

In 1605, when Captain Weymouth sailed into Plymouth Harbor, in England, with five kidnapped Indians and glowing stories, Sir Ferdinando Gorges was commander of this fortified seaport. His interest was excited, and he was energetic in the affairs of the Plymouth Company which was established a year later. It was he who took the leading part in outfitting the two ships of Captain John Smith's unsuccessful expedition in 1615. In following years he continued to send out vessels, chiefly for fishing, and in 1620 obtained new charters for the Plymouth Company, which made it wholly independent of its old rival the London Company. Forty men sat in council as directors, and they were known as the Council for New England. They had a monopoly of trade, could exercise martial law, and could expel intruders. With too little capital they sought to increase it by selling parts of the lands they controlled, and this land extended from about the latitude of Philadelphia to that of Quebec. Thus were the "Mayflower" Pilgrims able to buy their lands outright, and for fifteen years all settlers based claims to the land upon rights granted by the Plymouth Company.

Other settlers now began to come. In 1622 Thomas Weston

sent out a colony to Wessagussett, twenty-five miles north of Plymouth. They had troubles, partly with the Indians, and also because they were mostly rabble, and they were glad to return to England in a year. Then in 1622 came Thomas Morton, agent of Sir Ferdinando Gorges, with thirty followers, to Merrymount, where their methods of life did not please the Plymouth settlers, and Captain Myles Standish stopped them in 1628. In 1625 came Captain Wollaston to the site of what is now Quincy. Soon he carried his group off to Virginia, and Morton took possession of the place in his stead.

By 1628 other settlements were dotted here and there. A few were at Nantasket and more around the Piscataqua River, in what is now York County, Maine, and Portsmouth, or near by, in New Hampshire. Samuel Maverick was living on Noddle's Island, now East Boston, and William Blackstone was on the Shawmut Peninsula, now called Boston.

In 1622 Sir Ferdinando Gorges and John Mason obtained a royal grant to all land between the Kennebec and Merrimac Rivers. Colonizing also followed this. The Dorchester Adventurers, a company of merchants in the shire town of Dorset, had sent vessels after fish for some years prior to 1623, at which time they set up a village as a fishing station on Cape Ann. A squabble soon arose with the Plymouth settlers, who claimed jurisdiction that far north. Roger Conant adjusted the dispute, and was soon chosen manager of the Cape Ann Settlement. Soon the Dorchester Adventurers abandoned their enterprise and left the little colony to shift for itself. Conant found them a better location at Naumkeag, now Salem. Then followed the building up of this colony under John Endicott, while a royal grant gave it all the land from three miles north of the Merrimac to three miles south of the Charles, and from the Atlantic to the Pacific. This latter ocean was then assumed to be a little way beyond Hendrick Hudson's great river. This grant lapped over the Gorges-Mason grant, and there were other complications, so that Endicott was sent over promptly, superseding Conant. After some dispute

Poquanum selling Nahant to Thomas Dexter

From an old lithograph

The "Eagle" ran from Boston to Nahant

First, in 1818

as to authority all was amicable and the place was named Salem, the Hebrew word for peace.

Then came the greatest movement of all, under the corporation bearing the title of the Governor and Company of Massachusetts Bay, which brought John Winthrop to the foremost place among the founders of New England. Before Christmas of 1630 seventeen ships had brought over more than a thousand people. Disputes over grants and authority continued. Endicott attempted to settle Charlestown from Salem, and the Gorges claimed Maverick and Blackstone and others were their tenants because of a special grant to Gorges' son. Perhaps the Gorges interests were too unscrupulous in some of their actions. The actual wave of immigration overwhelmed all these claims, however, as it poured over Charlestown, Boston, Roxbury, Dorchester, Watertown and Cambridge. The Puritans occupied the country. By 1634 over four thousand English had come over, and a score of villages were founded around Massachusetts Bay. Houses, roads, fences and bridges were building and farming was begun. Thousands of cattle grazed in the pastures and swine were plenty. In one year, soon after this, three thousand immigrants came to these villages, which soon pushed out in every direction, forming many new settlements. This Puritan exodus to New England ended about 1640. It was wholly English, the exceptions being too few to affect the general statement. Thereafter, for a century and a half, or until after the Revolutionary War, a population in New England of about twenty-six thousand multiplied and developed in notable seclusion. The settlers were homogeneous in social condition and in blood. They were thrifty and prosperous, industrious and of good behavior. The needy and shiftless, who usually make trouble in new communities, were barred out as far as possible, and were comparatively few. From these twenty-six thousand have come, says Fiske, one-fourth the population of the United States.

In these days of easy travel and large steamships it is hard to visualize the magnitude of the exodus of over twenty thousand people in twenty years from comfortable homes in England to the American wilderness. Not a factor of life was as easy as it is today. Shelter, light, clothing, fuel, transportation and food were mostly very different and far more troublesome. The face of nature, that today seems not dangerous, then had real perils, and winter, wilderness and distance, if they only meant inaccessibility, carried enough of the thrill of adventure to satisfy any one and to daunt the timorous. Far different is it today, when the milk bottle is on every doorstep with the daily punctuality of sunrise, and one can admire every spring the freshly painted billboard landscapes, and live by the side of the road and sell gasolene to the multitude.

CHAPTER II

THE INDIANS

THE many Indian tribes that inhabited North America prior to the coming of the white man were very different in their habits of life. Some were more or less wandering, and some were home-loving, with gardens and other accompaniments of a home life. Some were warlike and some were peace-loving, though life in the wilderness, with neighbors not always pleasant, necessitated readiness for serious conflict on the part of all. The story of the Indians and their lives, and social and political methods, is interesting. Many tribes were developed far beyond the savage barbarian stage, with rites and ceremonies which, while pagan, were dignified and systematic, and showed an adherence to orderly methods, proving a civilization.

Boston and all the best localities anywhere around it were used by the Massachusetts tribe of the Algonquin Indians, who were between the Taratines and Pawtuckets on the north, and the Narragansetts and Pequots on the south and west. It is said they had a population of over a hundred and fifty thousand, and could muster three thousand warriors into the field of combat.

For the two score years before the settlement of Boston, vessels had been sailing the coast, fishing and trading, and they were not always honest. Kidnapping and other mistreatments were too common. While the Massachusetts Indians were not naturally so hostile or warlike as many other tribes, there was reason for whatever dislike or retribution they might have shown or exercised. Here was a population, many times outnumbering the Puritans who were to come, who occupied the best places around Boston Harbor, and who might hardly be expected to give up their holdings without a struggle.

In two years this condition was changed. A plague came and "the country was in a manner left void of inhabitants." What this pestilence was is disputed. Many have called it smallpox, but Englishmen of that time knew smallpox. One in four was pock-marked. Yet Bradford called it an infectious fever, although he recognized and named smallpox when it raged among the Indians in 1733, seventeen years later. This plague began in 1616 and was ended in 1617. In 1621 Governor Winslow, from Plymouth, on an excursion to the interior, says, "thousands of men have lived there, which died in the great plague not long since." William Bradford writes they were not "able to bury one another and their skulls and bones were found in many places laying still above the ground, where their houses and dwellings had been, a very sad spectacle to behold."

> "It was in this way," as that eminent Christian Divine and close student of the precepts of his Master, the Rev. Cotton Mather, charitably observed eighty years later, "the woods were cleared of those pernicious creatures to make room for a better growth."

The citation is from Charles Francis Adams, "Three Episodes in Massachusetts History."

The Indians around Lynn and north of Boston as far as Maine were ruled by Nanapashemet, or the New Moon, one of the greatest Sachems in New England. His summer home was on Sagamore Hill in Lynn, which is the hill nearest Nahant. Nahant Street and Newhall Street go up a part of it, while the highest point lies between the two and east of Sagamore Street. Nanapashemet escaped the great plague of 1616 and 1617, but was killed by the Taratines from the North, in 1619, at Medford, where was his second house, or winter home. Governor Winslow visited it in 1621 and describes the late Sachem's house as a well-fortified place where he had tried to make himself safe against the deadly vengeance of his enemies.

Nanapashemet had three sons, Wonohaquham, Montowampote and Wenepoykin, sometimes called Winnepurkit. The former was Sagamore in the Mystic River region, and was commonly known as Sagamore John. Montowampote was commonly known as Sagamore James. His wife one writer called Nahanta, and another says she was Wenuchus, daughter of Chief Passaconaway. They were married in 1629, when the Sagamore was twenty years old, and lived on Sagamore Hill in Lynn until 1633, when he and his brother, on the Mystic, were victims of the serious smallpox epidemic of that year. Montowampote is said by one writer to have journeyed to London in 1631, armed with a letter from Governor Winthrop chiefly to protest against his defrauding of twenty beaver skins. He was received there with respect, but could not stand the life or the food, and was glad to return to his clams and succotash in Lynn or Medford. Wenepoykin was born in 1616, the youngest son of the great chief Nanapashemet. In 1633, at the death of his brothers, he became Sagamore of Lynn and Chelsea, and after the death of his mother in 1677 he was Sachem of all Massachusetts north and east of the Charles River. He was proprietor of Deer Island, which he sold to Boston. He was called Sagamore George, and sometimes George Rumney Marsh. This chief was taken prisoner in the Wampanoag War in 1676, and died in 1684, after returning from slavery in the Barbadoes to the home of a relative in Natick. His wife was Ahawayet, daughter of Poquanum, who was Sachem of Nahant. The name "Nahant," like many others, appears to have been an old Indian name, and not one given by the white settlers or explorers, although the whites often gave Indian names to places.

There is record of the name Mattahunt, and also of Fullerton Islands. But the name "Nahant" persisted. It is properly pronounced with soft "a" in both syllables, and often spoiled in mispronunciation. Charles A. Hammond, elsewhere mentioned, has had exceptional opportunity for acquaintance with the Indian language of a western tribe, and from this deduces the reasonable theory that the original Indian name was "Na-an." The Indian fondness for the soft "a" and the Indian simplicity of language are shown in the suggestion of twins offered by the word in this form. It would be assumed that the twins would be Little Nahant and Great Nahant, but this might not be the case. Hammond points out that from the Indian vantage point on or around Sagamore Hill, Little Nahant would be blanketed by Great Nahant, and the twins would be Great Nahant and the Bass Point section, joined by the low-lying marsh land. This theory is interesting and plausible, even though no record neglects the two added consonants now in the name. These might, nevertheless, come from the inaptitude of the English language for soft-spoken syllables, and be a product of English occupation of the territory.

Whittier, in his legend "The Bridal of Pennacook," tells that Winnepurkit, as Sagamore George was often called, wooed and won Weetamoo, the daughter of Passaconaway. It appears, however, to have been his brother Montowampote, Sagamore James, who married a daughter of the famous old chief, but her name was not Weetamoo. As Whittier tells the story Weetamoo was once escorted to her father's place, among the White Hills to the north, by a distinguished group of her husband's warriors. Later, when the visit was over, old Passaconaway sent for Winnepurkit to come and get his wife. The reply was abrupt, to the effect that as he had provided escort one way the father should do like courtesy for the return trip. The old chief refused and there was a deadlock. The story tells that the distracted wife started off alone, and was lost in the rapids she could not master in her canoe. One of the several trails up Chocorua Mountain, the newest one, is named Weetamoo trail. Here appears to be the new woman stepping out and claiming a part of life's glory; but perhaps mere men named it, after all.

Poquanum is called Duke William by William Wood in his "New England's Prospect," and depositions in the Salem court records show that he was also known as Black Will. In 1630 he sold Nahant to Thomas Dexter for a suit of clothes and a plug of tobacco. In 1633 some vessels hunting for pirates found Poquanum on an island in Portland Harbor, and hanged him for the alleged murder of a white man, who, according to all accounts, deserved the killing. But before this Wenepoykin had mortgaged Nahant to a man in Charlestown for twenty pounds or so; and in 1630 a Swampscott farmer claimed to have bought Nahant, Swampscott and Sagamore Hill; this time Black Will sold again.

It may not be said that these transactions, and only a few among many have been cited, show dishonesty by the Indians. They were suddenly brought in contact with new ways, and some mortgage, deed, or court record or other thing meant nothing but confusion to them. The act of Black Will in taking vengeance on a white man does not prove much, either, in days and among people where other forms of law and order were unknown. Black Will may have been something of a rascal, but what has been told does not prove him so, and the Indian's association with the white man seems not yet long enough to acquire the latter's own brands of rascality and double dealing. In any event, Poquanum has been dead a long time and on the strength of the old saying he ought now to be a very good Indian. It may not be said, either, that the Indians were exceptionally ignorant of the values of their lands and livings. Indeed, not so many years later, as Van Loon says in writing of the Treaty of Westminster of 1674, the astute Dutch relinquished their hold upon New Netherlands in exchange for peaceful possession of sugar-raising lands in Guiana. "They swapped New York Harbor for a swamp in South America." Curious things can happen in new lands.

In 1602, when Gosnold visited our shores, he discovered land on Friday, May 14, according to Purchas' "Pilgrim." Sailing along the shore he anchored near a place he called Savage Rock. Bancroft, in his "United States History," and others have assumed this was Nahant. A boat went off to them containing eight Indians, all dressed in skins save one. This one wore a full suit of English clothes, which he could have obtained by trading. Maybe this was Duke William, and that when he traded with Farmer Dexter his suit was worn out and he needed another.

There is earlier mention, perhaps meaning Nahant, than this visit of Gosnold. Various writers, in citing the old records of Thorwald's visit to America, agree that probably Nahant was the place he praised. Returning from Rhode Island in the year 1004, after a two years' sojourn there, he "sailed Eastward and then Northward, past a remarkable headland, enclosing a bay, and which was opposite to another headland. They called this Kiarlarnes, or Keel cape" from resemblance to a ship's keel. This seems to have been Cape Cod. "From thence they sailed along the Eastern Coast of the land to a promontory which projected — probably Nahant — and which was everywhere covered with wood. Here Thorwald went ashore with all his companions. He was so pleased with the place that he exclaimed — 'Here it is beautiful, and here I should like to fix my dwelling.'" There was fighting with the Indians and Thorwald was mortally wounded. He instructed that he should be buried on the headland, "and plant a cross at my head and also at my feet, and call the place Krossanes — The Cape of the Cross — in all time coming." If the Scandinavian records and traditions are correct, the Northmen, as they were called, visited this country repeatedly in the eleventh and twelfth centuries.

The various settlements soon tried to substantiate their claims to their land by getting deeds from the Indians, and this involved many depositions which are now of record. Yet all these dickerings, mortgaging, buying and selling naturally led to great confusion of ownership, much of which will become more evident as the story of Nahant is told. The town of Lynn was repeatedly obliged to defend its proprietorship in Nahant in court actions. Nahant at this time, according to William Wood in his "New England's Prospect," was "well wooded with Oakes, Pines and Cedars. It is, besides, well watered, having, besides the fresh springs, a great pond in the middle, before which is a spacious marsh. In this necke is a store of

Old Johnson Homestead
Gateway nearly opposite Town Hall entrance

Home of Joseph Johnson
Formerly on Nahant Road

THE INDIANS 17

good ground, fit for the plow; but for the present it is only used to put young cattle in, and weather goats, and swine, to secure them from the woolves; a few posts and rayles, from low water marks to the shore, keeps out the woolves and keepes in the cattle. One Black William, an Indian Duke, out of his generosity, gave the place in general to this plantation of Saugus, so that no other can appropriate it to himself."

The first white settlers in Lynn appear to have ensconced themselves in what is still recognized as Woodend, named for the Wood family, one of whom was this William Wood. Another "end" was Breed's End, down near what is now Breed Square, and there was Graves End. It is interesting to note the white settlement somewhere around the vicinity where today's Union and Chestnut Streets meet, while not very far away, on Sagamore Hill, around Sagamore, Nahant and Sachem Streets, was the Indian settlement. This sort of mostly peaceable infiltration occurred all around the Boston Harbor vicinity. Apparently the Indians, never so hostile as some Indian tribes, were terribly disheartened by their losses in the great pestilence of a dozen years earlier, and by their war with the Taratines. Nanapashemet was chief of a great tribe. His sons were chiefs of small groups, broken in spirit. Furthermore, they may have welcomed probable aid in beating off their fiercer war-loving enemies. A common enemy is a good uniter. In any event, the two sorts of settlements appear to have lived together, and to have done business together, in far greater harmony than the history of other places meeting other Indian tribes can show. What would have become of the Plymouth settlement of a half hundred or so people, in 1621, if the Indians had been numerous, strong, alert and jealous of encroachments?

The Indians also had a superstitious dread of the white man, and some of them believed the strangers held the demon of the plague at their disposal, and had let him loose upon the red man in those dreadful disease years. This kept the tomahawks quiet for a while. They cursed the settlement at

Plymouth, but did nothing else, although the Narragansett tribe tried conclusions once by sending in a bundle of arrows wrapped in a snake skin, with the reply that most histories tell about. The location at Plymouth seems to have been a fortunate accident. It was for a time the safest from attack. Further south were the Pequots and the Susquehannocks, who were more powerful and more ferocious.

The incident of the purchase of Nahant by Thomas Dexter of Chief Poquanum, or Black Will, is commemorated on the town seal of Nahant. This, according to the town records, was designed by the selectmen and accepted at the annual town meeting on March 13, 1875. The selection of a subject never seemed fortunate, for Dexter's title to Nahant was successfully contested by the town of Lynn, because Poquanum, in his ignorance, had obtained money several times by mortgaging or selling Nahant. It is said that he gave the place to Lynn in the outset. Yet as a curious and rather spectacular happening it will serve as a point of interest. Town seals are rarely designed by great artists.

There is an Indian legend of Swallows Cave, on Nahant, which is told in print, for example, in the "Manuscript" for November and December, 1827. This little magazine does not seem to have qualities which would endear it to modern readers, and the story takes the length of a short magazine article to tell a simple, brief tale. A party of Narragansett Indians on the war path were driven out of the village of Lynn in King Philip's War, and fled over the beach to Nahant, taking refuge in what is now called Swallows Cave. The writer uses this name, but says it should be called Indians Cave. A witch woman in Salem, called "Wonderful," told the settlers where these Indians could be found, and when an attack was about to begin this same woman appeared and drew the white defenders of their homes off with dire forebodings and tales of trouble. She persuaded them to treat with the Indians and make peace. The effort was successful because the Indians had unwittingly fled to a small peninsula, a sort of cul-de-sac, from which there was no escape. The entire band of red men agreed to return to their own tribal homes and fight the white men no more, and they were allowed to depart in peace. Apparently the story can be classed with many another, and carefully labelled interesting, if true. In so far as age is a merit, the tale was in print over a hundred years ago.

CHAPTER III

THE FIRST OF LYNN

LYNN was an early Massachusetts settlement. It originally included Saugus, Lynnfield, Reading, Swampscott and Nahant, and was known as Sawgus, or Sawgust, until 1637. A 1647 Almanac gives a list of towns with dates, and says that Lynn began in 1629. The first white men known to have been inhabitants of Lynn were brothers, Edmund and Francis Ingalls. A family record says the former came from Lincolnshire in England to Lynn in 1629. Another account says they came to Salem in 1628 and moved over to "Sawgust" the next year. Edmund was a farmer and settled on what is now Fayette Street near Goldfish Pond. He was drowned, says Lewis in his "History of Lynn," in 1648, by falling with his horse through the Saugus River bridge on Boston Street. He had nine children, six of whom were born in England. They and their mother recovered damages from the General Court, "there being a court order that any person soe dyeing through such insufficiency of any bridge in the Country" should be paid compensation. Here, almost at once after the establishment of a government, is a form of public liability set up.

Francis Ingalls lived at Swampscott and was a tanner with the first tannery in New England, on Humphries Brook. Then came William Dixey, who was an employee of Isaac Johnson, and who says in a deposition of July 1, 1657, that he and others "met with Sagamore James and some other Indians who did give me and the rest leave to dwell there or thereabouts, whereupon I and the rest of my master's company did cutt grass for our cattell and kept them upon Nahant for some space of time; for the Indian James Sagamore and the rest did give me and the rest, in behalf of my master Johnson, what land we would; whereupon we sett down in Sawgust and had quiet possession of it by the aforesaid Indians, and kept our cattell in Nahant the summer following." Lewis enters his coming under date of 1629, from which 1630 is perhaps the first year cattle were kept on Nahant. Dixey later moved to Salem.

William Wood came to Lynn in 1629 and lived there about four years during which he wrote "New England's Prospect." He went to London, where his book was published in 1634. He says he wrote "because there hath been many scandalous and false reports passed upon the Country, even from the sulphurous breath of every base ballad monger."

The year 1630, when John Winthrop, the first Governor of Massachusetts, came to Boston, saw many people added to Lynn. Among them was Allen Breed, the ancestor of the family still well represented in the city, and with descendants on Nahant mentioned elsewhere. The Allen Breed Chest is an antique of the Essex Institute in Salem. Thomas Dexter was another early comer, of whom more must be said because of his connection with Nahant.

Dexter owned eight hundred acres of land on Saugus River. He was known as Farmer Dexter, and he seems to have prospered, although his claims to the whole of Nahant were overridden in the courts. He was one of those men who seem destined, as James R. Newhall said, "to make a sensation wherever they are." He was of a fairly irascible disposition, and an early incident was a quarrel with Governor Endicott of Salem over the proper season for pruning a pear tree, perhaps the immortal pear tree brought over by the Governor, and in recent years still pointed out on the Endicott farm in Danvers. In 1632 he was bound over to keep the peace, and again he was set in the bilboes and disfranchised and fined for speaking disrespectfully of the government; also he was fined for being "a common sleeper in meetings." There seems no doubt that Dexter was a man of enterprise. One of his schemes was for a stone breakwater to protect Long Beach and give easier access to Nahant. Colonial authorities were indifferent to the plan, and others thought the undertaking too great. In another scheme he carried over in boats a considerable quantity of good soil to Egg Rock. Then he wanted to straighten Saugus River. But with all his speculative schemes he was a useful and worth-while citizen of old Lynn, who gets this attention here because so many of his plans had to do with Nahant. Newhall tells much more of Dexter, but his accuracy is questioned.

This year also saw Christopher Lindsey here, an employee of Thomas Dexter, usually called servant in those days. Lindsey kept his master's cattle on Nahant, and a hill was once called Lindsey's Hill. E. J. Johnson says Lindsey lived on the hillside westward from Bass Beach until his death. Many think Spouting Horn hill was "Lindsey's Hill." He died in 1668. He was wounded in the Pequot War, and a petition to the court in 1655 states that he "was disabled from service for twenty weeks for which he never had any satisfaction." He was awarded three pounds, and here is an example of very early attempts at compensation for injuries in war. Lewis says Lindsey's daughter Naomi was the wife of Thomas Maule of Salem, the famous Quaker who was indicted for publishing a book maintaining the truth as he saw it. Then he published the "Persecutors Manual," in which he said he had been five times imprisoned, three times deprived of his goods, and three times whipped, besides many other abuses. The way of the transgressor of general public opinion was hard at times. Today many people spend more money than they have to avoid a contumely, real or imagined, which seems severe, although it does not include whipping or other corporeal inflictions.

Altogether, about fifty men and their families came to Lynn in 1630 and settled in desirable parts of the town, occupying from ten to two hundred acres or more, upon which they were practically squatters. Before the land was strictly divided and fields fenced, cattle were kept together in one drove and guarded by one man called a hayward. The sheep, goats and swine were kept on Nahant and tended by a shepherd, or more than one. These shepherds, of whom Dixey and Lindsey seem to have been two, apparently lived on Nahant, perhaps with their families. The impermanent nature of these occupations, however, not only precluded them from being called real settlers, but made any accurate record or present-day knowledge of them on Nahant quite impossible.

These early residents of Lynn had town meetings every three months for the regulation of their public affairs. They cut wood in common, and drew lots for the grass in meadows and marshes. "The chiefest corn they planted, before they had plows, was Indian grain, and let no man make a jest of pumpkins, for with this food the Lord was pleased to feed his people to their good content till corn and cattle were increased." They cultivated fields of barley and wheat, using much of the former for malt for beer. A malt house was an important adjunct of these settlements. Water was rather a dangerous drink in England in those days of some crowding and no sanitation, and the beer-drinking habit was fixed and was brought along to the new country.

The first houses were rude structures covered with thatch or bundles of sedge or straw. A common form was eighteen feet square, with a sleeping chamber under the roof reached by rude steep stairs more like a stepladder. Better houses were built two stories high in front, sloping down to one story in the rear. Burnt clam shells were used for lime for plastering. Windows were small, opening outward on hinges, and with very small panes. People burned about twenty cords of wood a year, and ministers were allowed thirty cords.

Lewis says Lynn was incorporated in 1630 by the admission of its freemen to the General Court, there being no other acts of incorporation for several of the early towns. Boston, Charlestown and Salem had no other form of incorporation.

In this year an order was passed by the General Court regulating wages, naming not over sixteen pence a day "if they have meat and drink." This order was soon rescinded and wages were left unlimited "as men shall reasonably agree."

Lewis also tells the story that two of these early settlers

went to Nahant for fowl, and separated. One of them killed a seal on Pond Beach, and, leaving him, went after some birds. Returning, he found a bear feeding on the seal. He shot the bear, wounding him only, and then beat him with his gun until it broke. Then the bear chased the man into "Bear Pond," where he stayed until his companion came to his rescue and the bear went off. Returning to town they told their neighbors, and fires were kept burning on the beach through the night to keep the bear from getting out of Nahant. In the morning they killed him. It was not wise to let such animals roam on cattle ranges.

Here was a town set up, where three years earlier was only a wilderness and the Indians. Some years later, in 1686, the settlers got a quitclaim deed from the Indians. This was only a wary move, which was executed also by other North Shore towns, to perfect a title. Grants from various proprietary companies in England, with authority from the King, disregarded any ownership by the Indians. Nevertheless, the Indian deeds appeared to clinch the ownership.

Up to 1634 the General Court was composed of all the freemen, and a freeman had to be admitted as such by each locality. Any complete attendance left the villages unguarded, and there had been trouble with Indian raids from tribes to the north. In this year eight towns sent three representatives each, — Boston, Charlestown, Roxbury, Dorchester, Cambridge, Watertown, Lynn and Salem. Here seems to have been the beginning of representative government. About this time it was ordered that "no person shall take any tobacco publicly, under pain of punishment, also that every one shall pay one penny for every time he is convicted of taking tobacco publicly." Perhaps this acted like a tax and brought in revenue. Sumptuary laws and luxuries taxes are nothing new, it would seem.

In 1635 the intent of the settlement to keep Nahant for pasturage was waived because of the importance of fishing. Nine men were given permission to plant and build at Nahant and possess land for the purpose, but if they did not further

The Great Hotel on East Point

Showing several enlargements

The Nahant Hotel and Surroundings

From an old pamphlet, about 1832

the fishing industry, "but either do grow remiss or else do give it quite over," their land was to be forfeited to the town. Marshall, in his history of Rockport, says that in this same year, 1635, a small vessel sailing from Ipswich to Marblehead was wrecked and all hands lost but two, — Anthony Thacher and his wife. The small island where this disaster occurred was ever after known as Thacher's Island, a name it bears today, and its twin lighthouses are seen at Nahant. One of the vessels bringing more settlers from England in this year was the "Hopewell," a name which was used on Nahant, as is elsewhere mentioned.

In 1636 four companies of militia were called out to fight the Pequot Indians. One of these was commanded by Captain Nathaniel Turner of Lynn, who lived in Nahant Street and owned most of Sagamore Hill. Again, in 1637, Lynn furnished men for an expedition against the Pequots. In this same year a number of families moved from Lynn and began a new settlement at Sandwich. It was also in 1637 that the name Saugust, or Sawgust, was changed to Linn. Lewis says the name was chosen as a compliment to the Rev. Samuel Whiting, who came from old Lynn in England. Old Lynn was called Lynn Regis, or King's Lynn, and is an old English town. In 1880, when St. Stephen's Church in Lynn was built, a stone was sent over from St. Margaret's Church in Lynn, England, and built into the structure. It bears the inscription, "St. Margaret's Church, Lynn, England, to St. Stephen's Church, Lynn, Mass., U. S. A., 28th June 1880."

Lewis says that in this year, 1637, the General Court ordered that no person should make any cakes or buns "except for burials, marriages and such like special occasions." Corn was made legal tender at the rate of five shillings a bushel. These were the days of much bartering and little cash, so there was need for some standard other than coin or scrip.

In 1638 the lands of Lynn were divided or allotted to the settlers, who before that had taken and used as they liked. A committee was chosen and the farms were laid out with boundary lines, at least in those parts most desirable for cultivation.

The woodlands and pasturage were not divided or laid out, but were kept as common property and called "town commons." The whole of Nahant was in the latter class, and was not divided until 1706. All through the early records are curious and interesting orders or regulations. This year saw one relating to woman's dress: "No garment shall be made with short sleeves; and such as have garments already made with short sleeves shall not wear the same unless they cover the arm to the wrist." After all, Lewis says, legislators are not always as harmlessly employed as in cutting out dresses for women, and he said this nearly a century ago. A curious punishment appears to a man who lived in Lynn a short time and committed a serious offence. In 1642 he was ordered to be whipped, to have his nostrils slit and seared, and to be confined to Boston Neck, out of which he could not go on pain of death. He was obliged to wear a "hempen roape about his neck, the end of it hanging out two foote at least, and so often as he shalbee found abroad without it he shalbee whiped." He was also fined.

The year 1643 saw iron first worked in this country, and the place on Saugus River has always been known as the old Iron Works. Thomas Dexter, mentioned elsewhere, and Robert Bridges seem to have been the promoters. Iron tools and iron ware were of course wanted, and shipments from England did not relieve the scarcity. Bridges took specimens of ore to London, and a company was formed which later got out seven or eight tons a week. Several workmen came over from England especially for service at this place, and a village grew up around it. Later, a controlling interest in this plant and in one or two others was acquired by William Paine of Ipswich. Paine became one of the wealthy men of the time and finally moved to Boston. He was in England in 1598 and died in Boston in 1660. This iron company was encouraged by all sorts of grants from the General Court, so much was the industry desired. Among other things there was exemption from taxes for ten years, — a modern practice which seems to have the grace of antiquity.

In 1651 appears another court order on the "intolerable excess and bravery" of dress. They ordered that no person whose estate did not exceed two hundred pounds should wear great boots, gold or silver lace, or buttons or silk hoods, ribbons or scarfs. So here is the very modern habit of "Keeping up with Lizzie" found not to be so modern. But the courage to frown upon extravagance has diminished to the zero point.

Reaching the year 1657, at a town meeting in Lynn it was voted "that Nahant should be laid out in planting lots, and every house holder should have equal in the dividing of it, no man more than another; and every person to clear his lot of wood in six years, and he or they that do not clear their lots of wood, shall pay fifty shillings for the town's use. Also every householder is to have his and their lots for seven years, and it is to be laid down for a pasture for the town; and on the seventh, every one that has improved his lot by planting, shall then, that is in the seventh year, sow their lot with English corn; and in every acre of land as they improve, they shall, with their English corn, sow one bushel of English hay seed, and so proportionate to all the land that is improved, a bushel of hay-seed to one acre of land, and it is to be remembered that no person is to raise any kind of a building at all."

Dexter was afterwards given permission to tap pine trees on Nahant, as he had done before for the purpose of making tar. It is easy to see, in this encouragement to cut down forests and make farm land, the beginning of an onslaught on the trees of Nahant which resulted in a treeless town, except for a few scrub cedars.

And so is shown, perhaps dimly, what was happening around Nahant during a time before the white man settled here, and more immediate interest is enlisted. We dig up, accidentally, a heap of clam shells, or a stone tool or weapon of the Indians; or maybe a few old bones. A cast-iron shot reminds us of battles fought off shore whence may have come a scattering fire. Probably the main street of old Nahant — once called

Washington Street, as was customary in so many towns, and now called Nahant Road — was developed from a trail in the woods to a cart path and then to a road. Crooked streets in old towns usually mean just that.

> Not a country highway only
> Is this old road,
> Winding crookedly as it does;
> Tediously over the hills
> And along the quiet creek;
> But more a pathway
> Through a land of wondrous
> Scenes and impressions.

Considering the early settlement of Nahant there is first the period of use as pasturage or for wood-cutting; and even in 1657 it is seen, by the vote of the town of Lynn as quoted, that no buildings were to be erected. There is the deposition by William Dixey in 1657 that about twenty-eight years earlier he cut grass and kept cattle on Nahant for "some space of time." There were many depositions in the various court actions arising from the confusion of Indian sales and grants. Their unfamiliarity with grants and deeds led to trouble. But these lawsuits give information of value, as in the Dixey deposition. In 1676 it appears that Lynn established her title to Nahant in the courts, and in 1686 Lynn seems to have fortified it by a deed from the Indians which relinquished whatever claim they may have had. Yet in 1687 Edward Randolph asked Governor Andros for a grant of Nahant. His plea was denied.

In 1706 Lynn voted to divide Nahant among the townspeople. It had been "commons," used by all in common for pasturage or for wood-cutting under restrictions imposed by the town of Lynn, its owner. A committee chosen for the purpose made this division, and cut the town into 208 lots, the smallest about a quarter acre and the largest about eight acres. They made eleven strips in Great Nahant, each forty rods wide with a one-rod road between them. They were called ranges and the roads were called range roads. The cross roads of Nahant's main roads today are partly these old range roads, though widened to two rods by taking half a rod from each side. The strips of land in the ranges are therefore now thirty-nine rods wide. These roads run northeast and southwest, at least across Nahant Road. In places, as on Pond Street, the original one-rod road has not been widened on both sides, and the old McBurney house lot on the corner of Prospect Street juts into Pond Street. Pleasant Street, between Town Hall and the Public Library, is the only one which does not run through from water to water. Wharf Street at Willow Road is a continuation of Pleasant Street, but swings out easterly conforming to arrangements made with adjoining property owners when Wharf Street was built through to Nahant Road. It is claimed that these streets all run through to high-water mark, and that no one has any title to land at the shore within these street lines.

Range One was most of East Point, called the Ram Pasture in early days. The line between Ranges One and Two was easterly of Swallows Cave Road. The line between Ranges Two and Three was about where a northeast and southwest line runs through the old wharf, or between the Fay and Paine estates. Between Ranges Three and Four the line follows Cliff Street at Bass Beach fairly closely, but continues southwesterly where Cliff Street bends westerly away from the range line. Between Ranges Four and Five the line runs through Whitney's Swamp, and would cut the wing of the Whitney Homestead. Between Ranges Five and Six is Pleasant Street; Range Six is from Pleasant to Summer; Range Seven from Summer to Winter; Range Eight from Winter to Ocean; Range Nine from Ocean to Pond; Range Ten from Pond to High; and Range Eleven westerly from High Street. On Bass Point the range lines were about as follows: Range One, Baileys Hill and other land as far as Trimountain Road; Range Two, Trimountain Road to Old Willow Road, now discontinued over the government land; Range Three, from Willow Road to Range Road on one side of Relay House yard; Range Four, Range Road to Flash Road; Range Five, Flash Road to Bay

View Avenue; Range Six, Bay View Avenue to Lynn Harbor. Little Nahant had one range line about where Little Nahant Road is. Confusion of intersections which would come in the low land between Great Nahant and Bass Point was avoided by not dividing this land, which was doubtless considered of small value.

Besides these cross roads laid out so accurately and regularly this old committee report of 1706 is interesting for what it says about roads already in use. By their description there can be little doubt that some principal streets are now following the lines of old roads or cart paths. "A highway over Little Nahant two poles wide on the West end and soe running over the beach unto Great Nahant" appears to be the present main road, now widened to three rods. Toward Lynn it turned sharply down on to Long Beach, identical or nearly so with the cart path through the sand as now, and as used within a few years when road construction over the beach deflected traffic on to the sand for a time. No road was possible over the sandy ridge which was the only dry land connection with Lynn. This ridge has been described as of dry, loose sand, with some small stones. A horse and rider might get over it, but assuredly no vehicular traffic for its length of two miles or so. "Also a highway, two pole wide, on the Bay side, over to Bass Neck, and soe over to Mr. Taylor's lott; Mr. Joseph Jacobs' lott, and Moses Hudson's lott unto the other highway," which is now Flash Road. This is now Castle Road from Nahant Road to Flash Road. "And soe on the Southwardly side of the hill to about ten poles above Calf Spring and running slanting up the hill into the old way, and soe running on the North-east end of James Mills his land and soe on to the first range in the Ram pasture." This road is Spring Road from Nahant Road around Mitchell's Corner, by Calf Spring, and on to Nahant Road again, although a short stretch of it was along or near a range road now called Pond Street. The hill which the report mentions with this road is now called Sunset Hill. By some curious and now unknown accident the name of this hill was changed. Formerly it was Fox Hill, and it was so entered upon the Alonzo Lewis maps. Sunset Hill was on High Street just above the cemetery chapel. Today Fox Hill is the hill over near Castle Road and Fox Hill Road; Sunset Hill is the former Fox Hill; while the former Sunset Hill has no place name. It is not clear from this committee report if the main road up the hill and by the present schoolhouse, cemetery and police station, between Spring Road and Pond Street, was laid out by them, but the main road was Spring Road and Pond Street to avoid the steeper hill and be convenient to the spring. "Alsoe a highway two poles wide from the highway by the spring over into Bass Neck and soe through the ranges to the Southermost range on said neck." This is what is now Flash Road and partly Castle Road. "And a highway one pole wide over the Westward end of each range on Great Nahant; and a highway one pole wide on the Northwardly end of each range on Bass Neck." These appear to be what is now Willow Road. "And a highway one pole wide over between the range of lots on each side of Little Nahant," being in part what is now Little Nahant Road.

Spring Road, formerly called Calf Spring Road, ran by the spring whence came its name. The committee of 1706 "left about an acre of land joining to the highway by the spring to accommodate cattle coming to the spring." This old spring was a pure water spring not many years ago, and probably would be again if it were cleaned out and the scrub growth cut away from it. It is about twenty feet in front of the old wooden town barn which the town built on this acre. The land became the property of the town of Nahant when it became a separate township in 1853. If High Street were continued it would run over the spring. Only a part of this acre is now owned by the town. The balance was sold and is now occupied by the J. T. Wilson & Son mill and yards.

This committee report probably was accepted, although there is no record of the acceptance. It was recorded with all the separate lots and owners' names. Lewis, in his "Annals of Lynn," under date of 1706, says he has made a complete map of Nahant on a large scale, on which the lots are shown with the names of the original proprietors and of the present owners. An accurate copy of this old map is owned by the Nahant Public Library, the gift of Samuel Hammond in 1916. It was formerly owned by Samuel H. Russell who for years was a summer resident of Nahant, mentioned elsewhere in these annals. This copy was drawn by Charles A. Hammond and is dated 1871. Its inscription says it is made by Alonzo Lewis and John Q. Hammond. Whether these two men collaborated on it, or Hammond added to it and improved it, there can be no doubt that it is a very important piece of Nahant history.

And now a little more citation from old records, this time from the journal of Obadiah Turner as used by James R. Newhall. Speaking of a trip a little into the interior in 1630 he says:

> Wee did see some reptiles and serpents. And two yt wee saw had rattils in their tails, wherewith they made a strange whirring noise much like ye noise of ye rattils of ye night watch in London, only not so mighty a rattil.

In 1631 he writes:

> Wee had goode hope yt by this time our towne might become some famous and be faire in comlie habitations. But wee have been much put to it to get materialls of ye right sorte wherewith to build. In Salem they now have some bigge sawes, wherewith to make boardes. But few come to us, as the way hither is hard to travell by reason of ye stumpes and rockes yt be in it. And likewise ye people there much want their own bordes. So wee must do as wee best can with our axes and adzes and smaller sawes, and what few bordes wee can from time to time make out to haul hither. Wee have stone in plentie, but no mortar wherein to lay them. And we have abundance of clay yt might bee used in ye making of brickes, but none of us have ye skill to rightlie molde and set up ye killen; and if wee had ye mortar would bee wanting.

Of 1632 Turner writes in one place:

> Ye winter still continueth mightie cold insomuch yt ye sea be froze far into ye offing. Wee can go to Nahauntus on ye ice. Our houses be half buried in snow. And wee have to strap boardes to our feete whereby wee may walke on ye snow, wch wee call snow shoes.

Bass Beach in Foreground, Canoe Beach Beyond
Stone walls of original hotel standing after the fire

Farthest East — One of the Nahant Hotel Group
Probably built in the 1820's. Lately used by Senator Lodge for book storage

THE FIRST OF LYNN

In 1638 an entry reads:

> Some going down to Nahauntus on the thirde day last did see two ravenous wolves; being ye same I think yt tore in pieces goodman Lakeman his cow. But they could not shoot them, for they were too quick into ye woodes there.

In 1643 good hours were established thus:

> This morning ye watch did begin ye blowing of their horns wch is to be in this wise. One to starte from ye hill near ye roade to Nahauntus and walk westerlie; ye other to starte from ye forke of ye roades at ye west end of ye common lands and walk easterlie. Ye two to meet at ye halfe way post both stoutlie blowing their hornes all ye way. They to starte one hour before ye rising of ye sun, and to walke some hastilie, and returne back without stopping. And whatsoever houses they find without a light or some token of stirring therein they are to reporte. And at nine of ye clocke at night they are to doe likewise onlie reporting all such houes as have lights or other tokens of ye people not being abed. And this is ye regulation to make ye people industrious and keepers of good hours.

Another entry in the journal of Obadiah Turner notes the completion of fifty years of Lynn:

> It is now fiftie years since this now famous town was first begun. Wee have grown from ye small beginning of about a score of poore pilgrims dropt as it were in ye sauvage wilderness, to be a people well to do and manie in number. And all this by God his blessing for which his name be praised.
>
> Wee have good houses and gardens and large fields well cleared and sufficient for growing all wee need and more for exchange for such from abroad as wee desire; for it is always with a people yt their cravings increase with their means. Wee have horses and cattle and piggs and fowles in abundance. And have wee not enow with all these. So let us thank God for his undeserved bountie and purge our hearts from all uncleanness.
>
> We have butchers to supply us with flesh meat and fishermen to supply us with fish both fresh and salted, likewise clams and other meat from ye sea. And we have smiths, carpenters and bricklayers; shoemakers, weavers and manie other handicraftsmen to make and mend for our comfort. Who, then, are better provided than we. And for ye same we doe againe and without ceasing thanke God. But above all doe we bless his holie name for our gospell privileges,

for our abundance of good preaching and diligent catechising; likewise for the faire schooles wherein our children are taught.

Wee prospered under Charles ye firste; we prospered under Cromwell and ye Commonwealth; and wee yet prosper under Charles ye second. But wch was ye greatest prosperities I do not rightlie know.

The Turner journal is partly if not largely imaginative, though presented to the public by a man who also did serious historical research which is important. In these "Annals," which quote several times from the journal, care is taken not to use citations for any historical value, but only to give an impression of these early times and ways. It is the flavor which is sought, and, judged by comparison with the abundance of other material, the flavor is correct even though synthetic.

Rambling among old laws and old ways is so pleasant an avocation that it may be overdone, while the present aim is to give enough of them to yield a tang of the times. One result of such an exploration is to see the uselessness of boiling over on some question or other that may seem of deep moment. As people get older, or study history, the perspective widens, and they can see important things get less important. The vital need in any generation seems to be to keep awake and alert. There is sense enough in the world if it is used. There is capacity enough for the work of the world if there is will and willingness. Many basic factors are not alterable, and history's tale is not wholly of old things gone by, but partly of a continuous recurrence. Even the Ten Commandments do not suffer because of their age, and they do not need rewriting, but only rereading.

CHAPTER IV

EARLY NAHANT

THE vote of 1657 encouraging the cutting of trees and making of pastures; the rights to settle on this commons land given to men engaged in fishing; certain inaccuracies in the division of this commons by the committee of 1706; and the squatters who seem to have moved in here without any accorded rights or permission, — these things seem to have made Nahant a battleground which would have been good for lawyers. For a time lawyers were barred from some of these early settlements. Doubtless they may ever do more harm than good, but doubtless this may be said of the followers of any other trade or profession. As communities grew, and laws and regulations controlling men's actions necessarily multiplied, men studied in the interpretation of statutes and policies were important. Lawyers who use their wits to protect the guilty may be detrimental to a community. Any specialist is liable to similar criticism. But specialists are necessary. Life is too confused and complicated for any one person to know very many factors of it.

It would seem that from out this welter of confusion on Nahant lands, present-day titles might be found too incomplete for comfort. In fact, however, they are much less so than in many another old town, and most towns of the period were settled more or less loosely, with their lands afterwards divided. George A. Dary, a careful and reliable Boston conveyancer whom many Nahanters remember, was a student of Nahant lands and titles, and never considered them so wanting that any trouble could result. Of course there were a few exceptions, but these arose mostly from later transactions not connected with these early methods and mixups which so far have been considered. Nowadays Land Court titles are popular and desirable, and there never has been difficulty in registering Nahant titles.

The Lewis and Hammond map, to which reference has been made, is too large to reproduce in this work. A smaller map by Lewis is pictured here because it shows roads and names, although too small to show property owners. There is also shown a Lewis map of Lynn which is interesting. Note that in 1838 no street crossed Broad Street toward the water except Nahant Street, and that the present Ocean Street district, full of residences, is marked farm land from Lynn Harbor to Swampscott. Indeed, people now living can remember when Humphrey Street was called the new road, and the old road to Swampscott was less direct. The old part of Ocean Street is the Swampscott end. Nahant Street ran from earliest times to the sandy beach over which was the only access to Nahant. Nahant Street was also a street of Quakers, and as late as 1840, with a dozen or twenty families on it, only one was not a Quaker. Lynn had many Quakers, and separate schoolhouses were used where no others could attend. When Lynn was first divided into wards, all the Quakers were put into one ward wherever they lived; geographical lines were ignored with this important sect.

Even after this division of Nahant among the citizens of Lynn, which seems to have been a legal and proper process, and upon which land titles in Nahant today mostly rest, lawsuits were not over. On September 28, 1706, the town of Lynn voted that after the commons lands were divided every person should have liberty at all times to pass and repass over any other person's land for necessary access to his own land, provided he cut down no tree in so doing. This might have made trouble if legal or enforcible, but probably it was not aimed at Nahant. The common lands of Lynn were in seven divisions of which Nahant was called the Seventh. By its layout with range roads, to give ready access to the beaches as well as to the various lots, there was little need of crossing each other's land. There were, however, settlers claiming ownership by right of occupancy.

In 1708 Dr. John H. Burchsted of Lynn brought suit of trespass against Hugh Alley, Jr., at Nahant for trespass on land the former had bought of Joseph Collins, Jr., and Samuel Newhall, to whom it had been allotted a couple of years before. Reference to the old map by Lewis & Hammond shows that Lewis placed this land of Collins and Newhall as two adjoining lots extending from what is now Cliff Street down the hill westerly to the range road between Ranges Four and Five. This road was never a town road, and as laid out by the 1706 committee it ran parallel to Pleasant Street, northeast and southwest, as did other range roads in Great Nahant. It started from what is now Nahant Road, then a main road also, in such a position that the westerly wing of Whitney's Hotel, now the Whitney Homestead, would rest upon it. The location on Cliff Street of this Collins and Newhall land shows that its limits were from nearly over to the northerly side of the "Lodge Villa" land to about a half or two-thirds across the Fred R. Sears estate land. Alley claimed this land because he had held and enjoyed it for "above fifty years last passed." Alley further claimed eight acres Lynn had given for services in the Pequot War. This service was probably by his father in 1636, but the alleged grant of land may have been some time later. Alley lost his land and soon after moved to Lynn. Again the depositions give interesting information. They show that Hugh Alley, Sr., lived at Nahant as early as 1647. He appears to have been the second known inhabitant. The first was Thomas Graves, as is shown in an indenture dated 1656 between Joseph Armitage and the citizens of Lynn, which uses the phrase "near unto ye place where Thomas Graves' house stood." In the Alley case one Susanna Fferne deposed that she was born in Nahant and could remember Alley's occupancy of the land he claimed for thirty years, or back to 1678. No doubt Hugh Alley, Sr., settled here in 1647 or 1648, and had six children born here.

Probably his wife was a daughter of this Thomas Graves who is the earliest known settler. Alley appears to have opposed all decrees of Lynn or the courts and kept his residence in Nahant, and his son after him, until this final scrimmage in 1708. Benjamin Collins and others deposed, in this legal battle, that the land in controversy was given to Hugh Alley for his services in the Pequot War, and the land was called the Hope Well. Another, John Lewis, testified that he had plowed this land for Hugh Alley from year to year for forty years. Benjamin Collins also testified that Hugh Alley had another field within fence, "where his house stood, some distance from ye land in controversie." One Joanna Alley mentions her mother-in-law Mary Graves, and apparently in this deposition is the evidence that Hugh Alley married a Graves. This document states that the house of Hugh Alley was standing in 1673 or 1674. These various depositions show that the rest of Nahant, outside of these Alley holdings, was at the time used only for pasturage.

It was this Pequot War which finally brought a death judgment, curiously made, to Miantonomo, the Narragansett Indian chief. As a captive, according to Indian customs, he would meet death and torture, but his captors were warned by their white allies not to kill him. Puzzled but obedient they sent him to Hartford and then to Boston, so John Fiske says, for the white man's judgment. The government was also puzzled, for they did not want him alive. They referred the matter to a synod of clergymen from all over New England, which was in session in Boston, and their advice was asked. A committee of five of them recommended death, and Miantonomo was sent back to Hartford to be slain by his Indian captor's tomahawk.

There seems some question if Graves and Alley were the first and second permanent settlers on Nahant. E. J. Johnson, in his "History of Nahant," says the evidence shows it, but goes on to say that Lindsey and Fferne lived here about this time. The statement of Susanna Fferne that she was born here has been cited, and she remembered back to 1678.

There is also the peculiarity, which may need adjusting by those sufficiently interested, of the 1706 committee mention of James Mills. They say, referring to what is now Nahant Road, "and soe running on the North East end of James Mills his land." This would indicate no Alley land recognized along this road in 1706. The 1708 deposition of Collins places Alley's house "some distance from ye land in Controversie," which was the Hope Well land already located, if the Lewis map is correct. E. J. Johnson agrees with this location, but avers that this Alley house must have stood in from Nahant Road, probably on the north part of the Sears lot. But the northerly part of the Sears lot would appear to lie within the Hope Well lot, and therefore not answering the description of "some distance away." Again, Joanna Alley, as quoted by Johnson, testifies that she saw her mother-in-law Mary Graves put James Mills in possession of "ye aforesaid house and land that was formerly in ye possession of Hugh Alley about thirty three years since." This would be in 1673 or 1674. It seems confusing, therefore; and what actually happened may only be guessed, as E. J. Johnson worked long and hard on the question with only this indistinct outcome.

If the Hope Well lot was where the "Lodge Villa" and Sears estates are now, and if Hugh Alley, Jr., lived "some distance away" in 1708, and if James Mills took over Hugh Alley's house in 1673 or 1674, probably at the death of Hugh Alley, Sr., in January, 1674, then it seems clear that the house Mills assumed and occupied, as mentioned by the committee dividing Nahant in 1706, was the house of Hugh Alley, Sr., while Hugh Alley, Jr., lived in from what is now the main road. Probably this would be along the side hill westerly from Cliff Street but farther in than E. J. Johnson places it. Lewis, in his "Picture of Nahant" (1845), says the James Mills house was about six rods southeast from Whitney's Hotel.

Hugh Alley, Sr., most prominent of the few early Nahanters, came from England in 1635 in the ship "Abigail" bound for

New England. If he married Mary Graves, as E. J. Johnson suggests, probably it was before he settled in Nahant, as the first two of his eight children are not recorded as born in Nahant. The children were Mary, John, Martha, Sarah, Hugh, Solomon, Hannah and Jacob, born between 1642 and 1663. The son Solomon was killed in King Philip's War. The son Hugh is the only son coming into Nahant history, as already mentioned. The daughter Martha married James Mills, here mentioned, who was employed by his father-in-law. The piece of land called "Hope Well," Johnson says, was probably named after the ship "Hope Well" which arrived at Salem in September, 1635, with Joanna and Mary Graves among its passengers. These were "probably" daughters of Thomas Graves, as they came to Nahant where Graves was settled.

People from farther away than Lynn used Nahant for pasturage, and apparently some of the early residents were temporary. They were employed to care for the cattle and sometimes went when their jobs were ended, although a few stayed longer. Joseph Jacobs married a daughter of Hugh Alley and acquired a considerable acreage on Nahant but finally moved away. John and Michael Lambert were others who appear here, and Christopher Lindsey. Others have already been named.

The year 1717, Lewis says, found Nahant without an inhabitant, James Mills having died and his family moved away. His house and land became the property of Dr. John H. Burchsted, who in December sold it to Samuel Breed. Lewis states that Breed "built a house where Whitney's Hotel now stands." The exact locations of all these older houses remain more or less indefinite. It may be said, however, that these early residents all seem to have chosen this protected hillside, with its southwesterly exposure, for their homes. Doubtless there were exceptions in the cabins of the herdsmen who were here temporarily. All these early houses were crude and bound to be superseded by better structures, and in the later construction it was natural to use material from the old buildings.

William Wood

Frederic Tudor

Alfred D. Johnson
Town Clerk

Washington H. Johnson
Selectman

These contained well-seasoned logs, or if they had any hewn timber this would be used because the process of preparing this material was arduous. As for sawed timber, none was made on Nahant, and to haul it over the beach from Lynn meant trouble, also encouraging the use over again of material from these outgrown houses. Thus it is that seldom are the earliest houses in existence. The method of construction did not yield a very durable result, and this also helped toward their disappearance. Whether this early Samuel Breed house replaced the Mills house, which had come to him from his wife's father, Hugh Alley, or whether the Mills house was not in this exact location, may not be stated. In either event, old timber may have been used in the Breed house. No one can tell.

E. J. Johnson in his history of Nahant does not seem clear in his statements about the Breeds. In one place he says it is "uncertain whether Samuel Breed Senior lived at Nahant previous to 1717, when he purchased his land there: but his two sons were both living there in separate houses before 1739." Elsewhere he says, "The Breed family were among the first families to make their permanent home at Nahant, Samuel Breed having lived there previous to 1706." Samuel Breed, Sr., married Annie Hood in 1690. She was a sister of Rebecca Hood who was married to Hugh Alley, Jr., in 1681. This Breed and the Hood family, who now appear in the picture of Nahant, were from the Lynn families of early settlers, and their antecedents and family connections are easily found in various books or by reference to material at the Lynn Historical Society. Samuel Breed, Sr., who was born in 1669, was a son of Allen and Mary Breed, the first Breeds in Lynn. Samuel Breed, Jr., son of the former, was born in 1692, and E. J. Johnson says he was born in Nahant. Yet Lewis says that 1717 saw Nahant without an inhabitant, after James Mills was driven out by Burchsted. Nor do Lewis and Johnson agree which Samuel Breed, father or son, bought of Burchsted. Their ages in 1717 were forty-eight and twenty-five. Lewis says it was Samuel

Breed, Jr., while Johnson says it was the senior, who married Annie Hood, and conveyed his purchase to two of his sons, Samuel and Jabez, in 1735. The senior Breed had several children, some of whom, Johnson says, were born in Nahant. In any event, it appears that Samuel, Jr., and Jabez Breed, brothers, and sons of Samuel Breed, Sr., were both living on Nahant in separate houses in 1735, and that the former lived where is now the Whitney Homestead, formerly Whitney's Hotel. Johnson finds that in 1738 Samuel Breed is designated "Inn Keeper" in a deed. This would probably be the Junior, and Johnson says it was. He was commonly known as "Governor Breed," probably because he was very small in stature. Nicknames have a way of being ironical. His wife was Deliverance Basset, so named because born after her mother's release from prison in the witchcraft orgy in 1692. Several Lynn people were engulfed in this tragic mist of superstition, by which a few young girls could cry out successfully against their elders. Perhaps some today would like similarly strong capacities. There are fogs hard to dispel in any age, so that opinions rarely are known to be wholly enduring. Those who think of the Salem witchcraft period without drawing a lesson from it need to be reminded of the old adage about the inhabitants of glass houses. The wheel comes full circle. Astrologers were ridiculed, and now scientists say the planet Jupiter affects the spread of bubonic plague. Deliverance Basset was a daughter of William Basset, Jr., and Sarah (Hood) Basset, the latter a daughter of Richard Hood. William Basset lived on Nahant Street in Lynn. The custom of choosing names with a meaning was more common in earlier days, though often seen even in modern times. Perhaps the names Prudence and Patience have been relegated to the places where dead dreams go, but other instances occur, even on Nahant of today. Samuel Breed, Jr., had several children, one of whom was Nehemiah Breed who acquired his father's property, and it was then inherited by an only child, William Breed, born in 1759. The Breeds moved to Lynn in 1817, and Lewis says they remodelled the house or hotel in 1819 for Jesse Rice, its new proprietor. It is interesting to note that William Breed had a son Daniel, a grandson William N., and a great-grandson George Herbert Breed. The latter was well known to Nahanters, and his wife was Edith H. Gove, herself a Nahanter until her removal to Lynn.

Jabez Breed built a house, Johnson says, which together with his share of the Breed land he sold to Richard Hood in 1738. The house was across the street from the Whitney Homestead. This Hood was born in Lynn, a son of Richard Hood. He married Theodate Collins in 1718 and had nine children, of whom Abner became the Nahanter, owning most of the considerable Hood holdings here. Johnson says they amounted to fifty-three acres, and that Abner came to Nahant at the age of five, with his father. A daughter of Richard Hood, Theodate, married Jeremiah Gray. In 1741 Gray built a house on land given by his father-in-law, Richard Hood. This house Gray sold in 1758 to Jonathan Johnson, soon after which there seem to have been three families living on Nahant,—Samuel Breed, Richard Hood and Jonathan Johnson. Gray and Jabez Breed had gone, and no record appears of any others remaining here.

It is interesting to see that the Breeds appear to have owned more land here at one time than any other family until Frederic Tudor of more recent times. Dr. Burchsted seems to have been a purchaser of many of the smaller holdings arising from the division of 1706 among the people of Lynn. Most of these folks had no personal interest here and were ready to sell at once. Dr. Burchsted sold sixty acres to Breed in 1717, and the Hoods had acquired fifty-three acres when Abner Hood came into possession. The Hoods and Breeds owned nearly all the land in the first four ranges, or nearly up to what is now Wharf Street as a westerly limit, while both had holdings still farther westerly. This appears to be the origin of the concentration into one ownership of the property later known as Whitney's Swamp, through the sale by Breed to Jesse Rice, and by Rice to his son-in-law, Albert Whitney. Mrs. Alice C. McIntosh, a granddaughter of Jesse Rice, says that Rice added to the house in 1820, building the easterly end. The exact years of any remodellings or addition is not important, though it could be settled by references to the old deeds, at least as to who did the remodelling. In any event, it was done for Rice or by Rice, who then or soon after bought it. Rice kept the hotel on the old site from 1817 to 1841, the date of Whitney's purchase. It was long known as the "Rice House," and is so mentioned by Nathaniel Hawthorne. Albert Whitney continued the hotel business in the location as "Whitney's Hotel," until 1883. Then, after some years' interim, it was opened in 1896 as the "Whitney Homestead," under which title it has been and is now operated by sons and daughters of Albert Whitney. Thus comes down to present days what is doubtless in part the oldest structure on Nahant, and the oldest hotel on Nahant. Probably it was a small place in Breed's day, for there does not seem to have been much to attract to Nahant, with its almost island difficulty of access. Certainly parts of the building reach back before the Revolution, perhaps even to Breed's building of 1717 or a little later. The present proprietor is Mrs. Alice C. McIntosh, a well-known genuine "Nahanter," as those born and bred here are sometimes called. She has lived here a great part of her time, although several years of her married life were spent elsewhere.

Richard Hood, before mentioned, was born in Lynn in 1692 and died in 1764. He moved to Nahant in 1738 or 1739. He was a son of Richard Hood of Lynn, who was born in 1655 and died in 1696, and a grandson of Richard Hood, who is said to have come from Lynn Regis in England before 1650, and who died in Lynn in 1695. He bought the Humfries farm on Nahant Street. Abner, who came to Nahant in 1738 or 1739 as a boy of his father's family, was born in Lynn in 1733 and died in 1818 at Nahant. He was married at the age of fifty to Keziah Breed, daughter of Benjamin and Ruth Breed of Lynn. These people were all Quakers. Abner Hood was a selectman of Lynn and did other public service. The Society of Friends finally decided that to hold public office was worldly and unseemly for their people, and he held no further positions. Some years later, apparently after 1800, he built a house up the hill toward Bass Beach, on what is now the Upham estate, and lived there, owning all of his father's Nahant property. There were five children, Abner, Richard, Theodate, Benjamin and Ebenezer, born between 1784 and 1790. The latter two were twins. The Nahant property was divided among the four sons, of whom Benjamin had the old homestead of his grandfather. This was in 1820. Benjamin and Ebenezer married into the Phillips family of Lynn, which later had representatives living on Nahant. From these two came the later Hoods well known on Nahant. A son of Ebenezer was Elbridge, father of Elbridge Gerry Hood, who was a Civil War veteran well known to many Nahanters now living. His daughter, Abby May, is Mrs. Thomas Roland, another real Nahanter. From Benjamin Hood are descended four sisters very well known here until their deaths. One was Ann Maria, wife of Dexter Stetson, while the Misses Julia Pond Hood and Ann Amelia Hood were familiar figures. They lived for some time in a house on Castle Road, while it was about the only house there, and after the death of the Stetsons, the two unmarried sisters, with their niece Helen Stetson, lived in Lynn. They owned the house on the northerly corner of Nahant Road and Pond Street. Miss Helen Stetson bequeathed money to the Congregational Church and to the Nahant Public Library as memorial funds. The fourth sister, Louisa Phillips Hood, was the wife of Albert Wyer, who, with his son, developed a large ice business in Lynn, which is now combined with others into the ice deliveries company which serves this vicinity. Other Hood descendants have drifted away from Nahant, until today none of the name and belonging to the family are living here. These four sons of Abner Hood all lived on the Hood property, occupying four adjacent houses on the right-hand side of the road coming down from Bass Beach, and across the street from the Whitney holdings. The original Hood house, inherited by Benjamin, was about where now is the gardener's cottage of the Upham estate, and was taken down, except the wing, which was moved to Summer Street Court and made into a cottage occupied for years by Charles H. Palmer and family and now owned by Fred B. Libbey. Ebenezer built what is now known as the Elbridge Hood house owned by Mrs. Thomas Roland, a great-granddaughter of Ebenezer Hood. Richard built what is now known as the Rice house, across Nahant Road from the head of Wharf Street, and more recently familiar as the home of George W. Kibbey. On Richard Hood's removal to Lynn he sold to Charles Bradbury who sold to Jesse Rice, elsewhere mentioned. Abner, Jr., inherited his father's place up the hill toward Bass Beach. He sold to John C. Gray, a summer resident, who in turn sold to Dexter Stetson, the same Stetson whose wife was a daughter of Benjamin Hood. This house Stetson kept as a hotel or boarding house. When Upham bought this property the house was moved. A part went to Short Beach, made over into a store and a house for James C. White; and a wing went to Spring Road, made into a house for David Robertson, and subsequently was moved back to Emerald Street, and became the property of Thomas F. Coakley.

It is interesting to see how the Hoods are entwined in all the Nahant families of this period. In 1739 Jeremiah Gray married Theodate Hood, daughter of Richard Hood, the first Hood on Nahant. Gray built the house subsequently owned by Jonathan Johnson, the first Johnson on Nahant. Johnson's third wife, from whom the large family of Nahant Johnsons are descended, was a granddaughter of Hugh Alley, Jr., whose wife was Rebecca Hood, a sister of Annie Hood who married Samuel Breed, Sr., in 1690. Samuel Breed, Jr., married Deliverance Basset, whose mother, Sarah Basset, tried for witchcraft in 1692, was a daughter of Richard Hood of Lynn and an aunt of the first Richard Hood of Nahant. Thus the Hood family was represented in all three of these early Nahant homes, as well as in the Alley family earlier on Nahant, but gone in the later half of the century, and with their house not standing.

The third family living on Nahant, in or before 1770, was of Jonathan Johnson. He was a son of Jonathan Johnson who came to Lynn in 1706, and married Sarah Mansfield in 1710. They had two sons and four daughters. One of the sons, Edward, born in 1721, has numerous descendants now living in Boston and Lynn, with some becoming summer residents of Nahant. He was a private in Captain Farrington's company at the battle of Lexington. The other son, Jonathan, born in 1723, was the original Johnson on Nahant. He enlisted in a cavalry regiment under Major Graves for the French and Indian Wars, and thus gained the common title of Trooper Johnson. On his return he lived in Marblehead. He first married Katherine Brummage in 1745; second, Susanna Farrington in 1753; and third, Ann Alley, widow of Thomas Williams and daughter of Benjamin B. Alley, who was a son of Hugh Alley, Jr., mentioned elsewhere as one of Nahant's earliest settlers. Thus the well-known family of Nahant Johnsons trace descent from the beginning of the town. He bought out Jeremiah Gray in 1758, and some time later, perhaps soon after this later marriage, he moved to Nahant, where three sons were born, — Benjamin, 1771; Joseph, 1776; and Caleb, 1778. He was farmer, fisherman and chair maker. His experience proved his metal, and he lived out an interesting, hard-working life until his death in 1799 while living with his son Caleb in the same house that he had bought about forty years before.

These three sons of Jonathan learned the shoemaker's trade with a half brother, Thomas Williams, serving an apprenticeship of seven years. Benjamin married Betsey Batchelder in 1795 and lived in Lynn. In 1798 Caleb married Olive Hartwell, daughter of Jacob Hartwell, who with his family used to visit Nahant. In 1814 Ward Hartwell, a brother of Olive, perished in attempting to cross Long Beach in a storm and after dark. He lost his bearings and drove into the surf. The children of Caleb and Olive Johnson were Mary, 1800; Welcome William, 1803; George L., 1806; Clara,

1808; Edward Augustus, 1810; Caleb Hervey, 1812; Daniel W., 1815; Olive Cornelia, 1817; William Frederick, 1819; and Charles Warren, 1823. Caleb was a fisherman, owning an interest in one or more of the fleet sailing from Nahant. He went fishing for over fifty years, and served as captain on the "Dolphin," the "Jefferson" and the "Lafayette." After his retirement from active life he continued to own a share in one or more of the little fleet which had furnished his life occupation. He died in 1867.

The third Nahant son of Jonathan Johnson was Joseph, who was born in 1776 and died in 1854. He married first, in 1797, Mary Cox from a Salem family; and second, in 1819, Betsey Graves from a Reading family. For a few years after his first marriage he lived in Lynn, but soon returned to Nahant and built his house there. The children were Joseph, 1798; Jonathan, 1800; Francis, 1802; Eliza, 1806; Pamela, 1808; Washington Harlow, 1811; Dolly Madison, 1813; Walter, 1816; Daniel Alfred, 1820; Edwarde Kirke, 1822; Frederick Henry, 1825; Franklin Everett, 1827; Mary Graves, 1830; and Edmund Buxton, 1832.

Joseph Johnson was part farmer and part fisherman, while a little sign marked "J. Johnson" on a corner of his house signified it as one of the early small inns of the town. It was built soon after 1800, and was removed long since. The land was used by C. Hervey Johnson, a son of Caleb, on which to build two houses now standing on Nahant Road next westerly from the post office block, and on the same side. The old Johnson house was nearer the street than these and stood about midway of the present lot. A painting and an early photograph of his homestead are in the Nahant Public Library. In 1872 or 1873 it was moved back to Central Street and altered, so that it does not resemble the old Joseph Johnson house. It was the home of Welcome J. Johnson for many years and is now owned by James A. Coles. The homestead of Caleb Johnson, after so many years' service as the "cradle of the Johnson family," was torn down in 1896 to make room

Home of Frederic Tudor
Later enlarged for the Nahant Club

The "Old Castle" at Bass Point
An early Nahant hotel

for the Henry Sigourney house now across the street from the post office block. The house stood a little easterly from the Sigourney house. Many photographs of it are extant, and there is a painting in the Public Library. This house was standing so recently that many people not very old can well remember it.

CHAPTER V

EARLY EIGHTEEN HUNDREDS

The year 1800, by an interesting coincidence, finds the same three homes the only ones on Nahant, as have been mentioned for the year 1770, and they are occupied by sons of the earlier owners, — Nehemiah, son of Samuel Breed; Abner, son of Richard Hood; and Caleb, son of Jonathan Johnson. Caleb's father, Jonathan Johnson, had been dead about a year. Caleb's brother, Joseph, was living in Lynn, though soon to return to his native town. Just when he came back to Nahant seems indeterminate. E. J. Johnson says the old house dated back to 1812, while E. B. Johnson places it from 1800 to 1803, and says it was either the fourth or the fifth house on Nahant at that time.

The house which disputes the fourth place among Nahant houses of about this time was one at Bass Point, located about where Edward E. Strout's house stands today, owned by his heirs. Lewis says this house was built as a hotel by Captain Joseph Johnson of Lynn in 1800. Another writer says it was built in 1802. In 1803 it was burned and at once rebuilt. It was owned and operated at one time by Nathan Silsbee, and was used as a hotel until 1840, when Silsbee sold it into the family of John Phillips, who was the first mayor of Boston and father of Wendell Phillips. This is the building known to the present generation as the "Old Castle." It was used for a summer residence by two sons-in-law of Phillips, the Rev. George W. Blagden, pastor of the Old South Church in Boston, and Dr. Edward Reynolds, father of Dr. John P. Reynolds who lived for so many years on Nahant Road next to the village church. Two sons of Phillips, George W. Phillips and the Rev. John C. Phillips, built houses on portions of the Old Castle estate. This Joseph Johnson is sometimes confused with Joseph Johnson of the other and larger Johnson family of Nahant. The former was not even of the same Johnson kin, or at least not nearly enough related to be so recognized. He and his family disappeared from Nahant after Silsbee took over the property.

Thus has been traced the five houses on Nahant soon after the year 1800. Three have been torn down, — the "Old Castle," the Johnson Homestead and the Hood Homestead. The Joseph Johnson house has been moved and remodelled so that it has no outward resemblance to the house of over a century ago. The Breed house, now the Whitney Homestead, is where it always stood, and although it has been extensively enlarged and remodelled, it still remains in part the oldest house on Nahant. In the interior, old doors, cupboards, ceiling beams, door latches or other fittings show that parts now in useful existence reach back to these older times, doubtless to 1758, and probably to a still earlier time, as has been shown elsewhere in these "Annals." No further attempt will be made to give the respective ages of Nahant houses, although others that are around the century mark in age will come into mention in this narrative.

It is interesting to look again at the Nahant of this period. The town was barren of trees and presented a pleasant stretch of open land, cool and delightful in summer. Visitors had begun to come. Driving from Boston or other points, a stop was often made at Lynn, perhaps at a hotel in City Hall Square then much used for this purpose. Here at least people waited for a low tide, and then going down Nahant Street crossed the beach on the hard sand, picking up the old road at Little Nahant. This road, as a main road, wound round by Calf Spring, along what is now Spring Road, joining the present Nahant Road at Pond Street and continuing its present course as far as Bass Beach, where it dwindled to a cart path onward to the Ram Pasture. There it apparently turned and came back, running off down Willow Road as far as Boat House Beach, or Longfellow Beach. Just where these old cart paths went is vague, but there were no cross roads, only country lanes, unbuilt and ungraded. Castle Road meandered over to Bass Point, and Flash Road was a cart path connecting into it. All of the houses took in boarders or provided meals, often "cooking up" for good-sized parties. Nahant Road from Spring Road up over the steeper hill and onward to Pond Street soon came to full use, as both roads and vehicles were improved so that the hill was no obstacle. And so the nineteenth century began for Nahant.

Any story of Nahant cannot pass far beyond the year 1800 without coming upon other men who had greatly to do with its development. One of these was Thomas Handasyd Perkins, a wealthy Boston merchant, born in 1764 and died in 1854. For him is named the Perkins Institution for the Blind, of which he was the chief benefactor from its beginning in 1833. He was also a liberal helper of the Boston Athenæum and the Massachusetts General Hospital. He chiefly financed the old Granite Railroad in Quincy, one of the first useful railroads in the country. An interesting memoir of this man was written by his son-in-law, Thomas G. Cary. One incident related is of his presence in Paris in the fateful years of 1794 and 1795, when with James Munroe, later President, then Minister to Paris, he witnessed an entertainment by the guillotine, seeing sixteen persons beheaded in fourteen minutes. Under the date 1817 Lewis says "this year Hon. Thomas H. Perkins built the first stone cottage on Nahant." Miss Emma F. Cary, a granddaughter, once wrote that it was built about 1823. She says the stone was brought from Weymouth in a vessel in which the workmen lived while they were building the house. There was also a summer house, like a little rock temple, on the summit close to Spouting Horn, but this was struck by lightning and destroyed long ago. This property came into possession of Mrs. Thomas G. Cary, a daughter, and thence to grandchildren. Three of these were familiar to old Nahant, — Miss Emma F. Cary, whom many Nahanters will remember; Mrs. Elizabeth Cary Agassiz, wife of Professor Louis Agassiz and President of Radcliffe College;

and Mrs. Cornelius C. Felton, wife of Harvard College's President Felton. In 1821 Perkins and William Paine bought for $1,800 of Nehemiah Breed, elsewhere mentioned, all of the first range on Nahant, which was called the Ram Pasture. Other purchases were added to this until the tract comprised about what is now known as the Lodge and James places. These men apparently bought with the definite idea of building a hotel, and at once proceeded to get subscriptions for this purpose. In September, 1821, the "Columbian Centinel," one of the Boston newspapers of the time, carried a notice summoning all who were interested in the project to a meeting in Boston. The matter seems to have been delayed a little, but the new Nahant Hotel was opened in June, 1823. More about this hotel appears in this book elsewhere. There can be no doubt that Perkins had become a lover of Nahant, and believed a new and large hotel would fill a demand. Doubtless he also considered it a paying proposition. He was a leading Boston merchant, unlikely to enter upon merely chimerical schemes, for although a man may give time and energy to an enterprise merely for its benefit to the community, it rarely is for something usually satisfied by commercial activity.

Soon another figure appears in the person of Dr. Edward H. Robbins, who was actively interested in this new hotel. Dr. Robbins lived on what is now Swallows Cave Road, on the westerly side, owning the land lately owned by the Guild and Grant estates. The house set a little southerly from the Guild house.

Dr. Robbins was born in 1792, the son of Edward Hutchinson Robbins and grandson of Nathaniel Robbins, the latter a prominent lawyer in Boston, member of the Committee on the Constitution of Massachusetts in 1780, and a member of the committee on building the "new" State House from 1795 to 1798. He was Lieutenant Governor from 1803 to 1807. He was a descendant of Ann Hutchinson who came to fame in Massachusetts with the early Antinomian controversy. Dr. Robbins was in the business of woolen manufacture, which was badly hurt financially by the general business depression in 1829. He died in 1850. The property was soon after sold to Charlotte Boardman Rice, widow of Henry G. Rice, who occupied it in the summer time until her death. In 1882 the house was torn down and two houses were built for her sons-in-law, Patrick Grant and Samuel E. Guild. Judge Robert Grant, well-known author and until recently Judge of the Probate Court for Suffolk County, is a son of Patrick Grant, and spent many summers of boyhood and manhood in these surroundings. He was born in 1852. The Grant house, close to the cliff's edge, was later sold to Dr. Francis P. Sprague, and is now occupied by Ralph Lowell, elsewhere mentioned. The Guild house remained in possession of the family until its sale in 1927.

Another man important to Nahant in these early days was William Wood, who has been described as an eccentric bachelor. He was born on Bunker Hill in Charlestown in 1777, a son of David Wood who owned a portion of the hill. After a long and useful life he died in Canandaigua, New York, in 1857. He was a prosperous Boston merchant, in partnership with his brother, with business interests in New York and London. His hobby for the greater period of his life was the formation of libraries. The old Apprentices Library of Boston was an early one that he originated. This was in 1820. Then followed the Mercantile Library Association of Boston and New York. He also founded libraries in Albany, Philadelphia, and New Orleans. In 1839 he started the Mercantile Library in Liverpool, England. He seems to have been especially interested in this work for the sake of young men, workmen, clerks and such. He also established libraries in prisons and poor houses, churches, steamboats, merchant ships; and after much exertion in Washington saw results in an order from the Navy Department "for every ship bound abroad to take a suitable number of volumes for the use of sailors." The Apprentices Library in Boston has been called the first which he founded, but it was in 1819 that he started a public library on Nahant, as is told elsewhere in these "Annals." There is no record that William Wood ever lived on Nahant. For about a score of years after 1800 no houses were built or owned by summer residents. The townspeople all took boarders or served dinners, and the natural beauties of the place were attracting much attention. Resort here for a day or a week, or even a month, in this sort of way leaves no trace easy to unravel a hundred years later. Laborious search through county records doubtless would yield some information. For the most part, what is known comes from other contemporary evidence, — in letters, newspapers and pamphlets, and from any family's knowledge of its own antecedents.

Another of the early Nahanters was Cornelius Coolidge, also impressed with the beauties of the town and giving time and energy to its development. In 1824 he bought from the Hoods and Breeds nearly all the land between Rice's Hotel and the Ram Pasture, or westward from what is now Swallows Cave Road as far as a goodly strip beyond what is now Cliff Street. He laid out streets and sixty or more house lots. The "Columbian Centinel" for February 19, 1812, carries this advertisement:

> Cornelius Coolidge and Co., 53 Long Wharf. Now issuing from Sloop "Mary" and for sale, 70 hogsheads retailing molasses, 25 hogsheads high proof good flavored rum. From the sloop "Otho", 7 hogsheads retailing molasses, 13 ditto good flavored rum.

Allen Chamberlain, in his "Beacon Hill," gives most of the following information. Coolidge was a Boston merchant, son of Cornelius Coolidge and son-in-law of Moses Grant. Boston Directories list him as a merchant from 1803 to 1821. In 1823 he is listed as an architect and later as a building contractor and real estate agent. Apparently he was a land speculator and builder, but not to be allied with speculative builders of today, for his work was sound and substantial, and his architecture had merit. A report by a committee of the common council of Boston in 1833, relating to certain land transactions by the city, states that Coolidge had been "reduced from affluence to insolvency" as a result of the financial crisis of 1829. The report continues comment on this panic year and says that "many of our wealthiest families and citizens were ruined." Coolidge began building while still a merchant, but finally went wholly into the field of real estate development. He probably was the designer of fifty houses on Beacon Hill between the State House and Charles Street, besides many others elsewhere. By 1838 he seems to have regained somewhat his position in the business world, but at his death in 1843, at the age of sixty-five, he seems again to have lost, as he left no estate to be probated. He is buried in the family lot in the old Granary Burying Ground in Boston.

On Nahant Coolidge apparently planned more than he executed, although he was well started on his schemes. Recently the Public Library received, as a gift from Samuel Hammond, an original old notebook owned by Coolidge, which gives the early owners and "present" owners of all Nahant land west of Summer Street. This was the "great pasture," so named in other plans and deeds and other parcels, and it would indicate that this man had schemes evolving for the western part of Nahant that might have materialized but for his bad luck in 1829. He built the Bryant Cottage (now Paine), the Dr. Robbins (now gone), the David Sears (later Appleton, then Boyden, now Smith), the Hubbard (later Charles R. Green, burned in 1896), the B. C. Clark (later Amos A. Lawrence, now Arthur Perry), the N. P. Russell (later Miss Mary Russell, now gone), the Nahant House (later Peabody, now Fay), and the "Lodge Villa." The latter is said to be the last one of his ventures here, and is the nearest to its original condition of any of them. All of the others still standing have been remodelled out of any semblance to their originals, although in all of them, probably, there are parts of the old construction by Coolidge. This man is said to have met financial reverses again in the panic of 1837, the year which ended a boom of wildcat speculation and carried to ruin many not engaged in it. This boom and panic are described elsewhere, but this curious quotation is from a memorandum kept with records of the Nahant Church. "He failed

The Witch House
Stone lion still in his cave

The Maolis House, Ocean Street
"Witch House" in background

for want of capital and credit. New England was suffering under the democratic rule; a maxim attributed to Andrew Jackson, who was hated as no man has been hated since Jefferson, was that all who did business on borrowed capital ought to break. Perish credit, perish commerce, was another axiom. Till in 1837 a general bankruptcy swallowed up what little was left, happily including the democracy of that day." Coolidge was not through with his plans for Nahant and meant to do much more. He built the stone work, still standing, around the "old wharf," lately known as the residence of Ellerton James, which was afterwards built there. He gave the land for the Nahant Church on Cliff Street, which was erected in 1832, but not the present structure, as is told elsewhere. In losing Cornelius Coolidge probably Nahant lost a very much worth-while friend. Inquiry does not elicit further information about him, but he disappears from Nahant and none of his family or descendants belong to Nahant. Cliff Street, running southerly out to what is now Arthur Perry's estate, was called Coolidge Street and it stopped there. In his day only a cart way ran down the hill as Willow Road does today. Coolidge built his houses one after another and sold them. The exact dates or order of building is not given here, but it would be easy for any one interested to trace this out through the registry of deeds.

Another figure who appears in Nahant history at about this period is Frederic Tudor, who is probably the best known of all old Nahanters, though only by name to most. He was aggressive and eccentric, so that he has become a historic character of the town, the sort of whom many amusing and interesting stories can be told. His son, Frederic Tudor, writes of him as follows:

> In the earliest years of the century a young man just entering mercantile life, looking around him with a beginner's enthusiasm for unthought-of and cheap commodities to carry to new and dear markets, lit upon the ice which in limitless fields clothed his native lakes in winter. Even at that time, well-to-do people housed a little ice for summer's use, and to him occurred the possibility of

transporting this great absorbent of heat and producer of cold to tropical latitudes, where its value would be the greatest.

The substance was easily obtained, and to cut it into blocks convenient for handling cost very little. An uncertain but probably large part would be lost by melting; would there be a residue after storage, transportation and handling which could be sold at such a price that all expenses would be paid and a profit left over? The young man who considered this project was Frederic Tudor, the third son of Colonel William Tudor, a Revolutionary officer and friend of General Washington, and a lawyer of eminence. Born in Boston September 4, 1783, he was scarcely twenty-one years of age when he began to ponder the scheme of a trade in ice, and he had so well satisfied himself of its feasibility that in 1805 a cargo of ice cut from a pond on his father's country place in Saugus was actually loaded on board a schooner, and, in charge of himself as owner and supercargo, was shipped to the island of Martinique.

The project, of which this was but an attempt, a bare opening of what he calculated would grow to be a great trade with the Indies, was laughed at by all his neighbors as a crazy undertaking.

He confessed that one reason for sailing along with his novel merchandise was to escape the jeers of his acquaintances and the well-meant restraint of his friends; but as such things have no weight with the man who is possessed by an idea and seriously in earnest in its development, his chief reason was undoubtedly to watch the effectiveness of his precautions to preserve the ice, and to introduce the new product to its first market in the tropics in person.

So unaccustomed were the residents of the island to the properties of ice, and so unprepared to receive and use it, notwithstanding the efforts of his advance agents, that no real advantage was obtained from it, but the whole cargo arrived with trifling shrinkage, and the success of this most important part of the experiment was satisfactorily demonstrated.

From this time for many years his enthusiastic nature carried him forward, in spite of disasters, losses, accumulating debts and innumerable discouragements. He managed, in spite of his lack of money, even with a heavy load of debt which favoring fortune never lightened without soon involving him deeper by unexpected and improbable disasters, to steadily extend his business. For nearly twenty years his days and nights were spent in a continuous contest against adversity. In spite of innumerable reverses, which permitted only the slowest progress, he at last got his trade into a condition in which an ultimate reward of great profit was certain.

EARLY EIGHTEEN HUNDREDS

His early youth had been largely spent upon his father's country place, "Rockwood" (now the Poor Farm of the town of Saugus) where the homestead is still standing. Here he and his brothers and sisters indulged their taste for gardening, farming and country life, and entered actively into the study of nature and the making of agricultural experiments. They kept a record of their doings, mainly in the hand of the boy Frederic, who even then seemed overflowing with ideas and enthusiasm. Although he was the only one of four brothers who was not graduated from Harvard College, he had great fondness for letters and the company of cultivated people.

It was probably as a horticulturalist that he was best known to Essex and adjoining counties. Fond of the sea, he had, along with Colonel Perkins, Stephen Codman and others, been first to pitch upon that gem of the ocean, Nahant, recognizing its great charms as a summer resort. Originally a common belonging to the town of Lynn, and used from the earliest time as a pasture, the promontory had been stripped of what must have been a crowning beauty, — its forest trees.

Tudor, who had now made Nahant his home, set about to restore this feature somewhat; and in addition to the extensive gardens which he laid out on his own grounds, located and built the public roads, and planted and cared for trees on their margins. The promontory, being so bold and high, offered no shelter from the merciless arctic winds of winter; the site was dry, bleak and most unpromising for experiments in horticulture. But it was his characteristic both to test the unknown and to accomplish the impossible.

As the essence of sport is the surmounting of obstacles, so without this stimulus perhaps his efforts as a gardener would have failed to interest him. His success should be measured not only by results, which were considerable, but by the difficulties successfully overcome and the permanent character of his improvements. During his life his garden was kept in the most advanced state of cultivation, the products frequently taking the highest prizes. The results were due to his own knowledge and care, assisted by such native Yankee talent as he could find about him. He never employed a trained and educated gardener. It was his pleasure that the community should enjoy free what had cost him so much. Admission to the gardens was always readily granted, and when the fruit was ripe, all the children of the town were invited to come with baskets, and to fill them during the day. Afterward they were entertained by a sumptuous collation.

He made many attempts to discover valuable seedlings, but

met with no substantial success, although he spent years in costly experimenting; nor did he need this glory. He won credit enough in his hard-earned success in covering his loved Nahant with trees, now, nearly thirty years after his death, in their prime, and by his generous expenditures in public improvement for her benefit. His method in planting and transplanting was principally to provide artificial shelters. He used to set out hardy and quick-growing trees as wind barriers to protect those of slower growth and greater shade-giving qualities, which, when they had grown to sufficient size, would support each other in resisting the wind, after the protecting trees were removed. No one who should visit Nahant at the present time can understand the utter incredulity with which his attempts at tree planting were regarded by his contemporaries, so magnificent is the outcome of his perseverance.

The first growth of Balm of Gileads has now nearly all disappeared, and the protected trees now stand secure, handsome elms and maples, some of them two feet in diameter.

He lived to see all his concerns in a flourishing condition, and died on the sixth of December, 1864, in the eighty-first year of his age. He possessed such an originality of thought and language and conduct as to be remarkable and make him a most entertaining companion. He had a deep sense of religion without cant, and was charitable, yet with discriminating justice. He possessed a romantic, even poetic nature, and his hard life never subdued his finer feelings or diminished his sympathy with his fellow men.

This account by his son is the greater part of an article used by E. J. Johnson in his history of Nahant. This history was published in 1888, and a reference by the writer shows the article was written about 1884.

It was in 1820 or a little earlier that Mrs. Delia Tudor, mother of Frederic Tudor, was a frequent visitor to Nahant. She built the stone house which was bought by her son in 1824, Johnson says. Lewis, under date of 1825, says, "This year Frederic Tudor, Esq., of Boston built his beautiful rustic cottage at Nahant." The discrepancy may not be real, as it is likely that Tudor either had to do with the original building under his mother's name, or that he added to it or remodelled it after he took over ownership; or, what is perhaps more likely, the whole building operation may have extended from 1824 into 1825, during which time the transfer was made. In this latter assumption the statements of both Lewis and Johnson would be correct. The building is the central part of what is now the Nahant Club on Nahant Road, easily distinguished because of its old stone walls. The exterior is not much altered, as the changes have been liberal extensions without reconstruction of the older part. Johnson says that Tudor's first effort in public improvement was to plant a row of Balm of Gilead trees on each side of the main road from the hill near Short Beach to Summer Street. Prior to this William Wood and Thomas H. Perkins had planted elms from Summer Street to the Breed house, now the Whitney Homestead, along the main road. There are many trees, like the row of maples on Spring Road, planted by Mrs. J. P. Putnam, which were established in later years, but it may be said that the street trees of Nahant that are as old as Tudor's work here are the results of his efforts. This is especially true of the magnificent elms on Nahant Road.

The following letter dated 1849 is quoted by Johnson, and is mostly cited again as follows, for it gives a good contemporary account of what Tudor was doing:

> Among the many beautiful features of Nahant, one of the most beautiful is the residence of Mr. Tudor. We called to see his place on the occasion of a recent ride to our famed and favorite Nahant, and were politely received by our friend Mr. Wm. F. Johnson, to whom we express our thanks for his attention.
> The cottage and garden of Mr. Tudor are well worth a visit, and certainly deserve a mention to the public.
> The cottage is built of stone which was collected at Nahant, of a coarse or dark granite which is quite abundant there; the roof is covered with hemlock bark, giving the building an ancient appearance, which seems to be a taste the proprietor studies.
> Mr. Tudor's garden contains over two acres, and is inclosed by a very substantial fence, about seventeen feet high, which not only protects it from intruders, but prevents in a great measure the effect of the violent wind. He has a large collection of very fine fruit trees, many of them beautifully trained on fences, giving them a very tasteful and ornamental appearance. One cherry tree, with its branches trained horizontally, covers a space of over five hundred square feet; some of its branches are about twenty feet in

length, extending each side of the trunk perfectly straight. The pear trees look exceedingly well, considering that it is an unfavorable season for the pear crop in this vicinity, owing to the late frost in the spring.

His plums are worthy of notice, all looking finely, and, notwithstanding the depredations of the curculio, many of these trees are loaded with the finest plums.

There are many interesting experiments in shading trees from the sun in the hottest part of the day, which have proven quite successful. All his experiments are tried in the most thorough manner. Among the many experiments is one quite novel of capturing insects; he has suspended in his trees between two and three hundred small bottles, partly filled with sweetened water, into which all flies, bugs and moths are enticed and drowned.

Great quantities have been destroyed in this way. During two weeks of the dry weather in June there were captured about five hundred thousand bugs, and in thirty-six hours on the nineteenth and twentieth of June, one hundred and eight thousand were taken.

Although his principal interest is in trees, yet he has a portion of his grounds dedicated to Flora, and a beautiful marble figure of this goddess is in the centre of this department.

When we take into consideration the fact that one-half of the community think that nothing can be grown successfully at Nahant, and twelve years ago not one in a hundred could be found that believed it, no one will deny that Mr. Tudor is entitled to a great deal of credit for his persevering efforts, for by them he has established the fact that the barren soil of Nahant will yield to the industry of man as well as other places. And quite an interest has been aroused in many of the inhabitants of Nahant, which it may not be improper to attribute to the example of Mr. Tudor.

Besides the gardens, Mr. Tudor has quite a farm, raising large quantities of beets and carrots. He has harvested the past season about fifty tons of hay; although he has never yet devoted his attention personally to that branch, yet there is no reason why he cannot have one of the finest farms in the country. In addition to gratifying his own private taste, Mr. Tudor has not neglected the public, as any one who resides on Nahant cannot fail to observe.

The many fine trees on each side of the road are living witnesses of the fact, and the many hundreds of trees scattered about on the hills. It must have required an unusual degree of care and expense to have brought them to their present thriving condition.

In short, the entire appearance of the peninsula has been changed, and the beautiful contrast between the green trees and the wild ocean make the spot doubly interesting to the lover of nature or the seeker of pleasure, for all of which the future generations cannot fail to be unmindful, and to remember him with gratitude.

Tudor bought up all Nahant land he could get, apparently, until he owned a large portion of the western half of Great Nahant, and Fox Hill, now so called, and other considerable areas on Bass Point. Among his holdings was the Great Marsh as it was early called, reaching from Short Beach out across what is now the Town Play Ground and Bear Pond. This marsh was not divided up by the 1706 committee who apportioned Nahant among the people. It was kept by the town of Lynn, apparently because unsuited, mostly, for tillage. Part of it was later given to Alonzo Lewis, the historian and surveyor often cited in these annals, as a reward for his services which were so valuable and so largely without other recompense. From Lewis it passed to Tudor. Incidentally it is interesting to note that the Lewis house in Lynn will be remembered as standing, in dilapidated condition, nearly across Washington Street from the Newhall Street junction. Within a few years it stood alone on its lot of land of about a half acre. Recently stores have been built along the street and the old historian's house is hidden by them. Tudor built ditches through these marshes and made them largely usable. On a part between Calf Spring and Bear Pond he made an orchard which many Nahanters will remember, and which was surrounded by a very tall fence, the tallest of all windbreak fences that Tudor built. Poles like telegraph poles were used in its construction, all thoroughly braced, as indeed they must have been, for they withstood a great wind pressure, and were never blown down until decayed. The posts and framework remained standing after the slatting was gone. This slatting, put on vertically, was about an inch and a half wide and spaced about an inch apart. The height of this remarkable fence was at least twenty-five feet, and some people remembering it say it was thirty feet. The orchard was of pear trees, or chiefly so, and folks now living can remember fine fruit there, though the place was run down and out of condition.

Another of Tudor's orchards were the apple trees covering the land now bounded by Spring Road, High Street, Coolidge Road and the cemetery, including the land where now stands the Maolis Club. Forty years ago this orchard still yielded a good crop of fruit, though practically neglected for many years before that. Gradually the yield diminished, while the several houses on this tract caused the removal of the trees. A few are left. One of the new owners who built there, E. W. Bourne, took care of the half dozen or more trees on his lot and brought them back to look healthy and clean. The present owner, Aaron Hershenson, is also caring for them. Though they are old, doubtless proper treatment will bring a reasonable yield of fruit again, and they are still able to be an ornament to his place.

Tudor also built the old stone barn on Spring Road at the corner of High Street, which was not then, or until within a dozen or fifteen years, cut through to the cemetery east gates. With the widening of range roads to two rods, as is required of all town roads, a corner of the stone barn juts into the street, but the building is an old landmark and curiosity, and it is to be hoped it may not come to an earlier end on that account. The stone wall along Spring Road at that point — a wall which originally extended up beyond Emerald Street — is built with the wall of the barn, as an inspection of interlocking stones will show. This barn was a fruit storage building and was never used by Tudor for any other purpose. The remains of racks for fruit storage were recently, perhaps are now, to be found there. He also used it for curing tobacco, which he tried to grow in Nahant, but without much success. In recent years it was fitted up for use as a stable, and is now used for storage only.

The gardens described in the quotation already cited were adjacent to his own house. They were irregular in shape. There was a peach and plum orchard reaching out close to

Along Bass Beach toward the Mifflin House

Mifflin House, formerly Samuel A. Eliot
Decorated for fiftieth anniversary celebration

Ocean Street and to the driveway to what is now the Nahant Club. These driveways to Ocean and Winter Streets are the same as Tudor built them. The orchard extended down Ocean Street northeasterly across from the junction of Tudor Street as since built. This was also enclosed in a tall fence, but not so tall as the one on the marshes. It was fifteen to twenty feet high, and a picture shown herein is better than further description. From its northerly corner another tall fence went slanting away from Ocean Street and turned again in behind the homestead, enclosing more gardens. These and the "South Garden" soon to be described, were kept in good condition by Mrs. Tudor, after her husband's death, for many years. All trace of them has now disappeared, except for shrubs and trees around the homestead. The grass tennis courts of the Nahant Club are on the site of the peach and plum orchard.

The remaining Tudor orchard needing mention is the South Garden, across Nahant Road from the Tudor Homestead, and occupying the land now used on Nahant Road by the Burr, later Newell, and the Dabney, later Parker, houses. The westerly line was exactly the line against the old South Field now occupied on Nahant Road by the Hopkins and Wilson, later Bacon, places. The South Garden extended down to Willow Road, thus including land on the latter, now occupied by several houses. This was an orchard containing all sorts of fruits and was surrounded by another tall fence, again not so tall as the tallest of them. On the Nahant Road line this fence was different. It was of posts, rails and slats, similar to what has been described, but was veneered with bricks. These bricks were two by two by eight inches, half the width of commonly used bricks, and were laid up against the slatting with a mortar which got a clinch in between the slats. It was laid in design, basket pattern, with interstices. All in all, it would seem to be of very short-lived construction. But it stayed in place well, and when taken down in the late 80's whole sections of this thin brickwork, a square yard or more, could be handled, perhaps a difficult performance at any time with full-sized bricks laid solidly. Some of these bricks were used to pave the front entrance path to the house on Ocean Street later owned and occupied by Charles Davis. Because of this wall the garden was often called, forty or fifty years ago, the "Brick Garden."

The heavy gateway to this garden was at the corner of Winter Street. In the other Nahant Road corner stood a tall wooden water tower with a large tank, providing artificial watering in dry times. In the 80's, when the gates were left open, as often happened after the fruit-picking season, school children used to scamper across the garden and up the stairs and around the platforms of this tower. Many Nahanters can remember doing so.

The "Boston Journal" for October 5, 1858, contains the following account of a garden party given by Tudor to the townspeople. The citation is from Johnson's "History of Nahant:"

> The first event of the above nature in our peninsular history occurred last week upon the premises of Frederic Tudor, Esq. By invitation kindly extended to all the inhabitants, a large party met on the afternoon of Saturday the 2nd of October inst. Cider, perry (made from the juice of the pear) and merry making, conviviality and good feeling generally were the order of the day. Here were gathered in abundance the rich fruits of the earth. The first cider mill ever seen at Nahant was put in operation, and the first cider was received from the hand of Mr. Tudor by the oldest inhabitant (Uncle Caleb), and drunk with an appropriate toast.
>
> The delicious beverage ran freely from the press, and was as freely dealt out to the multitude, who, by smiling faces and pleasant remarks, evinced their appreciation of its merits. Then followed the manufacture of perry, which was universally pronounced most excellent. In addition to two barrels of cider distributed at the gathering, and near a barrel of perry, six or seven other barrels of cider are yet to be made, and large quantities of fall and winter apples and pears are yet to be gathered.
>
> Some interesting and appropriate remarks were made upon the occasion by Mr. Hammond, who addressed the party in response to a call. Allusion was made to the present condition of Nahant in regard to fruit, etc., as compared to a few years since, when, under the auspices of Mr. Tudor, fruit and ornamental trees were

introduced and their culture encouraged and promoted. Then Nahant was comparatively barren, unsheltered from the driving storms of winter and the fierce rays of the summer sun; now the finest varieties of fruits are comparatively abundant, and shaded walks and groves greatly enhance its native attractions.

Some one present produced the "Atlantic Monthly" for August, from which Mr. Hammond read a portion of an article in which the writer makes disparaging mention of Mr. Tudor's ugly fences and scrubby pear trees. Suffice it to say that the statement, when brought in contrast with the facts in the case, exhibited altogether a sorry contrast. No expression of indignation followed, but twice three deafening cheers for Mr. Tudor gave evidence of the prevailing feeling.

Retiring from the scene of the cider making, the party, each provided (even to the ladies) with a bottle of pure juice of the apple or pear, were conducted by Mr. Tudor to his large garden orchard on the south side of the peninsula. Here in every direction upon the lap of mother earth and hanging from the trees were the finest of fruits in the greatest abundance. Free to all, "As God gave to me, so I give to you," was the generous sentiment of the host. Here, in eloquent volumes, did these pear trees pronounce the "scrubby" epithet a misnomer.

Wishing Mr. Tudor length of days in which to enjoy the fruits of his labors, the merry and happy party repaired to their homes, long and gratefully to remember the pleasant and interesting occasion.

Then follows a paragraph telling that in all, about eighty or ninety barrels of apples were grown on Nahant that year, together with many pears and some butternuts and walnuts. The largest quantity, except for Tudor, is named as grown by Charles Amory, who lived in what is now known as the Dr. Dwight house on Cliff Street near the corner of Willow Road. Many people can remember fruit trees here reaching up Cliff Street to what is now Vernon Street.

The stilted reportorial phrasing and wording of this newspaper article is curious. It contains about all the bromidisms that could be squeezed in. Traces of it are still fairly common in news writing today, but not in such "great abundance." The "Mr. Hammond" is John Q. Hammond mentioned elsewhere in these "Annals."

Tudor built the famous Maolis Gardens, which have a chapter to themselves, and Marginal Road, with its heavy stone sea wall on the shore side. This wall stood intact for a half century or so, needing little repairs, but has gone to pieces rapidly of late. Probably a gradual throwing out of place by the action of frost is the chief cause of the trouble.

Tudor was sufficiently eccentric to be the basis of many stories. One is that in his search for a carpenter, for whom there was steady employment on his many buildings and improvements, he gave each applicant a first job of shingling the roof of a small shed. He made the unusual stipulation that the shingles were to be laid upside down, butts up, beginning at the ridgepole. Several job hunters refused to do so foolish a thing, until finally one said 'twas nonsense but he would do it. Next day Tudor found the job done in a workmanlike manner, though wholly useless, and ordered the man to rip the shingles off and put them on right, saying he only wanted to be sure he got a man who would obey his instructions.

Another story is of Alfred D. Johnson, long time town clerk and founder of Johnson's Nahant Express. At the launching of a little fishing vessel on Nahant, Johnson delivered the principal address. He eulogized graciously the summer resident for whom the vessel was named, and whom Tudor did not like. Next morning on his rounds attending to his express business he called on Tudor, who rushed out to greet him, and insisted on his coming on to the porch to meet a guest, who was a stately looking man of apparent importance. But the introduction was to Daniel Webster, and Johnson was presented as the one who was "greater than God, for he had made a man out of X Y after the Lord Almighty had failed to do so."

The Nahant Public Library has a copy of a rather rare book entitled "The Trees of America," by R. U. Piper, M.D., Woburn, Massachusetts, and dated 1855. This is one part of what was apparently intended to be a rather compendious work on the subject. It was presented to the library by Samuel H. Russell. Dr. Piper lived in a little house at the corner of Valley Road and Ocean Street, where the Valley Road schoolhouse now stands. The house was known, almost until its removal, as the Piper Cottage. It was owned and occupied later by Patrick H. Winn whom all Nahanters will remember, and was torn down when the schoolhouse was built. The book in question, so far as may be judged by the part that was published, hardly had important horticultural or botanical merit, but it is said that Tudor became interested in Dr. Piper and encouraged his work, probably with financial assistance. In return the Doctor liberally mentions Tudor and his work on Nahant, and some of his illustrations show Tudor, perhaps standing under the tree which is depicted. The illustrations are poor. But it is said that Tudor by will provided that the Doctor should have what amounted to a salary as long as he was engaged in this work. This might have been a life job, for there is no end to the pursuit of such a subject. One summer a pleasant young man appeared in town, sought the Doctor's acquaintance unobtrusively, and finally boarded in his house. Becoming intimate the Doctor told him of his plans and of Mr. Tudor's aid. The young man thereupon advised the Doctor that such a provision could be and probably would be broken, and that he would do well to hasten to the business of getting a lump sum settlement. The Doctor did so. Later it was said that this young man was sent to Nahant for the purpose which he accomplished, — of ridding the Tudor estate of what might well become an unwelcome beneficiary. This story comes verbally from a well-known lawyer later agent for the Tudor interests, and may not be correct in every particular. The connection between Dr. Piper and Tudor is, however, established by the book, and this explanation answers a question often asked about the book. Longfellow writes from Nahant one summer, about 1858, of a talk with Tudor and Dr. Piper in which they told him of their plan to plant Iceland with trees and thus enable that island to grow wheat.

Dr. Piper was a versatile genius, a surgeon who had written a book on some feature of surgery, and while on Nahant, partly a teacher of drawing and painting. He constructed a clever outfit for sketching expeditions, all carried in a box mounted on wheels. In Civil War times he was afraid of a bombardment of Nahant, and a cannon dragged up near his house by practical jokers and fired gave the Doctor a real sensation. The "Home Guards" of this period were augmented by Dr. Piper in a green sash, as surgeon of the company. He made rather a comical figure, and the company was nicknamed the "Piper Guards." Later on, removing from Nahant, he lived in Washington, where he was a microscopist and handwriting expert.

Thus is presented a great Nahant figure, Frederic Tudor. Other men have loved Nahant as he did, and have given time and energy to her welfare. Perkins, Dr. Robbins, Coolidge, Wood, — these are names of men of means and energy who assisted greatly in the development of the town. But because Tudor planted trees, which the town lacked, because he had great personal interests here, and because of his peculiarities, he is a more outstanding figure of importance than others. A discrepancy in the dates of birth and death may be noticed. If Tudor was born in 1783, and died after his birthday in 1864, it might be said he died in his eighty-second year, while his son, as quoted, speaks of it as his eighty-first year. Whether this is a misprint, or whether the present writer may be introducing an argument similar to that on when the twentieth century began, which never seemed much in question, may be left for others to determine.

After Tudor's death his widow, Mrs. Fenno Tudor, carried on with the same spirit, but, lacking his experience and some of his ability and enthusiasm, his undertakings gradually lost their prime condition, and later were left to time's destruction. Today a hunt is needed to find traces of what gave him so much pride and pleasure, except his trees, which still grace our town.

The numerous lands he had acquired, scattered all over town, passed by inheritance to a group so widely spread in residence that a corporation was formed to facilitate the passing of titles as the land was sold. This is the Nahant Land Company, still owners of more vacant land than any others, in spite of considerable sales. This company is often named as a real estate trust, so long has it functioned, while essentially it is only an estate to be settled.

Tudor is said to have named three things he wished to do, all of which came to pass, — to ship ice to the Indies; to have six children; and to make trees grow on Nahant. The results of Tudor's great ice enterprise seem to have been all he could have hoped. He came to eminence as a merchant, with Tudor Wharf over in Charlestown, and a Tudor building on Court Street, in Boston, located where Young's Hotel served the public for so many years until it closed in 1927. He obtained exclusive privileges for ice cutting on ponds around Boston. One of these was Walden Pond, made famous by Thoreau. Another was Wenham Lake, and mention may be found of this in Kipling's "Second Jungle Book." Here, in the story entitled "The Undertakers," the Adjutant Bird tells how a sailor on a great boat unloading white stuff threw him a piece. Never had he felt such excessive cold, and when his spasm was over there was nothing at all left of the food. "The adjutant had done his very best to describe his feelings after swallowing a seven pound lump of Wenham Lake ice, off an American ice ship, in the days before Calcutta made her ice by machinery." In "Walden" Thoreau writes, "Thus it appears that the sweltering inhabitants of Charleston and New Orleans, of Madras and Bombay and Calcutta, drink at my well." The "Ice King" was the most famous of the Tudor ice ships, and is pictured herein. A return cargo was found of East Indies products, though American cotton goods had destroyed a former trade in Indian equivalents. The homeward trip, says Morrison in "Maritime History of Massachusetts," was not so cool as the outbound voyage, and there were other discomforts. It is said that on the arrival of a vessel it was not uncommon to see a pack of terrified dogs running up State Street, in Boston, pursued by an army of Calcutta cockroaches.

CHAPTER VI

HOTELS

In these first fifty years after 1800, hotels played so large a part in Nahant life that a large space must be given to them. The residents of the town, probably all of them, took boarders or furnished meals long prior to 1800 as they did long afterwards. People now living came to Nahant and boarded, fifty years ago or so, in the old Johnson Homestead across the street from the present Town Hall. But none of these houses was built as a hotel. The first building constructed as such was the one at Bass Point, built and run by Joseph Johnson and Nathan Silsbee from 1803 or earlier until sold for a private residence in 1840. It was burned a year or two after building and was promptly rebuilt, as told elsewhere.

An advertisement of this hotel in 1802 seems up to date in its claims for perfections, and its light frankness seems also in keeping with good present-day practice:

> Joseph Johnson informs the public in general and the valetudinarians and sportsmen in particular, that he has reopened a House of Entertainment on the most delightful, pleasant, airy and healthy spot on Nahant, where he will be found ready furnished with every good thing to cheer the heart, to brace the frame, or to pamper the appetite. His house is commodious and neat, in the vicinity of the best fishing and boating on the peninsula; and he keeps a neat sailboat always afloat for the accommodation of his friends. To the other inducements he adds his respectful invitation; and while he will attend his guests with delight, he assures them that every favour shall be remembered with gratitude.
>
> > Friend to pastime, foe to care,
> > Come, enjoy our sports and fare.
> > Come, and stay a week or so;
> > But if uneasy, haste to go.

The "Log Cabin" of "Tippecanoe and Tyler too" Times
Replaced by present home of Arthur S. Johnson

Steamboat "Ulysses" at Tudor Wharf, 1870
Foreground, stone boat with stone for rebuilding wharf,
sunk in September gale, 1869

It has been argued that the use of the word "reopened" in this notice means opened after rebuilding, and that therefore it was built and burned before 1802. Lewis specifically mentions this fire as in 1803, however, and gives the exact time, even to the hour of the day, with some details about the escape of the occupants. It would seem that such details must have come from some authentic source to Lewis, and that Johnson's use of "reopened" referred to some hotel elsewhere and was an attempt to attract old patrons. In later days this building was known as the "Old Castle" and was said to be haunted, perhaps by the ghosts of revellers. It was taken down in 1903, when the late Edward E. Strout built his home a few rods away.

Samuel Breed was designated "Inn Keeper" in an old deed of 1738, and if he was an inn keeper his house was an inn. This means that what is now the Whitney Homestead reaches farthest back among Nahant hotels. It was not, however, built as a hotel, and in 1817 the last Breed moved to Lynn and Jesse Rice took over the property. A wing was added in 1820 or a little earlier, which made it certainly a building for hotel purposes primarily. This was the easterly end for a dining room with sleeping rooms above.

June 13, 1821, the old "Columbian Centinel" carries this advertisement:

> Jesse Rice would inform his friends and the public that he has lately made an addition to this house of a large hall and sleeping chambers, so that he will be able to give better accommodations to parties than he has heretofore, and will have large accommodations for boarders. He assures the public that no pains shall be spared on his part to give perfect satisfaction to all who may honor him with their company.

This hotel was called the "Rice House," and is the one mentioned by Hawthorne and other writers of this period. Rice started the first line of public conveyances between Nahant and Lynn.

Then there was the Nahant House built by Cornelius Coolidge about 1820, later owned by George Peabody and lately by Dudley B. Fay. Albert Whitney came to Nahant to keep this hotel, and in 1840 Jesse Rice, whose daughter Whitney married, sold the Rice House to his son-in-law.

In the meantime one of the four Hood houses mentioned elsewhere had been built about 1819 and kept as a public house until 1826 by Richard Hood. Then it was sold to Charles Bradbury, who sold to Jesse Rice in 1840. Rice kept this as a hotel until 1861. It was said that during its early years many English officers came here for entertainment, more or less disguised as civilians. This is the house, still often known as the Rice House, setting close to the street line, on Nahant Road across from the head of Wharf Street.

Whitney kept "Whitney's Hotel" until 1883. He built the long wing on the westerly end of the building in 1859. An advertisement in the "Lynn Mirror" of June, 1841, is of

WHITNEY, FORMERLY RICE HOTEL, NAHANT

This long established and well known house, having been recently repaired and newly painted throughout under the immediate direction of the subscriber, is now open for the reception of permanent and transient guests. It is delightfully situated upon one of the most pleasant retreats of Nahant. Every exertion will be made to merit the favor of the public. Patronage respectfully solicited. Meals 50 to 75 cents.

A. WHITNEY.

JUNE 16, 1841.

N.B. — Parties can be accommodated with a yacht of eighteen tons, with all fishing apparatus.

After closing from 1883 to 1896 it was reopened by a daughter of Whitney as a boarding house, and was called the "Whitney Homestead," under which title it is still operated by members of the family.

The Nahant House, which Whitney gave up in 1840, was soon sold to George Peabody and remodelled into a private house.

Then should be mentioned the Joseph Johnson house on Nahant Road, which bore a modest sign "J. Johnson." It

was built early in the century, 1801 to 1803. It cared for both permanent and transient guests. When Joseph Johnson died, in 1854, his son Edmund B. Johnson kept the house as a hotel or boarding house until 1867.
But nearly all these early houses catered to summer visitors. Dexter Stetson, who bought the Abner Hood, Jr., place, now a part of the Upham estate, took boarders. The Artemus Murdock house, now the house of the "Edgehill" group nearest Nahant Road, was another. The Jonathan Johnson house, or Mrs. Ann Johnson's, as it was later called, was where the post office block now stands. This was moved to the corner of Willow Road and Wharf Street, and lost its identity in the larger construction now known as the "Rockledge." The Bulfinch house on the corner of Nahant Road and Ocean Street, now owned by Philip Young, was another. The Tudor Homestead, now the Nahant Club, was at one time kept as a boarding house by Mrs. A. E. Robinson, who later bought the Murdock property and developed the extensive "Edgehill" buildings. The "Trooper" Johnson Homestead, later the home of Caleb Johnson and his son, C. Hervey Johnson, now the Sigourney estate, was at one time rented to Frederick Rouillard of Boston, once of the well-known old Julien House at the corner of Congress and Milk Streets. Later on Nahant he kept a small place near by and served fish dinners. The oldest part of Hotel Tudor was a small cottage on the corner of Nahant Road and Summer Street, just westerly from the Francis Johnson house, later Mrs. S. J. Melvin's and now E. J. Hutchinson's. It was owned by Samuel Perkins and occupied by his family until 1842. Between 1842 and 1854 Mrs. William Cary owned and occupied this house, which had become familiarly known as the Aunt Sam Perkins house. Perkins was a brother of Colonel Thomas Handasyd Perkins, who is mentioned elsewhere. In 1854 Frederic Tudor bought it and moved it to Willow Road, where he enlarged and rebuilt it. It was used as a private house, occupied for several years by Dr. Dix, and then as a summer hotel known as the Hood Cottage, so named because

it stood on land formerly owned by the Hoods. Still later it was bought by William Catto, who remodelled it in 1893 and opened it as the "Hotel Tudor."

Mention should be made of the "Bay View House," still standing close to the streets at the northerly corner of Willow Road and Summer Street. It was opened as a hotel about 1869, and was, though remodelled, the ell of the Dexter Stetson house, formerly owned by Abner Hood, Jr. Thomas Demster was one of the first proprietors, afterwards the first manager of the Bass Point House.

But the hotel which overshadowed all of these and made them minor matters was, of course, the great Nahant Hotel on East Point, the district formerly known as the Ram Pasture. Mention has been made of Colonel Thomas H. Perkins, and that he and William Paine were the signers of an invitation to those interested in this hotel project to meet in Boston in September, 1821. The notice appeared in the "Columbian Centinel" for September 15. In June, 1823, the house was opened and the following notice appeared in Boston papers. It seems to follow the perfervid description method which has been noted in other excerpts:

> This magnificent establishment is now open for the reception of visitors to the most delightful spot on the American Coast for health or pleasure. It is impossible to select a residence which combines so many natural and artificial advantages.
>
> Located in the bosom of the ocean, the air is salubrious and inviting; while the spacious bay, continually presenting the fleets of commerce, with the hills, verdant plains, islands, villages and country seats, extending from the heights of Scituate to the peninsula of Cape Ann, form a panorama unrivalled in any country.
>
> The numerous projecing cliffs afford excellent sites for the angler, from whence even old Izaak Walton would have thrown his line with pleasure, and looked abroad upon the wilderness of water "in moral contemplation wrapt."
>
> The hotel is capacious and fitted up with every convenience, where the superintendent, Captain James Magee, so distinguished for his gentlemanly deportment and kind disposition, is most assiduous to make every one happy and comfortable. There are floating, hot, cold and shower salt water baths, billiard rooms,

bowling alleys, a beautiful marine hippodrome which twice in twenty-four hours is laved and rolled smooth by the waves of the ocean; and numerous interesting walks for health, exercise and amusement. In truth, Nahant is the chosen domain of youthful Hygeia, the pleasant summer residence of the invalid and of all those who seek enjoyment or require relaxation from the cares of business life; whether they flee from the sultry clime of the South, or the "Stir of the great Babels" of commerce, there they can be at ease and keep cool.

Captain Magee was a relative of Mrs. Perkins, and a curious reference is made to him in an account owned by the Nahant Church, which says: "He commanded a little steamer called the 'Tom Thumb,' which I believe ran to Chelsea and perhaps to Nahant. T. H. Perkins, Sr., is sponsor for this: On one occasion he was on board the 'Thumb,' when Magee, in a loud voice, putting his head into the little companionway that led to the engine, cried, 'Mr. Engineer, how many inches on the Thumb?' 'Two and a half, sir,' replies the engineer. 'Then give her another stick of wood, Mr. Engineer.'" What makes this anecdote curious is that there seems to have been no "Tom Thumb," certainly not among the early steamers, while Tom Thumb, the dwarf for whom it might be assumed the craft was named, was a very diminutive little man in the Court of King Arthur. It seems doubtful if any of these crafts seemed small at the time, and therefore skepticism arises as to the name, the time and the boat.

The following year a further account adds to the description:

> The hotel itself is a large stone edifice, containing seventy chambers, in a number of which are recesses for beds.
> There is a dining room fifty feet in length and of sufficient size to accommodate one hundred and twenty-four persons at table; besides these there are several private parlors and a capacious stable, a handsome bathing house for warm and cold baths, a machine of peculiar construction for bathing in the open sea, excellent boats for sailing and fishing.

This notice is signed by Durant & Johnson, who managed the house until 1827. J. L. Homer, writing in 1848, says:

The original cost of the land, hotel and outbuildings was about $60,000, which was divided into shares of $100 each. It was carried on several years after its completion, with very little advantage to its proprietors, however, by the late James Magee, Esq., a gentleman of fine epicurean taste, and by Messrs. Johnson & Durand. In 1825, the original stockholders being a little sick of their bargain, having never received a dividend upon their investment, the hotel was sold at public auction, at the depreciated price of $14,000. The purchasers were Colonel Thomas H. Perkins and Dr. Edward H. Robbins, who enlarged its dimensions considerably by adding to it the easterly wing, which is now used as the principal dining room for the lodgers. This improvement cost several thousand dollars. Messrs. Perkins and Robbins sold the hotel again, in 1842, to its present proprietor, Mr. Drew, for $25,000. This gentleman made a great bargain. Owing to a combination of circumstances, it is now valued at more than double that sum.

After Messrs. Perkins and Robbins became the purchasers of the hotel it was carried on several years for their account by different individuals, none of whom succeeded so well as the proprietors expected they would, with perhaps one exception. In 1833 Mr. R. W. Holman, now of the United States Hotel, became the agent of the proprietors, for whom he acted until about 1840, driving a moderately prosperous business at all times. During one season under his management, I am informed, the hotel cleared about $6,000 in three months, — a pretty fair business, this. Mr. Holman was succeeded in the agency of the proprietors by Mr. Drew, who, in 1842, as I have before stated, became sole proprietor of the establishment, and since that time has been blessed with a run of prosperity which must have been highly flattering to his feelings and grateful to his purse. The present season has been successful beyond any previous one.

One of Drew's advertisements says that "an extensive garden has been laid out, and many other improvements for the pleasure of visitors. Parents are informed that a school for children will be kept on the premises." A letter written in August, 1848, and published in Homer's pamphlet of 1848, shows that some backbiting was going on, perhaps from jealousy at Drew's success. The letter takes pains to say that it does not allude to persons who follow the same business in Nahant, "for so far as Nahant is concerned they mind their own affairs; but there is a class of people who, having no business of their own to attend to, busy themselves in instructing persons far more competent than themselves." It would seem that no generation is free from the busybody. The greatest howls are howls for the other fellow's piece of cake. In 1852 Drew sold to Rand & Sons of the old Sagamore House in Lynn. One reference says it was sold to a group of Lynn people. They enlarged it again until it reached the form presented by the large lithograph pictures of it. These were advertising material, and many are in existence. The Nahant Public Library has two, and one hangs on the walls of the Maolis Club house. Some years ago a roll containing thirty or forty of these was found in Lynn, and they were dispersed to as many people. In 1854 Paran Stevens, the most noted hotel man of the times, was its manager, with J. E. P. Stevens. It was remodelled again, but not enlarged, in 1855. It was lighted by gas, then unusual for a country place, and it is said to have represented a total investment of well over $300,000. Telegraph wires connected it with the world, so says a contemporary writing, but it is doubtful how much of the world was reached. Morse's invention was first used over short distances about 1835, and yet it was 1858 before any regular and useful telegraphic service was set up between Lynn and Boston. Steam heating was installed in the hotel in 1859, to enable a longer season, which was so advertised. Much of the patronage was from the South and from Canada. The slavery agitation grew violent and war was imminent and patronage fell away. The management apparently used every effort to make 1859 a successful season, but it was the last season the house was opened. Gilmore's band, the most famous military band, perhaps, that this country has had, was engaged. A concert program for August 29, 1857, by an Englishman, George Henry Russell, shows the "Celebrated Songs of That Period." He sang "Life on the Ocean Wave," "The Gambler's Wife," "The Song of the Shirt," "The Newfoundland Dog," "The Ship on Fire" and "Cheer, Boys, Cheer." The house closed on October 1, 1859. The end was reached.

In the summer of 1861 the furnishings and fittings were sold at auction. Many things thus found their way to scattered ownership about Nahant, as well as to a wider field. In its later years it was known commonly both as the Nahant Hotel and the Nahant House. The original Nahant House, already mentioned, had passed to private ownership and occupancy, and no distinction was longer necessary. The hotel was burned on September 12, 1861, and is described as a magnificent sight in its destruction, visible, because of its commanding position, far out to sea and for many miles along the coast. The ruins, which were notably of the older stone part of the original building, were left standing for many years. Photographs of them are extant, as in the Nahant Public Library, and an old Prang chromo dated 1867 shows them.

The billiard hall of this famous outfit still remains, the most easterly building on the estate of the late Senator Henry Cabot Lodge, who used it in recent years for a book storage room. It is a dignified, well-proportioned little building, ranking among the older structures of Nahant. Another part of this hotel group, not burned, was moved to Short Beach, where it now stands, owned by J. C. Shaughnessy, and long the home of his father. It is the first house eastward from the beach on the shore side of Nahant Road. It is said that this was the private quarters of the proprietor, Paran Stevens, and there is a little gusto in the explanation that here Mrs. Paran Stevens lived, in this simple cottage, because she afterwards became such a social lion — or lioness.

This seems to be the story of the great hotel, the greatest of its time, and of the general hotel business on Nahant during a long period. Bass Point is newer, and has a chapter to itself, as likewise the Maolis House which was closely associated with the Maolis Gardens.

A little pamphlet entitled "Letters from Nahant," dated 1848, and with no author named, says, "It is now over twenty years since the erection of the Hotel, which took place in 1820, and from that time Nahant has grown to be one of the most

Henry Cabot Lodge

Public Library Trustee

Joseph T. Wilson

Elected over one hundred times

Edmund B. Johnson

Town Treasurer

Walter Johnson

Highway Surveyor

celebrated watering places in the country." "A night's sleep at Nahant, in hot weather, is a luxury nowhere else to be enjoyed; if ice is a luxury at Canton, so is a bed at Drews, of a hot August night. To be appreciated it must be enjoyed; no one can describe its invigorating influence."

An editorial in the Lynn "Mirror" of July 16, 1835, reads:

> Nahant, if we may judge from the carriages which daily pass over the beach, continues to be the favorite resort for pleasure and comfort. The fresh, cool breezes after the still sultry days passed in the city are very refreshing. The advantages of sport in fishing and gunning, the romantic and rural appearance of the place, and the excellence of the public houses will continue to make this a favorite retreat. We made an excursion there last week with a party of friends and found the place alive, with ladies galloping on horseback; fishing and shooting in whatever direction we turned our eyes. We called at the house of our friend Rice, a hotel, one of the oldest in the place, which for neatness, stillness, convenience, pleasantness and abundance of good fare, and, what is important in these days of pressure, reasonable of charge, we should recommend to the patronage of our friends and the public.

An advertisement in the Lynn "Mirror" of September 23, 1826, says that a coach will run from the Nahant Hotel twice a day, at 8 A.M. and 3 P.M., connecting with coaches for Boston, Salem, etc. Fare, fifty cents each way. The times of running were changed to suit the tides, as access over the beach was difficult at any time near high tide. Another advertisement of the same year is for a fisherman for the Nahant Hotel. "Robin Adair" was a favorite ballad of the time, and the Lynn "Mirror" of April 28, 1827, quotes a parody from the "Evening Gazette" on the purchase of the hotel by Perkins and Robbins:

> Who bought Nahant Hotel?
> Robbins, I hear.
> Pray, will it turn out well?
> Oh, never fear.
> Will all the mirth and glee
> That we were wont to see
> Be all revived by thee,
> Robbins, my dear?

> Without a steamboat nought
>   Comes off Nahant.
> This has he also bought,
>   So I have learnt.
> Hot, cold, seasick or so
> Down we'll for ninepence go;
> Budge not by land or sea,
>   Robbins, I sha'n't.
>
> But now thou art cold to me
>   East winds prevail.
> Yet soon shall verdure be
>   O'er hill and dale.
> Then will grasshoppers sing,
> Then will thy chowder bring
> Crowds. Oh! — this is the thing,
>   Robbins, all hail!

This effusion would not find a place in any anthology, except, perhaps, of worst poetry, if the "Sweet Singer of Michigan" had not pre-empted all that space. The various excerpts are given to show the times. Another paper in 1827 says:

> On Saturday last six hundred persons left Nahant for Boston; we are glad to find that visitors at this pleasant retreat are again becoming frequent. On Monday nearly three hundred people dined at the Nahant Hotel and were excellently well accommodated. One company, composed principally of members of musical choirs of several societies of the city, to the number of nearly two hundred, dined at tables extending the entire length of the three piazzas. Among the visitors at the Hotel this season are numbers of our southern friends, and if we may be pardoned for introducing the name of a lady, we should mention that Mrs. Randolph, the daughter of the venerable Thomas Jefferson, was one of them.

This sounds like a society column, but today a society column would have to apologize for not introducing the name of a lady. Another citation from a Salem paper in the same year reads:

> Nahant contains about a dozen dwellings, and has about three hundred and five acres of fertile land under high cultivation. . . . Nahant has long been a place of resort in the warm season for the fashionable and gay from the metropolis who are in pursuit of amuse-

ment and recreation, and for invalids from the vicinity and interior of the country, who are in pursuit of health, in the most oppressive heat and sultry weather of summer. . . . Immense quantities of seaweed are cast by the ocean on the beach and shore of the peninsula. Not less than three thousand tons a year are conveyed to the mainland by the farmers. . . . The number of visitors at Nahant this year has never been equalled. Strangers are enticed here from the more southern cities. The point of attraction is Nahant, which, like the orbit of a circle, encloses all the taste, elegance and fashion of the country. The balls are splendid and gay, the conversation lively and amusing.

Nahant seems to have had variations from this most fashionable life, in the time now considered, before the Civil War. George William Curtis in "Lotus Eating," in an article "Nahant," says of it:

Nahant would not satisfy a New Yorker, nor, indeed, a Bostonian, whose dreams of seaside summering are based on Newport life. The two places are entirely different. It is not quite true that Newport has all of Nahant and something more. For the repose, the freedom from the fury of fashion, is precisely what endears Nahant to its lovers, and the very opposite is characteristic of Newport.

This book was first published in 1852. Apparently changing managers and varying business success at the big hotel, which certainly set the pace for a time, made a difference in the speed of life and society which is reflected in descriptions of succeeding years. Nahant still appears, however, as remarkable for its time as the two or three best known resorts or hotels of California or Florida are notable for today. Another attempt to picture the life of the period for summer-time Nahant will be the following article, which is the entire report made by Professor Felton, once President of Harvard College, of a lecture by his brother-in-law, Professor Agassiz, in 1854. Professor Felton evidently enjoyed writing about the Nahant he also loved so well. A copy of it was sent to Senator Lodge by the Hon. Robert C. Winthrop for the Nahant Public Library in 1898 or 1899, and it was published with some other material on Nahant by the Library in the latter year.

NAHANT IN 1854

The attractions of Nahant the present season appear to have surpassed all former example. It is a wonderful place. It seems as if the agencies of nature had kept in view, while forming it, the special wants of the good people of Boston and their summer visitors. While the tri-mountain peninsula was shaping for the purposes of a large commercial city, with its harbor and beautiful islands, fitted alike for the ornaments of peace and defenses in war, the same beneficent agencies were also cutting out the promontory of Nahant for a summer retreat, to which the future citizens of the three-hilled town might flee from the hot air of the city, to refresh themselves with the cool breezes of the sea. The new hotel, with its spacious accommodations, has been opened opportunely for the unusual heat of this summer, and gasping multitudes have rushed hither for fear of melting down and running away on the parched and dusty mainland.

Nahant, however, does not agree with all constitutions or suit all tastes. To some, the rugged rocks that bound its shores are a barren and a dismal spectacle; and "old ocean's gray and melancholy waste" but a tedious and monotonous picture. The bracing air is too much for them. In half an hour they fall into a slumberous state, from which neither the splendor of evening nor the freshness of morning can arouse them. A desperate headache and preternatural stupidity deaden the joy of social intercourse and make the unhappy victim feel as if, in running away from home, he has left all his pleasures and all his duties behind him. You may see him, Ulysses like, sitting sadly on the shore and looking wistfully toward the distant horizon, content to die "if he may once more see the smoke leaping up from his dear native land." "Lasciate ogni speranza o voi ch' entrate" would be his motto if he had his wits sufficiently to think of one. But even in these pitiable cases, a few days of suffering open the way to a very tolerable state of existence. The gods have placed labor before virtue; and pain heightens the sensation of pleasure when it comes. The iron band around the head gradually loosens its pressure; the swollen eyes subside into their natural cavities; sleep relaxes his hold and contents himself with ten or a dozen hours out of the twenty-four. Signs of animation show that the case is not so desperate as was at first supposed and life regains some of its old interests, as to a man recovering from a trance. You may see the convalescent strolling languidly over the rocks and even looking out upon the sea, as if the notion were beginning to dawn upon him that there is, after all, something in it not unworthy of his attention. A week or a fortnight generally works a radical cure; reconciles the man to his mortal condition, and to Nahant.

These are exceptional cases. To most men, women and children Nahant presents a welcome refuge during the excessive heats of our summer months. The merchant gladly escapes from his counting house; the lawyer from his office; the clergyman from his study, to enjoy the rest and air of Nahant. Men of business easily reach the city by the morning boat, and after a day of delving in the dust of the town, return eagerly to a late chowder and a soothing cigar and a cool night for sleeping. And after all Nahant is not such a dreary rock as some people, who ought to know better, suppose. There is a pleasant valley between its craggy barriers with soft green turf, and running waters, and thick-leaved trees, worthy to be the scene of another Decameron. The Ice-King, who cools the tropics with the harvest of our winters and who seems born for victorious struggles with natural difficulties, has planted beautiful lines of trees over the peninsula, which grow and flourish in spite of summer's heat and winter's cold. May he live a thousand years, and may his shadow, personal and arboricultural, never grow less.

There is variety enough in the society here, whether we look at the permanent settlers who occupy the cottages, or the more flighty elements that change from day to day. Hither comes the youthful dandy, with the suspicion of a mustache on his lip, and a cigar in his mouth. Middle aged men and old men, fat men and lean men, stout ladies and slender ladies, disport themselves on the rocks, and repair the waste of exercise by the daily chowder, prefixed to the far fetched luxuries of a city dinner. A fleet of yachts dot the sea with their white sails and afford topics of interest, when other subjects of conversation flag. The morning concerts and evening dances at the hotel fill up the time and employ the heels and voices of the performers, as well as the ears and eyes of the spectators in the most agreeable manner. The spectacle of the yacht race, the other day, drew the beauty and fashion of Nahant to the cliffs; and the birds of the sea spread their snowy plumage for the sport under the inspiring presence of gay multitudes of ladies —
> Whose bright eyes
> Rain influence and adjudge the prize.

Nahant is the resort, also, of men of thought and letters. Prescott, to be sure, has deserted the rock on which he used to perch himself, and set up his workshop of history among the shoemakers of "the pleasant town of Lynn." But he wrote "Ferdinand and Isabella" and the "Conquest of Mexico" here; and it remains to be seen whether "Philip the Second" will come off as well among the leather and prunella of yonder sole hammering town. If history has retired, Eloquence and Poetry and Science have come. Winthrop is here, the orator and statesman, who won his laurels at an age when most men are still toiling unknown to fame. He is at present retired from public life, but only to enter the scene of his former triumphs with energies invigorated and renewed, and with a mind more amply stored with the wealth of learning and experience for the high service of the country. Longfellow is here musing on the "Sea and Shore," and doubtless meditating some rhythmical theme, to be as immortal as the harmonies of the deep. Agassiz has pitched his tent upon the rocks where he can gather his beloved fishes around him and subject them to his microscopic analysis. It is said the finny tenants of the sea already know the philosopher, who has done so much to sound their fame all over the world. They surrender themselves cheerfully without hook or bait, bob or sinker, for the good of science, into his hands. Sourel, the artist, is at work taking their portraits; and any fish may well be content to have his delicate tissues, admirable frame work and splendid coloring, rescued from the obscurity to which most ichthyological beauties are doomed, far down the dark depths of the sea, and to sacrifice a few draughts of his watery existence to be endowed with the immortality of a chapter in the great work on the embryology of the animal kingdom, which has been so many years preparing. St. Anthony preached to the fishes; they came up in their several ways to his call; they listened with great edification to the texts and doctrines of the godly man. But the sermon over they plunged back again, and like so many human hearers of the word, resumed their ancient wriggling courses. All the odd fish, star fishes, sea urchins, shovel sharks and the like find the way to the workshop of Agassiz, but none of them get back again. Perhaps they chose to remain; perhaps they prefer their lot; for they are forthwith thrown into bottles or casks and continue in liquor the rest of their days.

A solitary ramble around Nahant is, however, the greatest pleasure one can enjoy. It is pleasant to hear the singing at the concerts; it is pleasant to talk with friends, lying on the grass or stretched uneasily on the rocks; it is pleasant to drive or ride with a lively party on the long beach; it is pleasant to look upon the lovely faces gathered here from the north, south and west; but it is a deeper pleasure to sit on the massive piles of syenite that stand so firmly against the encroachments of the waters, and listen to the tones of the ocean as it sweeps up against the grey cliffs from its mysterious depths; to gaze upon the sparkling crests of the waves as they chase each other with "laughter innumerous" up to the shore, and play hide and seek in the sea-worn caves, which they fill with their multitudinous voices; to watch the fleets of commerce which daily cross the horizon, flying on their woven wings to every part of the world; to speculate on the messages they are bearing and the fortunes that await them on their adventurous ways. Sometimes the blue expanse seems crowded with them; at other times only here and there a single sail glimmers in the light. The changing colors of the sea are a never failing spectacle of beauty. The play of purple, blue, green, and the flash of the foaming waves as they break along the rocks; the march of the clouds across the sky, and now and then a fog-bank slowly and majestically sweeping landward and hiding all behind it like a solid wall, give to the contemplation of the sea an infinite and unsatiating variety.

> There is a pleasure in the pathless woods;
> There is a rapture in the lonely shore;
> There is society where none intrudes;
> By the deep sea, and music in its roar.

Nahant has not only its picturesque attractions but its scientific interests. There is much in its geological formation deserving the attention of the visitor; and so thought the inmates of the hotel. They seized upon the lucky circumstance of Agassiz's presence to invite him to give a lecture upon the geological structure of Nahant; and Friday evening was appointed for this novel entertainment. At a quarter past eight o'clock the spacious drawing-room was converted into a hall of lecture, and the fashionable company assumed the appearance of a learned society, occupied with the investigations of natural science. Everybody knows the personal appearance of the great philosopher; everybody has listened to the solid and earnest eloquence with which he discourses on the laws of Nature, and how impossible it is to escape the charm which concentrates every thought upon the lecturer and his theme.

At the appointed time the room was filled, and after a few moments of whispered communication and rustling of garments, the lecturer mounted the table, which was placed at the upper end of the room for a temporary rostrum. He was received with applause, and then in the midst of the profound silence, commenced. I can only give you the leading topics of the admirable discourse, which commanded the unbroken attention of the crowded and brilliant audience for more than an hour. Mr. Agassiz, in explaining the form of Nahant, made use of an excellent map, executed by Mr. Alonzo Lewis, the Historian, of Lynn, and illustrated the details of the structure by diagrams drawn on a blackboard.

Ladies and Gentlemen: Did I not know that it is in the nature and disposition of men to love change and variety, I should hardly venture to introduce among the guests of a place like this, dedicated to gayety, a question of scientific interest. This evening I propose to ask your attention to the geology of Nahant; to the structure of the spot over which we pass in our daily walks, in order to show how much instruction may be drawn from a subject apparently so circumscribed. Indeed, its features warrant a minute study of months, or even years, for we should constantly find new subjects of interest. To the student of nature, Nahant is a geological museum in miniature, in which he may examine on a small scale all the great features of the globe.

The outlines of a country do not furnish by themselves indications of the internal structure of the land. Nahant, for instance, which projects as a promontory in a west easterly direction, is by no means composed of rocks structurally connected in that way, but of bands of strata running exactly in the opposite direction.

In reality, Nahant consists of a group of islands, connected by low lands, and surrounded, on one side by the bay of Nahant, on the other by the harbor of Lynn. There is no set of rocks extending from the mainland to the end of the promontory. The strata cut across the peninsula, extending on the north through Beverly and on the south through Boston harbor.

The rocks are layers of clay-stone alternating in their succession from below upwards, with nodules of limestone. 2. Layer of clay-stone without such nodule. 3. Layers of syenite. 4. Layers of slaty syenite. 5. Layers of porphyry. 6. A large succession of layers of syenite, all of them intersected in almost every direction by dykes.

The rocks by no means are primitive rocks formed as they appear now. All the layers were deposited in horizontal position and consisted at first of materials differently combined from what they are at present. The hard silicious clay-stones were soft clay; the nodules of lime-stone forming alternate beds with the clay beds, were coral banks. The beds of syenite were beds of sand-stone, consisting of grains of quartz in clay-mud, with particles of iron and magnesian lime and other minerals. The slaty syenite contained some chloride; the porphyry some iron. Throughout the old peninsula the dykes are chiefly of hornblende. Now, if we were to take these materials as they are supposed to have been at the time of their deposition and to melt them in furnaces or subject them to the action of intense heat, as we subject the materials from which glass is made, upon cooling they would produce exactly the rocks we now have here, — the clays would become indurated, and we have from Nature's furnace a kind of coarse glass in the syenite.

It is the prominent peculiarity of Nahant to exhibit rocks which in their mineralogical appearance resemble the rocks of igneous origin, but in their arrangement and superposition, preserve all the peculiar features of regularly stratified rocks. This shows that this tract of land is one of the most beautiful examples of stratified rocks of aquatic origin, altered by the agency of internal heat and the eruption of melted masses into rocks of an apparent igneous origin.

The cause of this alteration lies deep under the surface and is apparent only at one spot — the black rocks of the northern shore, just under the window of my study; the dykes are of a later origin than the upheaval of the beds, since they run through the strata they have only filled the cracks formed by the process of cooling and the disturbance of the strata, during the transformation of the stratified rocks, by Plutotic agency.

This alteration of stratified rocks of aquatic origin by a subterranean agency of internal heat is not the only result of this change. The rocks have been not only altered in their mineralogic appearance, but their position has been changed from a horizontal into a more or less inclined dip, the direction of which is mainly north south, or more precisely north-east south-west.

This upheaval of the beds was caused by the action of the internal fires, on an axis of greatest tension, extending in the direction just mentioned.

This fact is conformable with the general structure of our shores, and owing to the degree of hardness of the successive alternate strata, has caused the alternate ridges and depressions of the country, and on a small scale, the different hills of the peninsula which run parallel to the coast in general. Such is the hill on which the hotel stands, which is separated from that on which the church is built by a low neck. Again, the highest hill on which the

Home of H. W. Longfellow, Willow Road
Burned in 1896

Fremont Cottage, owned by John C. Fremont, the "Pathfinder"
Built by Edward Phillips

village is built, is separated from the second by the marsh south of Whitney's hotel.

The direction of these hills and the strata of which they are composed is very important in showing the manner in which the peninsula has been formed. It is in fact the result of a great indentation in the mainland, which has produced the bay of Swampscott and the harbor of Lynn; and such indentations occur along the whole coast. The minor bays upon the northern and southern shores of the peninsula have been hollowed in the softer lands, alternating with the more durable ones, which rise as hills, and corresponding to these bays, we find everywhere the low necks uniting the hills; some of which would be real islands but for the accumulation of drift gravel and sand between them; as for instance Little Nahant and the hill of the castle,[1] south of the short beach.

If these structural features were well understood, a methodical search might be easily made of all the irregularities below water; and the safety to the entrance to Boston Harbor, now that ships so much larger than formerly are built, would not depend on the accidental discoveries of rising rocks, some of which have been found even within the last three months, but might be ascertained in their position by a regular examination. This is another of the instances of the importance of geological surveys, which, however, to be thus practically useful, ought to be prosecuted with a degree of minuteness and precision which no state has yet allowed to be applied in the surveys they have ordered and directed. Egg Rock affords a beautiful example of this connection with the mainland of apparently isolated islands. It is in reality the prolongation of the Spouting Horn Hill. The Graves are another hill running parallel with the general bend of the strata of the island, only more remote from the point than this is from the village, but bearing the same relation to it that the village bears to Little Nahant.

At what period the transformation I have spoken of occurred it is not easy to say, except relatively. No fossils are found here. The igneous action has obliterated all remains, except some traces very imperfectly seen in the lime-stone nodules. But the trend of these layers, if followed out, connects them with the coal beds of Marshfield. The deposition of the beds occurred at the time when the plants lived, which have formed the coal at Marshfield, or during the coal period. The American continent has been above water since the coal period. It is the oldest of the continents, and had its present conformation when Europe appeared only as a series of scattered islands or of archipelagos.

There is another series of facts observable here, of a very interesting character. Over the surface of Nahant, as well as of the mainland, large quantities of lava materials, pebbles and boulders, are thickly scattered, which are not the fragments of the rocks on which they rest. Many of the pebbles are rounded and polished; the large boulders are left standing in beds of

---

[1] Now known as Fox Hill.

small pebbles, in equilibrium; and sometimes on the ridges of hills, as for instance, Ship Rock — apparently having travelled over the whole space from Lake Huron and Lake Superior. These materials constitute a continuous sheet of unstratified sand, gravel, pebble and boulders. Where these are not found at present, they have been removed by rain or by the encroachments of the sea. Their internal arrangement, the form of the isolated pebbles, the nature of the surfaces upon which they rest, show plainly that they have been brought to their resting places by an agent capable of moving such immense masses of detritus from a considerable distance, and that the direction of the motion has been from the north to the south; for the rock, of which these materials are composed, can in every instance be traced to the north of their present position. From Labrador to the Rocky Mountains there extends a smooth, level and polished surface, over which these masses have been moved; and this surface is easily marked by straight lines, scratches, grooves or furrows, all of which point northward also. These have been made by the rocks and the pebbles in their onward course from the north southward. The question is by what agency these materials have been transported from their original position to the places where they are now found. No question in geology has perplexed to a greater degree the investigators of nature and few are more complicated. Upon the facts there is no discrepancy of opinion among observers; but they differ in opinion as to the moving agent. Some believe it to have been water. But an insuperable objection to this theory exists in the fact that the larger boulders are frequently uppermost, which could not have been the case if they had been swept along by a current of water. Again, the larger are angular, whereas the action of water is to polish the pebbles, subjected to its agency on all sides. Then the action of water is to wear away the softer materials more rapidly than the harder, thus producing irregularities. But, all over this worn surface, the dykes composed of harder materials than the masses at their sides, are nevertheless cut down to the same level. These facts seem to show that the moving agent could not have been fluid. The other theory is that the agent was ice. This is the opinion which I hold, though standing almost alone. The effects described must have been produced by a solid mass, keeping the pebbles together and moving along in one direction. I believe the mass to have been ice — in other words a glacial agency — a sheet of ice moving from the north to the south — like the existing glaciers, which produce all the phenomena we witness here — the rounded masses — polished pebbles — scratched surfaces — accumulation of loomy paste resulting from abrasion — boulders — in short, all the same features on a smaller scale. The theory of drifted icebergs is liable to the same objections as the theory of water action. The only difficulty is to account for the formation of such extensive glaciers and the origin of the motion. There are facts, however, which show that amazing changes have taken place in the temperature of our globe. The discovery of tropical animals imbedded in polar ice, is one of them. How these changes have been produced I am unable to explain; but it is only necessary to suppose that, in the glacial period, the meteorogical conditions should have produced upon extensive sheets of ice the same effects now observed, on a smaller scale, among the glaciers of the Alps, where great changes are seen from year to year.

With regard to the motion, we may observe that it depends, not so much on the slope down which a glacier moves, as on the amount of moisture that penetrates its mass, and the difference of temperature to which its lower end is exposed. A glacier may move as rapidly on an inclination of three or four degrees as of twenty degrees. Now a sheet of ice extending from the pole to the temperate regions would be affected by different temperature, as are the currents in the sea that flow to the south. The motion of these currents is not made by a sloping surface, but by a difference of temperature. The same phenomena would be produced by the same agency, in ice. It would move from the north to the south. Moreover, had these phenomena been produced by water, we should find indications of animal life in all their deposits. Again, water would not grind the materials into unstratified mud, and it would produce an undulating irregularity of surface. At Castle Rock we have the two classes of facts and the two agencies brought face to face.

I have already said that I cannot explain the cause or origin of the cold necessary to this extension of the glacial agency. But one of its wonderful results, showing the finger of Providence, was to grind the surface of the rocky layers over which the icy masses passed into the materials for the tracts of fertile soil, destined to the support of the animal kingdom, with man standing at its head. It may have been a secular winter — a geological winter preparatory to the spring, that led in the summer in which we now live. When the autumn and winter of this year of creation is destined to come, still remains to be seen.

HYPNODES.

"Felton was peculiarly susceptible to the soporific influences of Nahant air, so he takes for his signature the Greek word which means a sleepy fellow."
— NOTE BY WINTHROP.

CHAPTER VII

PROCESSION OF EVENTS

It is interesting to compare, or to group together, the events of the one locality under discussion with other happenings in the broader field of the world's activities. The year 1706, when Nahant was divided among the freeholders of Lynn, was the year of Benjamin Franklin's birth. In Boston, where he was born, the graves of his parents in the old Granary Burying Ground are visited today by those acquiring the historical flavor of the city. The following years saw bitter struggles for supremacy over the Indians; then the contests with the French, with the expedition to Louisburg under Sir William Pepperell, that man with the almost unique distinction of being an American knighted by the King of England; also the ill-fated Braddock expedition and Washington's experiences which aided him in his military work of later years. Then came the Stamp Act in 1765, the Boston Massacre in 1770, and the Boston Tea Party in 1773. In these latter years the three families of Breed, Johnson and Hood were living on Nahant, and descendants of the last two are still there. Feeling against the levy on tea ran high in Lynn, and at a town meeting in December, 1773, resolutions were adopted not allowing any tea to be landed or sold in Lynn, and pledging support to our "Brothers of Boston or elsewhere whenever our aid shall be required, in repelling all attempts to land or sell any teas poisoned with a duty." The closing of the Port of Boston after the "tea party" led to several meetings in Lynn; delegates were chosen to assemblies elsewhere, and a committee of safety was formed. Lynn men went to Lexington and four were killed there. In June, 1775, the Provincial Congress recommended the carrying of arms to meeting on Sundays, and other days when worship was held, by the men who lived within twenty miles of the seacoast. The Rev. John Treadwell, a member of the Committee of Safety, appeared on the Sabbath with his cartridge box under one arm and his sermon under the other, and went into the pulpit with his musket loaded. Three watches were stationed each night, one of which was on Sagamore Hill, overlooking Nahant Beach. Then came the Battle of Bunker Hill, where a Lynn regiment participated. Once, in 1776, there was an alarm at midnight, that some English troops had landed at Kings Beach, the next beach towards Swampscott from Long Beach, which latter is mostly in Nahant. In a short time the town was in an uproar. Many fled to the woods, but some soldiers were rallied and marched down to Woodend, where the alarm was found to be false. It was during this scare that a young officer, supposed to be on duty, could not be found. Lewis says that a little later he emerged from a large old-fashioned brick oven into which his fear had driven him. Perhaps he thought it better to be bad for something than good for nothing, but doubtless his mates saw not much difference.

Under date of 1777 Newhall makes entry, in Lewis and Newhall's "History of Lynn," of a curious custom relating to smallpox. This was a few years before Dr. Jenner introduced vaccination. Smallpox was a dreaded disease and pockmarked faces were common. Groups of people retired to convenient places with nurses and all the needed things and were inoculated with the disease. Taken in this way it was thought to be milder, and at least was probably less likely to prove fatal because of the more favorable conditions. "Lynn, Mass., May 14, 1777. There was a company of us went to Marblehead to have small pox." They took two doctors and a nurse. There were nineteen patients in all and all came home well. The memorandum bears the certificate from Marblehead authorities: "By virtue of this certificate permit ye within mentioned person, after being smoked, to pass ye guards. John Gerry." This sort of thing seems incredible, although perhaps it is fairly comparable with some medical or surgical practices of today.

The year 1783 saw the close of the wearisome war which, on the whole, was a gloomy period. Lewis says Lynn had one hundred and sixty-eight men in the Revolutionary War, of whom fifty-two were lost, besides the four killed at Lexington. The people of the time before the Revolution were a plain, plodding, matter-of-fact sort. Railroads and steamboats were not even imagined; the stage coach and omnibus were mostly unknown, and when a kind of coach appeared it was a crude vehicle, passing through Lynn twice a week on the way to and from Boston. A wealthy farmer kept a chaise, used mostly on Sundays or on an infrequent trip to a near-by town. People walked three miles and more to meeting on Sunday, or a man rode on horseback with his wife up behind him. Now they want the garage close to the front door. A family, perhaps, rode in chairs placed in a two-wheeled cart. A four-wheeled wagon was first seen in Lynn about 1770. The doctor went on horseback with saddle bags full of medicines, for apothecaries were rare. There were no lectures, libraries, theatres or concerts. Even shopping, dear now to some hearts, was difficult, as the shops were few and carried mostly only a limited variety of very necessary articles.

The flight of time in old New England was marked by sun dials out of doors and by noon marks and hour glasses within doors, though rarely by water clocks. Clocks were known, however. In 1677 E. Needham of Lynn left a striking clock and a watch in his estate. Judge Sewall wrote in 1687: "Got home rather before twelve both by my clock and dial." Twenty years later clocks were more plentiful. Early forms of oil lamps were used, with tallow, grease or fish oil, and soon candles were run in moulds. By 1750 the whaling industry brought about spermaceti candles, described as far better than the tallow candles of the period. As for heat, the early houses were very cold. Great fireplaces could not suffice. Around 1700 stoves are mentioned, though not in common use until later. Philadelphia fire stoves, later called Franklin stoves, came into use early. But the life and comfort of early homes centered around the great fireplaces in the old New England kitchens, with all their appurtenances which have now become curiosities sought and prized by the antique collector. Even up to a very recent date cold bedrooms were the rule in average houses, and feather beds were commonly used, with very heavy quilts and coverings. Many people can remember the use of warming pans, those articles now chiefly curiosities that fall down with a clatter whenever they are touched.

Our ancestors seem to have eaten chiefly with knives, spoons and fingers. Forks began to appear a little before 1700. In 1633 some one sent a table fork to Governor Winthrop, "for the useful applycation of which I leave to your discretion." The Pilgrims had a few mugs and jugs, but had little other earthenware and no china. China ware was not much known until Revolutionary times. Wooden trenchers were the table ware, and as late as 1775 at least one advertisement shows them to have been an article of common sale. They were simply hollowed-out blocks of wood. Pewter ware, however, was coming in about as America was settled, and the trade of pewterer was an influential and respected one in both New England and old England. Much old pewter is now extant in antique collections, but the old wooden ware has mostly disappeared. There was a little glass and it was valued, but by Revolutionary times it was quite common.

As for food, fish was very important, with corn, and a far more limited list than was available to later people, even before modern transportation brought foods from all over the world. As for potatoes, those that were mentioned were sweet potatoes. The Irish potato — a native of South America, but called Irish because Ireland grew it in large quantities — was introduced to America by way of England about 1745. Much has been written about every phase of this old colonial life and times. Lynn was a part of it and Nahant was a part of Lynn, which then included Swampscott, Saugus, Reading, North Reading, Lynnfield and Nahant; a district much larger than Lynn of today, and settled in several villages which grew and one by one sheared away from Lynn, the old third plantation, as it was called. Perhaps just the whiff of this old life, given in these few paragraphs, may be a reminder how far living has travelled and varied from the times these hardy settlers knew.

In religion these generations were all fundamentalists, as the name goes today, seemingly understood by all. Nothing on earth could be older than Noah's flood, and to doubt this was blasphemy. A vice-chancellor of the University of Cambridge discovered, in 1660, that man was created on October 23, 4004 B.C., at nine o'clock in the morning. The earth, in those times, was the center of the universe, around which all suns, stars and moons revolved. Even by 1800 the Copernican theory of the universe, with the old earth a speck among specks running at tremendous speed around the sun, was a dangerously materialistic doctrine to some professors in American colleges.

The year 1808 saw what was perhaps the only bull fight ever staged in New England, on the turnpike to Boston. Bulls and dogs were used. Raised seats for spectators made a proper arena, but the sport, crime or outrage (use any name) was not continued.

In the War of 1812 the schooner "Dolphin," owned at Nahant, was sold, from fear of the English cruisers, and the settlement was left without a vessel. Soon after peace was declared Caleb Johnson bought the "Jefferson," which had been used as a privateer, although she appears to have been of only fourteen tons burden, carrying one gun and twenty men. She was used as an excursion boat and for fishing until 1816, when she was sold and broken up. She was replaced on Nahant by a new boat named the "Dolphin." During this war it is said that the English ships frequently sailed by Nahant so near to Bass Point that the men on deck could be plainly seen, and fishermen were often captured or their catch requisitioned. E. J. Johnson says: "Mrs. Polly Hood remembered seeing Uncle Billy Breed ride from his tavern to Lynn on horseback, with a bag of money behind him, frightened at the appearance of the English ships."

In June, 1813, the English frigate "Shannon" approached Boston Harbor and challenged the United States ship "Chesa-

Tudor's High Fence around Peach Orchard
Across Ocean Street from present Davis House

The Last "Lone Tree" on Long Beach
About half way over, called the Half Way Trees

peake," lying in the harbor, to battle. The hills and house tops were crowded with spectators, many coming to Nahant for a better view of the encounter, which was in plain sight a few miles away. Such an event seems to have been a polite thing in those days, and safe to watch. The English vessel was the victor and sailed away to Halifax with her prize. A round cast-iron ball dug up on Nahant some time since brought the query as to whether it could have come ashore from that battle, but the only reason to suppose so appears to be that this engagement first suggests itself as a possible cause.

Brook's "History of Medford" says that about 1815, "when only a few persons resided at Nahant, it was the custom for families in Medford to join in parties to that beautiful promontory. From ten to twenty chaises would start together, and, reaching their destination, the ladies and gentlemen, girls and boys, would proceed to fishing from rocks and boats. Each one wore the commonest clothes and the day was passed in all sorts of sports. A fish dinner was an agreed part of the fare."

The year 1816 was the year without a summer, nicknamed eighteen hundred and freeze to death, with a frost in every month. A great horse trot took place on the turnpike, called one of the first of such in the country. The best time for three miles was a little over eight minutes. There is a record of an earlier race on Long Beach. The "Boston Gazette" for October 20, 1760, has an item as follows: "These are to notify all Gentlemen that there is a Horse Race to be run on the 23rd instant, at a place called Lynn Beach, for fifty pounds sterling. This money is given by private gentlemen as an encouragement, in order to procure a good breed of Horses. Any gentleman that pleases to put in a horse must deposit three pounds sterling as a reserve for stakes to be run for the next day. Any Horse that does not come within the distance by thirty rods is not to run again. Each heat stop a half an hour and rub." Evidently this hard sand beach was deemed the best place for such an event.

After the great business depression of 1829 and earlier the whole country had a period of expansion and ample business, and from 1830 to 1836 this was feverish. Western emigration had begun to what are now called the Central States, such as Illinois, Indiana, Ohio and Missouri. Ohio was the queen of the West. Great fortunes were made and lost in this decade of the 30's. Cotton was coming to be a great crop, and Mobile, Alabama, jumped its real estate valuations from four million in 1833 to twenty-seven million in 1837, whence it fell to seven million in 1838. Land speculation was wildly indulged, and in the East as well as the West. Paper was wasted, as much as at any time since then, showing valuable corner lots in hypothetical cities, where was only a wilderness, and where today the wilderness continues. The Erie Canal was built and then enlarged, and then land around the Great Lakes took on fictitious values. A conservative has been defined as a person who never likes to see a thing done for the first time, but a proper percentage of his qualities is always needed to leaven and sober the wild, booming optimism of times and events that move with a rush.

Lynn shared in all this, profited by the business activity and wasted money in the speculative orgies. There were about sixty streets in the city in 1831, and about one hundred and three in 1840. But in 1836 came disaster. Crops of all great staples failed. There were frosts in every month and much drought in many parts of the country. In fact, the troubles were in Europe as well as America. Large banks and business houses in England failed, many of them with obligations across the water. Business explosions were common everywhere. "Who has failed now?" seemed to become a common form of greeting as people met together. The recoil on Lynn, with its extensive shoe business, was overwhelming. Workers were fortunate who had home-raised pork and potatoes to rely upon. There were clams and eels and dandelions, with haddock cheap at Swampscott and Nahant.

The spring of 1837 opened gloomily for Lynn, and people were surprised when the Eastern Railroad Company announced it would build a railroad between Boston and Salem. A railroad was a new thing, and people supposed it would be impossible to get off the track in season to avoid the engine if it was within sight. Gangs of Irish laborers were set to work. Large-scale immigration was new, fostered by the railroad and canal building. There were about twenty-five miles of railroads in the United States in 1830, and eleven hundred miles in 1835. The building of the railroad through Lynn furnished some spare material from cuts, which was used in part on the streets. Union Street, and a piece of low land adjacent, was raised so no part of it was under water in the spring rains, as it had been formerly. It was then called Estes Lane. This railroad was opened in August, 1838, for public travel. From Salem onward the main line reached Portsmouth twelve or fifteen years later. The line from Salem to Lowell was opened in 1850, the Saugus Branch in 1853, and the Marblehead Branch in 1873. James R. Newhall writes that "in 1836 twenty-three stages left Lynn Hotel for Boston daily, and there were likewise numerous extras. They belonged to the great Eastern and Salem lines. Oftentimes they were well filled on their arrival at Lynn, and the cry 'stage full' fell upon the ear of the hurrying man of business in a way anything but pleasant. A great many, however, drove to Boston in their own vehicles. And there were numerous fast horses about town."

There was a rally in business in 1838, but it was of short duration. Troubles were renewed in 1839, when England suffered reverses again. Great banks went down, including the Bank of the United States. Politicians took up the subject, with "Tippecanoe and Tyler too" as a war cry in the presidential election in 1840. Log cabins were emblems, and hard cider, both carried in political processions. Enthusiasm ran high, — higher than in most campaigns mere moderns know. Log cabin style houses were built, including one example on Nahant. Alonzo Lewis, the historian and surveyor, planned it for Joseph G. Joy in 1841. The house on its site was called the log cabin, even to within the memory of present-day Nahanters, though the original was long since replaced. The logs for this house were brought by vessel from Maine by Dexter Stetson, the contractor, mentioned elsewhere.

The house, or its successor, is now owned and occupied by Arthur S. Johnson, who is a long-time summer resident of Nahant, well known in Boston as one of the makers and upbuilders of the Young Men's Christian Association of that city. He is a son of the late Samuel Johnson, who was also a summer resident, living in the house on Nahant Road opposite the "Edgehill" owned by J. Bishop Johnson and his heirs until recently. Samuel Johnson with his brother Edward C. Johnson, another Nahanter in summer, who lived on the shore at the foot of Pleasant Street, were for a generation heads of the well-known Boston dry goods house of C. F. Hovey & Co., and the former was frequently called, in brief, one of the pillars of the Old South Church. In 1921 his portrait was presented to the Old South Society, and an editorial comment on it in the "Boston Herald" set forth his many good works and said that "his greatest monument is the stately Old South Church on Copley Square." These Johnsons are not closely related to the large Nahant Johnson family so frequently mentioned herein, but they always have been strongly interested in all things relating to the town. They are, however, descended from Edward Johnson, a brother of Jonathan Johnson, the first Johnson on Nahant. Edward Johnson seems to have been one of those who went post haste to the Battle of Lexington, while his brother, "Trooper Johnson," living on Nahant and getting the news later, mounted his horse, so it is said, and galloped away for the fray, only to arrive too late to be of service.

In the same year, 1841, the first daguerreotype picture was taken in Lynn with a cumbersome outfit from France, where it had just before been invented. This was the first practical method for photography. It was later superseded by other ways which have been improved gradually to what is in common use today. The tintype, however, is a development from the daguerreotype, and has persisted in use even today because of the speed of the whole operation. This makes it available for amusement resorts, as there is no waiting for the finished picture, and it is in such uses that it is commonly found.

The gold rush to California, which gave so many men the title "forty-niner," saw many enthusiasts start away from Lynn. A list published in December, 1849, contains one hundred and seventy-eight names, including two women. A good short account of this is in an article by Warren M. Breed of Lynn, published by the Lynn Historical Society in September, 1926. Apparently an early starter was Edward Kirke Johnson of Nahant, a son of Joseph Johnson and grandson of the original Jonathan Johnson. His is the first name in the list above mentioned. His brothers Daniel Alfred and Franklin Everett Johnson, also went. Doubtless there were others from Nahant, but information is lacking. These three Johnsons all subsequently returned to Nahant. Alfred turned his given names around to avoid the inconvenience of using his middle name, and was Alfred D. Johnson. He was elected town clerk in 1857, and in thirty-four annual elections thereafter, and died in office in 1890 at the age of seventy. He also served on the school committee as noted in the lists of town officers. He was the founder of Johnson's Express, running from Nahant to Boston, of which more is told elsewhere. He built the house on Nahant Road opposite the Village Church, about 1845. It was subsequently owned and occupied by his brother, Franklin E. Johnson, until the latter's removal to the home of his daughter in Winchester, where he died. Alfred Johnson lived for many years on Prospect Street, owning a house occupied for a time by Henry T. Dunham and apparently built by Captain Henry Dunham, mentioned elsewhere. This house has been extensively remodelled since, and is now owned by Fred L. Timmins. Franklin Johnson owned the property adjacent, now used by the A. and P. store, and from there all the buildings down to Summer Street, which were at times divided into four stores, and which are very little changed today. The shop nearest Johnson's house will be remembered by many as "Gurneys." It was a small shop selling smokers' goods, a little candy, some fishing tackle and other oddments, and its proprietor, Captain William Gurney, was one of the characters of the vicinity on account of his dry, cackling humor. He was a brother to Serena, wife of F. Henry Johnson mentioned elsewhere. He died in 1898 at the age of seventy-eight.

Kirke Johnson, as he was known, was another of the characters of the town. He was an out-of-doors man, who knew much about nature and her ways, and who enjoyed telling nature stories to children. He was something of a faddist. Once he invited a boy to go to the Maolis Gardens and dine with him. The boy assumed a big fish dinner at the restaurant, but Uncle Kirke took him down to the rocks and shared a pocketful of nuts with him while he expatiated on the virtues of raw and natural food. Probably the boy did not care for the exposition or illustration.

Once, the story goes, illustrating his uniform politeness, a Nova Scotia lumber laden schooner ran down his dory when he was out fishing. He climbed aboard over the bow and appeared before the crew. It was about dusk and this was the first they knew of any man or dory. He took his hat in his hand, saying, "Good evening, gentlemen. You ran over my boat." They thought old Neptune was among them, for he had the long white hair and beard which graced his later years.

Kirke Johnson was a shrewd Yankee, with many ideas which almost came to fruition bringing fortune, but falling short in some particular and yielding only disappointment. As an example of this, it is said that in 1872 he was on the train to New York at the time of the great Boston fire, and knew that the wool district was gone, and Boston was a great wool center. At once he went around New York taking options on all the wool he could get, knowing that the price would rise. But with not enough money to cover his options, the dealers were glad to cancel them, for prices did rise. If he had carried his scheme far enough to take in a temporary partner with plenty of money, the execution of his plan would have been completed. With the options as held doubtless this would have been easy to do. At one time he sold cereals, proclaiming the virtues of the whole kernel long before the days of bran and whole wheat, which are now so common. On Nahant, at least, he made personal deliveries, and in a peculiar manner. He had a long bag into which he put his orders, one after another, with a string tied around the bag above each order. They were in geographical sequence, so that at each house in regular order he untied the top remaining string and delivered his goods. Filled and over his shoulder the bag looked like a huge sausage. Kirke Johnson died in 1891 at the age of sixty-nine, and one of the interesting men of the town was gone.

The outbreak of the Civil War found Nahant jumping into the fray with early enthusiasm. A meeting was held in the vestry of the Village Church on April 23, 1861, and a company called the "Home Guard" was formed. Luther Dame, the schoolmaster in the wooden schoolhouse on Pleasant Street just above the old Town Hall, was captain and drill master, and the company drilled mostly in the evening in the schoolhouse yard, still town property. Nearly every one fit for military drill enlisted. Arms were bought by subscription, and uniforms were purchased by the company members. Their first public parade was as a part of the Home Guard Battalion of Lynn on August 1, 1861. This was the group that was nicknamed the "Piper Guards," as related elsewhere. A flagstaff was raised on Bass Beach Hill, and when the Stars and Stripes were first hoisted on it, old Captain Henry Dunham, a veteran of the Mexican War, fired the cannon that assisted in the ceremonies.

Meetings were held in the schoolhouse, where subscriptions were raised and aid guaranteed to the families of men who should enlist for war service. On July 19, 1862, a town meeting was held "to see what action the town will take in relation to raising the town's quota of volunteers in response to the call of the Governor of this Commonwealth." Non-residents were invited to take a part in the discussion, and John E. Lodge, father of the late Senator Lodge, offered twenty-five dollars to each of the seven recruits desired from Nahant. James W. Paige offered the same sum to each of the first four who should enlist. Paige lived across the street from the Public Library, on what is now the Lawrence place, and was the father-in-law of Abbott Lawrence. Nathaniel Walker offered the same sum to the other three, and Frederic Tudor came up with the same amount to the whole quota. On August 30, 1862, another town meeting was held to "see what action the town would take" on raising the second quota for nine months' service. It was voted that the town should pay $200 to each resident enlisting to fill this call for men. The annual town meeting on March 14, 1863, appropriated $300 for aid to families of volunteers. The town records for this year give a list of twenty-nine men in United States service. In 1864 the town voted to remit all taxes for its volunteers, and on April 13 it voted to pay $125 for each recruit on a new quota. E. J. Johnson, in his story of Nahant, lists thirty-nine men as enlisted from Nahant, as follows:

1. Mortimer L. Johnson.
2. Charles Warren Johnson.
3. George F. Newhall.
4. William J. Johnson.
5. Patrick Riley.
6. Elbridge G. Hood (Captain).
7. Wilbur Hanson.
8. Alexander Webber.
9. John E. Wheeler.
10. Luther S. Johnson.
11. Edmund B. Johnson.
12. Edward J. Johnson.
13. Sidney C. Johnson.
14. Edwin W. Johnson.
15. Shepard H. Johnson.
16. Welcome J. Johnson.
17. John Simpson.
18. James Hogan.
19. Michael Mitchell.
20. Charles H. Palmer.
21. Otto Bush.
22. William L. Rand.
23. Charles T. Lawless.
24. Lorenzo P. Whitney.
25. Charles N. Babb.
26. Arthur J. Bulfinch.
27. William H. Perry, Jr.
28. George C. Neal.
29. John Williams.
30. George P. Stone.
31. Marcellus Kidder.
32. Daniel L. Seavey.
33. James Campbell.
34. John Henry Hood.
35. Nelson Tarbox.
36. George Tarbox.
37. Hervey H. Murdock.
38. Alfred Tarbox.
39. Theodore M. Johnson.

The list is not in order of enlistment, although Mortimer L. Johnson was the first to enter the service. The first two are the only ones who entered the navy, apparently, though the connections of the last ten are not given by Johnson. The last six enlisted in regiments outside of Massachusetts. About all of the old Johnson family returned to Nahant after the war, and lived and died on Nahant, but few of the others seem to

Nahant Road easterly from Summer Street
Jonathan Johnson house in center, on present site of post office block

Nahant Road easterly from Ocean Street
Signs for Maolis Gardens and "Ninepin" Alleys

have stayed in town for long. Captain Hood made his home here, and John Simpson, whom people will remember limping about with a cane on account of a war injury. Mortimer L. Johnson was an Annapolis man and remained in the navy and died a rear admiral. He was a frequent visitor to Nahant, where his father, Walter Johnson, always lived. Johnson says Nahant furnished forty-two men, though he names only thirty-nine, and the sum of all quotas was thirty-seven. The total expenditure by the town, exclusive of state aid, was over $6,500. The home activities for war service were much the same as people remember for the more recent World War, — sewing, boxes with food and small needs, and much worries. One of the summer residents wrote at the time:

> Nahant is very solitary and deserted this year. I stood looking down at the steamboat landing opposite — not a fishing boat, not a human being in sight; then the ghostly little steamer comes in, and the phantoms go over the hill towards the ruins of the burned hotel, and all is still and lonely again.

Many years later, in 1894, Luther S. Johnson, a shoe manufacturer and resident of Lynn, one of the Nahant Johnsons and Nahant Civil War veterans, presented a flag to his Nahant fellow soldiers. This flag is kept in the Nahant Public Library, but for years was taken out and used on Memorial Day and occasionally in other processions. A document accompanying the gift was signed by all but two or three G. A. R. men then living on Nahant. The group then included many who had moved here since the war, and of the thirty-nine names listed by Johnson, only nine appear on this paper, in a list of fourteen. For several years the few survivors of the G. A. R. in town were not men who enlisted from Nahant. Robert L. Cochran, Thomas J. Cusick and Patrick Linehan, though to be reckoned old Nahanters, came to town after the war. Linehan is the survivor, hale and hearty in this year of 1928, and a resident for over fifty years. Cochran was the long-time officer of the Board of Health and superintendent of sewers and water system, beginning service for the town in the 80's and ending with his death in 1922, at the age of seventy-six.

CHAPTER VIII

SUMMER RESIDENTS AND BOATING

J. L. HOMER, writing in 1848, says that so far as he can remember them the summer residents owning cottages at Nahant were T. H. Perkins, T. G. Cary, F. Tudor, heirs of Mrs. S. G. Perkins, Mrs. Phillips, E. D. Phillips, F. H. Gray, Charles Amory, Mrs. Gardiner Greene, heirs of John Hubbard, heirs of S. Hammond, David Sears, E. H. Robbins, William Amory, Mrs. Prescott Crowninshield, T. B. Curtis, the Misses Inches, T. Whetmore, B. C. Clark, Mr. Lodge, heirs of N. P. Russell, Mrs. Rice, and heirs of Joseph Peabody. Then we have a list of founders of the "Nahant Church," which is the correct title of the first church in town, whose building was erected in 1832 on Cliff Street. In September, 1831, a meeting of some of the subscribers was held in Boston. Colonel Thomas H. Perkins, Hon. William Prescott and Hon. David Sears were chosen a committee to secure a site for the church, and the proceedings of that day were signed by fourteen men: William Prescott, Jonathan Phillips, Nathaniel P. Russell, David Sears, Charles Bradbury, Frederic Tudor, William Appleton, Thomas H. Perkins, Samuel A. Eliot, Samuel Hammond, Peter C. Brooks, Cornelius Coolidge, William H. Prescott and Edward H. Robbins. William H. Eliot was secretary of the meeting. In 1834 a bell was provided, and the list of subscribers shows other old Nahant names: Abbott Lawrence, Thomas G. Cary, Stephen Codman, William Amory, John A. Lowell, Henry G. Rice, Benjamin C. Clark, John Hubbard, Stephen G. Perkins and David Eckley. Here in these lists are most of the summer residents of that time. Their houses were mostly at the eastern end of the town at or beyond Bass Beach or Cliff Street. A few were near the village, then clustered around the vicinity of Whitney's Hotel, and a few others farther north, notably the house built by Perkins, now known as the Cary House. George William Curtis in his article already mentioned writes pleasantly and descriptively as follows:

> Nahant is a shower of little brown cottages fallen upon the rocky promontory that terminates Lynn Beach. There is a hotel upon its finest, farthest point, which was a fashionable resort a score of years since. But the beaux and belles have long since retreated into the pretty cottages whence they can contemplate the hotel, which has the air of a quaint, broad piazzaed, seaside hostelry, with the naked ugliness of a cotton factory added to it, and fancy it the monument of merry but dead old days.
>
> The hotel is no longer fashionable. Nahant is no more a thronged resort. Its own career has not been unlike that of the belles who frequented it, for although the hurry and glare and excitement of a merely fashionable watering place are past, there has succeeded a quiet, genial enjoyment and satisfaction which are far pleasanter. Some sunny morning, when your memory is busy with Willis' sparkling stories of Nahant life a quarter of a century ago, and with all the pleasant tales you may have collected in your wanderings from those who were a part of that life, then step over with some friend whose maturity may well seem to you the flower of all that the poet celebrated in the bud, and she will reanimate the spacious and silent piazza with the forms that have made it famous.
>
> You step upon the steamer in the city, and in less than an hour you land at Nahant and breathe the untainted air from the "boreal pole," and gaze upon a sublime sea sweep, which refreshes the mind as the air the lungs. You find no village, no dust, no commotion. You encounter no crowds of carriages or of curious and gossiping people. No fast men in velvet coats are trotting fast horses. You meet none of the disagreeable details of a fashionable watering place, but sunny silence broods over the realm of little brown cottages. They stand apart at easy distances, each with its rustic piazza, with vines climbing and blooming about the columns, with windows and doors looking upon the sea.
>
> In the midst of the clusters, where roads meet, stands a small temple, a church of graceful proportions, but unhappily clogged with wings. It is the only catholic church I know, for all services are held there in rotation, from the picturesque worship of the Roman faith to the severest form of Protestantism. The green land slopes away behind the temple to a row of willows in a path across the field,

> whence you cannot see the ocean, and it is so warm and sheltered, like an inland dell, that the sound of the sea comes to it only as a pleasant fancy.
> This pretty path ends in the thickest part of the settlement. But even here it has no village air. It is still, and there are no shops, and the finest trees upon the promontory shadow the road that gradually climbs the hill, and then, descending, leads you across Little Nahant to Lynn Beach.

This quotation is only a part of the article, or essay, intended to give an impression of Nahant as Curtis saw it in the early 1850's. The large hotel was lapsing from its former glory, according to the writer. Steamboat service was regular and the town had become a summer resort of householders rather than hotel patrons. The place was quiet. He says there was a "feeling of its dulness on the part of the young." One reads and wonders just how many fold that feeling would be multiplied by the young of today, when quiet is no longer tolerable and contemplation a lost art; and if the pure air from the "boreal pole" will ever return on a visit. Not even Nahant's distance from buzzing cities prevents smoke, dust and odors altogether, while automobile gases are a near-at-hand vexation. Still, doubtless its air is better than any other.

Thus has been shown, in words mostly contemporary, a picture of Nahant for a generation or more prior to 1850, or to its incorporation as a separate town in 1853. Many other writings, in letters, magazines, newspapers and pamphlets, could be cited, but they perhaps would not add to the story drawn here. Nahant grew, in fifty years, from a place of three houses to a great resort with a large and wide reputation, chiefly as a hotel colony. Gradually the hotel life dwindled, and was succeeded by a summer cottage life, much of which is present today.

Other writings which are commonly mentioned are "The Home Life of H. W. Longfellow," by Blanche Rosevelt Tucker-Machetta; "Life of William Hickling Prescott," by George Ticknor; "Life Here and There," by N. P. Willis; and "Little

Journeys to the Home of American Authors" for March, 1896, by George S. Hilliard.

S. E. Morrison, in his "Maritime History of Massachusetts," writes the following, which is not quoted in continuity, but abstracted to include remarks about Nahant. It will be noted that some of his dates do not agree with this present narrative.

> Thomas Handasyd Perkins set a new fashion when, in 1817, he built a stone cottage just above the Spouting Horn at Nahant. This rugged peninsula at the north margin of Boston Bay — a miniature, even rockier Marblehead — had remained a mere sheep pasture for lack of a proper harbor. After the war several Boston families began boarding in the few native houses, and in 1818 crowds of excursionists came by the steamboat "Eagle." Samuel A. Eliot erected a worthy example of the Greek revival in 1821. Frederic Tudor, the ice king, built a tasteful stone cottage in 1825, established a remarkable garden, and set out elm trees. Like almost everything else Mr. Tudor did, the setting out of elms was scoffed at — no trees would grow on Nahant. The Tudor elms now make one of the most handsome avenues of trees in New England. Other mercantile families followed the dean of their order, and by 1860 Nahant exhibited every known atrocity in cottage architecture, and had fairly earned its jocose subtitle of "Cold Roast Boston." This peaceful capture of Nahant by the merchant princes began a process that has utterly transformed the New England sea front. Swampscott, for example, was a poor fishing village until 1815, and mainly that for another forty years. In 1842 a merchant of Boston offered $400 an acre for a farm near the present Ocean House, and the astonished native threw down his rake and ran for a lawyer to get the deed signed before the Bostonian came to his senses.

Yachting held the interest of Nahant people from the beginning of its history as a pleasure or summer resort. Good mooring grounds were an assistance. A man quoted by J. L. Homer in "Nahant," 1848, a little pamphlet, says the first privately owned decked boat ever moored at Nahant for the summer was the "Mermaid," of twelve tons, in 1832 or 1833. This is said to have begun yachting in Massachusetts Bay except for small undecked boats. She was owned here for two summers by Benjamin C. Clark, and was then sold to

William P. Winchester, who kept her until his well-known "Northern Light" was launched. The next yacht was the "Raven" of twelve tons, owned by Clark, for whom she was built. This is the Clark for whom Clark's Point was named and who lived in the house where now stands the home of Arthur Perry. "Like the splendid 'Northern Light' of Colonel Winchester, the 'Raven' has done good service for her owner, and won numerous laurels, which she bears as gracefully in her beak at the present time as she did when they were first acquired." The third yacht was the "Susan" owned by John Amory Lowell. She came soon after the "Raven" and was sold after one season to Phineas Drew of the "Nahant Hotel." The fourth yacht that had moorings for the whole season was the "Avon," of eleven tons, owned by Edward Phillips. Then came the "Brenda," of thirty tons, owned by David Sears. Next and last, up to 1848, the year of the article named, was the "Cloud," of twenty-two tons, owned by J. H. Gray, which came in 1847.

Benjamin Cutler Clark thus appears to have almost founded yachting except for small boats. He was born in Boston in 1800 and was a shipping merchant of the firm of B. C. Clark & Co. He was always interested in the sea and anything pertaining to it, and wrote and lectured on ships and ship building. He was an enthusiastic yachtsman and in 1830 owned the "Mary," a small half-decked boat. In 1856 he sold the "Raven" and built the "Young Raven" which he owned until his death in 1863. He bought his Nahant property in 1832 and was a summer resident for twenty-one years. In 1864 the estate was sold to Amos A. Lawrence.

One son of B. C. Clark was Colonel Robert F. Clark, whom many Nahanters remember, and who was well known as police commissioner of Boston. Another son, Arthur Hamilton Clark, born in 1841, continued his father's love for the sea. At the age of seventeen he was apprentice on the "Black Prince," and he was captain of the yacht "Alice" on her memorable trip across the Atlantic in 1866. Captain Clark commanded many ships and steamers both in America and in China. He was

SUMMER RESIDENTS AND BOATING

Lloyd's New York agent for twenty-five years, and only retired in 1920, living thereafter in Newburyport, where he died in 1922. He was the author of "The History of Yachting" and the "Clipper Ship Era."

There were pretentious regattas in those days. The Nahant Public Library has two notices of this sport, held under the auspices of Thomas Rand & Son, proprietors of the Nahant Hotel, on July 22, 1859, and September 5, 1859. Possibly the hotel interest might be suspected as partly commercial, but the lists of judges shows that the regattas were yachting events of quality. The former has five judges of whom Hon. C. Levi Woodbury is named as of Nahant, while the other four are picked from Boston, Salem and Swampscott. The latter has three judges, all Nahanters: George D. Oxnard, Samuel Hammond and Charles J. Paine. The Oxnard house is now standing, little altered, at the corner of Nahant Road and Summer Street. It was later owned by William B. Archibald and is now owned by Wallace D. Williams. Samuel Hammond lived in the well-known stone house down toward East Point, back from Nahant Road, and now owned and occupied by Samuel Hammond, son of the foregoing, whom all Nahanters know. Charles J. Paine lived in the house built by Cornelius Coolidge on Swallows Cave Road, later sold to John Bryant, Paine's father-in-law, and now occupied by a son, Frank C. Paine. General Charles J. Paine afterwards became the well-known yachtsman who, with the "Puritan," "Mayflower" and "Volunteer," successfully defended the famous America Cup. Both Hammond and Paine are remembered as familiar Nahant figures by many people not now to be called aged. J. L. Homer in his pamphlet tells of what he says was the first regatta held at Nahant. The following is a large part of his account of it. The boats are not all Nahant boats, of course, but came from various places round about.

> On the 19th of July, 1845, a regatta, which had been long talked of, came off at Nahant. It was free for all vessels of not more than fifty tons nor less than ten. The prizes offered were a silver cup valued at $50 and a suit of colors. An allowance of one-half a minute

per ton was made by the larger boats to the smaller ones on the difference of tonnage. The course run was from Nahant, round the Graves, outside of a station boat on the northwest side; thence round Egg Rock, on the north, back to the judges' boat off Joseph's Cove, Nahant. A very large number of persons from Boston and the neighboring towns were collected to witness the trial; all the eligible points for observation were thronged, and the bay in the neighborhood of the peninsula was studded with boats of every description, filled with spectators.

At half past three o'clock the contending yachts, eleven in number, all schooner-rigged, were ranged from east to west off the southwest bluff in the following order: "The Nautilus," 11 tons; "Avon," 11 tons; "Neptune," 11 tons; "Raven," 12 tons; "Pathfinder," 12 tons; "Naiad Queen," 15 tons; "Gipsey," 21 tons; "Alert," 22 tons; "Vision," 24 tons; "Odd Fellow," 30 tons; and "Cygnet," 31 tons. Their foresails and mainsails were hoisted, and each boat was held by a single line made fast to a separate mooring.

At a quarter past four the signal gun was fired, the moorings were dropped, and the jibs run up at the same instant. The start to lookers-on seemed a perfect one, and the beautiful appearance of the little vessels, as they flitted away together, elicited much admiration. The wind was from the southeast, consequently it was nearly a dead beat to the Graves. The boats started with their larboard tacks aboard, and headed for Broad Sound, running four and one-half to five knots. Immediately after filling away it was perceived that the "Vision," from having a slight advance at the start, had lapped the "Odd Fellow," and taken the wind out of her sails; the latter, however, soon kept off, took the wind out ahead of the former, and passed on ahead.

At about a quarter past four the "Cygnet," "Odd Fellow" and "Vision" tacked to the eastward. Strong indications of a wind more southerly probably induced this movement. The manœuvre, however, although well designed, was not completely successful, for notwithstanding the wind did haul slightly to the southward, the three large boats weathered the Graves with difficulty at a limping gate. The next boat was the "Raven." After passing half a mile beyond the wake of the others she tacked to the eastward and passed the Graves, going a wrap full. The "Alert" followed the "Raven;" the other boats were now a long way in the rear, and it was quite apparent that the matter was settled so far as they were concerned. Still, it was a subject of regret that they did not complete the distance named in the conditions of the race, inasmuch as the prize was offered only with a view of ascertaining

Old Stone Schoolhouse
Built 1819

Grammar Schoolhouse
Later the Police Station and Court Room

how far the pretensions of the different yachts would be justified by their performance.

The "Cygnet" and the "Odd Fellow" passed the Graves nearly together; next came the "Vision" with the "Raven" close upon her. Up to this period the "Raven" was in good time for the first prize, but it was considered that in working to windward her best play had been seen, and that on the return, in running at large, her raking masts and heavy draft would cause her to drop far astern of the larger boats, whose arrangements and ability for going free were supposed to be vastly superior.

Upon squaring away, however, this opinion proved to be ill-founded, for when half the distance between the Graves and Egg Rock had been made, it was obvious that the "Raven" had not only neared the head boats considerably, but had also dropped the "Alert" still farther astern. When abreast of Egg Rock one of the crew of the "Odd Fellow" fell overboard; in rounding to pick him up she lost some minutes. The "Raven" also lost some time by jibing her foresail and standing for the exposed individual.

From the commencement of the race the wind had been gradually increasing, and when the boats hauled on a wind under the lee of Egg Rock the breeze was quite fresh. They passed the station boat off East Point, Nahant, running at least nine knots, and came to abreast of the judges boat in beautiful style in the following order: "Cygnet" at 6.12; "Vision" at 6.14; and the "Raven" at 6.16, the latter boat taking the first prize, with some minutes to spare; the second prize was awarded to the "Vision."

By some it was thought that the allowance of time was too great, but others, more skilled in nautical matters, considered that if it were so, the prizes would both have fallen to boats of the "Raven" class, whereas it appears that neither the "Avon," "Neptune," "The Nautilus," "Naiad Queen," or the "Pathfinder" were, or could have been, within four or five miles of even the second prize, which was taken by a boat of twenty-four tons, in a close contest with two yachts of thirty and thirty-one tons. The distance sailed, about twenty miles, was performed by the leading boats in about two and one-half hours, which, considering the wind at the start, was excellent time.

This was not only the first open regatta held at Nahant, but apparently the first held anywhere around Boston. S. E. Morrison, in his "Maritime History of Massachusetts," says: "Off Nahant, on July 19, 1845, was held the first open yacht race in Massachusetts;" and he adds, "The fame of this regatta, the boats owned by her summer residents, and a huge new hotel, made Nahant the yachting center of Massachusetts Bay until the Civil War." The hotel was not "new," but was newly enlarged and remodelled.

Thus was yachting around Nahant two or three generations ago. The interest remained, variable according to the enthusiasm of the people. In later years, remembered by present-day Nahanters, two yachts were always familiar figures in summer time. One, the "Alice," was owned by Thomas Gold Appleton, brother-in-law of the poet Longfellow. A picture in the Public Library shows Appleton among his crew and others. This man started transatlantic yacht racing when in the summer of 1866 his yacht set sail from Nahant and crossed to Cowes in something over nineteen days. Charles A. Longfellow, the poet's son, was aboard, and Arthur H. Clark was captain. This was the first crossing in a small yacht, and it is said she was spoken in mid-ocean by vessels who supposed she was lost and astray and probably needing help. The famous trip of the "America" was in 1851, the same year she was launched. She was a larger boat, eighty-seven feet long, schooner-rigged, and sailed across with short spars and no special attempt at speed. She was refitted at Havre before entering races around England. The summer of 1928 promises to see the fifth race across the Atlantic, since the "Alice" showed how it could be done. On her trip, says W. U. Swan in "The Boston Evening Transcript," she carried full racing canvas and spars and a comparatively small crew. Six months later, in midwinter, came the first of four Atlantic crossing races, with three entries for a large stake. Succeeding races were in 1870, 1887 and 1905. The other yacht, the "Breeze," was first seen here when owned by Charles Minot, but will be chiefly remembered as owned by Samuel Johnson. Both these men are mentioned elsewhere. Captain William F. Kemp, also a well-known Nahant figure, was for many years captain of the "Breeze." A little earlier, perhaps in the 70's and 80's, these yachts had companions. There was the "Rebecca," owned by Charles H. Joy, the "Romance," at home off Joe Beach, and the "Halcyon" of General Paine's, with Captain Stone, who afterwards sailed the cup defenders.

The famous yachts of General Charles J. Paine were familiar here. Paine raced the "Puritan" against the "Genesta" in September, 1885, and was successful. The boat was built by a syndicate of enthusiastic yachtsmen of whom J. Malcolm Forbes, William Gray, Jr., and Charles J. Paine were a committee in control. After the races she was sold to General Paine, who afterwards sold her to Forbes. These men were all eastern or New England men, mostly of the Eastern Yacht Club at Marblehead, who wanted an eastern boat entered as a prospective defender of the America Cup. The New York Yacht Club had a prominent boat, the "Priscilla," which was defeated in the trial races. In 1886 Paine built the "Mayflower" himself, using no financial aid from outside sources. She was raced successfully against the "Galatea" in September. Again, in 1887, General Paine's enthusiasm was manifest. He built the "Volunteer," which successfully raced the English challenger "Thistle," which was built by a group of Scotchmen expressly to compete for the famous cup. On Friday, October 7, 1887, a public reception was tendered to General Paine and Edward Burgess, who was the designer of all three yachts, at Faneuil Hall in Boston. The reception was the idea of Mayor Hugh O'Brien, who called together a committee of citizens to assist in the affair. The city council of Boston passed resolutions of thanks to Paine and Burgess for their energy and progressiveness and for their triple victories. It was deemed a matter of local pride, as the boats were eastern boats, commonly known as Boston boats. These great cup defenders never sailed important races in this vicinity, as the trial and cup races were held outside of New York; but they were often seen sailing along the North Shore, and at anchor off Nahant, where General Paine was a familiar figure. The proceedings at this reception were put into book form, with illustrations of the great yachts and their rivals, at the expense of the city of Boston.

General Charles J. Paine was born in Boston in 1833 and graduated from Harvard in 1853. He married a daughter of John Bryant, who was of the firm of Bryant & Sturgis, whose business began in dealings up the American west coast and the Columbia River, later entering the East India trade. He owned the "Bryant" place on Nahant, which later was known as the Paine place, on Swallows Cave Road. General Paine was himself successful in business, chiefly in railroad enterprises. He was of the old Paine family, reaching back to a signer of the Declaration of Independence and numbering many other well-known men in later generations. He had a fine estate in Weston, where he spent much time, but Nahant frequently saw him during the yachting season. His military title came from the Civil War, where he was commissioned captain in 1861, and major and colonel in 1862. In 1865 he received the brevet rank of major-general. He was a little-known man, always retiring and apparently preferring to be inconspicuous. Yet those who knew of him and his achievements would turn to look at him, if they met him, as long as he remained in sight.

Then there were the famous dory races, for dory sailing has always been a popular sport along the North Shore. The best idea of this and of the glorious communion of souls down at the wharf is given in the article written by Mason W. Hammond, a brother of Samuel Hammond, some time in the 90's. Mason Hammond shortly afterward left Nahant and lived abroad until his death. "Bertie" Otis is Herbert Foster Otis. The Goves, Kemps and Covells were three families of that period, thirty or forty years ago, loving the sea and getting a living from it. Charles E. Gove kept Gove's fish market on Willow Road at the foot of Ocean Street. He had several children, only one of whom is now a resident of Nahant. One, George A. Gove, was for several years town treasurer, resigning on his removal from town. Charles E. Gove had a brother George H. Gove, who died in 1878 at the age of thirty-three. He was captain of the "Blanche," owned by Thomas G. Cary. He was twice married, to sisters who were daughters of

Joseph Johnson and sisters of Luther S. Johnson. His children are known by Nahanters today, though not living in town. One is Anna H. Gove and one Edith Gove Breed, widow of George Herbert Breed. Another is Joseph H. Gove. Captain Kemp had a large family, mostly now away from Nahant. A daughter Susan is the widow of Francis B. Crocker. A son, Charles F. Kemp, lives here, and is grand mogul at the wharf. He was prominently connected with the Emergency Fleet Corporation during the Great War, being senior fleet captain. He is "Kibe" Kemp. Another daughter of Captain "Bill" Kemp married a son of Francis B. Crocker, Richard H. Crocker, now connected with the Nahant Fire Department. Another son of the senior Captain Kemp is Captain Joseph H. Kemp, not a resident of Nahant, but a well-known skilful sea dog. It is he who has put so many of the United States Navy ships over their trial test trips. The Covell boys were sons of Samuel Covell, elsewhere mentioned. Neither Samuel nor Otis, these two sons, have lived on Nahant for many years. "Cruso" Robertson is "Hall" Robertson, more correctly R. H. Robertson, still a resident of Nahant and well-known harbor pilot for Lynn, Salem and Beverly. And there was George B. Taylor, who died in 1902 at the age of seventy-eight. He was keeper of Egg Rock Light before he moved to Nahant. His sons, Fred L., George W., B. Frank and Eben were familiar figures, though Fred was drowned in the 80's, as related elsewhere. George was "Buster" and Frank was "Tony," and these nicknames, meaning general popularity, clung to them. They were great chowder makers for fishing parties, and just a few years ago "Tony" was invited to Detroit, with all expenses paid and a fee besides, to show Detroiters how good chowder should taste. He refused, saying he could not do the subject justice so far away from home. He died in 1922 at the age of sixty-seven. And now for Hammond's article:

> Every seafaring people in the world have a type of boat peculiar to themselves and their needs. And the style of boat which is peculiar to New England is "the dory." To this flat-bottomed, flat-sided little boat more fishermen and seafaring men owe their lives than to any type of boat yet

invented. No "banker" thinks of going out of Gloucester without a nest of dories amidships, and many a merchant sailorman, when his vessel has gone pounding on a rock or shoal, and the big seas come combing over her in walls of green water, and none of the keel boats could possibly have "a life" in such a sea, has prayed for an old-fashioned, slab-sided Swampscott dory. How the boat happened to be called a dory is a mystery. They have in England a fish called a John Dory fish, but they have no dories. We have the dories and no John Dory fish, and there you have it. The first man that we know about who made a name and a livelihood by building dories was one John Lowell of Essex, Mass., and today his grandson is head workman in a shop of Emmons & Co., dory builders, in Swampscott, Mass.

Gradually the dory, from being a rough, flat-sided affair, developed. The fishermen who went after perch and lobsters from the beaches put sails in their boats to save rowing home with a heavy load of lobster pots and fish. At first they only sailed before the wind, and then they found that by lashing a board over the lee rail and steering with an oar they could beat to windward, and then they put in centerboards, and then they began building their dories with a "bilge" and a round bottom, and finally they decked them fore and aft and round the gunwale, so that the fisherman's dory of today is practically a big canoe. And can't they sail, though, and go to windward and live in a sea way and carry sail? Well, rather! Many and many a time the writer has seen Red Faced Johnnie Blaney of the Second Beach (who is not to be confused with any other Blaney whatsoever, because Swampscott is filled with them), beating his old green dory out between Egg Rock and Nahant and dragging whole sail through a tearing northeaster when the big coasters on the horizon were staggering under double reefs. With one hand on the tiller and the other holding the sheet which had been previously passed under a thwart, sitting on the rail with his body far out of the boat, Mr. Blaney would go bobbing along like a cork where any ordinary catboat would be all under water. Now Nahant, which is almost an island, being connected with the shore by a narrow strip of beach some three miles long, is close to Swampscott, and Nahant always has been and is now a great place for boys. Generations of sturdy New England boys who could swim like fishes and handle boats just as well as any man have grown up at Nahant and given place to other generations, and "Cupid," which is the great bathing place, has probably had more boys burnt black upon its hot flat rocks than any place of its size in the world, and there never was a boy who passed his summers at Nahant who was not fond of sailing and rowing small boats. Ten or fifteen years ago they used to race keel boats with big spritsails, and then when they grew older they raced catboats. But now Nahant is "dory mad." The epidemic struck the place three summers ago, when "Bertie" Otis bought "Buster" Taylor's old dory and proposed to deck her himself and rig her as a sloop. So he hauled her up and put her down behind "Perk the carpenter's" (his name is Perkins, by the way) shop and went to work at

SUMMER RESIDENTS AND BOATING 119

her while all the fishermen and boys stood round and gave advice. He put in "Hackmitack" knees and nickle-plated "gudgeons" and a deck strong enough to hold the Vigilant's crew, and then everybody said she would be top-heavy. Then he had his sails made by the most expensive sailmaker in Boston, and when they were finished they were about twice too heavy, "like awnings," as someone remarked, and then he nearly cut his finger off with a chisel and had to have the job finished by a carpenter. All in all, the rigging up of the old boat cost him just about the price of a new boat. At last the day came when the "Royal George," for so she was named, was to be launched, and the excitement was intense. All the fishermen predicted that she would instantly capsize or wouldn't steer, and all assembled to see her misbehave. On long pieces of joist placed upon sturdy shoulders she was carried to the beach. A picked crew, consisting of three boys suitably undressed, were placed in her; she was double-reefed, as it blew half a gale, and with a loud shout from the three men on her rail, and in a cloud of foam, the "Royal George" was shoved through the breakers, and not only did not capsize and did steer, but behaved beautifully, and the "Royal George" was the beginning of what is now a large dory fleet at Nahant. That summer other dories were decked and rigged and a pennant was sailed for, the races taking place every Saturday afternoon round the time-honored little course where generations of Nahant boys have sailed every species of boat. It is a little triangular course, each leg being about a quarter of a mile long, and it is usually sailed over three times. The writer, with an old dory which he bought for $12, had the honor of winning the Nahant pennant that year.

In the meantime, dory building in Swampscott had been progressing with giant strides. Warren Small, who never was known to build a "mean" dory, had produced a boat called the "Pointer," sixteen feet on the water line, carrying eight hundred pounds of ballast and five men, rigged with a jib and mainsail, and, if need be, a balloon jib and spinnaker, and this "Pointer," sailed by the Melzard boys, who always decked themselves out gaily in white duck sailormen's clothes and blue caps, beat everything. And then the Nahant boys had three or four dories built in Swampscott and raced them, but somehow they were not particularly satisfactory, and last winter they had four new dories built. And wasn't there a plotting and a planning and a rushing down from Boston to Swampscott, and Emmons, who built the dories, had his life made wretched with talk of weighted centerboards and wrought-iron knees, and what not, and so the winter passed away and the dories were built and the summer came and the dories were raced with varying success. Sometimes one would win, sometimes another, according to the wind and who was sailing them. At last it was arranged that there should be a grand regatta on Labor Day, — a regatta into which everything which could carry a sail should come in, independent of size. There was a class for sloops and catboats over twenty-six feet, for catboats twenty-two feet long and over, and for racing dories sixteen and one-half feet on the floor boards.

Then there was a class for fishermen's open dories, no restrictions as to sail or length, and a class for boats twelve feet long and under; also a rowing race for fishermen.

The prizes were cups in all the classes except the fishermen's, and they were to receive $10 first prize and $5 second prize. The excitement in Nahant was something tremendous. Every fisherman's wife had to give up her household duties to go to making sails. The old dories which had not been cleaned for years were hauled up, dried out to make them light, and scraped with glass and sandpapered, and finally pot-leaded to the plank shear, just like the "Jubilee." The wharf near the steamboat landing was littered knee deep with bowsprits and gaffs and booms and spinnaker booms and old sails and new sails, and in the little back room behind Father Taylor's shop nothing was talked about but the fishermen's race. There is a great deal of local rivalry at Nahant. As to dory sailing, the Kemp family think that the Kemp boys can sail a dory better than the Gove boys, and the Gove boys think that they can sail better than the Kemp boys, and the Taylor boys know that they can sail better than anybody else, and the Covell boys deny the claims of everybody who attempts to say that he can sail a dory better than the Covell boys. In the meantime, a dark and deadly plot was being hatched among the younger sons of the "summer residents" who did not happen to own dories. Word had reached Nahant in some mysterious way — some said that a Swampscott fisherman had told a Nahant fisherman while hauling traps — that the familiar old dory "Pointer" was laid up in a barn in the back of Swampscott, the name had been taken off her bow, every one had forgotten about her, and that with all her sails and ballast complete, she could be bought very cheaply and fitted up in time for the Labor Day race. Behind closed doors the matter was discussed in hushed voices. A subscription was taken up. In the early morning two of the conspirators drove stealthily to Swampscott and inspected the dory, found her all right, and after a little bargaining bought her, had her painted, rolled down to the water's edge, launched, and anchored off the Second Beach.

Labor Day morning broke clear and fine, with white, fleecy clouds driving across the blue, and a hard, blurry, northwest wind churning up the surface of the bay. The scene at the wharf was one of great activity. Swarms of boys in white duck sailorman's trousers and jerseys rushed up and down the gangway leading from the wharf to the raft below. The old sea dogs and fishermen looked to windward and predicted that there would be more wind before there was less, and that there would be a likelihood of some one being drowned if the wind didn't go down before the race began. The stake boat and judges' boat were anchored off the end of the wharf with red flags in their bows, a tin horn which was to take the place of the usual gun used upon such occasions was procured, and the judges, two in number, were chosen, and copies of the rules and courses were nailed up on the post office and "Charley Gove's" and "Bishop's" fish shops and Father Taylor's shop on the wharf,

Caleb Johnson
1778–1867

Joseph Johnson
1776–1851

Luther Scott Johnson
Donor of Ellingwood Chapel

C. Hervey Johnson
1812–1901

and then the fun began for the unfortunate man who acted as the regatta committee. Everybody began to kick. Some would deliberately and carefully read the list of courses and conditions and then hunt down the committeeman and ask him what the courses were.

One young man who had been getting his dory in readiness for a week beforehand was too shy to make an entry, and would not have started at all if one of his friends had not done it for him. Still another entered his boat not less than five times, once in writing, once by deputy, and three times in person. One man protested the entire fishermen's class, consisting of eleven sail, because he thought that fishermen's dories ought to be steered with an oar instead of a rudder. Another protested the entire fishermen's class because they had washboards. And everybody kicked about the courses. Some wanted them longer, some wanted them shorter, and in the midst of the hurly-burly the "Pointer" arrived from Swampscott and distracted the attention of the quarrelsome crowd. Then the wind began to "flatten" ominously. Lighter and lighter it grew until the question arose as to whether there was wind enough to sail the race at all, and every one began taking out ballast until the raft looked like an old junk shop, littered as it was with chunks of pig iron. At last two o'clock came; the inhabitants of Nahant flocked as one man to the wharf and the rocks near it. Then the committeeman explained to each fisherman separately, and then to the whole collectively, exactly what a one gun or rather one horn start meant. How that horn would blow, and then each class would be given five minutes in which to get across the line. The committeeman had resolved to sail in the race himself, and to this end he had procured a ducking punt so small that the boys named her in derision "The Constitution," after "Old Ironsides," and a crew as small in proportion as the punt. He proposed to start in the last class. Well, the horn sounded and the crowd on shore set up a mighty shout, and the first class drifted slowly down on the line ready for the start, when the skipper of a boat in the second class suddenly decided that he didn't like the course, and sailed up to the judges' boat and said he would like to have it changed. "You can't," said the judges. "All right," said the skipper, "I'll sail my own course and make the one other boat in my class do the same."

And so the second class went a course by themselves.

Then the racing dories started and then the fishermen's dories. Cruso Robinson, who sailed the dory with the curious rig which you see a picture of, thought that he would be very clever, so he took his boat way up behind the line and then came down with a rush through the fleet. But he came down too soon and got over the line before the horn sounded. "Go back, Cruso," everybody shouted at him. "You're over the line." Down goes Cruso's tiller, up goes the dory into the wind and crashed into the almost motionless fleet of boats waiting to start, and at this critical moment off goes the horn and then wasn't there a row! "Buster" Taylor lost his rudder, bowsprits were smashed, everybody shouted, hats went overboard, every one tried to pull his own boat ahead and push the other men's boats back, and so the fishermen's class started, and somehow or other, although he had caused all the trouble, "Cruso" managed to get out of the jam first and rounded the first stake boat ahead. And then "The Constitution," with the other boat in her class, started. Alas, "The Constitution," of which the committeeman had had great hopes, could not seem to go. There was not enough wind for her, although every pound of ballast had been taken out, and she was miserably beaten. And so the eighteen little boats, looking from the shore almost like toy boats, went sailing about the little course, and "Otie" Covell won in the fishermen's dory class, with "Buster" Taylor second. "Bertie" Gove fouled ten buoys and Buster, and then protested "Buster." In the meantime the second class finished and the judges refused to give the winner the prize because the boats went the wrong course, and then the winner came to the committeeman and made a row, and the committeeman, to make everything pleasant, gave him the cup, and then the judges were furious with the committeeman for not sustaining their decision, and said that they would never, under any circumstances, act as judges at Nahant again. In the meantime the "Pointer" had gone to windward like a steamboat and beaten her class handily, much to every one's surprise and chagrin who sailed against her, although the surprise an hour later was not so great when her real name was made known. Then "Kibe" Kemp won the rowing dory race, with Otie Covell second. So the "Kemps" and the "Covells" and the "Taylors," which represent the three great clans on Nahant, each had a share of the day's honors.

Finally all the boats were taken in to the moorings and the smaller boats tied to the raft. It so happened that the committeeman landed on the "Pointer" to inspect the visitor, and the "Pointer" had no tender, so when the committeeman and the jubilant crew wanted to go ashore they had to hail the raft and ask to have some one come out for them. It was noted that those on the raft whispered and smiled together a little bit, and some one on the "Pointer" thought he saw a man called "Pudge" silently transferring his knife and other valuables to the pockets of his friends, and when "Pudge" got into a very crank canoe and came paddling out, the idea became a certainty that if the crew of the "Pointer" got into that canoe they would certainly find themselves wallowing in the eelgrass and seven feet of water inside of a few seconds. So a deep-laid plot was laid to entice "Pudge" on board on plea of examining a broken centerboard, then silently enter the canoe, one by one, push off, and leave Pudge to swim ashore by himself. This scheme worked beautifully, only just at the last moment "Pudge" saw the departing canoe, and with one mighty leap just managed to land his toe on the gunwale. That settled it. There was a wild shout of laughter from the shore, a still louder shout of dismay from the canoe, and five heads appeared above water. The committeeman spent the better part of half an hour diving in the eelgrass for his knife and shoes.

CHAPTER IX

INDUSTRIES

NAHANT never was well suited to become an industrial town. Its isolation gave it a disadvantage over places nearer supplies and railroads. A manufacturing establishment using coal brought by water, and able to use water transport for its goods, is conceivable but has impractical factors. Doubtless people have pictured some manufacturing on Nahant, and at least one political circular of within thirty years has pleaded the desirability and possibility of factories on the low lands between Pond Beach and Lynn Harbor, near the Coast Guard Station. It seems unlikely that such development can come, but times change and conditions alter, and it is bold to prophesy from the assumptions that things will remain as they are. This, however, is a popular pastime with people, little and big, in their consideration of future affairs, even of international importance. The impossible is often achieved, and uncommon events happen quite commonly.

At the present time only two industries on Nahant do much more than supply the needs of the town. One of these is the commercial florist's business, built up and carried on by Thomas Roland. Roland came to Nahant in 1884, a young man, working as a private gardener until 1890, when he bought out the comparatively small greenhouse plant of Charles F. Johnson, son of C. Hervey Johnson and grandson of Caleb Johnson. Roland proved a man of exceptional skill and ability, who steadily added to his business and his reputation, adding more and more to his greenhouse plant on Nahant, and establishing a second one at Revere. He is today one of the best known, most successful and most highly respected men in his industry, past president of the Society of American

Florists, and long-time influential trustee of the Massachusetts Horticultural Society. He was born in England something over sixty years ago, but long since became a thorough citizen of his adopted country. He married Abby May Hood, a descendant of the Hood who came to Nahant among the early settlers. There are several children, including sons who now assist him in his business.

The other Nahant industry, which does most of its business outside of Nahant, is the building business of J. T. Wilson & Son, Inc., which was founded in Nahant by Joseph T. Wilson in 1868. It is now owned in his family and is conducted by an organization, including a son Fred A. Wilson, which was mostly built up around him before his death in 1914. It comes to its sixtieth year of business life in 1928, as Nahant meets the three-quarter century mark as a separate township. A list of the houses built by this firm in Nahant up to 1900 here follows. It is given in no attempt to show activity or accomplishment, but only because dates of construction are interesting as houses get older.

1868–69	C. J. Whittemore	House and stable remodelled
	Geo. W. Simmons	Greenhouse
1869–70	B. Schlesinger	House and stable
1870–71	F. R. Sears	House and stable
	E. F. Parker	Stable
	M. Carroll	House
	John S. Wright	Stable
1872	Maolis Garden	Dance hall
	Catholic Church	– –
	Chas. E. Gove	House
	George H. Gove	House
1871–72	Dr. R. M. Hodges	House and stable
	Geo. P. Upham	Greenhouse
	Town of Nahant	Church tower
	A. D. Johnson	Stable

INDUSTRIES

1873-74	A. A. Lawrence	Small house
	H. C. Lodge	Stable
	Jere Abbott	F. Henry Johnson house, alterations and stable
	John Mitchell	House
	John Coakley	House
	E. B. Johnson	House
	H. S. Johnson	Stable
	Miss S. H. Hunt	House
	Mrs. J. P. Putnam	House remodelled
1874-75	Samuel Johnson	J. Bishop Johnson house, alterations and stable
	K. W. Sears	House and stable
	E. E. Spooner	House moved and remodelled and stable
	A. A. Lawrence	House and stable
	Thos. Motley, Jr.	House (Whitney)
	Mrs. Wm. Amory	House
	J. C. Phillips	Stable
	Mrs. A. L. Moering	Stable
	C. F. Johnson	Greenhouse
1875-76	Geo. Peabody	House and stable
	Morris Higgins	House
	H. C. Lodge	Greenhouse
1876-77	W. A. Gove	House
	Independent Methodist Society	Parsonage
	E. J. Johnson	House
	Admiral Thatcher	House remodelled
	B. Schlesinger	Greenhouse
1877-78	Samuel Johnson	House (Kemp)
	George P. Upham	Godsoe House (Ingersoll)
	Mrs. B. L. White	House
	P. Linehan	House
	J. B. Johnson	Fish market
	Nahant Land Company	Dunham House
1878-79	A. Murdock	House (nearest church)
	Capt. S. R. Knox	House (Stacy)
	Lodge Estate	"Wharf Cottage"
1879-80	J. F. Anderson	House remodelled
1880-81	Gen. C. J. Paine	House remodelled
	Thomas Howe	House and stable
	Martin Kenny	House

1881-82	E. C. Johnson	House and stable
	Thos. Motley, Jr.	House
	Mrs. S. E. Guild	House and stable
	Patrick Grant	House
	H. C. Haven	House
	G. A. James	Greenhouse
	Edward Fallon	House
	J. T. Wilson	House
1883-84	E. W. Johnson	House remodelled
1884-85	A. G. Wilson	House
	F. H. Wilson	House
	F. H. Johnson	House and stable
	John Rooney	House
1885-86	J. Colby Wilson	House (now Davis)
	F. G. Phillips	House
	F. W. Bradlee	House remodelled
1886-87	Mrs. J. M. Warren	House remodelled
	John Flynn	House
	Geo. P. Upham	Greenhouse
1887-88	W. P. Dudley	House
	S. E. Smith	House and cottage
1888-89	Frank Merriam	House and stable
	I. T. Burr, Jr.	House and stable
	L. Curtis	House remodelled
	F. H. Johnson	Double house
	W. P. Dudley	Cottage
	S. E. Smith	Cottage
1889-90	Mrs. A. E. Robinson	House
	A. S. Dabney	House
	Mrs. C. C. Boyden	House remodelled
	B. F. Taylor	House
	J. T. Wilson	Stable
1890	E. W. Bourne	House (Bass Point)
	A. A. Barnes	House
	R. L. Cochran	House
	Mrs. Bridget Kennedy	House
1890-91	P. V. R. Ely	House
	Walter Dabney	House
	C. E. Parsons	House
	E. C. Johnson	Cole's house and stable

INDUSTRIES

1891-92	W. K. Richardson	House
	Charles Merriam	House remodelled
	H. G. Curtis	House remodelled
	Geo. P. Upham	Stable rebuilt
	P. V. R. Ely	Stable
	Michael Deveney	House
	George St. George	House
	Chas. D. Vary	House
1892-93	Dudley B. Fay	House remodelled
	Mrs. A. E. Robinson	House
	Geo. F. Shepley	House
	Chas. A. Sampson	House moved and remodelled
	A. S. Dabney	Stable
	S. E. Guild	House and stable
1893	Bass Point House	Additions
	Hotel Tudor	Remodelled
1894	Geo. A. Gove	House
	Frank A. Gove	House
	E. J. Johnson	House remodelled and moved
	Thos. Motley, Jr.	Stable
	Bass Point House	Rebuilt after fire
	Roger Killilae	House
	Michael McCormack	House remodelled
	J. Colby Wilson	House
1894-95	Chas. Davis, Jr.	House remodelled
1895	F. H. Johnson	Three houses on Pond Beach
	Hotel Tudor	Stable
	Sylvester Brown	Billiard room
	Sarah E. Smith	House
	F. M. White	House remodelled
	Whitney Hotel	Remodelled
	Nahant Club	Remodelled
	Geo. W. Kibbey	Stable
	Chas. W. Stacy	Cottage
1895-96	E. F. Chapin	House remodelled
1896	E. F. Chapin	Two houses
	C. T. Lovering	House remodelled
1897	H. Sigourney	Stable
1897-98	H. Sigourney	House
	J. T. Kelley	House
1898	C. D. Adams	Stable

1898–99	Fred A. Wilson .	.	House
1899	Wm. R. Wilson .	.	House
	P. Linskey . .	.	House
1899–1900	John Mitchell .	.	House and store
	S. H. Hunt estate	.	House remodelled

Closely associated with Joseph T. Wilson was his brother, J. Colby Wilson, who conducted the painting branch of the building business and also did much work out of Nahant. He was known and liked all over town, and was a shrewd Yankee of the old-fashioned type, — honest and steadfast, helpful and friendly. These two men were a closely knit pair, friends as well as brothers.

Albert G. Wilson, a brother-in-law of Joseph T. Wilson, was another long-time associate. He was superintendent for many years, up to the time of his death in 1927, and on April 1, 1926, he completed fifty years in one employ. He was dean of town officers, having served on the Board of Public Library Trustees since 1889, a thirty-eight-year period.

Except for these two business enterprises, a look back over the years recalls the usual stores and shops a town may be expected to support. Special mention should be made, however, of the grocery store on Nahant Road at the corner of Pleasant Street, where now stands the Town Hall. This business was started in a house farther down the street, built by George Johnson, a brother of Welcome W. Johnson, on the present site of the Leavitt House, across the street and a little westward from the Whitney homestead. Caleb Johnson, at the time the old Johnson homestead was rented to Rouillard, as related elsewhere, built and occupied a house across the street and just above this old grocery store. This house was also removed when the present Town Hall was built. Welcome W. Johnson married in 1827 and lived here, carrying on the business in the adjoining building, which had been started by his brother elsewhere. This was the grocery store and village post office familiar to old Nahanters now living. As Nahant grew as a summer resort this store prospered. John-

Old Village Store, Johnson House beyond
Both replaced by new Town Hall

Pleasant Street Schoolhouse
Built 1851

son's son, Edwin W. Johnson, succeeded to its management, followed by T. Dexter Johnson and George E. Poland. Dexter Johnson was a son of William F. Johnson and a cousin of Edwin. In 1902 Poland moved the business into the block now called the post office block, where it languished and finally went out of existence. This old store Nahanters living, as well as those long dead, patronized, even as children doing detested errands for their parents and spending spare cents for Black Jacks or Gibralters. Those were the popular forms of candy long before the days of the regrettable all-day suckers and gaudy colored swabs on a stick, with which today's children aim to be so uninviting, and succeed. Johnson sold Black Jacks before the Civil War. It was a hard stick of molasses candy, cleanly wrapped, and respectable to eat.

Welcome W. Johnson was town treasurer for several years, as is shown in the list of town officers. Edwin W. Johnson, known by his schoolmates as "Bumble," was long on the Board of Selectmen, but finally sold out his business interests on Nahant, devoting himself to other schemes, sometimes taking long chances for a high stake. He was in mining enterprises with his brother Caleb, who developed into a mining engineer or manager, spending most of his time in the West. Caleb built and owned the house on Nahant Road now owned by Wallace D. Williams, west of the post office block on the opposite side of the street. Edwin made many trips West, beginning at a time when the Indians were a menace, and at least once narrowly escaping capture by them. The story is told of an Indian raid, where Edwin stumbled over a box bearing his father's name, Welcome W. Johnson. It developed that the latter had sent a latest type of rifle to one of his sons by the express, which was raided, and the rifle stolen. It was afterwards recovered through previous friendship with the Indian chief. Later Edwin travelled through the West for a prominent New York fruit commission house, trying to get improved packing and so save the large losses then suffered between farm and orchard and market. Later he developed, for himself and his brother Caleb, a large orange grove in Florida. It was brought nearly to the time of heavy yield when two frosts, a few days apart, in the early 90's wrecked the enterprise. Struggling not too successfully in following years, Edwin Johnson died in 1912 at the age of sixty-nine. His father, Welcome W. Johnson, died in 1880 at the age of seventy-seven. Both father and son were fine looking men, as indeed were many of this Johnson family.

The Nahant Post Office was established in the "Nahant Hotel" in July, 1847, during Phineas Drew's progressive management of this hostelry. Later in the same year it was moved into the village, and for many years was in one corner of the old Johnson grocery store which has been described. The successive proprietors were postmasters. There was no delivery system during this period, people going to the office for mail, with mail boxes for all, as is common in small offices and small towns. Welcome W. Johnson was postmaster until his death, succeeded by Edwin W. Johnson and T. Dexter Johnson. In January, 1899, Thomas J. Cusick was appointed postmaster, the fifth in the life of the town, while George E. Poland owned and managed the store. Cusick was a veteran of the Civil War, joining in the Tenth Massachusetts Battery, almost a boy. He enlisted from Brookline but moved to Nahant in 1870, and after working for a while for John D. Reed in a store on Summer Street in a building now owned by D. G. Finnerty, he bought the house, nearly across the street, from Mrs. Tudor, and put a store under it. He bought out Reed in 1874. For a long time he conducted a grocery business in Boston, giving it up in 1900. He ran his Nahant store until 1920, when it was closed. Cusick died in 1927. A son, Dr. Laurence F. Cusick, well known on Nahant and perhaps the second year-round physician the town has had, has built up a large practice outside of Nahant as well as within the town.

The post office stayed in the old Johnson grocery store until 1901, when it was moved to the Johnson block on Nahant Road, where it has remained. In this same year, 1901, the post office was made a branch of the Lynn Post Office, which

INDUSTRIES 131

gave Nahant the mail carrier system usual in larger places. Cusick, formerly postmaster, was made superintendent of the Nahant Branch Office, and held this place until 1921, when he was succeeded by his daughter, Mary T. Cusick, who now serves so capably in this important position.

The Johnson grocery store, the old Johnson house next to it, and the Spooner house on Pleasant Street, formerly the house of E. Augustus Johnson, son of Caleb Johnson, were bought by the town of Nahant following authorization by the town in 1911. The buildings were torn down, together with several smaller buildings, excepting one small house on Pleasant Street just around the corner from Nahant Road. This house was moved there from Swallows Cave Road and once occupied the place of the K. W. Sears house, and was owned and occupied by Benjamin Crowninshield. This house, small enough to be moved through the streets, was rolled to the westerly side of Spring Road, near Nahant Road, and is now owned by Mrs. Harry R. Cummings. The new Town Hall was occupied in the fall of 1912, giving accommodations which were badly needed and which were intended to serve town needs for a long time. But all at once, with the advent of woman suffrage was an increase almost doubling the number of voters, and the limit of capacity for the Town Hall may be reached far sooner than was expected. This is a trouble many towns are meeting, and which is leading to a modified form of town meetings which perhaps Nahant will not face in the future. The town is of too small an area to grow to the large size which is making old-fashioned town meetings unwieldy in other places.

Fishing was considered a Nahant industry, naturally so, as with most other favorably located coast towns, before later methods and large enterprises met the increasing demands. There are early records that men were given the right to live here, on this commonly owned place where homes were prohibited, if they would pursue the industry of fishing. It was a sort of license to occupy for a specific purpose. Lewis says in "The Picture of Nahant," 1845, that in 1635 nine men, who were named, but who do not appear later among Nahanters, were given liberty to plant and build at Nahant and proceed in the trade of fishing. If they did not further the trade of fishing their lots were to be forfeited again to the town. The three families living on Nahant in 1800 were Hood, Breed and Johnson. The first two were farmers, who owned nearly all the land in the first four ranges, or about up to Wharf Street. The Johnson family were fishermen principally, including Caleb Johnson, although he also was a large landowner. A little later Caleb's brother Joseph moved back to Nahant, and fishing was likewise his chief occupation. It should be remembered that all these families catered more or less to the increasing tide of pleasure travel to Nahant. The honest dollar looked attractive in whatever place it might be found, in those days when money was scarce.

But little is known of early boats and crews and doings. In 1824 the schooner "Lafayette," which was built at Essex, was at Nahant. She was a thirty-ton boat of the old-fashioned sharp stern, full bows type. Her two skippers were the brothers Caleb and Joseph Johnson. It is said they were remarkable seamen, knowing their way around on the water as well as most people do amid familiar landmarks. E. J. Johnson says they had a compass aboard, but cared so little for it that it was often out of order. Caleb Johnson followed this trade for fifty years, or until an accident not of the sea made him less fit for this hard service. Joseph Johnson continued to go out in the "Lafayette" until he was an old man. The growth of trawl fishing, which was becoming conspicuous in the 60's, injured the older "bay fishing" methods. Competition with the new methods was hard, and soon the near-by fishing grounds were less productive to the fisherman. The industry, operated as a trade conveniently handled from the shore, has disappeared from the vicinity. While fishing as a pleasure still affords results, the "grounds" once so teeming are comparatively exhausted.

In 1844 the schooner "Foam" was built at Salisbury and was one of the first sharp boats built for fishing. She was much used in summer for excursion trips, and for bay fishing at all other times. She was a fast boat and brought home good fares, and was known as a lucky boat. She was wrecked at Phillips Beach in Swampscott, after parting her cable during the gale of September 8, 1869.

In 1858 winter lobstering began at Nahant and soon this used forty men and four vessels. It was a profitable business, but soon lobsters were exhausted from places within reach. A thousand lobsters, and more, have been taken from a hundred pots, while half that number was a common fare. Laws were enacted to protect the diminishing supply. This decreased the legally available quantity. Prices advanced, encouraging catches of illegal sizes or ages, and today the once common lobster of waters around Boston is both rare and expensive. The price is so high that a few still go for them locally, but it is not a lucrative occupation. Boston markets, fed by supplies from far afield, or rather a-sea, now supply fish of all sorts to even the most salty of seacoast towns — unless it be a place like Gloucester, which has reached out for the new methods of the industry and made them her own.

On February 11, 1858, while fishing was still an industry in the town, a sixteen-ton schooner, the "Charles Amory," was launched from Nahant, the first vessel ever built here. Walter Johnson was chairman of the exercises at this event, and Alfred D. Johnson was the orator of the day. These three names will all be found mentioned elsewhere or in the list of children of Joseph and Caleb Johnson. Charles Amory, for whom the boat was named, lived in what is now the Dr. Thomas Dwight estate house on Cliff Street. He was interested in the Massachusetts Humane Society, which for a long time "caused our whole coast to be supplied with life boats and apparatus to relieve the shipwrecked from a dreadful death." This citation is from Johnson's address of that launching day. Many will remember the little sheds frequently seen, located at points nearest good launching places in storms, and containing boats and life-saving equipment. One of these was on Longfellow Beach, the little cove next easterly from the steamboat wharf and "Fremont" place. Johnson concluded his address in the following words: "Go, then, little craft, from this spot, whence you have sprung into existence, to the waters, towards which you are steadily pointing, and upon whose bosom you are to find your future home; and may this gilded hand which adorns your prow ever successfully point out to your gallant crew a haven of safety from the stormy dangers through which you will successfully bear them. May you combat the stormy waves for years, remaining, as now, the favorite of all, the pride of your owners and crew; and may no one ever have cause to regret that you bear the honored name of Charles Amory." This event of the times was followed by music, tea and dancing at the home of Jonathan Johnson. This house has been described, on Nahant Road, where the post office block now stands. This boat was finally sold to owners in Scituate. Some of the vessels engaged in fishing industry at Nahant were the "Dolphin," "Jefferson," "Sally Ann," "Caroline," "Lafayette," "Josephine," "Foam," "Fairy Queen," "Spray," "Susan," "Greyhound," "Faustina," "Fashion," "Charles Amory," "Lizzie Phillips," "Frederic Tudor," "Signet," "Fox," "John Randolph," "Raven," "Evergreen," "Unity," "James and Isaac," and "General Marion." The list is probably not complete, but is large enough to show a considerable industry for so small a community as Nahant. Most of this material on fishing is from Johnson's "History of Nahant." This fishing industry from Nahant centered around Nipper Stage, where Tudor Wharf now stands. Fish flakes and all the varied equipment of the business were on both the adjacent beaches. The little Crystal Beach just inside the wharf and Curlew Beach beyond were scenes of activity. In those old days the catch was sometimes a thousand pounds a man, all carried to Boston market the same day.

Worthen Gove came to Nahant to sail a yacht for the proprietors of the Nahant Hotel, taking out fishing parties. He was the drummer for the Civil War "Home Guard" troop. He was one of the owners and crew of the "Spray," and this group had a boat built for them and named the "Frederic Tudor," but she proved too small and was replaced by the "Lizzie Phillips," which some people can remember. J. Bishop Johnson and his crew sailed in the "Zeppie."

One of the men early engaged in winter lobstering was Francis Johnson, a son of Joseph Johnson and a member of the old firm of Johnson & Young of Boston, established in 1842. He went fishing at an early age, making his first voyages in the "Lafayette" of the Nahant fleet. Later he commanded, at various times, several of the vessels. Then he was captain of the steamer "Housatonic," which ran from Boston to Nahant in 1828 and 1829. Francis Johnson, commonly known as Captain Frank, owned and lived in the house built about 1827, on the corner of Nahant Road and Summer Street. It was later owned and occupied by his daughter, Mrs. Sarah J. Melvin, who died in 1914 at the age of eighty-six. A son of Francis Johnson, Francis H. Johnson, was also well known in the fish industry, but as a Boston marketman and not a fisherman. For many years he spent his summers on Nahant, building a house on Willow Road in 1885, for his own occupancy. Later he developed other property, including the Johnson block on Nahant Road, also called the post office block. At the time of his death in 1918 he owned ten or a dozen houses, and had proven himself a believer in real estate in the town. He turned what was a pebble ridge, on the shore between Bear Pond and Ocean Street, into house lots. Here were three houses built in 1895, westerly from his own house, and a fourth built there at a later date.

Fishing as an industry seems to have been important from the beginning of the town and as long as there were fish in near-by waters. Mention has been made of early grants of permission to live on Nahant "commons" given to certain men so long as they engaged in fishing. Nothing is known of the extent of this work in the early days except that it was considered a very valuable food supply. Perhaps the first mention of this business in the old records is in 1635, when Joseph Rednap was voted a grant of land and permission to live on Nahant "for the purpose of pursuing the trade of fishing." In 1669 is an interesting entry, though not pertaining to fishing, that Robert Page of Boston was "presented for setting sail from Nahant, in his boat, being laden with wood, thereby profaning the Lord's Day." Lewis says the second inhabitant of Nahant of whom there is any record was Robert Coats, who was probably a shepherd or a fisherman living in town a short time.

Perhaps the only fishing vessel ever built at Nahant was the "Charles Amory," which was designed by Edward J. Johnson, a son of Jonathan Johnson, and grandson of Joseph Johnson. Edward J. Johnson was one of the Nahant contingent of Civil War veterans, and his spare, erect figure, with eyes always afire with spirit, will be remembered by many people, perhaps as a marcher with his comrades in Decoration Day events. He was a student of Nahant history, and after his death in 1901, at the age of sixty-nine, many old deeds and other Nahant papers from his collection were given to the Nahant Public Library. He served on the Board of Selectmen for several years ending with 1878, and was on numerous committees, including the public library committee. In 1886, in connection with a general history of Essex County towns, a "History of Nahant," written by Johnson, was published. It has been drawn upon liberally in the preparation of these present writings, which, however, are using much material far outside the scope of that work. Johnson's son, Jonathan Edward Johnson, was an Episcopal clergyman, meeting death too young, in 1908, at the age of forty. A daughter, Florence A. Johnson, is a genuine Nahanter through her lifelong residence here, and is well known as an efficient teacher of long service in the public schools of the town. Another daughter, married and away from Nahant, has a son, Frederic Manning, whose wife is the daughter of Ex-President Taft.

Of course farming or gardening was always an important adjunct of life in old days. Many acres were under cultivation on Nahant, and there were fields of grain and considerable

Lynn — Old Boston & Maine Station from Central Square
Burned in the great Lynn fire of 1889; Union Street on left

Ellingwood Chapel

yields of vegetables. The big barn on the Johnson homestead was the scene of many husking bees followed by the generous farm suppers which are so often told about as bright spots in the country life of those times. Those were the days of a simpler life, when a bumper crop did not bump the farmers so much, husbands had less competition with chow dogs, and yearnings less often outran earnings.

The making of shoes was a Nahant industry in the days when shoes were made in scattered small shops. Lynn was early prominent in this industry, but even far-away places had these little shoe shops. Even within thirty years materials for shoes were shipped out to the homes of New England to be put together, although machinery was rapidly replacing much hand work. These early shops were little square buildings ten to fourteen feet on a side, with a pitched roof affording a stowaway garret. They were low-ceiled and easily became stuffy. Benches for from two to six workers were provided, and their tools and materials made a crowded room. Heat was furnished by a small fireplace in early days, and later by stoves. The work was piece work, and a worker took materials for a day or sitting — what he wanted to do, or had time to do, interspersed with his farming and fishing, for not many of them devoted all their time to shoe making. This came to be called a "seat of work," and apparently inspired the phrase heard today, "to take out a seat of work" on a person, usually meaning to start a campaign of talk or action against him. To many people this saying is very familiar, while others do not know it, showing a rather local habitat.

A good sample of one of these old shoe shops stands on the grounds of the Lynn Historical Society, where it has been restored, in appearance and furnishings, as nearly as possible to one hundred years ago — as if the workers could be expected to return to it after a while. There were several of these little shops on Nahant, — one a room in a corner of a barn, another over the grocery store, while at least one was a little separate building such as has been described. This building still stands on Harmony Court, though descended from its high estate to later use as a henhouse. They had local names, says Johnson, such as "Invincible," "Band Box," and "House of Commons." On a bad day for fishing they might be crowded, — a few loafers would do it, — and then came attempts to consume tobacco and smoke out the whole outfit. Some of the sewing or binding was often done by the women in the houses. Thus hard work prevailed. It is said to have been the days when the Board of Education was the scrubbing board, and girls did not have to be careful to take exercise enough to enable them to wear ear rings without stooping. The people were a hardy lot, the sort from whom are springing so many of the great of the world.

The shoe industry conducted in this way died gradually. Around the 1850's machines began to do the work, and in a few years factories superseded shops, although some work was still sent out, perhaps with the stock all cut up ready for sewing. Lynn grew to be a shoe manufacturing city, probably headed in that direction originally because skilled shoemakers settled there and gave supremacy even in early days.

In discussing Nahant industries mention should be made of town employment. In 1926 around $30,000 was spent for labor by the several town departments using manual labor. This is employment for many men, in a small town, and this annual pay roll is exceeded only by the two industries before mentioned, which deal chiefly out of town. It grew to this size from small beginnings, but perhaps was always more or less in the same proportion to the total number of inhabitants.

It is evident that Nahant is today, as it has always been, practically a residential town, though accompanied in its progress throughout by a typical shore resort development in one or another part of it. The Maolis Gardens was an early example, and later years have seen most of the merely transient visitors going to the Bass Point section, which was built up for the purpose. The natural attractions of the town and its proximity to cities made both developments, — for residents and for visitors; but as they do not fit together well it was fortunate that the two came finally to different parts of the town. Crowds and amusements for crowds are noisy and troublesome to people who seek their homes for rest and quiet. Even the Maolis Gardens, which had not the transportation facilities of today, were considered troublesome, looked at askance, as it were, and Tudor was criticised by neighbors for setting up such an institution in the midst of the quieter home seekers.

CHAPTER X

MOSTLY NAUTICAL

THE projection of Nahant into the waters of the approach to Boston, while giving Lynn a harbor, has always meant some danger to shipping. From the beginning the shores of Nahant could tell of wrecks. Lewis, in his "Annals of Lynn," says a vessel was wrecked on Nahant rocks on February 18, 1631. In a "great snowstorm" on December 17, 1740, a schooner was wrecked on Nahant rocks. On February 14, 1755, a schooner from Salem was cast away on Short Beach. On February 6, 1757, two merchant vessels from London, valued at a hundred thousand pounds, were wrecked on Lynn Beach. February 8, 1766, an English brig was cast away on Pond Beach, and in 1769, in a September storm, a sloop was "driven ashore at Nahant." The year 1772 saw a fishing schooner wrecked on Long Beach with loss of life, and in 1788 there was another wreck at the same place. Near the southern end of Lynn Beach, which was out toward Little Nahant, a Scotch brig, the "Peggy," met her fate in December, 1795, and many lives were lost. In May, 1827, a schooner from Maine was driven ashore on Long Beach, or Lynn Beach, as it was then often called. A coffee laden schooner was wrecked on Shag Rocks in March, 1829, with "all hands lost." These rocks are near Pea Island and Swallows Cave. A brig with a cargo of sugar and molasses was wrecked on Long Beach on December 17, 1836. On December 15, 1839, during a great storm, a schooner from Philadelphia for Boston was wrecked on the rocks near Bass Point, with loss of life. Another wreck on the southern end of Long Beach was the Belfast schooner "Thomas," loaded with wood, on March 17, 1843. Then came the Nova Scotia brig "Exile," wrecked on Long Beach on November 21, 1851. Her deck load of wood was washed ashore, furnishing material for fires which assisted in the work of saving lives. It is said that a thousand people gathered on the beach that night to watch and help. Another vessel, a schooner from Bristol, Maine, for Boston, went ashore on Long Beach September 30, 1856.

In November, 1840, came a storm on a high run of tides with a great sea outside. Lewis says, "and the swell of waters was immense, passing for several days entirely over Long Beach, so that not only the harbor, but the marshes of Lynn, Saugus and Chelsea were a portion of the mighty sea. There was no safety in approaching the level shore; but it was a grand and terrible sight, to stand upon Sagamore Hill, or some other elevation, and view the fearful devastation of the waters. Nahant appeared to be severed forever from the main, and ocean to be passing the bounds of its ancient decree."

It was the great storm of April 16, 1851, that brought destruction to the stout steel frame structure of Minot's Ledge lighthouse, so plainly visible from Nahant and replaced with the present dovetailed stone tower. This ill-fated lighthouse was operated for the first time on January 1, 1850, and so was of very short life. There was a wreck on Nahant in that year, but not in that storm. The greatest storm of which there seems to be much record, if not indeed the greatest of all for Nahant, was on January 17, 18 and 19, 1857. On the 16th the thermometer dropped to fourteen below zero. Throughout the storm it showed similarly cold. Lewis says that in Lynn it was twenty-two below. Lynn Harbor and all the coves of Nahant were frozen over, while the water between Nahant and Swampscott was full of loose ice. On Sunday the 18th snow came, with winds increasing to a hurricane. All travel was suspended, and not until Tuesday the 20th did any railroad train get through Lynn. There were eleven engines in the Lynn station at one time. The great boom of the waves at Spouting Horn was heard all over Nahant. On the 19th, as the storm abated, wreckage was found strewn along the shores. Egg Rock seemed smothered by the surf, and spray dashed up at East Point higher than the hotel. On the noon high tide great waves mounted over Canoe Beach, dashed across the low land, and emptied overboard again in the cove west of what is now known as the James estate. Around the rocks by Swallows Cave the seas swept into the cove, Joe Beach, cleaning out the wharf and every other part of everything movable or not firmly set in place. The low lands were full of water from Whitney's Swamp across to Dorothy's Cove in front of what is now Hotel Tudor. Crashing over Pond Beach the seas filled the meadows. Both Long and Short Beaches were washed over. Thus, as E. J. Johnson says, Nahant appeared like a group of islands wrestling in the furious waters. Next day the sky was clear and visitors began to come to view the grandeur of the ocean. They brought the news of the wreck of the bark "Tedesco," laden with wine and salt from Cadiz. This is the wreck of which an old print is now among the much sought items of print collectors. One may be seen at the Nahant Club. She went ashore on the Swampscott side of the bay.

On June 8, 1858, the schooner "Prairie Flower" from Salem for Boston suddenly capsized off Nahant with loss of life. February 2, 1859, saw the British bark "Vernon" driven ashore on Long Beach. She was from Messina for Boston, with a cargo mostly of fruit. In 1860, on January 6, three men walked across the ice in Lynn Harbor from the foot of Commercial Street to Bass Point. This is farther out than most people can remember for this feat, remembering that Bass Point at that time was the point now owned or used by the Bass Point House. Bass Point as a name for that whole wing of Nahant is of recent origin, replacing the name Bass Neck. The new lighthouse at Minot's Ledge was finished in 1860 and lighted first on August 22, going into regular service on November 15. On February 7 and 8, 1861, there was a phenomenal drop in temperature of sixty-six degrees in eighteen hours, to a low of twenty-one below zero. On December 10, 1864, the schooner "Lion" from Maine was cast away on Long Beach with loss of life. Then there were wrecks on Canoe Beach, — the "Major Ringold" and another. Coming down to the recollections of present-day Nahanters was the "Augustus Smith" from Nova Scotia for Boston laden with potatoes and turnips. This wreck was on Short Beach on December 21, 1883. The "Alsatian" came ashore near Spouting Horn in 1896. Then there was the three master "Charles S. Briggs" wrecked on Short Beach close to Little Nahant on January 31, 1899, and strewing her coal cargo all over the vicinity. Greenlawn Cemetery holds some of the victims of this disaster. There are others of more recent date which need not be named so specifically, one on the rocky beach by Marginal Road, for example, and another farther to the eastward. It seems a strange comparison of contrasts to cross the beaches of today on the well-made roads, finding so many people in automobiles seeking solace from hot weather, and recalling some of those other times when storm-beaten vessels heaved upon these same beaches, almost within touch, while the raging elements claimed a toll in lives and in almost unbearable discomfort. In 1898 Senator Lodge gave a list of wrecks which he had compiled, to be inserted in the town records as a method of preservation. It names them in twenty-five of the years back to 1740, with seventeen since 1800.

It is interesting to see what history tells about Long Beach, the slim connection with the mainland, important to Nahant because it bears the only road giving access to the town, and important to Lynn because it makes Lynn Harbor. From Thomas Dexter's early proposal to build a stone breakwater, which was discarded by the General Court, as the Legislature of the time was called, the importance of this protecting sand bar to Lynn seems to have been realized. It was only a ridge of sand, hammered hard by the waves, as tides ebbed and flowed, just as it is today; but above the usual high-water mark was only loose dry sand, so nearly impassable that passage to and from Nahant was only attempted as the tides allowed access to the hard-floored beach. Storms gullied through the ridge, but little if anything was done to fortify the work which nature had begun. Finally, by an accidental combination of storms, each doing a little more harm, action was necessary. In 1824, after a petition by the town of Lynn, the General Court appropriated $1,500, to which the town added a like amount, and a plank wall was constructed about half the length of the beach to prevent further encroachments. The importance of the beach aroused further action, and in 1837 Alonzo Lewis made a survey of it under the direction of Congress at Washington. A plan was submitted calling for the building of a sea wall the whole length of Long Beach at an expense of $37,000. The appropriation was not made by Congress, and the scheme fell with all efforts in its behalf unavailing. In 1841 the selectmen of Lynn voted to set three hundred cedar trees on Long Beach, and in 1842 one thousand more. These appear to have been cedar posts and not growing trees. There were frequent meetings of the selectmen at the beach to see what should be done and to inspect repairs. In several years more planks and posts were bought to aid the protection.

The first attempt at a road over the beach, except in conjunction with some proposed sea wall or breakwater, seems to have been in 1847, when about $1,300 was raised by subscription, chiefly by Nahanters. The first house at Little Nahant was one built to accommodate the workmen during this roadmaking. The town of Lynn afterwards appropriated $1,000 to complete the road. It was built under the direction of Alonzo Lewis. In 1847 the selectmen went two or three times to examine the beach with relation to the proposed road, and on September 5, 1848, accepted the "new road lately made over the Nahant Long Beach." During several of these years by-laws and regulations were in force to prevent the removal from the beach of sand, gravel or stones, to the injury of this strip as a dyke. The taking of seaweed was also regulated. This was sought as a fertilizer, and the people of Lynn wished to reserve it for their own use. In 1848 and 1852 acts of the Legislature went into effect carrying similar prohibitions or restraints.

Spouting Horn Cottage
Built by Thomas H. Perkins

In Front of Hotel Tudor
Willow Road, named for large willow trees formerly bordering it

On the 17th of March, 1851, there was a great storm, and on the 16th of April a greater one, often called the greatest in two centuries. During the former, tides were driven entirely over Long Beach at several points and Nahant was an island. Flooding the marshes across the harbor did damage to the railroad bed. The April storm was worse. This was the one that wrecked the lighthouse on Minot's Ledge. A continuous sheet of raging water lay between Lynn and Nahant. Seven successive tides inundated the beach, badly gullying the recently built road, covering it with sand, and making it impassable. The sea flooded the lower part of Beach Street, now Washington Street, over the Lynn line, and washed away everything weak or movable.

After these storms it became apparent that something must be done for the protection of this strip of land so important to Lynn as a harbor protection, as well as to Nahant as a land connection. Lynn appropriated $5,000 and a line of red cedar posts was set along the ridge with stone, sand and sea débris worked around them as compactly as possible, in the hope that the sea would itself make further accretions. A guard was thus formed which served a very good purpose. Many Nahanters of today can remember this line of posts, set three or four feet apart, standing out of the ground three feet or so, and holding up a ridge very much higher than any part is today. These posts and their installation were under the direction of Lewis, who seems to have studied the problem here and was intrusted with the execution of the plans adopted. This new dyke also replaced the old plank breakwater which had guarded a part of the distance. This was practically a plank trough filled with sand, and was destroyed in the storms of 1851, which did so much other damage. A part of this story of the beach is taken from Lewis' "Picture of Nahant." Alonzo Lewis, who had charge of so much of the work on this beach, was getting old and died in 1861. The story of the road and the beach has other interesting features, some of which are recollections difficult to verify or to date accurately.

It is said that Frederic Tudor interested himself in the

problem, and through him the grass grown on the dykes in Holland was planted in the sand. This is commonly called Bermuda grass, but its technical name is Ammophila Arenaria, and its proper common name is Marram grass. It is used as a sand binder in many places. Cape Cod and the Golden Gate Park in San Francisco know it well. Even its Greek name means sand lover. Certainly it has done wonders on Nahant Beach. When one realizes what storms have done to this neck of land, and how the ridge is gone, the guarding posts are gone, and the general level lower than at any time in a half century, it does seem foolish for those now in control of this strip to allow this great sand binding grass to be harmed by the newly developed tribes of auto maniacs, who, like the proverbial poor, seem destined to be with us always. Yet injury is done, and at this time the grass is so worn off in occasional places that any such storm as some that have been described, combined with the extreme high tides that happen on a new or full moon at a time when sun and moon are nearest the earth, seems sure to break through the beach defences. The combination of conditions favorable to this happening does not come often, but it has come before and can again. Apparently the lowered ridge may make things easier for the old storm king. There is such a thing as a false sense of security after the sea has lulled people for so many years without raging at its worst. Of all the various forms of protection that have been provided, this dune grass is the sole survivor. Need it be emphasized that it is wise to protect this in its full strength and extent? There are other storms than those mentioned that washed over the ridge and the road. As late as the 70's, so tells a Boston man recently, there was more than one storm when a man could not get over the road without getting wet ankle deep in the splash of the waves, while not avoiding a more thorough drenching from the spray.

 In March, 1875, the town in town meeting voted to lay out Long Beach Road seventy-five feet wide with thirty bound posts placed on harbor side. This was done under the direction of Frederic Tudor, Jr. Along the straighter part of the beach, from the Lynn line toward Nahant for over a mile, and on the harbor side, was set a line of hubs, similar to boundary markers as commonly used. The line of them was slightly curved to exactly an arc of a great circle of the earth. When the grass did not conceal them one could look along the line of posts and see in a mile or more just what is the curvature of the earth. To visualize it in this way was clearer than to describe it, or try to see it in other ways. Some of these posts are said to be in their places yet, but some have been moved or taken away altogether.

It was in 1845 that first a group of Nahanters met at the Nahant Hotel to forward the building of a gravelled road across the beach. Some thought it was not practical to put gravel over the sand, and favored a plank road. A committee was chosen, as a result of this meeting, consisting of Josiah Quincy, Frederic Tudor, John H. Gray, Phineas Drew and Caleb Johnson. They were to ascertain the cost of a road, receive subscriptions, and ask for assistance from the town of Lynn. Other schemes were afoot, for the Lynn "Whig" for September 13, 1845, quotes a correspondent of the "Transcript" as saying the committee will probably report in favor of building upon Nahant Beach a branch of the Eastern Railroad. The road was finally made by spreading gravel over the loose sand and was built about one rod wide. It was completed in the summer of 1848, and is the one suffering, as has been told, in the two storms of the spring of 1851. But it was repaired, and from year to year it was improved and widened. The successive steps are not interesting or important to trace. In 1864 an appropriation was made to build a wall out from Little Nahant, and in 1876 it was extended. In 1880 it was voted to regrade the road at Little Nahant and build the wall which appears to be the present stone retaining wall on the up-hill side. As late as 1870 a proposition was up to lay a plank road at the Lynn end of the beach.

In 1846 Nahanters had petitioned to the Legislature

to be incorporated as a separate town, but the move was strenuously opposed by Lynn and came to naught. In 1853 the agitation was renewed and the attempt was successful. Apparently Lynn did not oppose so strongly. Why not, is now conjectural or mere impression, but it is said that the recent troubles and expenses on the beach made Lynn willing to give over its control, and so the line between Lynn and Nahant was set, as it now stands, as close against what might be called the mainland as it is possible to get. Yet there followed a struggle with Lynn for the possession of certain rights on Long Beach until the courts decided that all rights had passed to Nahant by the act of incorporation and the establishment of boundary lines.

As an almost yearly matter, after Nahant became a separate town, there were appropriations of a few hundred dollars to repair the breakwater on Long Beach, until finally the tenacious grass was so well established that the protecting line of posts was disregarded and allowed to rot away and disappear. It will surprise many people to know that at the annual town meeting in 1891 it was voted to employ the noted landscape architect Frederic Law Olmstead to plan Long Beach, so there would be two roads to Lynn, and with suitable planting and other embellishment. Of course nothing came of the scheme, or results would be manifest today. The roadbed was improved, as years passed, until in 1912 the town remade the entire length at a cost of about $53,000. This expense was borne by the town except for the sum of $4,000 which was contributed by the State from its funds for highway construction.

Near the Lynn end of Long Beach on the harbor side a few acres of land were owned privately and had been devoted to various uses until for many years prior to 1900 nearly all of it was a boat-building and repairing establishment operated by Allan Hay. Here also was one of the familiar sheds of the Massachusetts Humane Society. This outfit was never very neat or desirable. Such establishments cannot be beauty spots, and in its later years it was in a run-down condition which further detracted from its appearance. On the sea side were two amusement places, both through changing proprietorships, reaching back many years. The land on this side was owned by the town of Nahant, and these proprietors were tenants. One place was operated by Soule & Son and was a hotel of some size. Restaurant, barroom and bathhouses made this an active hostelry during the summer season. Just below it and adjoining was an amusement park with restaurant and other appurtenances. This place seems originally to have been known as Seaside Park. There is a large photograph in the Nahant Library which shows it, with its swings, merry-go-rounds and other appliances, and with a sign over the entrance bearing its name. The date of the photograph, perhaps, can be approximated by the figure of a man on one of the early bicycles of the old-fashioned pedal type, the first after the early ones, which were propelled with feet on the ground, walking or running. This latter kind of bicycle, known as dandy horse, or later as hobbyhorse, antedated the forms operated by pedals which seem to have been made practical around 1850 or a little earlier. Probably they were not common for some time after that. The annual town reports show that Samuel Soule of Lynn paid rent to the town of Nahant beginning in 1863 and perhaps earlier. It was about 1855 that Soule built a small hotel here, close to the Lynn line. It was burned a few years later and at once rebuilt, on a larger scale. For some years Soule kept it in partnership with George Taylor of Lynn. Then he bought out Taylor and ran it alone until 1882 or 1883, when it was enlarged and his son, Frank Soule, was taken into partnership. After Samuel Soule's death, Fitzgerald, McDonald, Payrow and Trafton were successive managers, until in 1901 the place was cleared of buildings. The large building was sold to Carahar Brothers of Nahant and moved by them across the beach and up to the summit of Little Nahant, where it now stands.

In 1900, after much debate and deliberation, the Metropolitan Park Commission of the State of Massachusetts took over the beaches, including land on the sea side of Long and Short Beaches, and on the harbor side of Long Beach. The town of Nahant acceded to this, in fact, its officials suggested it, but reserved to itself a fifty-foot strip containing its road. Within a year or so all buildings were removed from the Lynn end of the beach, including the old boat yards, which the Park Commission bought from their owners. A little later, in 1903, the present State bathhouse was erected, the traffic road built behind it, and conditions were as people have now become accustomed to them.

The following quotation is from the selectmen's report, in the Town Report of 1885:

> Long Beach is the only road leading to and from Nahant, and we might add that its good roadway, its fine situation, and its charming views form one of the chief attractions of the town, not only to its own residents, but to those of adjoining towns. A drive over Long Beach road upon a summer's day or evening is, indeed, an event worthy of considerable effort and sacrifice. This beautiful avenue, with its attractions preserved and protected, as they have been in the past, is peculiar to Nahant. Deprive it of its natural beauties, or make it in the least dangerous to travel, and our peninsular will sink below the most commonplace of towns; but carefully keep and zealously guard it against the encroachments of the despoiler, sacredly maintain it as a pleasure park, as a place where all can enjoy a quiet drive with perfect safety, and we can offer to the world an attraction that is unequalled on our coast.

Any story of the beaches and the beach road should mention the two trees which were on the sea side about halfway over from Little Nahant, called the halfway trees. They were poplars, always badly weathered and leaning toward the quieter west part of the compass. No one knows exactly when they were set there, but they were weatherbeaten in the 70's. Perhaps it was in the 90's that one of them succumbed. A photograph taken in 1893 shows only one. This last reminder of an old landmark was blown to pieces in a heavy shower on July 31, 1916. The situation is an exposed one, but doubtless a clump of trees, assisting each other against the weather, would grow there, or anywhere along the beach, if given some soil and food and support.

The first steamboat service of any kind out of Boston seems to have been to Nahant, or to have included Nahant in its run. There was a reason for this. Even in the early days, before the town became a famous resort with hotels, it was a popular place for picnics and for excursions or visitors who would get a dinner or night accommodation at the few houses, all of which seem to have catered to this sort of trade. But the access over the beach was more or less difficult and always dependent upon the tides. It was natural, therefore, that a steamboat might look for good patronage by running to Nahant. Morison, in his "Maritime History of Massachusetts," says, "Beyond a daily summer service to Nahant, which began in 1818, Boston had no steamboat facilities until 1824, when a Maine corporation established a line from Boston down east." The statement is interesting but needs slight modification to agree with what is here written.

The "Massachusetts" was the first steamer ever seen in Boston or vicinity. She was built in Philadelphia in 1816 for the Massachusetts Steam Navigation Company, a group composed of Salem and Portsmouth hardy adventurers into new fields of investment. This was about ten years after Robert Fulton's initial voyage on the Hudson River. This latest and up-to-date vessel was about a hundred feet long and one hundred and twenty tons' gross measurement, with a crude form of walking beam engine. No good picture of her is extant. Her propulsion was by groups of vertical oars rather than the later revolving paddle wheels. On April 25, 1817, she left Philadelphia for New York, but broke down on the way and got to port partly in tow and partly by a sail set on the single mast she had. She arrived at Salem on June 5 after much more delay, and was repaired and altered rather continuously during her whole existence, so that confidence in her ability to reach a destination was impaired, and it seems that people patronizing her did so chiefly from curiosity and when time was no object. During July and August of

1817 this steamer made excursions to Gloucester, Marblehead, Nahant and Boston, so the Salem papers say. In the fall she was sold and was wrecked in an attempt to go south to Mobile, Alabama. The new adventure into steam shipping was financially disastrous to this Salem company, and they seem to have dropped their enterprise. These early steamboats give emphasis to the old slander why boats are of the feminine gender. They were coy, uncertain and hard to please.

A smaller steamer, the "Eagle," was built in Connecticut and launched in April, 1817. She was of eighty-two tons' burden and ninety-two feet long. Just what she did in 1817 is not very clear from available records, but the Boston newspapers in 1818 carried an advertisement that the "Steamboat 'Eagle' leaves this morning for Nahant at nine and returns to Boston at twelve noon. She will return to Nahant precisely at three and leave there at half past six." Another Boston notice says she arrived a few days since from Nantucket "for the purpose of gratifying the inhabitants of this town and vicinity with the repetition of those pleasant excursions down the harbor, with which they were so much delighted last summer, in the steamboat 'Massachusetts.'" Other advertising of this season shows that she ran to Hingham. From the files of the "Columbian Centinel," however, there seems no doubt that in 1818 and 1819 the "Eagle" ran chiefly to Nahant.

J. L. Homer writes: "With some thirty others, in the year 1819, I was a passenger in the steamboat 'Eagle,' Capt. Wood, the first boat, I believe, that ever ran to Nahant regularly. She made three trips a week, that year, to Nahant, and three to Hingham. Capt. Wood was a gentleman of the old school, a man of polished manners, good conversational powers, and hospitable feeling; there are but few of that stamp now in existence, the race is fast disappearing, and, I am apprehensive, will soon be extinct." "The 'Eagle' was usually three hours in making her trip to Nahant, and the same time back; and she was considered a wonderfully swift boat." This was written about 1845 and already the writer

Joseph's Beach in the Seventies

Four houses on the beach: right, George Peabody, Thomas B. Curtis, John Amory Lowell; left, Charles R. Green; others are less prominent

Nahant Road westerly, before High Street crossed to the Left

"Truck House" on corner, on lot now occupied by Police Station

thinks he sees signs of modern froth and superficiality. It is only an example of what is said in every generation, that the Golden Age lies behind us. It was said in old Greece and ever since. As it never has been true, perhaps it is not true, and never will be true for anything like the reasons which commonly cause the sighing statement.

The steamboat "Massachusetts" later mentioned seems to have been a second of the name. Picture and description are different for the two, and there is record of disaster to the first. This second "Massachusetts" appears to have been built in Philadelphia in 1817. She is advertised (see the "Salem Register" for the summer of 1820) to run from Boston to Salem, touching at Nahant and Marblehead, as was likewise the "Eagle." It looks like two boats, with competition. The "Eagle" continued running on this line through 1821, and was then sold and broken up. The second "Massachusetts" ran until 1825. Here follows a list of the steamers running to Nahant. Of course they showed rapid development from the uncertainties of early design and construction, but no specific comment is important for most of them.

1817	"Massachusetts."
1818–25	"Eagle" and "Massachusetts" (2d).
1826–27	"Patent."
1828–29	"Housatonic."
1830	"Rushlight" and "Housatonic."
1831	"Fanny."
1832	"Connecticut."
1833–35	"Hancock" and "Fanny."
1836	"Mt. Pleasant."
1837	"Kingston."
1838	"John Jay."
1839	"Thorn."
1840	"Hope."
1841–47	"General Lincoln" (1st).
1848	"Nahanteau."
1849	"King Philip."
1850	"Suffolk."
1851	"Norwalk."
1852	"Clifton."
1853	"Queen of May."
1854–61	"Nelly Baker."
1862	"Nequasset."

1863	"General Berry."
1864	"Clinton."
1865	"Orient."
1866–76	"Ulysses" and "Meta."
1877	"Eliza Hancox."
1878–80	"Meta" and "Eliza Hancox."
1881–83	"Nahant," later the "General Lincoln" (2d).
1884	(No boat).
1885	"General Bartlett."
1886–87	"Julia."
1888–89	"Anita."
1890	"Frederick de Bary."
1891–1903	"Frederick de Bary" and "City of Jacksonville."
1904	"Mt. Desert" and "Beebe."
1905	"New Brunswick" and "Favorite."
1906	"Cimbria" and "Pokanet."
1907–10	"General Lincoln" (2d) and "Governor Andrew."
1911	"General Lincoln" and "Cape Cod."
1912	"General Lincoln" and "Martha's Vineyard."
1913–16	"General Lincoln" and "Machigonne."

Besides this list there is evidence that boats running to Maine, after 1824, stopped at Nahant. Newspapers for 1826 mention the "Legislator" as stopping at Nahant on her way to Portland and Bath. This list is quoted from Johnson's "History of Nahant," and the source of his information is not known.

The "Housatonic" was captained in 1828 and 1829 by Francis Johnson, one of the Nahant Johnsons, a son of Joseph Johnson and grandson of Jonathan Johnson. This gave him his familiar title of "Cap'n Frank." Probably the best known of all these boats was the "Nelly Baker." She was built expressly for this line by the Nahant Steamboat Company of which Daniel C. Baker of Lynn was a prime mover. He was Lynn's third mayor in 1853, her fourth year as a city. This steamer was named for Baker's daughter, and was of three hundred and three tons' burden, one hundred and fifty-three feet long. She was considered the fastest boat in Boston Harbor. During the Civil War she was used in southern waters as a transport and hospital ship. She was sold in 1866 and seems to have been rebuilt and renamed, as all trace of her disappears. In the early 80's another Nahant steamboat company was formed of which a prominent Nahant summer resident, E. Francis Parker, was the leading spirit. They built the "Nahant," which ran for three years with indifferent financial success, and was then sold to the Nantasket Steamboat Company who renamed her the "General Lincoln."

The year 1884 was the first year with no boat from Nahant to Boston, after sixty-seven years of continuous service. During the summer it seemed a great lack, this absence of boat transportation to Boston, and at a special town meeting in December the question was raised if the town should ask authority from the State Legislature, by a special act, to subsidize this service. There was a tie vote of 39 to 39, but the selectmen nevertheless proceeded to ask for and get a special act allowing the town to spend not over $2,500 a year for this purpose. At another special meeting on May 15, 1885, this act was unanimously accepted, and $2,500 for a subsidy was appropriated. It would appear that some good arguments were used in the interim between these meetings, to turn a tie vote to a unanimous yes vote.

Then began a hunt for a boat, and here comes upon the scene a figure familiar to old Nahanters, Captain Joseph B. Ingersoll, who in his later years made his home on Nahant, buying a house on Willow Road, second eastward from "Hotel Tudor." Captain Ingersoll and Joseph T. Wilson, chairman of the selectmen, scoured the coast to find a steamboat for service in 1885 and some people who would run her on the Nahant line. The best they could get in the short time before the season opened was the small screw propeller steamer "General Bartlett." Ingersoll was captain. Prior to this he had been pilot on the "Nahant" under Captain A. W. Calden, whom many old Nahanters remember, and had begun on the Nahant to Boston run in 1870 on the "Ulysses." Then followed the "Julia" and "Anita" with Captain Ingersoll, until, after many conferences with Frederick De Bary of an importing firm in New York which owned two steamers desirable for this service, contracts were made under which the "De Bary" and "Jacksonville" were operated for fourteen summers beginning in 1890. Ingersoll was captain of the former a part of the time, in the later years. During this period the De Bary interests were sold to the Clyde Steamship Company which continued to operate. The two boats were used on the St. John's River in Florida in the winter season, and this made a desirable business combination for them. Finally, however, it was deemed a hard trip along the coast, and the Clyde Company gave up sending them north. The boats were of light draft and received a bad battering around Cape Hatteras on more than one run between the two routes of business. Captain Ingersoll retired in 1904 and died on Nahant in 1913. Captain Thomas W. Lund will be remembered in this service with these boats, because of their long use here. Subsequently he was the Clyde Company's port captain at Jacksonville, Florida. The Clyde Company then ran other boats until after 1906, when they gave up and declined to renew the contracts. These various contracts were made with the town of Nahant and called for specified trips to Tudor Wharf for which the subsidy was to be paid. Bass Point had come to the front as an amusement resort, and most of the traffic was to the Bass Point Wharf.

Then came the formation of the Boston, Nahant and Pines Steamboat Company, which took up the service in 1907 and continued until 1916. Fred A. Wilson of Nahant was president of this company, and most of the money was from Lynn investors. Lawrence F. Sherman, then a young man living on Nahant, since moved to New York, was the leader in organizing this group, and was its manager during the whole period of its operation. The company bought several boats and hired others. Its first purchase was the "General Lincoln" and "Governor Andrew" from the Nantasket Steamboat Company in 1907, and these two boats were run together until the "Andrew" was burned just prior to the opening of the season of 1911. During these years of operation an attempt was made to establish service from Nahant to Revere Beach, where a new amusement pier was built. No success attended. Part of the trouble was in getting light draft boats in to the

Revere Wharf, Revere Beach being a long beach with shoal water extending an unusual distance from land. This company met very indifferent financial success. In 1916 the line stopped, chiefly because the next season saw the government using, even commandeering, all craft which were useful for war purposes. They took the "Machigonne" and one or two smaller boats and service to Nahant was suspended. There seemed no incentive to continue, and as quickly as possible, although it took several years, the affairs of the company were settled and the company went out of existence. Since that time there has been some service to Bass Point, but nothing continuous or very persevering. The first year was 1924, when the Dixon Line started running. The automobile appears to be the popular means of locomotion, and the steamboat no longer is the easiest way to get to Nahant.

Two steamboat disasters, the "Eastland" in Chicago and the "Slocum" in New York, were followed by a heavy increase in requirements on the part of Federal government for excursion steamers. This meant more men, more small boats carried, and some alterations, with more rigid inspection. The Nantasket line, with whose fares the Nahant line felt it must keep pace, was rated an inside line, and the Nahant line an outside line with heavier requirements. Here was another handicap which bore heavily. Protests that the Nahant line ran only in summer, and was never more than ten minutes away from beaching possibilities, were unavailing. It was classed with lines which ran the year round, meeting the greater stress of winter conditions, and which were several miles from land at some parts of their runs. Thus ended a business venture into which many people entered with an enthusiasm which the years of experience modified. It is said that at least some of this company's stockholders felt that not all who dig are archæologists.

The "Ulysses," which ran here in the 70's and earlier, also touched at the Point of Pines. This place had a large hotel and was a prominent amusement resort hardly remembered as such by any one under fifty years of age. The wharf was below the present Pines Bridge on the Boulevard, and some of the old piling of it may still be seen. A channel was dredged to allow so deep draft a boat as the "Ulysses" proper access at all tides. The "Meta" which ran during part of this same period as well as later, made landings in Lynn in some seasons. She was a smaller boat, fit for the shallower channels. She touched at the old Black Rock Wharf, all trace of which has now disappeared.

Then from 1894 to 1918 were the regular runs of the Lynn Steamboat Company with the "E. W. Rice," the "Canestota" and a third used at times on Sundays and holidays. These ran to the Relay House Wharf in Nahant and to Breed's Wharf in Lynn. They could compete favorably with the old barge lines to Nahant, but the coming of the street railroad took off the edge of the business and made further operation less profitable.

A citation from an address delivered in Boston about 1836 may well close this story of steamboats. It was by J. L. Homer.

> Of the progress of steam and the increase of steamboats in our own country, we all of us have a familiar knowledge. Thirty years ago there was not one in existence in the civilized world; now there are thousands of them, crowding every bay and river from the Penobscot to the Missouri, and their number is increasing with a rapidity which knows no bounds.
> The introduction of steam carriages into America is an event of so recent occurrence that none of us can be ignorant of its importance, as identified with the growth and prosperity of our common country. When we remark the progress of these flying machines, with their long trains of cars and passengers, dashing on with fire and smoke through towns and villages at the rate of twenty and thirty miles an hour, we are forcibly reminded of the remark that the steam engine is the most brilliant present ever made by philosophy to mankind.
> And as it is the opinion of many wise men that steam is as yet in its infancy, who knows but some who are here congregated today may, before the year 1850, travel in a floating palace at the rate of thirty miles an hour. Dr. Lardner informs us that he has proved by repeated experiments that when the speed of a boat is increased beyond a certain limit, its draught of water is rapidly diminished,

and that he has no doubt that the increased speed of steamers is attended with a like effect; that, in fact, they rise out of the water so that, although the resistance is increased by reason of their increased speed, it is diminished in a still greater proportion by reason of their diminished immersion. If this theory is correct, and I see no reason to doubt it, what is to prevent the occurrence of which I speak.

An interesting feature of this address of 1836 is its reference to a comparatively recent development of speed boat built to get out of the water and decrease her resistance. For larger boats, to which the prophecy was applied, increase in size, weight and stability became the more important factors; but still they are driven through the water at greater speeds than the speaker dares to name. One might wish this prophet had spoken of other things, but doubtless he could not anticipate all the elements of today's high-speed life. Especially hard would he find it to appreciate the fact that the faster we go the less important is our errand.

CHAPTER XI

THE SEA SERPENT

BURKE said, "Superstition is the religion of the feeble minds." There are few people who have not at least some one pet superstition, while in many a generation past it played an important part in life. Not far from Nahant were enacted the scenes of the Salem witchcraft delusion. But there was a time when the fabled sea serpent appeared at Nahant, with suitable showings also at other points along the North Atlantic coast. Of course, there is no such animal, and never was nor ever will be such an animal — or reptile, if he is a reptile. A hundred years or more ago he made so much news for the newspapers and chat for the chatterers that some space must be allowed in order to tell about him. His existence was supported by people whose credibility may not be questioned. And yet it is questioned. The problem seems to be, did some prehistoric monsters survive in the ocean depths, breeding their kind in successive generations, and did one finally stray from its habitat to be seen by men. It might be an example of variability in the activity of a species, which is one of the sorts of things which made evolution possible, — that evolution which was finally spread upon a generation which could say scientists believed men descended from monkeys. This is another instance of a thing that is not so, and never was and never will be so. These "are nots," "were nots" and "will nots" are very dogmatic at times. But scientists never did say such a thing, that much is certain.

An early mention of the friendly sea serpent is in the journal of Obadiah Turner, other citations from which are given elsewhere. Under date of September 5, 1641, he writes:

Prof. Louis Agassiz

From "Life, Letters and Works of Louis Agassiz." Published by Macmillan Company, 1896

Henry W. Longfellow

From "American Men of Letters" Series. Published by Houghton Mifflin Company, 1902

William H. Prescott

From a photogravure of a drawing by George Richmond, Esq., R.A. Published by A. W. Elson Company, Belmont, Mass.

John Lothrop Motley

From etching by W. H. W. Bicknell. Published by A. W. Elson Company, Belmont, Mass.

THE SEA SERPENT

> Some being on ye great beache gathering of clams and seaweed wch had been cast thereon by ye mightie storm did spy a most wonderful serpent a shorte way off from ye shore. He was as big round in ye thickest part as a wine pipe; and they do affirme that he was fifteen fathom or more in length. A most wonderful tale. But ye witnesses be credible, and it would be of no account to them to tell an untrue tale. Wee have likewise heard yt at Cape Ann ye people have seene a monster like unto this, wch did there come out of ye sea and coile himself upon ye land mch to ye terror of them yt did see him. And ye Indians doe say yt they have manie times seene a wonderful big serpent lying on ye water, and reaching from Nahauntus to ye greate rock wch we call Birdes Egg Rocke; wch is much above belief for yt would be nigh upon a mile. Ye Indians, as said, be given to declaring wonderful things, and it pleaseth them to make ye white peeple stare. But making all discounte, I doe believe yt a wonderful monster in forme of a serpent doth visit these waters. And my praier to God is yt it be not ye olde serpent spoken of in holie scripture yt tempted our greate mother Eve and whose poison hath run downe even unto us, so greatlie to our discomforte and ruin.

Here is mention of clams cast up on Long Beach by the storms. Even as this is written in 1927, nearly three hundred years later, another storm has cast up clams in such profusion that many barrels are collected and sold to the markets. Some of them are called sea clams and some are quahogs, or quahaugs, as was the old Indian name for the large, round clam.

The greatest furor at Nahant over the sea serpent seems to have been in 1819, although it is said to have been seen at other places in the two years previous. In August many hundreds of people gathered on Long Beach on two days, attracted by the rumor that his snakeship was to be seen. Depositions were taken which tell of its appearance. It was said to be from fifty to seventy feet long and as large as a barrel, moving swiftly through the water with head up. In 1849, at a lecture in Philadelphia, Professor Louis Agassiz said:

> I have asked myself, in connection with this subject, whether there is not such an animal as the sea serpent. There are many who will doubt the existence of such a creature until it can be brought under the dissecting knife; but it has been seen by so many on

whom we may rely, it is wrong to doubt any longer. The truth is, however, that if a naturalist had to sketch the outlines of an Ichthyosaurus or a Plesiosaurus from the remains we have of them, he would make a drawing very similar to the sea serpent as it has been described. There is reason to think that the parts are soft and perishable, but I still consider it probable that it will be the good fortune of some person on the coast of Norway or North America to find a living representative of this type of reptile, which is thought to have died out.

The prominent Boston merchant, Amos Lawrence, is quoted as writing in a letter in 1849:

> I have never had any doubt of the existence of the sea serpent since the morning he was seen off Nahant by old Marshal Prince through his famous masthead spyglass. For, within the next two hours I conversed with Mr. Samuel Cabot and Mr. Daniel P. Parker, I think, and one or more persons besides, who had spent a part of that morning in witnessing its movements. In addition, Col. Harris, the commander at Fort Independence, told me that the creature had been seen by a number of his soldiers while standing sentry in the early dawn, some time before this show at Nahant; and Col. Harris believed it as firmly as though the creature were drawn up before us in State Street, where we then were. I again say, I have never, from that day to this, had a doubt of the sea serpent's existence.

Samuel Cabot, who is mentioned in this letter, was an early summer resident of Nahant and the great-grandfather of Senator Lodge. He wrote to Colonel T. H. Perkins under date of August 19, 1819:

> I got into my chaise about seven o'clock in the morning, to come to Boston, and on reaching Long Beach, observed a number of people collected there, and several boats pushing off and in the offing. I was speculating on what should have occasioned so great an assemblage there without any apparent object, and finally had concluded that they were some Lynn people who were embarking in these boats on a party of pleasure to Egg Rock or some other point. I had not heard of the sea serpent as being in that neighborhood, and I had not lately paid much attention to the evidences which had been given of its existence; the idea of this animal did not enter my mind at the moment. As my curiosity was directed toward the boats, to ascer-

tain the course they were taking, my attention was suddenly arrested by an object emerging from the water at the distance of about one hundred or one hundred and fifty yards, which gave to my mind, at the first glance, the idea of a horse's head. As my eye ranged along, I perceived, at a short distance, eight or ten regular bunches or protuberances, and at a short interval, three or four more. I was now satisfied that the sea serpent was before me, and, after the first moment of excitement produced by the unexpected sight of so strange a monster, taxed myself to investigate his appearance as accurately as I could. . . . After remaining some two or three hours on the beach, without again seeing him, I returned toward Nahant, and in crossing the small beach, had another good view of him for a longer time, but at a greater distance. At this time he moved more rapidly, causing a white foam under the chin, and a long wake, and his protuberances had a more uniform appearance. At this time he must have been seen by two or three hundred persons on the beach and on the heights each side, some of whom were very favorably situated to observe him.

Marshal Prince, named in the Lawrence letter, was James Prince, marshal of Massachusetts, and he wrote a letter to Judge Davis, under date of August 16, 1819, from which the following is taken:

I presume I may have seen what is generally thought to be the sea serpent. I have also seen my name inserted in the evening newspapers printed at Boston on Saturday, in a communication on this subject. For your gratification, and from a desire that my name may not sanction any thing beyond what was actually presented and passed in review before me, I will now state that which, in the presence of more than two hundred other witnesses, took place near the Long Beach of Nahant on Saturday morning last.

Intending to pass two or three days with my family at Nahant, we left Boston early on Saturday morning. On passing the Half-Way House on the Salem turnpike Mr. Smith informed us the sea serpent had been seen the evening before at Nahant Beach, and that a vast number of people from Lynn had gone to the beach that morning in hopes of being gratified with a sight of him; this was confirmed at the Hotel. I was glad to find I had brought my famous masthead spyglass with me, as it would enable me, from its form and size, to view him to advantage, if I might be so fortunate as to see him. On our arrival on the beach, we associated with a considerable collection of persons on foot and in chaises; and very soon an animal of the fish kind made his appearance.

His head appeared about three feet out of water, I counted thirteen bunches on his back; my family thought there were fifteen. He passed three times at a moderate rate across the bay, but so fleet as to occasion a foam in the water; and my family and self, who were in a carriage, judged that he was from fifty to not more than sixty feet in length. . . . The first view of the animal occasioned some agitation, and the novelty perhaps prevented that precise discrimination which afterward took place. As he swam up the bay, we and the other spectators moved on and kept nearly abreast of him. He occasionally withdrew himself under water, and the idea occurred to me that his occasionally raising his head above the level of the water was to take breath, as the time he kept under was, on the average, about eight minutes. . . . I had seven distinct views of him from the Long Beach, so called, and at some of them the animal was not more than a hundred yards distant. After being on the Long Beach with other spectators about an hour, the animal disappeared, and I proceeded on toward Nahant; but on passing the second beach, I met Mr. James Magee, of Boston, with several ladies, in a carriage, prompted by curiosity to endeavor to see the animal; and we were again gratified beyond even what we saw in the other bay. . . .

Then, for another example, comes Benjamin F. Newhall of Saugus, a man of high standing and reliability, who said:

As he approached the shore, at about nine A.M., he raised his head apparently about six feet, and moved very rapidly. He came so near as to startle many of the spectators, and then suddenly retreated. I could plainly see what appeared to be from fifty to seventy feet in length.

An odd little volume, entitled "A Romance of the Sea Serpent or the Ichthyosaurus," was published at Cambridge in 1849, which gave information on various sorts of sea monsters. During succeeding years there came reports of his appearance at different points on the North Atlantic coast. Some were so obviously fabricated to attract visitors to shore resorts that doubts multiplied, and more and more the existence of this great sea rover was discredited. In 1849 a Swampscott man, a credible and respectable citizen, went before a justice of the peace and swore to a statement that while walking on Nahant Beach he saw this monster on

August 3 in the early morning. In later years little has been
heard of him, and the story today brings only a smile, which
may only be a reminder that the farmer said of the circus
giraffe before his eyes, — there was no such animal. To go
into the newspaper accounts of the visitation would add little
further information, and the excitement of the time is vividly
shown in a writing by J. L. Homer published in 1848, the same
publication which has been used elsewhere for other citations.

> In 1817 his majesty the sea serpent appeared for the first time in
> Massachusetts Bay. I remember this fact well. His advent at
> Nahant produced an intense, a fearful excitement, among all classes
> in Boston. The late Marshal Prince seized his masthead spyglass
> and took several observations, the result of which he published in
> the "Columbian Centinel," then edited by his friend Major Russell.
> Mr. Prince was a most worthy and estimable old gentleman, a little
> near sighted, and at times somewhat passionate and enthusiastic;
> in a word, he was just the man to see the sea serpent. He discerned
> the teeth and tongue of the monster most distinctly, almost with
> the naked eye; but when he brought his telescope to bear, oh, ye
> gods, what discoveries he made. The eyes of the serpent were dis-
> tinctly seen; and when his majesty condescended to extend his
> tongue for the purpose of lapping his large and illustrious jaws, after
> eating a barrel of mackerel, there were no bounds to the ecstacy of
> Marshal Prince's delight. The bumps on his back exceeded those
> on the back of the cruel Richard, of English history, some dozen or
> twenty.
>
> I shall never forget the excitement produced by the first accounts
> received in Boston of the arrival of the sea serpent in our lower har-
> bor, nor the consequences which grew out of that excitement. The
> whole story, at this distant day, now almost thirty years, would be
> deemed incredible. Salem witchcraft was no touch to it, in one
> respect. There was not an old lady at the North End who did not
> shake in her shoes, and some of the clergy and many respectable
> citizens, partook of this unamiable and childish feeling. It was even
> feared, by some of the most timid, that, if he once condescended to
> leave his native element, as the shipbuilders and their accommodat-
> ing scribes call simple salt water, he would overtop all the houses in
> the city, occasionally peeping into the scuttle of some gentlemen in
> the vicinity of Mount Vernon Street, for the purpose of getting a
> tidbit, or spiriting away some Irish maiden lady, of fair proportions
> and good face. Depend upon it, there was a terrible excitement in

Boston and vicinity when the sea serpent first visited these shores. The affidavits published at the time on the subject, from fishermen and the crews of Eastern coasters, would fill a volume of five hundred octavo pages. Expeditions to capture the monster were fitted out, without number, from Boston, Salem, Marblehead, Gloucester, and other places on both the North and South shores. The prices of whaleboats and harpoons fluctuated, like those of railroad and other fancy stocks of the present day.

Captain Rich, an enterprising and experienced seaman, commanded the first boat that was fitted out. Much was expected of this expedition; but it turned out to be a dead failure, notwithstanding a temporary shed, of extensive dimensions, was put up in the vicinity of Faneuil Hall for the reception of his majesty and the accommodation of the universal public. Since that time he has been seen on our coast and elsewhere, periodically; but though frequently pursued, he has never been taken.

The sea serpent first made his appearance on our coast in 1817, which was the great year for seeing him. He moved about Boston Bay, in almost every direction, sticking chiefly to the North Shore, the waters near Cape Ann, Half Way Rock, Nahant, etc. Sharks and horse mackerel were constantly in attendance on his majesty. Bulletins in relation to him were issued from Gloucester during the travelling season, and published in the "Boston Gazette," "Centinel" and "Palladium," then the leading journals of the city, but now all defunct, and their editors all dead.

In 1818 his snakeship made his appearance again, and was seen by hundreds of respectable individuals, who described him, very minutely, as he looked to them, and partly under oath. In 1819 he appeared again, and continued on the coast throughout the summer. About this time the infidels of the South began to laugh at the Yankees, and to insinuate that they were too credulous on this subject. The "Centinel" resented the insult, and threw back in their teeth the burning words, southern scoffers, in the following paragraph from a September issue: "It is perhaps owing to his established harmlessness that he has not long since been taken. Had he exhibited the ferocity at first attributed to him, or occasioned the death of a single seaman or fisherman, the whole coast would have been alive with his adversaries, and our southern scoffers, if they pleased, have long since seen his skeleton decorating the hall of our Linnæan Society."

This citation has a word or two altered in order to preserve continuity where some parts are omitted. Homer himself seems to have been a bit of an advertising agent, for he admits a part in trying to induce "unsuspecting people to flock to Nahant, to see the monster wag his tail and eat mackerel, while they themselves ate chowder and drank wine."

It is time to say again that there is no such animal and never was nor ever will be any such animal. It was only a couple of big mackerel sharks, or more likely a school of porpoises, perhaps consciously arranging themselves in single file while they disported, in order to provide entertainment for summer visitors and profits for seashore summer hotel keepers. Some of the proprietors of the old Nahant Hotel were canny and diverted their patrons with amusements much varied. Did they impose this on the public as a grand hoax? Doubtless they did not discourage rumors of the arrival of this great marine attraction. But was there a sea serpent? His story seems to have been handed down a couple of generations, for people have asked of Nahanters now alive when they were going to see him again. Seriously, too many people are unable to enjoy and appreciate what they cannot understand, and the skeptic's non-belief is no particular source of content or comfort. To disbelieve a thing too definitely may be a sign of narrowed vision, for it is to be commonly observed that those who know most are least dogmatic upon new material brought to their notice. Quoting the words of Truherne, in his "Centuries of Meditation," it may be said that "you will never understand the world aright until the sea floweth in your veins, till you are clothed with the heavens, and crowned with the stars." To reach this condition may seem superhuman, and yet any consideration of the great men of the world's ages convinces one that intellectually or spiritually they did achieve it.

Returning to the sea serpent, the subject of his career may be closed with a couplet from Sir Walter Scott:

> And better had they never been born
> Who read to doubt or read to scorn.

CHAPTER XII

PUBLIC LIBRARY

THE age of public libraries is reckoned in so many different ways that some definitions are needed. Most early libraries were subscription libraries, similar to present-day circulating libraries, although in towns the initial payment may have been omitted. The impetus given the public library movement probably was due more to Benjamin Franklin than to any one else. In 1732, while he was a young man, he was chiefly instrumental in setting up the "Philadelphia Library Company," mother of subscription libraries in America. The later actions establishing libraries supported by taxation are not the beginning of the public library movement. From the first the earlier institutions were for the benefit of the many, and the fees were usually small and supposed to be no deterrent to joining. Later experience showed that fees hinder library progress, and today the great public library movement is almost wholly with free public libraries.

The earliest public library in Massachusetts appears to be that of Franklin, which was established in 1785 through the generosity of Benjamin Franklin for whom the town was named; then came Harvard, in 1808; and the third oldest public library in the State is at Nahant, founded in 1819. It was started through the efforts of William Wood, mentioned elsewhere as a man establishing many libraries. Unlike many other friends of such institutions, he was interested to set up a collection of books rather than erect a building. He was also interested in tree planting at Nahant, as the following letter, of which the original is owned by the library, clearly shows. He seems to have mixed up the Hoods and Johnsons somewhat in his address, which is to Joseph Johnson, Abner

Entrance to Maolis Gardens
Barge in foreground

Barge at Lynn Station
Byron Goodell in barge

Hood, Richard Hood, Caleb Johnson, Benjamin Johnson and Ebenezer Johnson:

BOSTON, April 8, 1819.

SIRS: — I have collected from various quarters about ten hundred volumes of books, for the purpose of forming a library at Nahant under the following conditions, viz.: These books, and all others that may hereafter be given to the School and Library there, shall be placed under the immediate trust of yourselves, and the teacher of the school shall be empowered to hire them out to any respectable person, who will deposit the value of the work, at four pence half for the small volumes and nine pence for the larger, and the said teacher shall render a weekly account of money received, and at the expiration of each month the amount collected shall be deposited in the Savings Bank, in Boston, to remain there until the month of April, then, the amount shall be expended in forest trees, and shrubs, annually to be planted in such parts of Nahant, as the committee shall judge most proper, in order that your pleasant abode may be rendered delightful by shade. As soon as you agree to the above conditions the books will be forwarded by

Your Obt. Servt.
WILLIAM WOOD.

This document betrays more or less unfamiliarity with Nahant on the part of William Wood, because Benjamin and Ebenezer, addressed as Johnsons, seem to have been Hoods. The paper agreeing to these terms is signed by six men, — four Hoods and two Johnsons. It reads as follows:

Mr. WILLIAM WOOD.

SIR: — We the inhabitants of Nahant have received your letter of the 8th inst, with the books collected in Boston to form a Library at this place, we jointly and severally agree and pledge ourselves to appropriate any and all moneys that may be received by loaning the Books to the purchasing Forest Trees and Shrubs, annually, and plant them in such situations in this place as shall be most proper to give beauty and shade to Nahant.

JOSEPH JOHNSON, Jr.
ABNER HOOD
BENJA. HOOD
RICHARD HOOD
EBENEZER HOOD
CALEB JOHNSON

Note the opening phrase, "We the inhabitants of Nahant," and then the six signatures. William Breed had moved away and Jesse Rice seems to have been considered a newcomer, not enough of a Nahanter to participate in such a matter as responsibility for tree planting and a public library.

This library was housed in the "old stone schoolhouse," which was finished in this same year 1819. The school teachers acted as librarians. The success of this enterprise, either as a public library or a tree planting scheme, seems doubtful, and no record or memory tells about it. The books were apparently whatever any donors chose to give, which meant some rather useless volumes, although very many were of excellent quality and fit for any public library at any time. Perhaps the most notable gift was a prayer book used in the Court of Queen Anne, and described as "once the property of George IV of England." It was presented by the wife of Christopher Gore, Governor of Massachusetts in 1809, and United States Senator from Massachusetts a few years later. It is bound in full leather with the royal monogram in gilt all over the covers. Another reason for a lack of success in this undertaking was the neglect to provide means for its maintenance. Wood cannot be blamed for this, as doubtless it is often well to let people do something for themselves rather than do all for them. Almost anything will work if the people will. Too much reliance on others resembles the flea on the dog. Then it may be said that public libraries were new and their use not a habit — indeed, neither was much reading, for average people.

In any event, some years later this public library is found languishing. In 1851 the "old stone schoolhouse" was torn down and replaced by a wooden building, and the library was moved into it. Cases were provided for it, one of which is still in existence in the office of Thomas Roland. Probably the library never wholly stopped circulating, but it fell into extreme disuse. Carelessness lost many books, which were taken away and not returned. A book is a peculiar article in this respect, and very dangerous to lend. Its loss is so probable that many book lovers never offer to lend books and regret requests to do so. It takes extreme care to avoid carelessness by misplacement and forgetfulness. An attempt was made, at the time of this removal, to collect these books from about town. A committee was appointed by the school district and many missing books were found. They were identified by the words "Nahant Library" written across each title-page. This resurrection was brief and the library was mostly forgotten. All of the books had become old, though not worn out, and many were wholly out of date. In 1853, when the town was incorporated, it assumed ownership of this library and gave it in charge of the school committee. Until 1870 it remained unnoticed and probably to many unknown, though occasionally a book was taken out, and often never returned.

The transition from subscription libraries to free libraries was gradual. The first movement in this country for establishing free public libraries was in 1847 and was made by Josiah Quincy, mayor of Boston. In that year Boston, by special act of the State Legislature, was empowered to establish a free public library and support it by taxation. The first State to pass a general law legalizing such libraries was New Hampshire in 1849. The town of Peterborough, New Hampshire, claims to have the first free public library organized in this country. In 1833 Peterborough voted to use a certain sum of money for this purpose. In 1851 Massachusetts passed a general law permitting all towns and cities to use money from taxation for public libraries. The movement became popular, and by 1894 over two hundred towns had free public libraries of over a thousand volumes each, with a total of about two million volumes. This was nearly as many as were in all the public libraries of all the other States. Private gifts and bequests have done much to aid the public library movement.

In 1870 some public-spirited citizens proposed that Nahant should support a free town library, and at the annual town meeting in March, 1871, three of these men — Edward J.

Johnson, Alfred D. Johnson and Joseph T. Wilson — were chosen a committee to organize and equip such a library. Fifteen hundred dollars was appropriated for the purpose. The library was then moved from the schoolhouse to a room in the Town Hall, which was fitted up for its use. On February 17, 1872, the Nahant Public Library was opened. H. H. Scott, master of the grammar school, the highest school in town, was first librarian. The library committee purchased the books and the selectmen managed the library. In 1872 Dr. J. Nelson Borland was added to the original committee, making four members, who served until March, 1876. During this time the town appropriations were liberal, amounting to over $9,500 for the five years. At the end of this period of building up a public library, there were about four thousand eight hundred volumes. Dr. Borland was a well-known summer resident, lover of Nahant, who subsequently moved to Connecticut, so that few people now living remember him. His daughter married James Jackson, who was a member of a prominent firm of bankers in Boston. A grandson is James Jackson, who was recently State Treasurer of Massachusetts. Dr. Borland was very popular on Nahant, and the town lost a good citizen in his removal elsewhere.

At the annual town meeting in March, 1876, the first Board of Public Library Trustees was elected, and according to the town's instructions had full control of the institution. The same library committee were chosen trustees, — Dr. J. N. Borland, E. J. Johnson, A. D. Johnson and J. T. Wilson. In 1877 H. C. Lodge replaced Dr. Borland as trustee, and began the forty-seven years of service which ended only with his death in 1924. In 1878 H. Shepard Johnson replaced Edward J. Johnson. H. Shepard Johnson is mentioned elsewhere as Shepard H. Johnson, which is according to the records. He was always known, latterly, by the former name. He was a son of C. Hervey Johnson and grandson of Caleb Johnson, and served several years on the school committee of the town as well as upon the Board of Library Trustees. These four trustees were elected annually until 1879. At the annual meeting in 1878 new by-laws were adopted under which the public library trustees were to be chosen one each year for a term of three years. At the next annual meeting, accordingly, Joseph T. Wilson was chosen for three years, Henry Cabot Lodge for two years, and H. Shepard Johnson for one year. Johnson was re-elected in 1880 for a three-year term, and William S. Otis succeeded him in 1883, serving two terms, or until 1889. Otis lived on the southerly side of Nahant Road, nearly across from the present post office block, in a house still standing and owned and occupied by Miss Kate Reynolds. It was sold to Otis by C. Hervey Johnson, as mentioned elsewhere. In 1889 Albert G. Wilson succeeded Otis as a library trustee, and served on this Board until his death in 1927. No further changes came in the trustees, consisting of H. C. Lodge, J. T. Wilson and A. G. Wilson, until J. T. Wilson's retirement in 1897 after serving twenty-six years. Herbert F. Otis was elected to fill the place but did not desire the office, and at once resigned. Fred A. Wilson was chosen to fill the vacancy, was elected in 1898 for the two remaining years of the term, and has served ever since. The Board continued from 1898 to 1924, a period of twenty-six, nearly twenty-seven years without a change. Senator Lodge died in November, and the vacancy was not filled until the annual March meeting in 1925, when Mrs. Wallace D. Williams was chosen for the unexpired one year of the term, and re-elected in 1926 for the full three-year term. A. G. Wilson died just before town meeting in 1927, and Winthrop T. Hodges was elected for one year. These long terms of service make various members of this Board the deans among Nahant office holders. J. T. Wilson served twenty-six years, Senator Lodge nearly rounded out forty-eight years, A. G. Wilson served thirty-eight years, and Fred A.Wilson, thirty-one years, to 1928.

In 1879 the town provided money to build an addition to the public library room, which had become very badly crowded, both for book-shelf room and public space for patrons. This is the one-story ell on the old Town Hall building on the northerly side, or toward the old school yard. This space continued to hold the Public Library until 1889. In the meantime another addition was built on the rear of the building, for school purposes chiefly, and this left available a small room on the second floor which had been used as a recitation room. This was assigned to the Public Library, and was used as an overflow room. Thus the library continued until its removal to the present Public Library building.

The library was originally open, for the delivery of books, on Saturday afternoon and evening. In the summer season of 1875 it was opened on Wednesday evening as well, and in 1877 it was opened Wednesday evening in the winter season and Tuesday and Thursday evenings in the summer season, all in addition to Saturday afternoon and evening. This arrangement continued until removal to the present building. There were no magazines and no reading room during this period. The library room was only about twenty by thirty feet, and had three book alcoves in each end, with a large shelf space on the wall between the windows. Rails and counter enclosed the public space. It was an interesting room, finished in two woods, black walnut and white ash, with twisted pillars and carved heads on arch keystones, all more or less according to Eastlake style. Many Nahanters remember it well.

Several small catalogs in pamphlet and leaflet form were published before 1878, and in that year they were made over into one catalog. Again, in 1886, all leaflets were made into one general catalog. Several bulletins were issued after that. During this period the catalog question was a serious one. Without a reading room the library had no attractions for patrons, who liked to be able to send children for books and who therefore needed catalogs in order to make selections. It was becoming a custom among libraries, now become a confirmed practice, to use no general catalogs, though bulletins of books on special subjects are very desirable.

The library circulation fell off as the newness disappeared, and reached the more normal volume of around eight thousand a year in 1890. At that time there were about seven thousand five hundred books on the shelves. The report published in 1880, the first report made by a Board of three trustees, was signed by H. Shepard Johnson, chairman. The report for 1881 was by H. C. Lodge, chairman, and this report for the first time urged "upon the town the necessity of erecting at an early day a fireproof building for the library." Senator Lodge wrote and signed these reports until 1888, when appeared the first report written and signed by J. T. Wilson. Lodge was still chairman — in fact, he held that title until his death, but his increasing duties elsewhere placed more of the detail of the trustees' work upon the other members. This 1888 trustees' report again pointed to the need for more accommodations in a public library building. In 1889 Samuel H. Hudson, who had been librarian for several years, made a comprehensive report, and pleaded for more appropriation, more catalogs and more room. This same year he declined reappointment and was succeeded by Jonathan E. Johnson, son of Edward J. Johnson. During this first twenty years or more of the library the librarians were teachers or young men wanting to help their way through school or college. The open times of the library fitted the spare time from other occupations. Hudson, son of Samuel Hudson, who lived on Pleasant Street where William F. Waters now lives, graduated from Dartmouth College and is today a prominent lawyer of Boston. Johnson graduated from Harvard University and became an Episcopal minister. Neither of them came back to Nahant to live. The school teacher librarians were as temporary as teachers are apt to be, although Charles J. Hayward, a very popular man, nearly ranked as a Nahanter through his marriage to Alice C. Whitney of an old Nahant family.

The trustees' report for 1890, issued in March, 1891, urged a new library building, and that a committee be authorized to investigate the question. This was done, and a year later the trustees suggested two sites, — one the Spooner lot, where the building now stands, and one the Johnson lot, where now is the post office block. Another lot was later added to the list, — the George Johnson lot at the corner of Nahant Road and Summer Street, next easterly from the Village Church. The trustees sent out ballots to all voters, to get an expression of opinion, and as a result the present public library lot was purchased. Competitive plans were invited from six Boston architects, and the trustees were assisted in their selection from them by the head of the Department of Architecture of the Massachusetts Institute of Technology. But the prices ran too high. High money rates prevailed in that year, and a reconsideration of the plans had to be made to fit it better to the lot and surroundings. Mr. E. W. Bowditch was called into consultation as a landscape architect. On May 14, 1894, ground was broken, and the corner stone was laid on July 23, with Masonic ceremonies, by the Grand Lodge of Massachusetts, assisted by Mount Carmel and Golden Fleece Lodges of Lynn. The contents of the corner stone were arranged by Edward J. Johnson and Fred A. Wilson, a committee chosen by the trustees for this service. The trustees acted for the town in all the preliminaries, and were the building committee. This is not good general practice, but in this instance there was practical business and building experience represented in the membership. The new library building was opened on June 1, 1895. At that time, and until the building of the new Town Hall in 1912, the room now the children's reading room was the selectmen's room, and the room now chiefly occupied by the bird collection was the town clerk's and town treasurer's room. The library used the rest of the building. The bookstacks, of a modern type still much used in new installations without much change in thirty years, had a capacity of twenty-eight thousand volumes, and most of those interested doubted they would live to see them overcrowded. The number of volumes in the library at that time was about half this capacity. The old shelf system of cataloging was abandoned, and the new decimal system allowing indefinite extensions was introduced. This meant recataloging the entire library. Of course, a complete card catalog was a part of the result, and this has been kept up to the minute ever since. A card catalog can entail all the

Latest Type of Barge, with Glass Sides

Winter Barge
Rather stuffy

PUBLIC LIBRARY 177

time that can be given to it. The amount of cross indexing that may be done is almost without end, and it all makes for efficiency and for the convenience of library users. Not nearly so much of this as is desirable has been possible. Yet the library stands today in a very comfortable position among the libraries of the State.

Almost at once, after moving into the new building, began the collection of material relating to Nahant. Photographs, programs, pamphlets and clippings, anything that was Nahantiana was sought and was begged and borrowed, or bought when a little spare money allowed. Today, after thirty years of this effort, there is a collection of such material that has become valuable and interesting. Things that cost nothing, at the time, but a little care, or maybe the cost of an amateur's photograph, are today unobtainable. The library was deemed the appropriate place for such a collection, a sort of museum of Nahant, and the trustees believe their action was desirable.

Prominent today in the building are two collections: One, in the small room, is a collection of mounted birds, mostly Nahant specimens, made by Albert J. Richards and bought for the library by a special appropriation of the town in 1925. This collection of several hundred specimens is a fine one, as fine as any in the county except at Salem. Bird lovers find it very useful. The other, in the long side entrance hallway, is the Herbert Foster Otis Collection of Indian Relics, given to the library by Mrs. Otis after his death in 1921. This collection is important, even to the student, though not such an item as would commonly be found in a country library. An interesting part of it is a series of colored lithographs of the sort made around three-quarters of a century ago and now much sought by collectors. Otis was almost a lifelong summer resident of Nahant. He was a son of William S. Otis before mentioned as a trustee of the library, and a lineal descendant of James Otis of Revolutionary times. He was very much interested in all that related to Nahant, and a collector of divers material making a curious and varied assortment in a little building made especially to hold it. For years he lived in the house owned by the Hoods on the corner of Nahant Road and Pond Street, now owned by H. W. Robinson. In 1913 he built his house on Nahant Road down toward East Point, on the land formerly occupied by the house of Samuel H. Russell, which was burned in the "great fire" of 1896.

Almost at once, after opening the new library building, patronage began to increase. In a few years the circulation proportional to the population was the largest among Massachusetts public libraries, and it has remained so. There were frequent consultations with C. B. Tillinghast, long-time librarian of the State Library and chairman of the State Library Commission. From these many things were tried, some of them new to libraries. Interlibrary borrowing was the outcome of one of these conferences, and Nahant was used as a trial place for several things. Some were kept and some discarded. The town appropriations were fairly liberal, though never, even to the present time, larger than the average of Massachusetts towns of similar valuations; while in some other towns appropriations are much larger than this average. Tabular figures tell of over twenty-three thousand volumes circulated in 1926 at a cost of around twenty-five cents a volume and seven dollars a patron; and these figures include the expenses of the reading rooms, which are liberally used, and of the upkeep of the building and grounds.

The public library is an educational institution of great value, and it should be maintained at its high level of efficiency. The appropriations have not mounted, with the increasing costs of the past decade, as have others, but the time has come when a further expenditure will make greater efficiency. To increase regularly the annual appropriation by about one-third would yield a fifty per cent increase in the value to the town. It is a remarkable institution to find in so small a town, thanks to the judgment of the people in providing for it. As a town asset it should be allowed to go on at its maximum possibilities. It has been economical out of proportion to other town departments, but the time has come to give it a little of the increase which other departments have received. A comparison of the various branches of the town's endeavors is given elsewhere. It is said that contentment consists not of much wealth but of few wants, and that efficiency may be an overrated virtue. Yet the best thoughts of the world are in writing, mostly, and easy access to them adds greatly to the comforts and attractions of community life, in addition to their important assistance to learning. In keeping Nahant among the best of residential towns, the Public Library must be kept top notch, which means both efficiency and expenditure. It may be that the prime educational institutions for some are the Chocolate Sundae School and the Movie Academy; but even these pass as influences, while real education remains important, and easy access to its means is a desideratum for any town.

CHAPTER XIII

THE MAOLIS GARDENS

On the North Shore of Nahant, about one-third of the way over from Pond Street to Ocean Street, is a cold spring running out through the ledges into the ocean. It is close to the sea; indeed, storm waves can reach it, but it is a spring of pure water. Early known, it was called the North Spring, and picnic parties soon found its vicinity a desirable place for a day's outing, for here was fresh water near at hand, and close to the ocean which they came to enjoy. The rocks of the shore afforded plenty of places fit for rude fireplaces where outdoor cooking could be done. The combination of qualities for picnic purposes was so desirable that parties were there almost daily, while military companies, Sunday schools, and all sorts of organizations brought large groups to the land around the North Spring.

This gave Frederic Tudor the idea of making a summer resort here, which was quickly developed into an amusement park and picnic grounds. Not long before 1860 another spring was discovered farther eastward and about a hundred feet westward from Ocean Street. This he named Maolis Spring, which, it is mostly agreed, was a reversal of the name of the Biblical Pool of Siloam, which recalls Reginald Heber's old well-known hymn:

> By cool Siloam's shady rill,
> How sweet the lily grows.

The new amusement park was named Maolis Gardens. There are many accounts of this place, but two from which material for this chapter is largely drawn are by Charles A. Hammond and Caroline M. Foye. These people were both born on Nahant. The former is a son of John Q. Hammond,

THE MAOLIS GARDENS 181

prominent Nahanter of seventy-five years ago. The son has been away from Nahant for years, but his sister, Caroline V. Hammond, was so long a teacher in Nahant's public schools that few people are better known here. Mrs. Foye was a daughter of Annie E. Johnson, granddaughter of Jonathan Johnson and great-granddaughter of the Joseph Johnson whose father, Jonathan Johnson, was the first progenitor on Nahant of the large Johnson family. Mrs. Foye's father, Charles B. Johnson, was connected with this Johnson family.

A sort of advertising description of the time, says of the Maolis Gardens:

> This is one of the most attractive summer resorts in the United States. These gardens offer great attractions to the pleasure seeker and to those in search of health and quiet. Its grand ocean scenery, its delightful walks and drives, its quiet retired nooks, are all peculiarly attractive to lovers of the sublime and the beautiful. To that large class afflicted with mental exhaustion and nervous diseases, Nahant offers especial attractions by the variety of its scenery. This delightful spot is very accessible to the city. Steamer "Ulysses," Captain Calden, leaves India Wharf for Nahant three times a day. The Gardens can also be reached via Eastern Railroad to Lynn, and thence by coach along Lynn Beach. On the grounds is a commodious dining hall where parties can be furnished with a good dinner; also shades and tables for parties bringing their own provisions. To parties of ladies and children Maolis Gardens is a most delightful place.

Tudor bought this piece of pasture land containing several acres, extending from Ocean Street to Pond Street, and from the water up the hill nearly to the top. The present Maolis Street enters Ocean Street nearly midway of the extent of the Gardens on Ocean Street. He enclosed it with high slatted fences, similar to those described as around other parts of his property. Here the fence was about ten feet high. He planted trees, moving some that were nearly full grown; made flower beds, built shades and pavilions, swings and tilt boards. There was a bear den, ice-cream pavilion, and cages for other animals. The North Spring was covered with a rustic roof supported by the cliffs on the shore side and tall ledges to seaward. The dining hall was close to the cliff edge, where the proverbial biscuit could be tossed into the ocean. A large dance hall was first in the rear interior of the place, and later was moved out close to Ocean Street in the upper corner of the Gardens, where in the decadence of the establishment this dance hall could be let and used separately. An original feature by Tudor was the installation of stoves in the open pavilions, with fuel furnished, which parties could hire for the day, and cook their own dinners. The entrance to the Gardens was about fifty yards up from the present sea wall on Marginal Road. Above the entrance was the ticket office with other management spaces in the same building. A narrow gate close to the building admitted foot passengers, and a wide gate adjacent toward the ocean admitted carriages. Along the Ocean Street side, between the gates and the water, were horse sheds of the sort still to be found near country churches, although today they house automobiles, if they cover anything. At the time the Gardens were opened the admission was five cents for adults and three cents for children. This seems to have been liberality on the part of Tudor, although things inside were sold, much as in amusement parks of later years; and there were concessions, such as the balloon man, the candy man, and the tintype artist.

Down at the right from the entrance gate, and below the carriage sheds near Ocean Street, was Maolis Spring, which Tudor had walled up to make a circular pool about eight feet in diameter. On the land side the wall was fifteen feet high, or more, and on the shore side about four feet high. On each side a flight of winding steps curved around the stone work of the pool to the shore level. On the masonry over the pool was a marble slab inscribed "Pool of Maolis 1859." Up on the land side a similar inscription was applied in gilt over a painted space on the stone work.

By a curious coincidence it was found that "Maolis" was the name of a Greek hero, who won renown at the battle of Navarino, and to whom the Greek nation owes its independence. Tudor had a brochure printed, telling about him.

Over near the North Spring one of the pavilions was an octagonal shade with a large shell at the peak of the roof and with large clam shells fastened along the roof lines. Inside the fittings were marble. Steps around the octagon, five in number, dropped down to a pool and a fountain. This fountain was the statue of a boy covered with sea shells and holding a horn. It cost over $2,000 and was considered a wonderful work of art. A clever umbrella-like contrivance overhead caught the water from the fountain jet and dropped it back into the pool like a constant shower of rain. In later years this pavilion was used as an ice-cream saloon and the pool was filled in and floored over. The fountain was stored in the cellar of the bowling alleys, which were another part of Gardens' equipment. Those alleys were burned in the fall of 1880 and the statue was destroyed. On one wall of this structure was a series of small mirrors, set as in a window sash, but each was placed at such an angle that by standing on the right spot on the floor Egg Rock could be seen in all the mirrors by only moving the eyes to look into one after another. Then there was a tea house, and the Parasol, supported on one post or heavy pole, which slanted diagonally to the ground, leaving the pavilion wholly unsupported by anything reaching the ground within its limits. Later this was partly enclosed, and on the outside was a painting on the boarding labelled "Boys Playing Blind Man's Buff." On the inside another picture depicted a boy holding a skein of yarn for his grandmother, while others beckoned him to come along with them. This was labelled "The Trial of Patience." Still later this picture was hung in the dining hall.

The tea house, which was over toward the Pond Street side, was a small marble temple-like structure, tiled in colors and with a freize ornamented with shells. On a small table there was kept a little house made entirely of sea shells, enclosed with a rail to prevent handling. It was made by Mrs. Thomas P. Whitney, and was very attractive to children. Near here Tudor planted tobacco and later dried it in the old stone barn on Spring Road. Near by also was Moses Rock, cleverly arranged to yield water, and with inscriptions in Hebrew and Greek, "He smote the Rock and the waters gushed forth."

In another part were swings. One was a great swing, taller than telegraph poles, being about fifty feet high. The supports were great logs well braced, and the swing seat would hold several people. Though heavy and ponderous, the effort of one man could get it moving through a broad sweep, beating anything of the sort that children of the time could see elsewhere. And everywhere on surfaces large enough to allow it were rude paintings, illustrating all sorts of things, two of which have been described. In a group of trees, in a pen, stood a life-size bull made of clay and painted in natural colors. Around the gardens was statuary. Four pieces represented the four seasons. At one time the statue of winter, that of an old man, was moved over to the Witch House, across Ocean Street, where it made so ghastly an appearance that it was moved again. Some think that from this happening originated the name "Witch House," so well known even today.

Then there was dancing, flying horses, wheels of fortune, target rifle range, tilting boards, croquet and a Punch and Judy show. There were two trained bears named "Ben Butler" and "Jeff Davis," who were cared for by Roger Killilae, whom many will remember as a good old Nahanter, though not old at this time of the Maolis Gardens. The bears were led down to the ocean for frequent baths, and people enjoy telling how "Ben Butler" broke away from his keeper once, on his return from his dip, climbed through a screen in a kitchen window of the dining hall, and got well mixed up with some blueberry pies. After this he needed another bath. Then there were the Indians from Oldtown, John and Celia Barker, with the usual baskets and other trinkets. One summer the Eighth Regiment held its reunion here. Just after the Jubilee in Boston, in 1872, the French Band was here for a day, attracting the largest crowd ever at the Gardens.

But gradually amusement resorts grew up everywhere,

Easterly on Nahant Road toward Whitney's
Famous large willows in center; Wharf Street not built

The Old North Spring
About 1865

THE MAOLIS GARDENS

while the Gardens were less accessible and were not maintained in prime condition. Latterly they were rented to people who could spend little of their own money on them. In 1892 they were wholly dismantled and most of the buildings moved down to scows and taken by water around East Point over to Bass Point, where the Bass Point Hotel Company was developing its property. Those at all familiar with the old buildings can still recognize some of them, although they were mostly built over or changed to suit new conditions.

Some time during this period Tudor built Marginal Road with its heavy stone retaining wall toward the ocean and the tall stone wall toward the hillside. The "Lynn Weekly Reporter" for August 29, 1857, tells that along the large stones were painted a number of disconnected words, a sort of multiple anagram, which could be arranged into a proper sentence. The solver would win a valuable ring which Tudor had deposited with Paran Stevens at the Nahant Hotel on East Point. The duration of the contest, or the number of times repeated, may not be stated, but the prize was awarded at least once, to a Boston editor.

Mrs. Tudor willed the Maolis Gardens to the town of Nahant, to be kept forever as a public park and maintained somewhat as Tudor had originally planned it. She died March 9, 1884. The executors of her will wrote on June 27, 1884, of the bequest and set forth the provisions. This was read at an adjourned town meeting of July 1, 1884, and a committee was chosen to consider the matter. It was brought up for action at a town meeting on September 27, 1884. The town concluded that a country town did not need such a park and did not care to assume the expense of its maintenance, as required. It was therefore voted to refuse the gift, provided the sum of $7,500 be given instead, to build a public library building which should be known as the "Tudor Library." Apparently this was agreed to, and pending certain adjustments of Mrs. Tudor's will and estate the executors gave the town a bond guaranteeing this payment. Negotiations continued, however, and at the annual town meeting March 19,

1887, the town voted to accept "Central Wharf" in place of all claims it might have under this will. After this time this wharf was officially known as "Tudor Wharf," but with only one wharf, except at Bass Point, the name was more or less unused. To say "the wharf" was adequate and easier.

Across Ocean Street from the Gardens was a hotel built by Tudor and called the "Maolis House." It was close to Ocean Street and between the present Maolis Street and Marginal Road. It was built of wood and opened about 1860. Later it was burned and replaced with the brick structure, located a little nearer the water, and which old Nahanters will remember, as it was standing at Mrs. Tudor's death in 1884. Soon after this it was torn down. Among its managers were Clarence Tibbetts of Lynn, Thomas Whitney, Joseph Libbey, and Mack and Searles. The latter were afterwards proprietors of the Relay House at Bass Point.

The prominent Maolis Gardens feature which remains today is the Rock Temple, or familiarly known "Witch House," on a rocky knoll above the corner of Marginal Road and Ocean Street, and now owned by George L. Richards, whose house is just above it. He has repaired it and restored it as well as could be done after its many years of neglect. It was designed and built for Tudor by John Q. Hammond. Hammond's son, Charles A. Hammond, then a boy of fourteen, designed its details of carved figures. Tudor wanted something the like of which had never before been seen, and gave Hammond *carte blanche* to go on and erect it.

In plan it is octagonal, with eight gables, each alternate one truncated, and all radiating from the center. The supports at each angle are columns of rough stone blocks. Each of these was carefully selected, chosen for some peculiarity of color or marking, water worn, or showing strange strata or veins. All were from the shores of Nahant, some brought from the farthest parts of the town. The superstructure was strongly framed and bolted down stoutly to the foundation ledge. Thus it has stood the gales of two-thirds of a century, though only supported on rock columns.

The roofs and gables were covered with hemlock bark and in each full gable was a round medallion, with one of octagonal shape in the truncated gables. These medallions were made of wood finely executed and gilded. At the peak of the building was a large wood carving of a beautiful shell with scalloped edges, upborne by two satyrs, and the whole gilded. The drawings for these were made by Charles A. Hammond from subjects taken from the "English Art Journal."

A few yards from the Witch House, to the westward, was a cleft in the ledge. A tradition has it that during the Salem Witchcraft orgy a woman and her daughter, refugees from that place of terror, lived in this cave for a time. With a little excavating this was made into a den eight or ten feet deep and a yard high and wide. This Tudor named the "Cave of the Lion" after which he provided the lion. Encouraging home talent he commissioned David Hunt, a rough stone mason who had worked for him, to carve in granite a life-size figure of a lion. By immense labor and perseverance, Hunt did two masterpieces, creations fearfully and wonderfully made. Placed in the cave one grinned out through stout iron bars, striking more or less terror into youngsters. The other was set up within the Gardens, facing the entrance gate.

The ornaments of the old Witch House loosened and fell as years rolled on, and it is a simpler structure today. But it still remains a dignified, stately pavilion, exciting comment for its wild natural beauty.

Around the curving corner of these two streets, and enclosing the Witch House lot, was a wooden fence, slatted with wide slats so that Tudor saw a chance to paint a sea serpent upon it, for Nahant was the favorite visiting place of this king of serpents, or should it now be called "ace" of serpents. He called out young Charles A. Hammond again, impressed with what he had done on the Rock Temple. He turned the boy loose in Dr. Warren's library in Boston, where he studied sea serpent lore, and then was painted this hundred foot serpent along the fence, a sight which old Nahanters still remember. It remained on view for several years, or as long as the fence lasted. By a familiar optical illusion caused by the slatted fence, the serpent at certain angles of vision mostly disappeared, leaving only a mass of several colors of paint. This added to its interest for children.

The Maolis Garden was a formidable piece of development by itself, as the hobby of a man engaged in large business of another nature. Added to what Tudor did elsewhere in Nahant, it shows the tremendous activity of the man. Doubtless it was his pleasure or his recreation to do these things, but it is fortunate for Nahant that his interests brought such a benefit to the town all down through these later years, yielding her chief beauty even today. Frederic Tudor was a great benefactor of Nahant. This considerable space is given to the enterprise because it was a very early example of amusement parks.

CHAPTER XIV

NATURE AND MAN

THE earliest landing place used extensively on Nahant was around the present steamboat wharf at the end of Wharf Street, near Marjoram Hill, and now often known as Tudor Wharf. This rocky point was called Nipper Stage, apparently from the quantities of "nippers," or perch, around it. It broke the undertow, as well as the force of the sea, from its full effect on the two sand beaches to the northward. The farther one, in front of Hotel Tudor, is now oftenest called Willow Beach. Willow Road skirts it, and both were named from a fine row of old willows, long since gone, along the water side of the road. Newer trees have been planted but are not yet of the size of the good old row of willows that old Nahanters remember. A steep bank, loose and shelving, was between the road and the beach. Gradually this was eroded by the sea, and in 1900 the town built the present concrete sea wall from about abreast of where Valley Road enters Willow Road, eastward along by Hotel Tudor. In 1905 the wall was extended westward as far as cottages now standing on the water side of the road, and in 1911 another section continued the wall to the eastward. The selectmen's report to the town, in the 1900 town report, says that all necessary relinquishments of private rights to the beach, or to the strip of land between the road and this sea wall, should be obtained before construction is started. The Hotel Tudor always had a bathhouse structure on the bank, and this privilege was continued. Later a claim was set up to another part of this newly made strip of land, but apparently it was not effective.

This Willow Beach was originally known as Dorothy's Cove, named for Dorothy Mills, daughter of James Mills, early

Nahanter. Old maps of the town carry this name, and it is a little unfortunate that old names with historic meaning cannot be kept. Recently a new road was named South Field Road, a dignified title recalling Tudor and old Nahant. A little later the name was changed, and the street now bears a pleasant name, Intervale Road, but with less meaning, either in appropriateness or historic value. It runs next above Willow Road between Winter and Ocean Streets. Perhaps it is as good a Nahant name as those of Summer and Winter Streets.

The beach nearest Nipper Stage is a little beach sometimes known as Sandy Beach and earlier as Crystal Beach. This is much protected by the Nipper Stage ledges, and was the most used early landing place, doubtless, for Nahant. Perhaps from here wood was carried off to Lynn and Boston two or three centuries ago. Here was the landing place for the fishing industry of Nahant, and on the slopes near by were the fish flakes for drying fish. From here it was loaded into boats again to be carried to Boston, although much was sold on the spot to those who came to buy it. Mrs. Abner Hood, known as Mrs. "Nabby" Hood, has told that many country people came to Nahant to buy both dry and fresh fish, lodging at the Breed Tavern. There was a spring near by that yielded plenty of good water. From here a path led up across field and swamp to the old Johnson homestead on the main road across from the present Town Hall. A cart path wound from this beach out around Marjoram Hill about as the road now goes, and continued westward along Dorothy's Cove, and seems to have gone up Valley Road to Calf Spring Road, which was a part of the main street of the town. Connecting with this a cart path, now Summer Street, went up to the main road. By these ways for years were fish and many kinds of stores, brought in by boat, carried to the homes of the town.

Off this Nipper Stage point was moored the fishing fleet, much as the yachts and boats of the town are now moored. In 1817 there was some sort of landing, for it was here that

the "Eagle" came, and it appears to have been used as a
steamboat landing until the opening of the new "Nahant
Hotel" in 1823. It seems doubtful if the "Eagle" came up
to any dock, at least, unless in very smooth water, and one
old account speaks of landing from the steamer in dories.
Some sort of a float was here, however, and irons in the ledges
remained long after as evidences of this. In 1823, with the
opening of the great hotel, this landing was less convenient
than one near what was sometimes called the "Swallows
House," partly because there was no road. Only the cart path,
starting from the main road at Summer Street, wound around
to Nipper Stage. At the new landing dories seem to have
been used, also, but construction of a wharf was soon begun.
A new road, now called Swallows Cave Road, was built by the
hotel people and Cornelius Coolidge, up the hill as it goes
today. From near the top a broad footpath and steps led
westward down to what is now called the Old Wharf. A house
later built upon it was the summer home of the late Ellerton
James. According to E. J. Johnson's description the waiting
rooms for this wharf were on the side hill and not down at the
wharf level. He says the building was an open, six-sided
structure with seats on the sides and end. "A passageway
ran through to a long flight of stairs which led over the ledge
to a narrow walk. Two ship spars had been laid from the foot
of these steps to a square wooden frame made of logs pinned
together. This framework was then filled with stones, making
a barrier against the sea, and upon this the ends of the spars
were fastened, and piles were driven, slanting in a westerly
direction, to deep water. On these piles a long plank walk
was made, at the end of which the steamboats made a landing
at all times of the tides. Subsequently Mr. Coolidge built
the sea wall, filling the space between the wall and ledge with
stone and gravel, which gave plenty of room for the wharf and
for the passageway from the wharf." The construction by
Coolidge is the present-day stonework with which Nahanters
are familiar. The early wharf described by Johnson appears
to be a small stone-filled log cribbing connected with land at

the ledges by a narrow runway made on two spars. Some piling and another runway, doubtless a "drop," gave access to the steamer at all tides.

Cornelius Coolidge built the Nahant House about 1820. It was the building which later became the residence of George Peabody, and still later of Dudley B. Fay. There were extensive remodellings, so that no semblance of the original building remains. A rivalry came between this Nahant House and the Nahant Hotel on East Point. The former was nearer the wharf and might be reaping a benefit from its location. Accordingly, the Nahant Hotel people built another wharf off from the beach adjacent to East Point southward, abreast of what is now known as the Paine Field. This was used in 1828 by the steamer "Housatonic." By this time Dr. Edward H. Robbins and Thomas H. Perkins had become chief owners of the Nahant Hotel, and this wharf was popularly known as Dr. Robbin's Wharf. The situation was too exposed, both for the durability of the structure and the comfortable docking by steamers, and it was promptly abandoned. The hotel company bought out the Coolidge interest in the former wharf, and by piling and timber extensions, which are shown in old photographs, made a good landing place which was used by the Nahant steamers until about 1870. E. J. Johnson says: "Lines of steamboats were now running their regular trips between Boston and Nahant, the 'Eagle' making one hundred and fifty trips that season." The statement cannot mean the season after 1828, for it appears that what F. B. C. Bradlee says in "Essex Institute Historical Collections," volume 50, for July, 1914, is reliable. The "Eagle" was sold and broken up after the season of 1821.

After the hotel at East Point was gone, the crowds travelling by steamboat were more likely to be seeking the Maolis Gardens on the north side of the town between Ocean and Pond Streets. The wharf needed repairs, and Mrs. Tudor, who carried on at Nahant after Frederic Tudor's death in 1864, built or reconstructed a wharf at the old first landing place near Nipper Stage. This was called Central Wharf, and was used for a

Once a North Shore Sight?

The "Old" Wharf, off Vernon Street
Stern-wheel steamer

steamboat landing up to 1916. Subsequently it has gradually yielded to age and infirmity, and little attempt has been made to keep it in good condition. Mrs. Tudor died in 1884, and after correspondence and discussion, her executors gave this wharf to the town of Nahant. Since that time it has been known as Tudor Wharf. Articles in Town Warrants mention it as Tudor Wharf. The absence of any sign, or particular need for a distinguishing title, has prevented the name from common use.

The wharf seems to have been important in the 70's, furnishing, with the steamboats, a desirable way to get to Nahant. At a special town meeting in September, 1873, it was voted that the selectmen be a committee to see if any suitable arrangements can be made for the existing wharves of the town; and if not, it was voted to petition the State Legislature for a special act permitting the town to build a wharf, and the committee was to report to the town recommending a location, if one could be built, and giving the cost.

At the annual town meeting in March, 1874, this committee reported a proposition from Mrs. Tudor to sell Central Wharf for $30,000 and the town voted to buy it. But in the March meeting of 1875 the selectmen reported that the purchase as authorized was inadvisable, as the wharf needed repairs and the amount of land to be ceded with it was too restricted. E. J. Johnson says that it was in 1875, after this deal failed of consummation, that Mrs. Tudor rebuilt the wharf, making it of about the size it is today, but the abandonment of the "old wharf" for steamer service was earlier, at least as early as 1870, and perhaps a year or two before that. The evidence is that Mrs. Tudor built the wharf in 1869 and further added to it a few years later.

Inside the wharf, toward Crystal Beach, there is maintained a raft and runway up to the wharf level for the use of small boats. On the same side of the wharf, or the approach to it, a masonry runway reaches from the road level down to low-water mark. This was built by the town in 1900 for the convenience of small craft, which could be drawn up on it for access for repairs or painting. In November, 1899, a storm wrecked the building used as an express office and wharfinger's store. A new one was built in the spring of 1900 and is now standing. This is on the shore side of the wharf. The old building, as well as the waiting rooms out on the wharf, were probably built in 1875. The coal pocket was a later addition. Photographs of some of the steamers lying at the wharf show no such structure. It was removed some years ago when it became unsafe. The other building on these premises is the Nahant Dory Club house. It was originally used in part for storage, but is now entirely a club room. It was built in 1906.

This Nipper Stage vicinity has therefore been for a long period the scene of marine activities. This means accidents, also, for the sea is often relentless. So there are drownings recorded, even back to early days, but not of old Nahanters. Many stories center around this locality: of the old fishing days; of the "drop" that dropped, letting a score of people into the water with Captain A. W. Calden plunging to the rescue; of a day when a mistaken engine room signal drove a steamer on, bringing destruction to small boats, and almost putting her nose into the beach; of Captain Kemp and "Buster" and "Tony" Taylor. There are always workers and loafers in such a place, and the little activities around a wharf interest young and old, the sea lover and the land lover. Interest in racing and fishing means yarns to tell, even beating those of the hardened golf bug; and they are not all just yarns. Not all fishermen can lie. Think of the Apostles. One of these yarns, usually fastened to a good-natured old Nahanter, often called the best-natured man in town, relates to a man whose wife had been ordered to take salt-water baths. They had never been to the seashore, but the man figured out how to proceed, and bought a pail and a rope one morning, and went to the wharf, which was near by. There he met this old Nahanter, who looked important and seemed to own something around there, and said, "How much for a pail of water?" "Ten cents" was the answer. He paid the money and drew his pail of water —

not a hard job, as the tide was in. That afternoon he went over again, and met the same man and paid another ten cents. Going to the edge of the wharf he threw over his pail, but the tide was out and it was a longer pull. Thereupon he exclaimed to the proprietor of the sea, "Gosh, what a whale of a business you must have done today."

About the year 1892, when the Bass Point House property was much enlarged, a wharf was built on the westerly side of Bass Point. This point, strictly named, is the point belonging to the Bass Point House, although the name has applied to this whole wing of the town for seventy years or more. From the time of its construction the Boston to Nahant steamers all landed there. A part of the trips, notably on Sundays and holidays, were run directly between Boston and the Bass Point House Wharf. Others made the round trip, landing at both this wharf and Tudor Wharf. Usually the contract with the town, under which the steamers received a subsidy, required certain trips direct between Tudor Wharf and Boston, for the convenience of business men using the service. This Bass Point House Wharf is still standing in its original location and size, though it has deteriorated, and has had new pile lines driven, partly because in certain weathers the exposure was bad.

In this same year, 1892, a wharf was built on the Relay House property, a long narrow runway out over shallows to a head accommodating steamer service to Lynn. There never was depth of water sufficient for the larger Boston boats, for which this wharf was not intended. From 1894 to about 1916 small steamers ran from there to Breed's Wharf in Lynn during a long summer season. In its later years of use steamers ran across the harbor to Revere Beach, where "Ocean Pier" had been built partly as an amusement pier and partly for this service. This Relay House Wharf is now standing in about its original condition.

Then there was another wharf, of which little trace remains, off Black Rock, the first cliff on the harbor side as one goes southerly along Castle Road. This ran to deeper water, and larger boats occasionally landed there. The "Meta" ran to Lynn from there, and the "Ulysses" touched there from Boston. It was used at one time for a coal wharf by Welcome J. Johnson, and Tudor Wharf also had coal landed there, but not regularly. H. Shepard Johnson, once in the hay and grain business on Nahant, landed hay at Tudor Wharf for a short time. After it came into possession of the town it was used only for passenger steamers. This wharf at Black Rock was built in the early days of Nahant as a town, and many people can remember the remains of its piling. Its location was not good for service, but apparently was chosen because it was sheltered and reached deep water easily. The waiting room on this wharf was moved back across Castle Road and remodelled into a house and owned and occupied by Dexter Stetson in his later years. Soon after his death his daughter and her two aunts, Misses Julia and Amelia Hood, who lived with him, moved to Lynn. When this building was made over, Stetson built into it some diamond-paned windows which were formerly a part of the old "Log Cabin" elsewhere mentioned.

The beach in front of Hotel Tudor, often called Willow Beach, with its concrete sea wall, has been mentioned. This was Dorothy's Cove. Then, next to Tudor Wharf is Crystal Beach, the little beach used earliest by fishermen. Next easterly, between Nipper Stage Point and Clark's Point, is the pebble beach usually called Longfellow Beach because the home of the poet Longfellow was on the side of the hill above it. Early maps call it Curlew Beach. Often it is called Boat House Beach, because here was one of the sheds, with boat and equipment, of the Massachusetts Humane Society. This was given up after the establishment of the Coast Guard Station on Short Beach in 1898. Old inhabitants heard this beach called Bolger's Beach, from Bolger and his little old shoe repairing shop that was there alongside the Humane Society building. The latter was up on the crest, fairly near the road and at the westerly end, against the Fremont property line. "Fremont property" was the old name for the house and land lately owned by Frank E. Johnson, a son of Francis H. Johnson and grandson of Captain Francis Johnson.

Continuing around Clark's Point, named for Benjamin C. Clark, an early summer resident who owned it and lived there in a house built by Cornelius Coolidge, the next beach is Joseph's Beach, commonly called Joe Beach. Clark's Point is now owned by Arthur Perry. Joe Beach is parallel to Vernon Street and extends to the old wharf, recently the summer home of Ellerton James. Then comes Irene's Grotto and Swallows Cave and Pea Island. The cave is worth seeing, a deep recess easy of access except at high tide, running underground a considerable distance, with a typical "chimney" at the inner end giving difficult access to open air again. The next beach stretches mostly abreast of the "Paine Field" near the junction of Swallows Cave Road and Vernon Street, and ends about at the James estate, where ledges again pick up the outline of the shore. The whole of East Point is mostly ledges, and the route around the shore turns westerly again before meeting another beach, which is Canoe Beach, adjacent to the entrance to the Lodge estate on East Point. There are little coves, some usable for bathing or landing, but no real beaches. Canoe Beach was also used by the great hotel, and in those days was sometimes known as Petticoat Beach. The next beach is Bass Beach, and the two are separated by Castle Rock, a projecting point which allows a half acre or more of land between the road and the sea. This whole vicinity was a sort of "Midway" for the hotel. "Midway" is a term used since the 1893 World's Fair at Chicago, to denote amusement enterprises which attract but have not quite the dignity of the main show. Old Nahanters can remember when Indians came to Castle Rock with their summer encampment and sold baskets and other Indian-made articles, just as they do now around summer hotels in the White Mountain region. In 1860 John Denier, a tightrope performer, walked fourteen hundred feet on a rope stretched high above Canoe Beach between Castle Rock and the hill of East Point. Bass Beach is still a favorite bathing beach, as it is well sheltered by pro-

Nahant," published in 1845, as follows: "Little Nahant is one hundred and forty rods long and seventy broad, containing forty acres. It is a hill consisting of two graceful elevations rising eighty feet above the sea, and defended by great battlements of rock, from twenty to sixty feet in height. On the southerly side are two deep gorges, called the Great and Little Furnace. Between them is Mary's Grotto, a spacious room twenty-four feet square and twenty in height, opening into the sea." It lies wholly to one side, easterly, of the main road over the beaches. Apparently a road, at first a cart path, connected it with Great Nahant since early days. Traffic over the sand beach, dependent upon tides, was from Little Nahant toward Lynn.

Long Beach is the greatest beach of Nahant, stretching for two miles or more of beauty. Here are trippers also, but the State, with its bathhouse at one end of this stretch of sand, does better with cleanliness. On the Lynn Harbor side the shore is mostly mud flats, with a bit of sand or pebble a part of the way, from the Lynn line down by Little Nahant as far as Castle Road. Boots that shed water are needed if one would explore very much. It is a pleasant area to look out upon. The flats are maligned a little in calling them mud flats, for they are clean looking and far from disagreeable.

These beaches seem to have been attractive as income producers, but fortunately they were always kept open and free from the peculiar growth of buildings which so often infects a beach resort. At the annual town meeting in March, 1870, it was voted to lease land on Long and Short Beaches at the discretion of the selectmen. Then in April, 1879, it was voted to lease land on Long Beach near Sand Point for a coal and wood wharf. Sand Point is on the harbor side just beyond the "Causeway" or wall towards Lynn from Little Nahant. This proposition was from Welcome J. Johnson, who was then in this business on Nahant. He was a son of C. Hervey Johnson. He proposed that the town sell Sand Point for this business. Nothing ever came of the consent to lease.

Turning with Castle Road toward Bass Point the cliffs

John Q. Hammond
School Committee

Welcome W. Johnson
Town Treasurer

William F. Waters
Town Clerk

Fred A. Wilson
Public Library Trustee

begin again at Black Rock. Beyond this is another beach, beautiful like the others, which used to be called Johnson's Beach. The name should be continued, for it is a reminder of the Johnson who built the hotel near there about a century and a quarter ago. West Cliff separates this from what was known as Reed Cove, abreast of the Relay House property. Then comes Bass Point, a rugged rocky point projecting a few hundred yards into the ocean. Easterly from this is Lewis Beach, and other coves and cliffs break the shore line to Bailey's Hill. This hill, a real hill, projects its entire bulk into the water, and is surrounded by cliffs and ledges against which great seas lash out in fury when tossed shoreward by storm and gale. Around from Bailey's Hill is Pond Beach, named because adjacent to Bear Pond. Bear Pond got its name from the bear episode mentioned elsewhere. Then comes another and smaller point, and Dorothy's Cove is met again and the circuit of the shores of the town is completed. Naturally all Nahant is a beauty spot. Some parts are hurt in community beauty by houses too closely set together, and some houses and other buildings are not things of beauty or joys forever. But this is true of almost every community. As a whole, Nahant remains a healthy, attractive country town, with comparatively few of the accompaniments that make a suburb ugly or otherwise undesirable. Still, there are those who like suburban districts. In these days, when content comes f. o. b. Detroit and a home is a sleeping place adjacent to a garage, it may not matter to people where they live.

The highest part of the main road of the town is the short piece where Ocean Street crosses it and for a few yards either side. The highest point on Nahant may be noted by a huge boulder in a field near Highland Road. An area of several acres in that vicinity appears to be of about the same level. But five feet or so marks the differences between several points on Nahant, such as at East Point, Bailey's Hill, Fox Hill, the summit at Little Nahant, or the hill above the cemetery. The elevation formerly called Cannon Hill is in the same class. It is the vicinity of the Moering estate, above the standpipe. Many of these old place names seem to have an origin past discovery. A search in vain has been made for Joseph's Beach and Bailey's Hill, for example, yet some one reading these lines may know all about it and wonder at the ignorance of others. These annals are prepared with the assistance and co-operation of many people, yet some one not approached may be the very one able to answer interesting questions.

Bear Pond has been filled in at the easterly end by its use as a town dump. Forty years ago it extended up to the junction of Pond Street and Willow Road. The water of the pond is brackish, by infiltration from the ocean, but freezes over for good skating, although open to winds which often make rough ice. There is a large spring over against the bank of the knoll on the southerly side, a vigorous spring of good drinking water and flowing so freely that it does not freeze over. It is within the pond, but flows sufficiently to remain fresh with brackish water all around it. On marshy ground near by grow cat tail and other wet ground wild plants.

It was always easy to find water on Nahant by digging wells. The South Field, across Nahant Road from the Nahant Club grounds, was called springy ground, with water near the surface. Likewise the field above the telephone station. Just below this, nearly across Spring Road from Charles F. Leavitt's house, was a shallow well, half in the road and half in the bank, stoned up six feet or more above the road level. This was almost an open spring. It is referred to in the town records, in connection with the laying out of Valley Road in 1865, as "the stone reservoir." Many people have believed this was "Calf Spring" of old mention, back to 1706, but this is not so. Probably Tudor built this well, and it fed a public watering trough fifty yards below and across the street. In 1883 Joseph T. Wilson built a well on his new place farther down the hill, and this new well interfered with the "stone reservoir" which afterwards ran nearly dry in dry times. Public water supply to the trough ended the usefulness of this old well and shortly it was filled in. Calf Spring was always an open spring, and is mentioned elsewhere, a hundred feet or less southerly from Spring Road.

About a mile off Nahant, northerly from Saunder's Ledge, is "Egg Rock," called in earliest times "Birds Egg Rock" because of sea birds nesting there. It is eighty feet or more in height and of about three acres area, with about an acre of arable soil, part of which, perhaps, was boated over there by Thomas Dexter as one of his schemes. In June, 1855, the town of Nahant voted to quitclaim this little island to the United States government for a lighthouse. On September 15, 1856, Egg Rock Light was first shown a white light, changed to red on June 15, 1857. It continued to burn red up to within a few years of its discontinuance, when it was changed to white again. The last night it burned was on April 17, 1922. The old lighthouse was rebuilt in 1897, a larger and more modern structure. To get to Egg Rock was rather difficult except in smooth water, but a framework landing bracketed out from the ledges was a later addition giving easier access. After the light was stopped the buildings were sold at auction, but an attempt to move one of them down to a scow for floating away was unsuccessful, and the house slid into the water and was not worth salvaging. Other buildings or remains stayed there until 1927. The State of Massachusetts took it over for use as a bird sanctuary, named after Senator Lodge, who looked out upon it for so many years, and in this latter year dynamited walls and the other works of man in order that the sea birds might not be disturbed by any suggestion not made by nature herself. Man has helped the world, apparently, but his help in Egg Rock's present destiny seems better when absent.

Several other lighthouses are seen from Nahant. "The Graves," a few miles southerly, is a comparatively new light of high power, started first on September 1, 1905. It is a double wink every five seconds. Farther easterly and farther away is Minot's Light, blinking its one — four — three every half minute. Minot's was originally a great iron frame structure with a house on top and was first regularly lighted on January 1,

1850. On April 17, 1851, it was wrecked in a great storm. Then a new light tower was built of granite blocks dowelled and dovetailed together, and the light was started again regularly on November 15, 1860. Until 1894 it was a steady white light, and then it was changed to its present appearance. In the spring of the young man's fancy described by the poet it is said to wink "I love you." Still farther easterly may be seen the slower and less nervous blinking of Boston Lightship.

The Long Island Light in Boston Harbor is older, dating back to 1819, though rebuilt more than once. At first it was a stone house, then an iron structure, and about 1900 the present brick building was erected. Deer Island Light is a range light, not visible from the western half of Nahant. This was started about 1890.

Over northerly Nahant sees Thacher's Island Twin Lights, down Cape Ann way, and dating back to 1773. The original towers were forty-five feet high and were replaced by one hundred and twenty-four foot towers in 1861. The lights always shone as now.

Southerly is Boston Light, another important Boston Harbor guide, familiar to Nahanters as a white tower and a revolving light flashing every half minute. This was started in 1716 and was the first lighthouse built by any of the colonies in North America. It was supported for a time by a tax on shipping, and the year of its first lighting was an early date in lighthouse history. The Eddystone Light only ranks eighteen years earlier. In the Revolutionary War this structure fared badly. It was partly wrecked by Americans while the British occupied Boston and was blown up by the latter when they evacuated the city. In 1783 it was rebuilt and with various alterations is the present Boston Light. Apparently it was not shown for a time in the War of 1812. About 1811 it was changed from a fixed light to the revolving light familiar today. In 1719 a gun was placed at the light to "answer ship in a fog," and this cannon is still at the station. In 1851 a fog bell was installed, in 1872 a fog trumpet, and in 1887 the present steam siren. Comments here made about variations in any of these lights do not refer to their brilliancy. Improved methods have changed most of them in this respect.

The Graves Lighthouse also has a booming fog horn which warns mariners and wakes sleepers not accustomed to it. There is a bell buoy on Fawn Bar, a few miles toward Boston, which can be heard on Nahant when the wind brings the sound in that direction. Then there is "Old Sunk," or "The Spindle," with a spherical cage on a tall iron column. It looks small from shore, but is large enough for a man to climb into if he can also get up the shaft. "Old Sunk" is the only above-water ledge tip of a ridge continuing seaward from Bailey's Hill. Recently a red guide light was set up on Tudor Wharf. Nowadays harbor pilots land there, getting back to their stations or houses more quickly than if returning by water. This light is a small power red light and was started December 24, 1920. It should not be mentioned as in the lighthouse class. A few years ago a bell buoy was placed down near "Old Sunk," and for a few weeks its clangor, and the infernal irregularity of it, threatened to depopulate the town. Beseechings, for once, were not in vain, and the offending noise maker was removed.

The question of the ownership of the beaches of Nahant seems to have been a live matter from the beginning of the town. Among the first printed documents of the new town was one in 1856, entitled "Extracts from the Records of the Town of Lynn, together with the Division and Names of the Original Proprietors of Land at Nahant and Reports Thereon." This was the report of a committee of three appointed by the town "to make investigations in relation to the rights of the town in the undivided and unimproved lands within its corporate limits." The committee was Francis Johnson, Alonzo Colby and John Q. Hammond. Hammond was secretary and prepared the printed report for circulation. It is a careful piece of work and ably presents the town's claims. It was accepted by the town as a report of progress. The committee was continued and enlarged by the addition of the Board of Selectmen, and instructed to take such action as the interests of the town required. This report quotes the records by which the committee of 1706 was chosen by the town of Lynn, and gives the entire list of allotments as later recorded, also, on the Lewis and Hammond map. Then it describes the method of laying out the lots among the proprietors of Lynn, and continues as follows:

> By the common law which we received from England, the seashore belonged to the Sovereign; but by an old Colony ordinance of 1641, it is declared that, "in all creeks, coves, and other places, about and upon salt water, where the sea ebbs and flows, the proprietors of the land adjoining shall have property to the low water mark, where the sea doth not ebb above an hundred rods, and not more, wheresoever it ebbs further."
>
> By this ordinance, which has been adjusted to the law of the land, the beaches which surround the peninsula of Nahant became the property of the commoners of Lynn, and were subject to their disposal in such manner as they might elect, not inconsistent with the public rights of navigation, fishing, fowling and bathing. Now it becomes important to know whether the commoners of Lynn ever intended to convey their rights to private individuals, or whether they intended to divide the lands held in common, and retain their rights in the beaches. At the time of this division of the common lands, and for nearly a century afterwards, in every annual town warrant there was an article as follows, viz.: "to let the Nahant beaches," and in the records of the doings of these meetings these "beaches" were let to some one or more individuals, the town receiving a consideration therefor; and in August of the same year of the division, stone were sold from the Nahant beaches by vote of the town. Also on March 3, 1711, "all of the shells that shall come upon the Nahant beaches for one year were sold to Daniel Brown and William Gray for thirty shillings," and at the same meeting, bits of land on which to set a house were granted to James Mills, Jona. Johnson, and two others. All of these facts, which are matters of record upon the town books of Lynn, show conclusively that the town still continued to assert complete control over the beaches, and to exercise all the rights of ownership of the same. That this was the intention of the town will still further appear by the action of the committee of division, for although the ordinance of the old Colony was at that time in force, which gave to the owners of the land adjoining, the shore to low water mark, yet they did not measure to that point, and enter the same on the town book, which they must have done in order to give title to it. Neither did they make

any allowance for such a privilege conferred upon some persons who would possess, on such a supposition, in some places nearly eight rods of shore. . . . Upon this head tradition points to the same conclusion, for the range ways are claimed to be for the use of the proprietors, to go to the shore for sea manure, which, by the old Colony ordinance, they would have no right to, but, upon the supposition that the shore belonged to the commoners, would be perfectly proper and right.

It is still within the memory of many that the people of Lynn have claimed and exercised this right, to take seaweed from these beaches, and to prohibit all persons not residents of Lynn from exercising this right.

In the year 1807 several inhabitants of Danvers were prosecuted for taking sea manure from the beaches, contrary to a vote of the town, and the court in its decision sustained the town in its right to pass such a prohibitory vote, and left it in legal possession of all the natural treasures which the sea might cast upon its shores. Thus it appears to your committee, in the light of these facts, that to the town of Nahant as the successors of the commoners of Lynn, belongs the soil of the seashore, subject, however, to public rights under the general law, and rights acquired by custom, prescription and adverse possession.

Then follows a discussion of the ownership by the town of certain lots not granted to individuals in the 1706 division. The committee continued its work, evidently, and at the annual meeting in March, 1859, the following resolution was passed and is a part of the town records:

Whereas the ownership and fee of the beaches, shore and strand surrounding the town, and also of the ground over which the highways were laid out by the committee by which the division of the land in the town was made in the year 1706, are claimed as the property of the town, and whereas divers persons owning land abutting on said beaches, shore and strand, and others, have obstructed the access thereto by erecting fences or buildings thereon or otherwise, and have in like manner obstructed said highways, and, by continuing such obstructions may possibly acquire rights adverse to those of the town and of the public;

Voted, That this town claims to be the owner in fee of the said beaches, shore and strand, and of the soil on which the said highways are laid out, subject always to the public rights of navigation, fishing, fowling and bathing thereon in such manner as may not be inconsistent with the laws and police regulations of the Commonwealth and this town:

That the town disputes and denies the right of any person or persons to the exclusive use of the said beaches, shore or strand, and the land over which the said highways are laid out or any part or parts thereof, or to any exclusive right of any air, light or other easement thereover, and also the right of any person or persons to exclude the public therefrom or from the use and enjoyment thereof for the purposes aforesaid, excepting those places in which the town or the selectmen thereof have granted or may hereafter grant any such exclusive right.

Then followed a vote to notify all owners abutting beaches of this action. It is not proposed to discuss the legal effect of these actions of the town, but they are interesting as showing a plain attempt to prevent the beaches from becoming private property. A former chairman of the selectmen, a competent lawyer, is said to have remarked that a look at what the town had done in these early days would cause some consternation. With the auto maniac abroad in the land, and with the whole eastern end of Massachusetts on wheels and headed for the seashore in hot weather, perhaps people willing to accept the care and responsibility of so-called private ownership are relieving the town of worry over rubbish and crowds.

At the March town meeting in 1874 it was voted to build a plank walk around Mifflin's Point to connect with the one built by George P. Upham. Since that time the town has maintained this plank path and its protecting guard rails or fences. It has been suggested that the town lay out a town footway the entire length of this path as it now runs, from Bass Beach around to Stony Beach at the northeastern end of Summer Street, and thus insure its remaining a public path such as it has been for so long a time. The path long antedates the building of the plank walk, and reaches back so far that no one can discover a time when it was not used by the public. There could therefore appear to be little question of damages to adjoining property, for it would suffer nothing new. Even the automobile traffic will not add to its use, apparently, for the auto maniac is not a walker and cannot get far from his motor car.

Model of Frederic Tudor's Ice Carrier, the "Ice King"

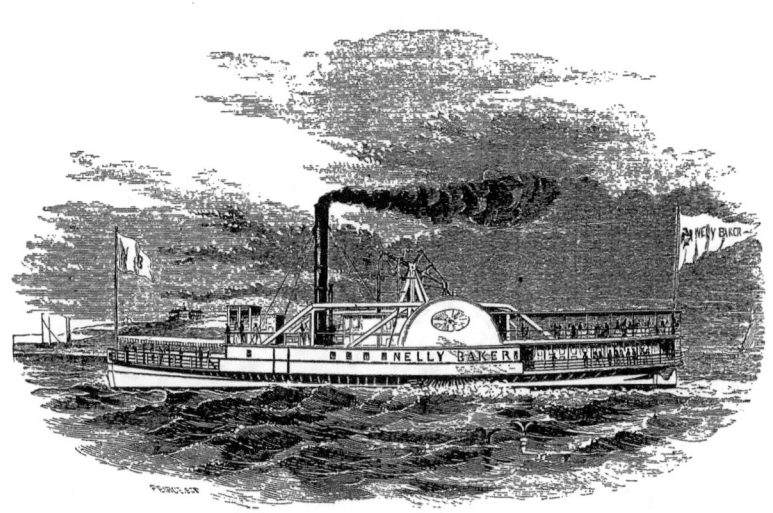

NAHANT STEAMER, NELLY BAKER.

Popular Nahant Steamboat of the Fifties

The same comments are made about the path through to East Point, which has a curious history. In 1865, on a petition of residents, including some summer residents, a road one rod wide was laid out all around the shore at East Point. Damages were set and money appropriated for them, and the report of this laying out was duly accepted. At once arose a discussion as to the location and difficulties of building, which delayed construction so long that the legal time limit placed on it was exceeded and the laying out was to be done over again. John E. Lodge, who bought the whole of East Point after the great hotel had burned, died in 1862, but compromise overtures were made by his heirs, or their representatives, that the town did not really want a road around the point but only a footpath access to it. It was proposed to cede a right of way between the two parts of the estate, as it had been divided, together with an adequately long path around the cliffs. This arrangement seems to have pleased everybody and was accepted. It was some time later that it was discovered that the town, perhaps through the ignorance or thoughtlessness of both parties to the plan, had given up a permanent way for a way existing only at the will of the owners. The transaction does not seem to reflect credit on any one. A cure now, as for the path around Mifflin's Point, is to lay out a town footway, and again damages would appear to be simple, because no person has ever lived there without the existence of this public privilege, and the added suffering on account of it may be tolerable. Perhaps the owners would co-operate to continue what has existed since the point was used for private residences, or to correct what appears to have been an error in the original deal establishing this public footpath.

In 1906 the town purchased Marjoram Hill, near Tudor Wharf, for a park, and in 1905 the low land behind Short Beach for a public playground. Both of these purchases were urged during several years by George Abbot James, who served as town forester from 1881 to 1908, and gave much attention to keeping the town in good condition while adding to its beauty by further planting of trees and shrubs. James lived at East Point, on the property bought by John E. Lodge, which was divided between his two children, Senator Lodge and Mrs. James. An only child, Ellerton James, served the town on many committees, and was giving his energy to one at the time of his death, in 1926. George A. James died in 1917. Both of these men were long-time summer residents and legal citizens of Nahant, whose interest in town affairs of all sorts was unceasing. They loved the town and were always ready to be of service to it.

This playground land was not originally allotted in the 1706 division of Lynn's common land. It was given to Alonzo Lewis in 1847 for his services to Lynn, and later sold to Frederic Tudor, whose successors were the Nahant Land Company. The title through Lewis did not seem to be clear enough, and in 1882 the town of Nahant quitclaimed to the land company. It was a formality to perfect the title, as the town had no claim. Tudor built ditches through the marshes he owned, both this playground and the marsh north of Bear Pond. Drainage was chiefly out across Castle Road through a culvert long called "Little Bridge." The land company deeds for sales near these ditches have stipulated that the drainage is not to be hindered. The ditches still function, but need clearing occasionally. They accomplished their purpose, and both pieces of low ground are dry enough most of the time, though often holding a very wet condition late into the springtime.

This description of the natural part of Nahant is mechanical, and intentionally so. Its beauties have been sung by others. Of course, when man steps upon a place he hurts it. It seems inevitable. Much that man does is not beautiful. It was an old hymn writer, Reginald Heber, who wrote the lines —

> Though every prospect pleases
> And only man is vile.

And Heber died over a hundred years ago and wrote of no particular place and not even of America. In a residential town much may be done to make community beauty. It only needs the right spirit whole-heartedly supporting proper regulations against the few who care nothing for the town and only for themselves and their imagined welfare. Proper building regulations conserve health and safety, but do less for beauty. The year 1927 sees a zoning committee at work preparing regulations which will help the town in good looks more than may any other measure. The recently adopted planning board by-laws provide another medium which may make Nahant attractive or keep it so. Neither of these agencies are operative through other town offices or boards, but both, and all together, and the whole people with them, are needed for the full development of any place toward what it should be and can be without undue pressure or hardship upon any one. The selfish and self-seeking will find the contrary, have already found the contrary, but the whole people only need to understand measures for conserving community beauty and welfare in order to back them enthusiastically.

There is still the problem of the bad looking house or grounds, but much may be done by example and pattern to enlist the pride of all. It is as easy to get the good in design as the bad, and as cheap, but care is necessary. Black and white or any colors tend to be too busily combined in this jazz time of living; brick can pollute a countryside; and wood and paint can yield a horror in form and color. There is the newly organized Nahant Garden Club, also in the field to help Nahant. The agencies which would make Nahant better are astir and only need public support. Doubtless they will get it, for the heart of the public is sound. A few recalcitrants can be noisy and troublesome, but this means all the more need for the many to stand solidly behind what seem to be measures for better surroundings, better living, and a better community.

Botanically and geologically Nahant is also interesting. Mrs. Joseph T. Wilson, an enthusiastic student of Nahant wild flowers, collected over two hundred varieties into an herbarium which she later gave to the Public Library. Unfortunately, herbariums need expert care and attention, and public library conditions are not conducive to their long life. Among the rarer things found here are the beach pea, the pimpernels, saltwort, sea rochette, seaside crowfoot and curled crowfoot. The two latter are very rare. Hudsonia tomentosa blooms along the way to Lynn in June. Then there is mossy stonecrop, only occasionally found in this country. Scotch lovage is scattered along the shores. Of several artemesias, one, the candita, is rare. There are rhodora, and cerastium arvense, the field chickweed. Pearlwort, of the same family, is on Nahant, and is rare. The seaside spurge is always a curiosity.

The town is a storehouse to the student of geology. Space does not permit telling about it. The lecture by Professor Agassiz is a part of the story. Some of the rocks are old, belonging to the earliest formations, and some have come from far away, moved here by glacial action.

Then there are sea gardens in all the nooks of the shores, with weeds, mosses and curious sea creatures. These things are commonly overlooked, but are present to delight the soul and reward the efforts of the seeker after knowledge and beauty.

CHAPTER XV

CHURCHES

THE early people of Lynn were a religious and church-going group. This is not redundancy, for today one may be either religious or church-going, and not the other. Escaping more or less religious oppression by their removal to America, settlers everywhere seem to have been rather strict themselves.

The first minister in Lynn seems to have been Stephen Batchellor, who came in 1632 and was driven out in 1636 for serious irregularities in conduct. Before 1632 doubtless there were laymen's services with prayers, readings, singing and amateur preaching. The year 1636 saw the coming of Samuel Whiting, who settled in Lynn and was minister here until his death in 1679, at the age of eighty-two. He was a very much loved and respected pastor. In 1637 this settlement took the name of Lynn, or "Linn" as the records have it, and this is said to have been a compliment to Whiting, who came from the town of the same name in Norfolk County, England. He was called "Father of Lynn" and the "Angel of Lynn" by enthusiastic admirers, and he certainly led his flock well and deserved the admiration he received. His second wife, who came with him to America, was a cousin of Oliver Cromwell. A simple shaft marks his grave in the "Old Burying Grounds" in West Lynn.

These present writings will not trace out the churches in Lynn, although they were for Nahant as well. Nahant as a community set up its own churches, though in far later years, because there was no village until after 1800. One old item of Turner's journal for 1646 is, however, interesting to quote:

> Allan Bridges hath bin chose to wake ye sleepers in meeting. And being much proude of his place, must needs have a fox taile fixed to ye end of a long staff wherewith he may brush ye faces of

them yt will have napps in time of discourse: likewise a sharpe thorne wherewith he may prick such as be most sounde. On ye laste Lord his day, as hee strutted about ye meeting house, hee did spy Mr. Tomlins sleeping with much comforte, his head kept steadie by being in ye corner, and his hand grasping ye rail. And soe spying, Allen did quicklie thrust his staff behind Dame Bullard and give him a grevious prick upon ye hand. Whereuppon Mr. Tomlins did spring upp mch above ye floore and with terrible force strike with his hand against ye wall, and also, to ye great wonder of all, prophainlie exclaim, in a loude voice, cuss ye woodchuck; he dreaming, as it seemed, yt a woodchuck had seized and bit his hand. But on coming to know where hee was and ye great scandal hee had committed, he seemed mch abashed but did not speake. And I thinke hee will not soone againe go to sleepe in meeting. Ye women may sometimes sleepe and none know it, by reason of their enormous bonnets. Mr. Whiting doth pleasantlie say yt from ye pulpitt hee doth seem to be preaching to stacks of straw with men sitting here and there among them.

As early as 1820 services were regularly conducted in the "Old Stone Schoolhouse" by the Rev. Samuel J. May, whose life was published in 1873. He came to Nahant at the invitation of several summer residents to act as tutor to their children, and he "conducted the services of public worship each Sunday morning." His Sunday audiences were thirty or forty in number. His teaching was also in this building, which was school, library, church and meeting place for any village affairs.

The first church at Nahant is properly called the Nahant Church, but through custom it is more commonly mentioned as the Boston Church and sometimes as the Union Church. The former name came to it because it serves only in summer and was started and is maintained by the efforts of the summer residents, who were always called the "Boston People," as most of them came from Boston. The other name is because its services are of various denominations.

"The increase of visitors to Nahant, attracted by the Nahant Hotel, opened in 1823, and by the construction of many cottages for private families on adjoining lands, suggested to Mr. William Havard Eliot — who lived, in the summer of 1831, in the stone house next to the present church, now occupied by Mr. Charles R. Greene — a plan for building a chapel where different religious sects might assemble, and, as our tablet expresses it, 'Unite in the worship of God.' " A subscription paper dated July 24, 1831, was circulated and at a meeting in September, in Boston, at the office of William Appleton, it was decided to proceed with the erection of a building. Colonel Perkins, Hon. William Prescott and Hon. David Sears were a committee, while Judge Prescott was chairman of the group and Eliot, secretary. The latter, the prime mover in the enterprise, died before the building was completed, and his brother, Samuel A. Eliot, took his place in this activity. The first service was on July 8, 1832, and was conducted by the Rev. John Gorham Palfrey of Harvard University. The wardens for that year were Samuel A. Eliot and Frederic Tudor. In 1834 the bell was presented by the ladies among the summer residents, and is the same bell now in use in the present building. In 1846, under the direction of the committee for that year, Charles Amory and John E. Lodge, the chapel was enlarged by the addition of two wings, making small transepts and adding sixteen pews. In 1862 this building was severely injured by a winter gale, and as a larger one was needed it was proposed to build a new chapel. F. C. Loring, John A. Blanchard and Samuel H. Russell were a committee to procure plans and estimates. It was not until 1868, however, that the old building was removed and the present structure built. This early building has been called a Tuscan type of chapel, and was of wood. Good photographs of it are extant, one of which is in the Nahant Public Library. The later building is the one still in use.

In the summer of 1868 this church was accommodated in the Village Church. "Under the direction of William Appleton, Esq., acting as committee for the year, services were conducted on the same plan as in their own chapel, both congregations sharing the sittings between them. The present chapel was opened in 1869 with dedicatory services on June 27 by the Rev. Andrew P. Peabody of Harvard University."

The land for the original chapel was given by Cornelius Coolidge, and a later additional tract was bought through the efforts of James W. Paige. A glance over the lists of wardens, treasurers and trustees reveals a group of names familiar to old Nahanters and containing many that are great in the history of Boston, Massachusetts or America. The list of preachers also contains the names of some of the greatest of their times. There never was a settled minister, as the church was only of service during the summer season; and each season has seen various denominations represented. The quotations and much of this information about the "Nahant Church" are from the Appendix to a pamphlet entitled "A Sermon Preached in Commemoration of the Founders of the Nahant Church at the Dedication of a Tablet Erected to their Memory June 22nd, 1877: by Andrew P. Peabody, D.D." A copy of this is in the Nahant Public Library and contains lists of preachers, wardens, treasurers and trustees up to 1877. Perhaps the notable name is of Samuel H. Russell, because of his long service as treasurer, beginning in 1863 and ending with his death in 1894, at the age of seventy-one. A successor in this office was Frank Merriam, who died in 1923 at the age of seventy-three. He was a Nahant summer resident from his youth. He married a daughter of J. S. Lovering, another well-known summer-time man, whose son, Charles T. Lovering, married a daughter of Frederick R. Sears. It is also notable that in 1862 Charles F. Johnson, grandson of Caleb and son of C. Hervey, began to serve as sexton in this church, and is in his sixty-sixth year in this position in this year (1928).

The Village Church, standing in its present location, was built in 1851. A copy from the old records reads: "In the year of our Lord Eighteen Hundred and Fifty, early in the month of September, a meeting of the inhabitants of Nahant was called to learn the opinion of the people in regard to a subscription paper that had been put in circulation by Welcome W. Johnson and others for the purpose of erecting an Episcopal Meeting House." This meeting was in the old stone school-house, and William R. Johnson was chairman with William F.

The "Alice" in Mid Ocean
Nahant to Cowes, 1866.   Painting by J. E. C. Peterson

Tudor's "Brick House;" Stone Fruit Storage Barn on Right
Note old type lamp post

CHURCHES 217

Johnson secretary. The project for an Episcopal church was reconsidered, and with several denominations represented, no one of which could hope to build, or maintain worship, ballots were taken to determine which should have preference. The result favored the Methodists, and the name Independent Methodist Society was adopted. A committee was chosen to raise money to erect a house of worship, and another to procure a preacher for the following winter to hold services in the schoolhouse. As a result the Rev. Harry M. Bridge officiated until April, 1851. It is told that people attended evening services, bringing their lamps with them, as the schoolhouse was not provided with facilities for lighting. Services in the old Johnson homestead are also noted, but it is suggested that these may have been in 1851, in the interim between the tearing down of the old schoolhouse and the opening of the new church building.

In the meantime the building committee were at work. They were Dexter Stetson, Joseph Johnson, John Q. Hammond, Francis Johnson, Jesse Rice and Walter Johnson. The present main part of the building, setting lower than now, and without the tower and later rear addition, was dedicated on September 25, 1851. The land was given by Caleb Johnson, who once owned most of the land along Nahant Road westerly as far as Pond Street. An addition to it was later given by James W. Paige. The eight hundred pound bell, still in use, was given by Dr. William R. Lawrence, who was a summer resident at Little Nahant, where he lived with his father, Amos Lawrence. The communion service was presented by a group of summer residents.

In 1872 came an unusual action. The town meeting warrant for March 7 contained this article. "To see if the town will appropriate money to raise the village church and belfry and put a town clock therein." Apparently no special provision was made for any ownership, and doubtless people knew it was proposed to build on land not owned by the town, so that ownership of what was done would actually vest in the owners of the land. There seems to have been some argument about it, for the vote finally passed appropriated money for a tower and clock, but contained the provision that "No part of the sum be expended to repair or beautify any church or building used for purely religious purposes." Probably a first thought would have been to put this clock tower on the town hall, but the more conspicuous position, visible over a greater area, made the church the best place for it. For years the town maintained the tower and clock and made annual appropriations for the care of clock and bell. Yet the bell was never bought by the town. Latterly, the question of the town's rights has arisen, and in recent repairs the town assumed liability only to the extent of protecting its clock, to which it might claim ownership as portable property. When this tower was built the church building was raised to its present level, providing the well-lighted basement used as a vestry and for Sunday school purposes. Formerly the bell hung in a little belfry on the front of the structure. The pulpit was high up in the air, as was the old custom. It was made and presented by Dexter Stetson, who was the builder of the church. The choir gallery was across the rear, also well elevated above the general floor level. Here was a little organ played by succeeding amateur performers; and here it was most difficult to be always quite stately and properly dignified, with the minister looking straight across the room over the heads of the congregation. In later years this was changed. The old choir gallery was removed, giving the space in the rear as now. The pulpit was lowered to a more comfortable location, and the choir was moved up to the corner at the right of the minister, taking out several pews that faced crosswise and were not very much used. Then in 1907 a pipe organ was installed, and in 1914 an addition was made in the rear, giving parlors above and kitchen below, and opening into the main church through a new doorway which necessitated the removal of the crosswise pews in the other corner. Thus the church came to its present appearance and facilities. It has always had a loyal band of workers, who have, in many instances, made it their church, regardless of the denomination with which they may have been affiliated in other places. The ministers do much to point the way toward liberality or restriction, but in the main it has been an open policy institution with a long list of preachers who have striven hard and capably and have done good in the town. A list of them here follows:

W. R. Clarke	1853–54	Oliver Huckel		1890
Henry W. Webber	1855–56	William A. Mansell		1890
H. V. Degen	1856	John Willetts		1890–91
Allen Gammett	1857	D. A. Denton		1891–92
C. N. Smith	1858–59	Will L. Holmes		1892–94
Stephen Cushing	1860–66	Frank E. Dodds		1894–96
Timothy Atkinson	1866–67	Clement E. Holmes		1896–97
George G. Jones	1868	Charles A. Bowen		1898
Joseph B. Hamblin	1869	H. McKinney		1899–1900
Wilbur F. Crafts	1870	F. M. Swinehart		1900–02
William E. Huntington	1871–72	David H. Jemison		1902–05
Davis W. Clarke	1873	Arthur S. Burrill		1905–08
Fales H. Newhall	1874	W. B. Ronald		1909–12
J. W. Dearborn	1874–78	Elmer Jones		1913–14
M. E. Wright	1878–80	Denver C. Pickens		1914–17
Jonathan Neal	1881–85	Frank S. Hickman		1917–19
A. W. Seavey	1886	Dwight M. Beck		1919–24
A. Lee Holmes	1887–89	E. E. Tillotson		1924–27

In 1876 a Young Men's Christian Association was formed, chiefly through efforts of Rev. J. W. Dearborn, then pastor. A piece of land on Summer Street was given by Mrs. Tudor, and a small building was erected. The association flourished for a while and then gradually faded to nothing. After some years of disuse the property was sold to Thomas Roland, who remodelled it into a house which he now owns.

The first Roman Catholic Church services were held in the Nahant Church on Cliff Street in 1866, or about then. The pamphlet published with the dedication of a tablet in this church in 1877 states that "the Reverend Patrick Strain of Lynn, and others of his church, preached and said mass for members of the Roman Catholic Church in the old chapel, till they built a chapel for themselves at Nahant." There is a discrepancy here, for the "old chapel" was torn down in 1868 and the Roman Catholic Church was built in 1872, with the tower added in 1874. People remember services in the Town

Hall, then the new Town Hall, on Pleasant Street, now occupied by the American Legion Post. Probably this was during this interim. Until 1902 this church was a mission from Lynn. The Rev. Patrick Strain, rector of St. Mary's Parish in Lynn, was in charge of it until 1893, when he was succeeded by the Rev. A. J. Teeling, then pastor of St. Mary's Parish.

In 1901 this church building was raised, providing a liberal basement used for church activities and bringing the structure to its present appearance. In 1902 the Nahant Catholic community was set apart as a separate parish, and the Rev. Francis P. Hannawin was pastor until 1913. The parish bought the Worthen A. Gove house as a rectory. This was the original Gove on Nahant, and the father of a family of sons and daughters, most of whom lived on Nahant for several years, while one, Charles E. Gove, spent his life here. He died in 1920, well within the recollection of even newcomers to town. This house was used as a rectory until 1916, when the property now so occupied was purchased. The Gove house was moved back to a location opening on Highland Road and remodelled. This allowed the more spacious grounds now enjoyed by the church and rectory. The 1916 purchase was known as the F. Henry Johnson house. Johnson was of the old Nahant Johnsons, as will be found elsewhere. A son of the same name, but known as Harry Johnson, has for years lived in summer in his house on Highland Road, until his death in 1927. He is of the firm of White & Johnson, with a summer shop on Summer Street. This house was renovated and somewhat remodelled, but without much changing its already dignified appearance, during the incumbency of Father O'Connor, who was succeeded by the Rev. J. F. Kelley in 1919, while the present pastor, the Rev. William J. Reardon, came in 1922. Before the church was built, a Sunday school was held in the schoolhouse, and in 1872 Mrs. Dwight established the school in the new building, where it was later carried on by Miss Veronica Dwight, a daughter and the sister of Dr. Thomas Dwight. Father Strain and Father Teeling, in later years, were both given the title Monsignor.

CHURCHES

The Roman Catholics of these earlier days were mostly the Irish. Just when the first Irishman settled on Nahant is hard to establish, but probably the first comer was John Farrell. He is said to have been here before 1840, but the Welcome W. Johnson list of inhabitants of 1847 does not mention him. His first home was in a stone shack near the ledge back of the street car station on the present Relay House grounds. This building was built by William Luscomb, grandfather of William Luscomb, later well known on Nahant. Then he built and occupied the house on Spring Road, northerly from Mitchell's Corner, now owned by P. J. O'Connor. John Farrell will be well remembered by old Nahanters. He died in 1885, aged seventy-seven. Perhaps the second Irishman to come to Nahant was Patrick O'Shaughnessy, father of James C. Shaughnessy, the latter well known in town today, where he has served as selectman and is now serving as assessor. The father first lived in a little house, now gone, near the Morris Higgins house. The latter was the first house in Short Beach Village, or Irishtown, as it used to be called. It was built by Samuel, or Nelson, Tarbox, who bought the land from Alonzo Lewis.

The 1847 list of inhabitants contains the name of Mrs. Donham, who is said to have been the widow of Michael Donham named as an early Nahant Irishman who went to California in the gold rush around 1849 and did not return. Another named Follen went from Nahant to California earlier than 1849. He is not related to Edward Follen who came later. Then there was Patrick Riley who enlisted from Nahant for the Civil War and whose name is on the Civil War Soldiers Monument in Greenlawn Cemetery. The five who apparently may be reckoned the earliest to come to Nahant and stay, with descendants also here, are John Farrell, Patrick O'Shaughnessy, Michael Carroll, Morris Higgins, and John Flynn, though Edward J. Hyde was born on Nahant in 1857, a son of William Hyde, who therefore dates back among the early ones. Coming down to fifty years or so ago there are many more, — Lane, Larkin, Killilae, Mitchell, Linehan,

Follen, Tierney, Waters, Rooney, Coakley, O'Connor, Kennedy and others. There are the Deveney's, several brothers and sisters, and James J. Deveney, son of Michael Deveney, has served on the school committee and on the Board of Assessors. Mostly these families were here throughout the recollection of many Nahanters now living, and they made up the community known as Irishtown, finally spreading out Flash Road on what is now government land. Later many of these Flash Road people moved their houses across the street, and descendants of nearly all these families are still in town. Most of these later arrivals came since the Civil War, and came from around one part of old Ireland. Irishtown, however, has been given up, by gradual removal to other parts of the town, and much more recently Italians have come in there so that the district may no longer carry its old name meaningly. These are also Roman Catholics, increasing the attendance at this church. Short Beach Village remains rather closely built up, but the newcomers have improved the appearance of much of the property.

Churches everywhere are arousing questions of their efficiency. Do they do their full part in education, to bring true life values to the front and eliminate the mad chase in wrong directions for pleasure and happiness. When people look back over the years they see clearly that their greatest moments were simple, and at the time unrecognized as superior to others reached by worry, effort and expense; and the Bible passage "consider the lilies of the field, they toil not neither do they spin, yet I say unto you that Solomon in all his glory was not arrayed like one of these" may be an epitome of life for an idle flapper or a youth with lip drooping to support a cigarette, but it needs a more accurate application, perhaps, by the churches. The "nots" in the Ten Commandments are too frequently mixed up and misplaced or omitted in every one's life. The churches struggle with financial burdens which should be removed. Complaint is made that parsons make the road to Heaven a toll road, but many a family spends far more for club dues than for church support. Yet the spiritual is important, and considered only as adult education the church is important, provided it does its work. With proper efficiency far greater sums could well be spent by any community upon its churches. People need to be told of some eternal verities. Not all things are mutable. The phrase, "as it was — in the beginning — is now — and ever shall be," has a resounding boom of fatefulness. But it applies to some factors of life, and should continue to boom, and not be resolved into a mere tinkle.

None of these Nahant churches have cemeteries, and the only one in town is Greenlawn Cemetery owned and maintained by the town. In early days there was a burial place near Pleasant Street, but it was practically private. A very early action of the town, at the third town meeting in 1853, was the appointment of a committee on a town cemetery, consisting of David Johnson, Dexter Stetson and Walter Johnson. They reported at the annual meeting in March, 1854, and the report was referred again to a committee of five, consisting of the same three with Washington H. Johnson and Artemus Murdock. They were empowered to buy a "suitable piece of ground" for a cemetery. At the March meeting in 1856 the committee reported the purchase from the heirs of Thomas H. Perkins of a lot in Range Eleven containing about two acres. In 1858 a street was laid out from the highway to the cemetery, and the place was named Greenlawn Cemetery. This street was exactly where the main avenue from Nahant Road runs today, and entered the lot near its northwesterly end. The northeasterly side was a few feet northerly from where the main avenue now broadens out to meet the circular part of the avenue. The other two sides were as they are now, on High Street southeasterly and along what was then a Tudor orchard southwesterly. About this time the town provided money for the stone posts and gates which many people will remember on this old line, in eighty yards or more from Nahant Road. Then came three additions to the area. First, in 1879, came the extension northwesterly down to Kennedy Court; second, in 1908, the purchase of the strip toward Nahant Road, about a hundred feet wide and from Linehan's land up to but not including the top of the hill; and third, in 1918, the inclusion of the land out to Nahant Road, part of which was occupied by the building first used as a schoolhouse and then as a police station. At a special town meeting in 1918 the town accepted the offer of Mrs. Luther S. Johnson to build a cemetery chapel, thus carrying out the intentions of her late husband. It was started in 1919 and dedicated on May 30, 1920. It was named "Ellingwood Chapel" in memory of Joanna Ellingwood Green, and Joseph Johnson, Jr., who were Luther Johnson's mother and father. Luther Johnson's grandfather was Joseph Johnson, son of the first Johnson on Nahant. Luther Johnson was a shoe manufacturer in Lynn, leaving benefactions to the Lynn City Hospital and other institutions. He always loved Nahant, his birthplace. In 1894 he presented his Nahant G. A. R. comrades with a flag which they carefully kept and which is now in the Nahant Public Library.

During the same year 1919 Mrs. Francis H. Johnson presented the town with the gateway on Nahant Road in memory of her husband. Mrs. James H. Beal gave a sum sufficient to build the fence and gateway on High Street, the old end of the cemetery. The town itself made an appropriation to move the police station across the street to its present location and to grade and improve the new parts of the area, and on Decoration Day, celebrated May 31, 1920, the work was completed to about its present condition. This year (1928) the town proposes a further extension along Nahant Road up to High Street.

Decoration Day has always been well observed at Nahant. For years a long procession, headed by a band and including town officers, firemen, G. A. R. men and school children, has made an impressive sight and a worthy tribute to the old soldiers, most of whom are gone. Some years ago the G. A. R. men feared no one would be left to do this interestedly, and set about enlisting the school children by special talks and a prominent part in the day's events. But now there is the American Legion, veterans of still another war, who may be relied upon to "carry on" this service of memory and of gratitude, which is equally felt by those who cannot participate

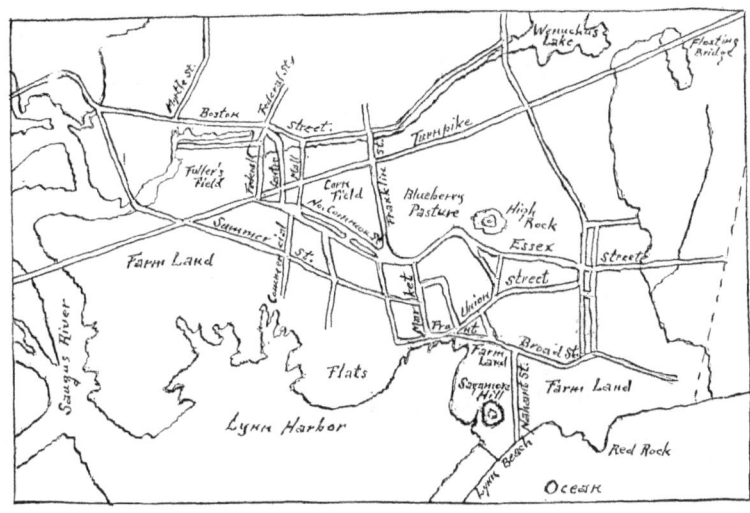

Lynn in 1838
No road to the shore except Nahant Street

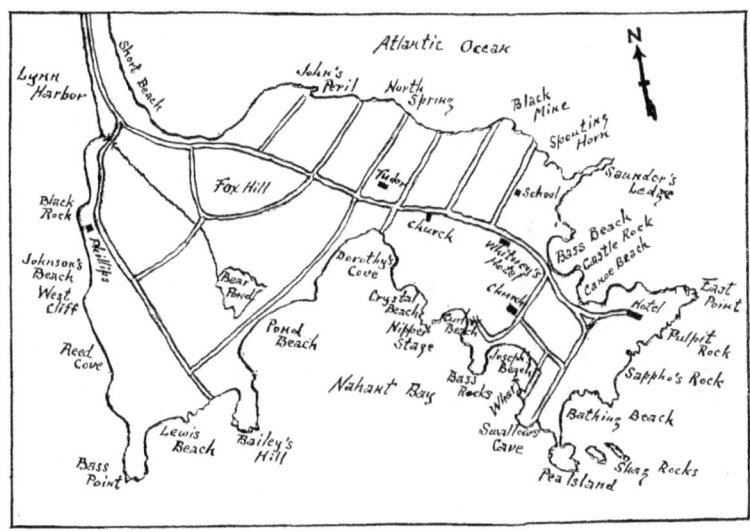

Nahant about 1855
From an old Lewis map

in the events. Mankind seems born to fight. Probably another fifty years will see still another group interested to continue, as those now so young begin to lay down their burdens.

Nahant has reason to feel proud of its cemetery. Its desirable location, its shrubs and trees, the beautiful Norman chapel and entranceway, all make it a place worthy to compare with any others. Indeed, these factors make it too attractive. Restrictions on the use of it have been tightened from time to time and may be more stringent. It is for Nahanters, and is too small to accommodate others, but it has been so used because of its beauty and because a lot in it is released by the town at a low price. In the very early days any one could get a lot, and so many did so that the available area was disappearing. Some people only wanted a little piece of real estate and never used their lots, selling them as years went on. Restrictions stopped this practice, but later on came other abuses and further restrictions. Probably there will always be people who would impose upon the generosity of a town, and so it must be rather strictly ruled that Nahant's burial place is for Nahant's own people.

The Civil War Soldiers' Monument was erected in 1866, and the American Legion Monument, a great boulder from the shore of the town, with a bronze plate, was placed in 1920. In 1858 a committee, of which John Q. Hammond was chairman, laid out the cemetery into lots and pathways, and the report of their work is extant, filed with the town clerk in March, 1859. Almost at once the forefathers of the town were moved from the old ground near Pleasant Street to the new burial place. It is said that the first burial in the new place, except perhaps for these removals, was of Alonzo Colby, who died in 1858. A formal dedication of Greenlawn Cemetery was held in 1859.

The disinterested services of Thomas Roland in the planting of trees and shrubs have assisted toward the fine result now evident; and the good work of Thomas P. O'Connor as gardener, performed with enthusiasm and interest, is also contributory.

CHAPTER XVI

TRANSPORTATION

It is impossible to say when the first public carriage from Nahant to Lynn began service. The growing of the hotel business made definite transportation important. Jesse Rice, of the Rice House, later Whitney's Hotel, is said to have established the first line of public conveyance. He came to Nahant about 1817. Definite service is advertised soon after, as in the Lynn "Mirror," in 1826, it is stated that a coach will run from the Nahant Hotel twice a day, connecting with coaches for Boston and Salem. This, of course, was dependent upon the tides. N. P. Willis writes:

> Road to Nahant there is none. The hoi polloi go there by steam; but when the tide is down you may drive there with a thousand chariots over the bottom of the sea. There runs a narrow ridge, scarce broad enough for a horse path, impossible for the rocks and seaweed of which it is matted, and extending, at just high-water mark, from Nahant to the mainland. Seaward from this ridge descends an expanse of land, left bare six hours out of the twelve by the retreating sea, as smooth and hard as marble, and as broad as the plain of the Hermus. For three miles it stretches away without shell or stone, a surface of white, fine-grained sand beaten so hard by the external hammer of the surf that the hoof of a horse scarce marks it.

There appears to have been some amelioration for the delays and waits for the tides, for accounts speak enthusiastically of the excellence of the punch at the Lynn Hotel near the Common, where folks could sip and read and talk until time to go on. The lumbering coaches were slow, as people travel today, but it is said that B. C. Clark, mentioned elsewhere as the owner of swift yachts, also owned fast horses.

By keeping horses on Nahant, in Boston, and at a stop on the turnpike, he could get to Boston in an hour in a light sulky, and this compares favorably with time today. Many men travelled over the road, but of course the steamboats came to increasing use as they were improved in speed and in certainty of operation. Then came a poor road over the beach in the late 40's.

The post office at Nahant, beginning in 1847, at once required rather positive functioning for handling the mails. The first mail carrier appears to have been Captain Henry Dunham, who used a small one-horse wagon or carryall which would hold four or five passengers. Dunham was born in 1794 and followed the sea from early youth, reaching the rank of captain at the age of twenty-one. He was in the Merchant Marine, on vessels from Boston and New York to foreign parts. He is said to have been the first to raise an American flag in San Francisco. He transferred to the United States Navy and was wounded in the Mexican War and retired. Moving to Nahant he built a house at the corner of Prospect and High Streets, enlarged and remodelled in recent years for Robert Amory. He died on Nahant in 1877. His son, Henry T. Dunham, was highway surveyor for several years. He was born in 1825 and died in 1907. It is said that he lived in the Alfred D. Johnson Prospect Street house, now owned by F. L. Timmins, for a time, or until Johnson bought it after 1857, and then moved to a house owned by Tudor on Ocean Street, below the S. Martin Johnson house now standing there. When E. Francis Parker, in the late 60's, built the house now owned by Albert Thorndike, this house of Tudor's was moved to between Valley and Willow Roads on the same side of Ocean Street, and was still occupied by Henry T. Dunham. Then in the late 80's he built the house on Pond Street later owned by Martin Curran and now by his daughter. Captain Dunham, while driving across the railroad tracks in Lynn, was struck by a train. It is said he was carried on the front of the locomotive from near Market Street into the station, and he was so badly injured that he was an invalid for the rest of his life. This was about 1868.

Near this time (1868) two other men started in this business, Byron Goodell and Edmund B. Johnson. Goodell came to Nahant and settled permanently, continuing in the transportation business until the electric cars arrived. Several of his sons and daughters and their children now live in Nahant. His home for many years was on Ocean Street in one of three houses later moved back on Tudor Street. This house has seen its share of moving. It was built as a Tudor corn barn on what was later the Schlesinger estate, and then remodelled into a house facing toward Pond Street. Later, or soon after 1869, when Schlesinger bought, this house was moved to Ocean Street. Goodell used a stable, built by Tudor, on the upper side of Maolis Street, which burned in 1880, and afterwards had an extensive stable outfit in the same locality between Maolis Street and the present Nahant Club grass tennis courts, with an entrance from Ocean Street just northerly from the tennis courts. At times, he kept forty horses. This property, owned by Tudors, was finally all cleaned up, about the time that the Maolis Gardens remains were cleared away and the various spaces divided into house lots. Goodell then moved down to Summer Street, using the house on the corner of Willow Road and a large stable just above it. Byron Goodell died in 1904 at the age of seventy.

The other line of barges to Lynn, set up by Edmund B. Johnson, one of the old Nahant Johnson family, was sold out in 1880 to George W. Kibbey, who operated it until the coming of the electric road. Kibbey had stables near Whitney's and latterly about where Robertson's Garage now stands, and later built the stable on Wharf Street, now turned into a garage and operated by his son, George H. Kibbey. Kibbey died in 1915 at the age of seventy-four. Some time later a third line of barges was opened by Carahar Brothers, who were James A., William H. and Bernard F. Carahar, of whom the latter is the survivor. James A. Carahar served on the Board of Selectmen, but died in 1908 at the age of forty-eight. In

TRANSPORTATION 229

1896, when the extensive Simmons holdings on Nahant were sold at auction, Carahar Brothers bought a considerable section at Little Nahant, including the peak of the hill to which the old hotel was moved by them from over close to the Lynn line. A part of this Bernard F. Carahar has lately developed into a shore resort with dance hall, bathing accommodations and other usual accessories. Carahar Brothers barge line ran almost wholly to serve Bass Point, which had grown as a shore resort, and the other two lines served chiefly the main part of the town. The Goodell line had direct service from the Nahant Wharf, later called Tudor Wharf, to the Maolis Gardens, when that resort was in its heyday of glory.

These barges naturally grew from small beginnings to long, side-seated vehicles holding twenty-five or thirty people, and were as comfortable as such conveyances could be, though hardly measuring up to present-day standards. Often they used three or four horses, especially to climb the hill *en route* to the Maolis Gardens. In winter time there were pungs with similar arrangements, but smaller, as the traffic was not so heavy. Straw on the floors helped to keep feet warm, and later charcoal burners were used to give a little heat. A lantern, sometimes smoky and smelly, furnished a little light. The Goodell and Kibbey lines interlaced their trips so that in summer time there was half hour service, or nearly that, with times set to meet trains to and from Boston. In the latter days of this service the fare was fifteen cents, with tickets at seven or eight for a dollar. Some years earlier, in the 70's or 80's, people travelling back and forth daily were carried for a dollar a week.

Soon after 1900 a trial was made of a motor barge, but it was too early in motor car development, and its ability to maintain any schedule was too uncertain. In 1904 it was proposed in town meeting that the town apply for a special act of Legislature empowering it to subsidize these barge lines at a thousand dollars a year for each of the three, and thus enable them to improve the service. But the electric road was in sight and the scheme failed. The natural end of the barges was at hand, pushed aside, as has been many another business, by what is called the march of progress. The barges disappeared, sold to other places and used, perhaps, for carrying school children from districts too remote for walking to school. In such uses barges may be seen today. Nahant barges were sold in Plymouth and Georgetown for this purpose. The word "barge" as applied to these vehicles has been thought peculiar to Nahant, although the dictionary has long defined it with this as one of its applications. People have even thought, because they were told to ride in a barge, that they were to get to Nahant by water.

These barges did not give evening service. Around five o'clock was the last trip up from Nahant, and at about half past six the last conveyance left Lynn for Nahant. On Saturdays, and at times on another evening, there were trips up after supper, returning about nine or half past. The barges to Bass Point ran through the evenings to suit their patronage. One could, however, hire a barge for two dollars, or even for a dollar and a half, which would take a half dozen or so to Lynn, wait around all the evening, and cheerfully get home around midnight. This was the transportation which the electric cars supplanted, yet few people who lived amid these conditions will say that they were more annoying than another group of possible vexations is today. Life moves onward into complexities of invention and achievement, but none of such things is sure to move life upward toward greater content and harmony with the world.

The earliest mention of any possible railroad to Nahant appears to have been in 1845, when a group met at the Nahant Hotel to consider if anything could be done to improve the communication over Long Beach. A wide-open discussion seems to have resulted, and one of the factors is indicated by an item in the "Lynn Whig" of September 13, 1845: "A correspondent of the 'Transcript' states that the committee will probably report in favor of building upon this beach (Long Beach, Nahant) a branch for the Eastern Railroad."

It might be interesting to speculate on how far from its present state the town would now be if this plan had been adopted.

The first mention in the town records of a street railroad appears to have been in 1861, when on January 16 a town meeting was held because the Lynn and Boston Street Railroad Company had given notice that it would petition the State Legislature for permission to extend their lines to Salem, South Danvers and Nahant. A petition was presented to the selectmen and recorded under this meeting, asking that the town refuse its consent. It was signed by thirty-seven summer residents, many of whom were not voters in Nahant. This meeting was called for the consideration of this one question only, and the town voted to reject the proposal by a large majority. In 1884 an article was petitioned into the annual meeting warrant by F. E. Johnson and twenty-two others, to see if the town wanted a street railroad, and it was referred to the selectmen who were to confer with the railroad company to find what was proposed. In the meantime legislation was again sought by the company, and the legislative committee asked the town to find out, at its annual meeting in March, 1885, if it favored the petition of the Lynn and Boston Horse Railroad Company for a right to extend its tracks to Nahant. The matter was disapproved by a vote of 91 to 25. Then in 1886 came the petition of the Nahant Railroad Company for a steam railroad over Long Beach. At the March meeting this was rejected by a vote of 94 to 6.

During these proceedings Joseph T. Wilson, who had begun his long services for Nahant, became acquainted with the street railroad officials, who saw, by their repeated defeats, that the town did not want them. Then they said to Wilson that they might as well wait, and whenever the town was ready to receive them they would proceed further. Wilson had never been a strong opponent in his personal opinions, as frequently expressed, but was strongly against the scheme until the people wanted it by a large majority. In the 1884 town report he stated, for the selectmen, that better transportation to Nahant "is imperative." He believed, particularly, that the summer residents should not be opposed to it, because they paid most of the taxes through which the town prospered. The dangers of turning a town, which was attractive because it was a country town, into a suburb, made possible by easy communication with a city, and without many factors which kept Nahant financially well-to-do, were all foreseen. Yet it was believed, by Wilson and such other proponents as also appreciated or apprehended these dangers, that sufficient safeguards of other sorts than difficult access would keep the place at as great a height of attractiveness as would be possible in any event. Bass Point was even then presenting many problems to a town that would be well ordered and of good repute in every part, and it was believed that the railroad would bring in people who would strive to keep the town a beauty spot, while doubtless also bringing others who cared little for community welfare, and who might want "three flatters" on small lots, for example, or to develop further a shore resort business not compatible with a residential district.

Thus the railroad question hung fire until 1887, when again in town meeting the opinion of the voters, this time on an electric road, was obtained. There were 127 against it and 50 for it. At the annual town meeting in 1900 the question was raised again, and by a yea and nay vote it was decided to postpone consideration indefinitely. By this time the selectmen, of which Wilson was still chairman, had become convinced that the road was coming. A few men, some recent comers to Nahant, were working actively for it, and their success seemed probable. The summer residents had mostly become acquiescent, though not wholly convinced that the movement was for the good of the town. Their own wishes were not so important to them. While they liked Nahant they could leave it and choose other places more desirable. In March, 1903, the town again expressed its opinion, and this time it was in favor of an electric road by 120 to 88.

Then followed an interesting period. The summer residents, seeing that it was coming, proceeded to form a corporation,

Maolis Gardens — One of the Stone Lions

Tudor's High Fence around Orchard near Bear Pond, Bailey's Hill in Background

Fence in this tumbledown condition about 1885

the Nahant Street Railroad Company, capitalized at $30,000. This was because it was thought better for the interests of the town to keep financial control within the town. Here, for the first time, Wilson became directly interested, and for the reason just given. His son, Fred A. Wilson, and Ellerton James were active in the affairs of this proposed company. J. T. Wilson had, of course, been offered stock and other "reasonable" pay for his services in getting the town to consider favorably some of the adventures proposed, but he was always immune even to "perfectly fair forms of graft." In the meantime another company, the Nahant & Lynn Street Railroad Company, was organized, with a majority of the stock owned out of town. It was capitalized for a much smaller sum. A hearing was given by the selectmen to the two companies, on the same evening. But just before this hearing the Nahant Company had been to the head of the company operating in Lynn, asking if they would build or operate or both, and had been informed that the line would not pay and under no consideration would they handle it. A prominent firm of Boston engineers and men with practical experience had been employed to estimate the cost of the outfit, all installed and ready to run with hired power, and their report called for an expenditure of over $160,000. This was a decided advantage for the Lynn-owned company. At the hearing their representatives promised five-cent fares, as the stenographer's record of the proceedings shows, and several other benefits only to be had from a line doing well financially. The Nahant-owned company, armed with their real evidence, could only promise to do as well as any one, and when asked about five-cent fares (the usual fare at that time) could only say they did not believe it possible, for the road was going to cost well over $100,000. Whereupon from all over a crowded hall came cries and cat calls at the utter foolishness of supposing any such expenditure would be required.

There were people at that time who did not believe that the Nahant-owned company meant business. James A. Carahar circularized the town as a candidate for selectmen in 1904, and stated that "it is their purpose to prevent the railroad being built." But of the sincerity of this company there can be no question. They had the capital subscribed, had obtained preliminary estimates, attorneys were at work on the legal features, and interviews were frequent with street railroad people. They only withdrew from a conviction that the investment was not wise and that any advantage of a Nahant-owned company hardly compensated for the risk. As for the risk, let the stockholders of the company that did build it bear witness today, although many argue that other methods would have brought better results. Other factors have given trouble and lack of patronage, and those not willing to cloud their wisdom of 1904 will attribute all troubles to these. But any suitable sinking fund for depreciation and renewals was never set up, and could not be, even before the automobile and the prohibition era were playing a large part. The gross income was never large enough to permit this important financing, even with the heavily increased fares. It is evidence of the sincerity of the Nahant-owned company that they promptly gave up their franchise, when stalling tactics could have postponed matters for a year or two, and the selectmen as promptly and in perfectly good faith awarded it to the other company.

The selectmen believed that the Nahant-owned company was as well able to serve the town as the other, and would be more likely to be friendly to the town's interests if a pinch came, and so, disregarding the promises of the Lynn company, they awarded the franchise to the Nahanters. But the latter were faced with their surprises at the expenditure required, and after considering the question thoroughly they begged leave to withdraw. A committee composed of Thomas Motley, Sr., William A. Hayes and Fred A. Wilson wrote a final report to the subscribers for the stock and expressed the opinion that no street railroad to Nahant could pay well enough to justify the expenditure. All of these considerations, by the two companies, by hearings, and in all talk about town, were upon the assumption of the nominal fare of five cents. Promptly after the award of the franchise, the Lynn-owned company perfected their arrangements and built the road. The hearing for this was on February 28, 1905, and the franchise was awarded on the same date. The company agreed to certain specified trips and petitioned for track locations. This petition was signed by the directors, who were Edward E. Strout, Clifton Colburn, George W. Belonga, James A. Carahar, E. H. Brann, Charles Cabot Johnson and Walter H. Southwick. It will be noted that most of these men are Nahant men. Most of the money was from out of town men at this time, also, and the capitalization had been heavily increased, so that the cat calls of the crowded first hearing on the subject were proven to have shown only ignorance, which is what such procedure commonly signifies. Then came a rush to build the road in time for use in the coming season. Edward E. Strout, a contractor of experience, was an active man in this construction. He had come to Nahant to live, building nearly on the site of the "Old Castle" property. He died in 1915 at the age of fifty-nine. By valiant efforts the road was regularly opened for traffic on July 20, 1905, with an official car and guests in the afternoon and passenger service in the evening. A few years later it was double tracked from Mitchell's Corner to Bass Point, with the loop in the Relay House yard, and thus it came to its position of 1928.

There was so much discussion of the electric road at the time it was approved by the town that it is interesting to see how closely the road followed the scheme laid out for it twenty years earlier. In the town report for 1886 Wilson discusses the question at some length, and the following are quotations:

> The anxiety and solicitude of numerous people or companies, outside of our town, to furnish us with railroad communication with Lynn, is really meritorious when regarded from the standpoint of their persistency. There are now some four or five companies anxious to enter the town with their railroad projects. First we have a steam railroad, either broad or narrow gauge, — anything

to accomplish their object. A petition for an elevated electric road was disposed of by the legislative committee. A petition from the Lynn and Boston Horse Railroad Company is in the hands of the selectmen. A street railway company, with electricity for the motor, petitioned last fall for a location in our streets.

This question of a railroad over Long Beach is becoming an important one, and some solution of it may have to be met in the near future. To our minds the least objectionable of all the schemes presented would be a surface electric road located on the Lynn Harbor side of the beach as near as possible to the water line. Have it cross Castle Road, near the bridge, and thence extend over the marsh, across Flash Road, thence through the valley. Such a location would save our roads from obstruction. This would, we think, practically save our beautiful drive, one of the principal attractions of our town. The solving of this question should be dependent upon what will add to the prosperity of the town. With such an object in view we doubt not but what, when the people pass upon the question, it will be decided for the general good of all.

Here, twenty years before the road is built, is laid down the location which was followed, and statements which show full appreciation of the general trend which would finally bring about the adoption of the improved transportation.

Then came the automobile, in ever-increasing quantity. Among other things this meant an advance in the methods of producing forgings. Street railroad companies everywhere stood and watched this, still using for street cars the old-fashioned, heavy castings, yielding a car weighing many tons, to be driven back and forth at great expense for haulage. Finally came the automobile bus, and this forced the street car to take notice. It was a competitor. It never should have been, apparently, for it does not cost nearly as much to drive the same weight on steel wheels over steel rails as on rubber wheels over gravel or concrete roads. But all unnoticed the light-weight vehicle had crept into the field, and everywhere there was consternation among the street car companies. Several years ago Nahant had a special committee of investigation, and reported against the bus and in favor of the street car. The report was accepted. Perhaps it now remains for the street car to become practically a bus on tracks, and thus achieve the economies which the bus has shown. Let it be gasoline driven, if need be. Indeed, street car lines are trying it. Whatever the outcome, it is said the street cars, perhaps, may in some places recover ground foolishly lost by too great a dependence upon the monopoly afforded by an exclusive franchise. All of this was indicated, eight or ten years ago, in the committee report which is above mentioned. This would seem to be true at Nahant, provided Washington Street in Lynn may be kept clear enough to afford reasonable passage. Over the beach the tracks are not in the travelled road, and are therefore free from the nuisance of a badly clogged passageway in midsummer.

Of course, the railroad at once found it could not operate at the five-cent fare which had been so frequently mentioned, if not promised, and at once came protests. For several years, perhaps even up to now, people grumble about the fares. The important factor, however, was the service. A reasonable service was important, and is so today, while the fare must be enough to allow a reasonable profit and maintenance in good condition. The automobile decreases patronage, and a fare may be so high that income will diminish and the purpose be defeated. It was a curious incident of the cry for lower fares that some of those who came to Nahant because it was a pleasant country town joined in it. They removed from suburban districts because they wanted less crowded surroundings, and then wanted the usual fare which had made those districts suburban and crowded, and might be expected to do the same for Nahant. Avoiding the suburbs they shouted that Nahant also be one, although such was not their intent. They only acted mistakenly. There are those who cry selfish to whoever would like to keep Nahant a country town. As well cry selfish to those who would make it a thickly settled suburb. A person is not selfish who wishes to live in the country and who would like to keep the town of his adoption in that class. By restrictions of various sorts Nahant has yet the chance to be what she likes as a residential place, but steps forward must be taken or the choice will pass and the trend of events will control.

Transportation by steamboats is discussed in another chapter. This service afforded the easiest means of getting goods down from Boston. With the establishment of a definite express from Nahant to Boston the boats were used almost entirely during the summer season. Boat service was for a hundred days, or beginning late in May and ending early in September. There have been many express companies doing service in Nahant, but the only one needing mention is the old Johnson's Express, founded by Alfred D. Johnson and his cousin Jesse R. Johnson. Johnson's Nahant Express was almost a Nahant institution, and almost "no man knoweth when it was not." It appears to have been started soon after Alfred Johnson's return from California — he was a forty-niner. This makes it an early express, as it is only twelve or fifteen years before that Harnden started what is said to be the first express doing that business and no other. The old stage coaches carried goods and passengers and the coach drivers did errands. On the death of its founder in 1890, Johnson's Nahant Express was taken over by Francis B. Crocker, who came to Nahant some years before to work for Johnson. He owned and managed it until 1923, when he stopped the service. Crocker was for years chief engineer of the Nahant Fire Department, and a well-known man of Nahant. He died in 1924, at the age of seventy-three, leaving a family, some of whom are residents of the town. Jesse R. Johnson did not stay in this business, so that few associate his name with it. On October 25, 1890, there was a special town meeting to fill the office of town clerk, made vacant by the death of the long-time town clerk, Alfred D. Johnson, who died on October 14. Resolutions were offered by H. C. Lodge, commending the faithful service of the former town clerk, one paragraph of which reads as follows:

> During all but three years of the life of the town, Mr. Johnson has served as town clerk, being chosen thereto at thirty-four

annual elections. The long term of office indicates not only the worth of his service, but the appreciation of his fellow citizens for his character, and for the manner in which he performed his duty. He served the town with zeal and fidelity, and his accuracy and punctuality, as well as his unfailing attendance at every town meeting, are well known to all his fellow citizens, and were rightly valued by them.

CHAPTER XVII

SCHOOLS

The first school in Nahant was in a room in the old Hood homestead, elsewhere mentioned. An old resident of Nahant, quoted by E. J. Johnson, writes that it was kept for twelve weeks in winter, and that his teacher was Nancy Carter. This room was always called the "School Room." When it began its service is not known. E. B. Johnson places it well back before 1780, or perhaps to the time when only the Hoods and Breeds had children to attend school. This was outgrown and superseded by the little red schoolhouse nearly across Nahant Road from the present Town Hall, on what is now the Sigourney estate. This house was earlier a shoemaker's shop. The seats were benches around the sides, with the teacher's table at one end. Here were accommodations for about thirty scholars. Clarissa Herrick was the first teacher in this building, and she married Richard Hood, son of Richard Hood who built the Hood Hotel, later the Rice House on Nahant Road, across from Wharf Street. The next teacher was Betsey Graves, who taught from 1812 to 1816, and who married Joseph Johnson in 1819. From a journal which she kept we have a list of the pupils in 1812, as follows:

Joseph Johnson.	Clarissa A. Johnson.
Jonathan Johnson.	George A. Hood.
Francis Johnson.	Harriet Organs.
Eliza Johnson.	David B. Mudge.
Pamela Johnson.	Albert Newel.
Mary Johnson.	Thomas Rich.
Welcome W. Johnson.	Priscilla Hitchings.
George L. Johnson.	

These Johnsons are all children of Caleb and Joseph Johnson, who were brothers and sons of the original Nahant Johnson.

Thomas Handasyd Perkins

Amos A. Lawrence

James H. Beal
1823–1904

Frank Merriam
1850–1923

Besides these pupils, entered as permanent scholars, there were transients, — Thomas and Amos Bulfinch, George and Henry Stone, Malinda Howard, Augustus Breed, Thomas and Otis Stone, Mary Stone and Nabby Breed. Here appears a considerable number of Stones, but the family seems not to have remained in Nahant.

Then in 1818-19 the "Old Stone Schoolhouse" was built, close to Pleasant Street, nearly across the road from the house now owned and occupied by William F. Waters, longtime town clerk. This was made from pasture stone and was about twenty-five feet square with a hip roof. There was a window on each side and two in the front, on each side of the entrance door. A sketch of this schoolhouse, hanging in the Public Library, was made in 1895 from a verbal description given by Edmund B. Johnson. The latter said that this building was erected chiefly through the interest of William Wood, who founded the library in this same year. The facts are not clear, except that from Wood's known interest in public libraries, it would seem likely that he was more interested in this building as a library than as a school. For many years it served the little village as church and hall, library and school, the public meeting place of the town. There was a bell in the cupola with the bell rope dropping down into the center of the schoolroom. Children of summer residents attended, at least while the Rev. Samuel J. May was a teacher. Here, so says May, as recorded in the "Life of Samuel Joseph May," published in 1873, the great historian Motley learned to read. It is said that Charles W. Eliot, famous Harvard University president, was also a student. He was a son of Samuel A. Eliot, who owned the Mifflin house. There was a sort of prudential committee that used to control the school, collecting the small sum allowed by Lynn for its maintenance, and soliciting more from those whose children attended it. For long years Joseph Johnson was a leader on this committee.

In 1851 this building was torn down and on the same site was erected the two-room wooden building which so many

Nahanters can remember and in which they attended school. It was dedicated on September 16, 1851. It is said to have been notable for a new system of ventilation, and was considered a thoroughly modern school building. For a time the upper floor was the schoolroom and the lower floor was an assembly room, but in 1853 a second school was established, so there were primary and grammar schools. Apparently the lower room was used also as an assembly room until the Town Hall was built in 1868. This school building had a cupola with the old bell hung in it from the "Old Stone Schoolhouse." It had double entrances with separate stairways and coat rooms for boys and girls. It was a comfortable commodious structure, up to the limit of its accommodations, and served the town well until the Valley Road schoolhouse was built. The old stone schoolhouse, and at first this newer one, only occupied a small plot of land, leaving not over ten feet all around the later and larger building. In 1854 the town bought the lot of about a half acre on Pleasant Street adjoining this smaller lot, and which is the school yard familiar in recent years. In 1853, the first year of Nahant as a separate township, a cellar and furnace were added to the school building. The town apparently began in 1858 to buy school books for the use of pupils.

In 1875 the small hall on the first floor of the Town Hall was set aside for school purposes, and a high school was established of which Charles J. Hayward was the first principal. This room remained about as originally equipped, until a little later the small anteroom on the second floor was used as a recitation room. Still later, in 1887, an addition was put on the rear of the Town Hall, affording a larger recitation room and other spaces for Town Hall purposes. And in a few years followed the one-story addition extending toward the Public Library and used as a police court room. This brings the old Town Hall to the condition it holds at present.

In 1880 a fourth schoolroom was established in hired quarters on Summer Street. This was the primary school, and a regrading of the three lower schools brought the system into

SCHOOLS 243

correlation with the high school, which was flourishing. In 1883 a new grammar schoolhouse was erected, up on Nahant Road near High Street, on land owned by the town and now a part of the cemetery grounds. This allowed the primary school to move from Summer Street into the Pleasant Street school building, and the arrangements continued until the completion of the Valley Road schoolhouse, in 1905. This building absorbed all the grades and the high school. The grammar school building was given over to the police department. The older building on Pleasant Street was torn down. The room in the old Town Hall building was left idle, and finally used as a basket ball room. Then in 1916 came the school building on Nahant Road, named the J. T. Wilson School, in honor of the man who for so many years headed the school department.

The long list of teachers needs no special mention except for a few of them. A list of men teachers is given for reference purposes, up to 1900, as frequently some one asks about them:

1854–55 . . . E. G. Partridge.	1879 . . . G. H. Eldredge.
1856–60 . . . Luther Dame.	1880 . . . G. H. Eldredge.
1861 . . . Luther Dame.		A. H. Kenerson.
J. Wesley Boyden.	1881 . . . A. H. Kenerson.
1862–63 . . . J. Wesley Boyden.	1882 . . . A. H. Kenerson.
1864 . . . G. A. Southworth.		W. P. Hood.
Wm. Reed, Jr.	1883 . . . W. P. Hood.
1865 . . . Wm. Reed, Jr.	1884–86 . . . Geo. M. Strout.
1866–67 . . . E. N. Smith.	1887 . . . Geo. M. Strout.
1868 . . . E. N. Smith.		A. E. Briggs.
E. H. Jose.	1888 . . . A. E. Briggs.
1869 . . . E. H. Jose.		C. L. Judkins.
H. H. Scott.	1889–90 . . . C. L. Judkins.
1872 . . . H. H. Scott.	1891 . . . C. L. Judkins.
H. D. Wyatt.		H. R. White.
H. V. King.	1892–94 . . . H. R. White.
1873 . . . E. C. Carrigan.	1895 . . . H. R. White.
C. J. Hayward.		A. B. Crawford.
1874–77 . . . C. J. Hayward.	1896 . . . A. B. Crawford.
1878 . . . C. J. Hayward.		O. A. Tuttle.
G. H. Eldredge.	1897–1900 . . . O. A. Tuttle.

There are three long-time and well-known teachers who may be mentioned. Miss Carrie V. Hammond taught from

1873 to 1914. Miss Florence A. Johnson began in 1881 and resigned in 1927. Both of these, upon their retirement, were honored by the people of the town, who tendered them receptions and gifts, in appreciation of their long usefulness. Miss Nellie M. Palmer taught from 1879 to 1904, the year of her death, and was loved and honored as a teacher of the little beginners of life. Miss Hammond is a daughter of John Q. Hammond, prominent in town affairs in early days. Miss Johnson is a daughter of Edward J. Johnson, who likewise was a town official and who was a lifelong resident of Nahant. Miss Johnson did notable work in encouraging the study of birds and flowers. An herbarium, prepared at one time, won a medal when exhibited at the Massachusetts Horticultural Society. It is now in the Nahant Public Library. These three Nahanters, in public school service, belie the old rule that local people are not the best for such positions, for they have done hard and faithful work full of good results. There is always a desire, in any locality, for residents of the place to fill public positions. It is convenient, and, of course, the applicants may be as fit as any others. But it is not commendable practice. Honest people do their best always, but there is an unconscious though real reliance upon a background of friends, able to bring more or less pressure upon public officials, which halts incentive a little. In the schools there is the possibility of hearings and a natural dislike of a school committee to make a stir over a resident in a small town. These factors may never take shape, but they are always in the wind. A teacher should, then, even for his own sake, seek employment away from home, where his full efforts are enlisted, and nothing else. There is more character building of young people by getting away from home and out on their own feet altogether. These successes for Nahant, as mentioned, do not affect the principle, for that was good luck rather than good practice. A school committee should always be able to say good-bye to a teacher with the least fuss and feathers. They are the judges of inefficiency or lack of co-operation. They should be able to say they want instructions obeyed. Of course, the committee may be wrong, but as some one must have power in the department, who is it to be? Some one elected for the purpose or some one acquiring the power in another way?

The various yearly reports of the school committee are interesting, but too long and numerous to be quoted extensively. It is rather curious to note that in 1872 J. T. Wilson, writing the school report, cites the need of training for proper use of leisure. This is a factor of education emphasized recently, and this reference to it of over fifty years ago has its significance. It reads as follows:

> We have already seen the hours of manual labor universally reduced, and it cannot be supposed that this decrease in the requirements of time for labor is at an end. Our hours of leisure are to increase, and for what? Upon the solution of this question depends our destiny.

All through these years the school committees have tried to steer clearly through the many issues of education, leaning not too far back lest they become unprogressive; nor too far forward to meet the latest erratic experiment. It is always a task. Between the fine arts and the useful arts, the vocational and the academic, the major and minor, the three "R's" and a widespread feast of learning, the humdrum and the imaginative, a rational course is hard to steer. Today outcries against educational methods are stronger than ever, for special reasons apparently not traceable directly to unusual educational inefficiency. Many still insist on drill, drill, drill, and many would even teach integral calculus before arithmetic, because the child should have the more imaginative during its more imaginative years. Until some of these things are settled, educational peace is not expected. The diapason of discordant voices at least shows divergences of opinion proving no clear road forward. An education that is "good behavior to the young, comfort to the old, riches to the poor and decoration to the rich" is certainly not abroad among the schools and colleges so largely as wanted and needed. The education of today, with its improperly digested accessories, is what leads so many men to lives of quiet desperation. Cures are possible but slow in arriving. Everywhere there is talk, but educators plod along, unheeding, mostly, the cries from obvious injury. Common sense is supplanted by a supersense, which is desirable as a team mate, but needing a harness and guiding reins or it cannot pull the load or find the right direction, and Phi Beta Kappa keys worn in a proper pectoral position are not sure guides to efficient leaders.

In a little town like Nahant the schools can step out in new adventures somewhat more easily than in larger places. Yet the greater need is for a steady policy without vacillations from pillar to post. Every change might well be for a while an effort to correct an identified fault, and never a mere branching into some new ism decorated with the gold lace and filigree of further theorizing. Theory is important, but in education the most important thing is, why is so large a proportion of people careworn and harassed? It is not an inevitable condition of mankind since Eve's fall, for enough in every condition of life are not so to prove its needlessness for most, unless misfortune overtakes them. Meantime, Obedience, Consideration and Concentration — three needs of people at work and living together — languish and fade. This is all old, very much as the faults of the flapper are revealed in the Old Testament. But old things are not necessarily outworn. Certain life values persist unchanging, — the verities; others shift about with the years and generations. What does education do to classify them for those who need to know the differences? Education is properly assimilated information. What about the assimilation? People are getting information the way the automobilist saw Rome, remembering it as that old burg where the roads were so rough. Of what use is the information or the visit to Rome? This preachment is, of course, not directed at Nahant schools, but at schools and schooling in general. Incidentally let every one be urged to read or reread Batchelder's "Keeping Up With Lizzie," a real compendium of economics and sociology applicable to present-day conditions, and a good story delivering a sermon without the "hard reading" which for many people attends any real study. Living is like a radio outfit. If it is not tuned in correctly not many stations can be reached, although the pleasures are all there waiting to be enjoyed.

In the fall of 1914 the Nahant High School was given up, following a vote of the town at a special town meeting in the previous June. The two last years were taken at the Lynn high schools, and the Nahant school became a junior high school adjusted as soon as possible to fit its pupils to step without trouble into the Lynn school system. In the fall of 1919 another class was sent to Lynn, giving three years of schooling in Lynn. This change was made because the Nahant High School was expensive and yet not getting commensurate value. It was too small. Not only was the cost deemed disproportionate to the results, but there were clear advantages in the pupils' contact with larger groups in larger schools. This connection seems now to be an undisputed part of the Nahant school procedure. The town pays tuition and transportation. It may be noted that this move to use the Lynn high schools was of much earlier origin. In 1893, and again in 1894, the school committee proposed to give up the high school at Nahant, and even said when it might be done, — a year or two later. But the transportation problem of the time made the plan too difficult, and it was abandoned. The town reports for these years tell about it. There is now more or less transportation about town, particularly from Little Nahant, which is the section farthest away from the school buildings. At times there has been a tendency to overdo this, but it is natural in these days when good housing demands that the garage door be not over twenty feet from the front door. Old Nahanters remember walking from anywhere in town, Little Nahant then having practically no homes sending children to school, down to Pleasant Street, where all the schools were located. This was two round-trip walks a day, and the weather seemed not the hindrance it is in these modern days. Either winters are more severe now, or the children are feebler, or the modern way decreases the sickness and death toll. There were no devices for drying wet clothing in the older days, so that in a comparison of all factors it would seem parents were then running a grave risk in allowing their children to go to school at all. Charles A. Hammond, son of John Q. Hammond, writes that for three years beginning in 1862 he attended the Lynn High School and walked back and forth each day to his home on Pond Street. The seven or eight mile walk appears to have done no harm, as this year (1928) finds him hale, and interested to tell his recollections of old Nahant, — memories which reach back to the early 50's.

Nahanters over forty-five or fifty years old remember the great high school "exhibitions" closing the school year in February. This was graduation and promotion time for all schools, but the climax was the high school graduation in the old Town Hall, which was always jammed to the doors, — perhaps the only time in the year when its size was inadequate. Declamations, essays, valedictories, music and other accompaniments of such occasions were turned on full blast. Many a boy, and perhaps girl, learned enough of standing before an audience to face a town meeting in later years. The old programs were very choice to those whose names appeared on them, and the participants were proud of their parts and did them well. Long drilling made real orators for the moment, and applause was heavy from good-natured audiences. In fact, the time needed for the preparation of these exhibitions was finally their undoing. It was decided that too much was lost from the curriculum work in the school system. The day of days was modified and softened until it seemed tame in comparison. In 1897 the closing of the school year was shifted to June, to conform to common practice, and to avoid the great summer vacation as an interlude breaking into a school year of work. About this same time it became necessary to have a superintendent of schools, and O. A. Tuttle, then master of the high school, was the first school superintendent for Nahant, a position which he occupied from 1897 until his resignation and removal from town in 1908.

Amusement Park of Late Sixties

Sea side of Long Beach, near Lynn line

Eastern Part of Nahant, 1856

Showing residents

SCHOOLS

In 1875 the town made a special appropriation called "education" for a free lecture course during the winter. This was a series of a half dozen or so lectures in the Town Hall. The course was engineered by the school committee and was continued each year. The winter of 1885-86 was the last year of them. They were omitted in 1878-79, apparently because of larger than usual expenditures in other directions. This was the time of great lecturers, and lecture courses and lyceums were common in cities and towns. On Nahant these were always well attended and a packed hall was the expected condition even in severe weather. Perhaps they might be called a forerunner of adult educational methods, of which more is heard in recent years. It is certain that Nahanters enjoyed and appreciated them. One of the prominent lecturers of that time was Colonel Russell H. Conwell, who came to Nahant frequently, and oldtimers remember his famous lecture, "Acres of Diamonds," which he delivered so many thousands of times that it is said to have enabled him to found the college which he headed for so long in Philadelphia. This has been published in book form, with some history of it, and may be obtained from the Nahant Public Library. Finally, in town meeting, some one raised a question as to the legality of town appropriations for such a purpose. The money could have been added to the Public Library expenditure, as this department has rather a free hand in spending public money for widespread educational purposes. But in any event, the day of those great lecture courses, with competent men touring the country to deliver them, was passing. It was increasingly difficult to arrange such a group as Nahanters wanted. Therefore they were dropped, and many people sorely missed what had been pleasure, profit and inspiration to their lives. Even the children profited, and the front row of seats was always filled with young folks not accompanied by parents, who were thus grouped together under the watchful eye of the chairman of the school committee, who introduced the speaker, announced the next event, and sat on the platform, able to quell any noisy fidgeting which the boys and girls might begin, to the annoyance of the rest of the audience. No doubt such an annual course of lectures would prove a good addition to the town's educational system today, but the heavily mounting expenses in other directions are too alarming to make this sort of thing an allurement to those who study town finances.

The school department annual expenses stayed under $2,000 until the early 70's. They did not exceed $4,000 until 1879, nor $5,000 until 1892, creeping a little over $7,000 in 1900. Further gradual increase ran them over $8,500 first in 1910, and over $10,000 first in 1915. In 1915 was the largest single year jump up to that time, amounting to nearly $3,000, reaching a total expenditure of slightly over $12,000. The salary list was increased about $2,200. From 1915 onward came heavy increases caused by many things, but no one item exceeds the salary increases which have been about $1,100 since 1915. The year 1920 saw an expenditure of over $20,000, and in 1922 it went over $30,000, since which time the town seems to have become accustomed to these large figures. With an appropriation increased to thirty times the figures of early days the school population has increased six or eight times. Do the children make better men, women and citizens? If not, there are faults to be corrected. If the schools are not turning out a bettered product the money is poorly spent. No doubt they are doing as well in Nahant as in schools elsewhere, but when educators see trouble and are at war with each other on its fundamental causes, the layman can only lament and hope for better things. A recent book by a prominent educational expert even bears the title, "What's Wrong with American Education," and this sort of thing arouses suspicion that inefficiency exists. The higher salary list is more than compensatory for increased living costs, and should provide better teachers. In fact, still higher salaries and still greater other expenditures would be entirely justified for Nahant, or any town, provided there was some assurance of a corresponding increase in efficiency of operation and quality of output. Educators are studying their problems eagerly, but too often pass important factors slightingly; for example, certain things are not taught in the homes as they should be. The schools have taken up health questions even where they should be adjusted by the homes; but in some phases of training it is common to find them starting out from what the home ought to do, instead of what the home does do. Too often they say of some item that it is not their job but the home's job.

A school physician for Nahant was established by vote of the town in October, 1906. Until within a few years the position was filled by Dr. Lawrence F. Cusick, a Nahanter mentioned elsewhere. In 1921 a school nurse was appointed, who has given valuable assistance since then to the building up of children out of condition. In 1913 the town passed a curfew law keeping children off the streets after early evening. The fire alarm system sounds it at a quarter of nine each evening, and doubtless many people believe it to be only a daily testing of the alarm system. The law itself, however, should certainly not be considered more honored in the breach than the observance, and there is need for its enforcement today.

In April, 1906, the school committee appointed a special committee to supervise decoration in the new Valley Road School building. It was composed of Mrs. Alice C. Wilscn, Mrs. Alice C. McIntosh and Miss Marion G. Lees. The first two were Nahant residents mentioned elsewhere, and the latter was one of the corps of school teachers. They developed a careful plan for pictures and other material, fitted to the various grades, using a town appropriation and getting many gifts. The committee continued its work for a few years with good results. One item of the decorations may be mentioned. A pair of old marble pilasters came from the "Old Stone Schoolhouse," and were given by William Wood when he was collecting books for the Nahant Library. Another item, not used, is the old bell from the same old building. This is in the Valley Road School building in storage. It was taken out and pounded with a hammer or axe in celebration of the Armstice ending the World War in 1918, and was cracked.

It should be mended, mounted in a frame, and used once a day or once a week to summons the school to some assembly, and to remind them of a century ago.

The school department began Americanization courses in 1921 and a school sewing system in 1922. The former is subject to the same faults as are common everywhere, partly that those most needing this help are not reached. Much good is done, however. The Parent Teachers Association was started in 1914, and, as is common everywhere, has had vigorous years and inert years. The good of such is commensurate to the effort put into them, and they may be a good adjunct to the school system.

It remains to speak of medals. In 1916 George Abbot James founded the Lowland Medal, named after Lowland, his estate at East Point. Dies were provided and a fund to carry it on indefinitely. The first medal was presented to the Nahant Public Library, as that institution affords the best place in town for exhibition purposes. The medal is in control of the school committee, and the presentation is made each year by Dr. Lawrence F. Cusick. It is given solely for proficiency in mental arithmetic. Then there is the medal of the National Society of Colonial Daughters, arranged through the interest of Mrs. Louis Curtis, and given each year for the best patriotic essay. This was first given in 1918. The Washington and Franklin Medal of the Massachusetts Society of Sons of the American Revolution was given first in 1920. Then in recognition of excellence in conduct Mrs. Lawrence F. Cusick gave a cup, beginning in 1922, to the class with the best record for the year. Mrs. Cusick was elected to the school committee in 1921 and served one three-year term, and then retired. Other prizes of various sorts could be mentioned, but they were more temporary. During the World War, Ellerton James gave a war savings stamp to pupils learning short poems out of a selected list, and many pupils became familiar in this way with a little good poetry which was not above their appreciation and enjoyment.

In the middle of 1921, at a special town meeting, it was

decided to have a school committee of six, instead of three, as had been the rule ever since the town was founded. It continues as six to the present day. The three additional members were elected at the annual meeting in 1922.

Among the unhygienic things to which parents subjected their children in earlier days were the common drinking cup and the slate. Many remember the pump and its ladle at the Pleasant Street school yard, near the street line, drawing water from a "good well." As for the slate, nearly every middle-aged person recalls it. About ten by fourteen inches, framed in wood, with the wood covered with red flannel to prevent noise. A wet sponge was supposed to clean it, but fingers wet in the mouth usually supplied a sponge deficiency. Even in 1926 two million of these were sold, throughout the country, but during the 90's annual sales often reached twenty-five million.

Thus is given a glimpse of many changes, not all for the better. Needs are not always met squarely, in these days when some folks want no Ten Commandments, while others are sore because there are not more. The law of the harvest, says one writer, is to reap where you sow. Sow an act and reap a habit; sow a habit and reap a character; sow a character and reap a destiny. Today, as another puts it, too many are mentally starving on a diet as nourishing to the mind as chewing gum to the body; infinite motion, but no sustenance. Educators have many problems.

CHAPTER XVIII

THE NEW TOWN

THE separation of Nahant from Lynn was not simple. Argument and persuasion and applications to the State Legislature extended over several years before the efforts to make a new town were successful. Perhaps the first of it was in 1842, when Jonathan Johnson and others petitioned the Legislature to "set off Nahant as a separate town." Lynn opposed it, though Lynn had seen several towns sheared away from the old Third Plantation, the last one being Swampscott, in 1852.

The act of incorporation reads as follows:

The Commonwealth of Massachusetts

In the Year One Thousand Eight Hundred and Fifty-three

AN ACT TO INCORPORATE THE TOWN OF NAHANT.

Be it enacted by the Senate and House of Representatives in General Court assembled, and by the authority of the same, as follows:

SECTION 1. That portion of the city of Lynn lying southerly of a line commencing upon the long beach leading to Nahant, at the sign post which gives the length of said beach, thence running westerly in a straight line at right angles with the course of said beach southerly from said sign post to low water mark, and running easterly from said sign post in a straight line at right angles with the course of said beach as aforesaid to low water mark, is hereby incorporated into a town by the name of Nahant, and the inhabitants of said town are hereby invested with all the powers and privileges and shall be subjected to the duties and requisitions of other incorporated towns according to the constitution and laws of the Commonwealth.

SECTION 2. The inhabitants of said town of Nahant shall be holden to pay all arrears of taxes which have been assessed upon them by the city of Lynn before the passing of this Act, and also their proportion of all county and state taxes that may be assessed upon said city previously to the taking of the next state valuation, said proportion to be ascertained and determined by the last valuation of said city of Lynn, exclusive of the valuation upon that portion of territory which now comprises the town of Swampscott, and said town of Nahant shall be holden to pay their proportion of the debts due and owing at the time of the passage of this act, from the city of Lynn, and be entitled to receive of the city of Lynn their proportion of corporate property now owned by said city of Lynn, such proportion to be ascertained and determined by the last valuation of said city of Lynn, exclusive of the valuation of Swampscott as aforesaid.

SECTION 3. Said city of Lynn and the town of Nahant shall be respectively liable for the support of all persons who now do or hereafter shall stand in need of relief as paupers, whose settlement was gained or derived from a settlement gained or derived within their respective limits.

SECTION 4. In case said city of Lynn and town of Nahant shall disagree in respect to a division of paupers, city property, city debts, or state and county taxes, the court of common pleas for the county of Essex are hereby authorized to and shall on application of said city of Lynn or of said town of Nahant appoint three disinterested persons to hear the parties and award thereon; which award when accepted by said court shall be final.

SECTION 5. The town of Nahant shall for the purpose of electing representatives to the general court to which the territory comprised in the city of Lynn is now entitled, until another appointment of representatives be made, remain a part of the said city of Lynn: and the inhabitants of said Nahant shall vote for the number of representatives which the city authorities of Lynn may decide shall be elected annually in town meeting; and it shall be the duty of the selectmen of said Nahant to preside at said town meeting and receive the votes; and the certificate thereof shall be made by the selectmen and certified by the town clerk of said Nahant, whose duty it shall be to make return thereof to the mayor and alderman of the said city of Lynn, within forty eight hours of the day of voting; and the votes so returned shall be counted by the said mayor and alderman as a part of the vote of said city of Lynn.

SECTION 6. Any justice of the peace in the county of Essex is hereby authorized to issue his warrant to any principal inhabitant of the town of Nahant, requiring him to warn the inhabitants of the town of Nahant to meet at a time and place therein appointed for the purpose of choosing all such town officers as towns are by law authorized and required to choose at their annual meeting.

SECTION 7. This act shall take effect from and after its passage.

HOUSE OF REPRESENTATIVES, March 28, 1853.

Passed to be enacted.

GEO. BLISS,
Speaker.

IN SENATE, March 29, 1853.

Passed to be enacted.

C. H. WARREN,
President.

March 29, 1853, approved.

JOHN H. CLIFFORD.

In accordance with the authority given by section 6 of the above act, Welcome W. Johnson, Justice of the Peace, issued the following warrant to Washington H. Johnson. These are two of the old Nahant Johnson family, sons of Caleb and Joseph, respectively, as told elsewhere.

COMMONWEALTH OF MASSACHUSETTS.

ESSEX, ss:

To WASHINGTON H. JOHNSON *of Nahant in said County,*

GREETING:

In the name of the Commonwealth of Massachusetts you are hereby required forthwith to warn the inhabitants of Nahant qualified as the law directs to assemble at the schoolhouse on Saturday, the ninth day of April next at three o'clock P.M., by posting copies of this warrant in at least two conspicuous places in said town of Nahant, there and then to act upon the following business, viz.:

1st. To choose a moderator.
2d. To choose a town clerk.
3d. To choose three, five, seven, or nine selectmen.
4th. To choose three or more assessors.
5th. To choose three or more overseers of the poor.
6th. To choose a town treasurer.

Joseph T. Wilson and Senator Lodge

About 1910

George Abbot James and Joseph T. Wilson

Fiftieth anniversary celebration, 1903

7th. To choose a school committee of three or more.
8th. To choose one or more surveyors of highways.
9th. To choose one or more constables.
10th. To choose one or more tything men.
11th. To choose one or more field drivers.
12th. To choose one or more fence viewers.
13th. To choose one or more surveyors of lumber.
14th. To choose one or more measurers of wood and bark.

15th. To transact any other business that may properly come before said meeting and that may be necessary for the organization of the town of Nahant, and to secure a division and settlement with the city of Lynn in relation to the public property and public debt. Hereof fail not and make due returns of this warrant with your doings thereon to me on or before said ninth day of April next.

Given under my hand and seal at said Nahant in said county this first day of April, A.D. 1853.

      Signed WELCOME W. JOHNSON,
             Justice of the Peace.

NAHANT, SS.   APRIL 6, 1853.

I have served this within warrant by posting up attested copies of the same in two conspicuous places in said town seven days before holding this meeting.

              W. H. JOHNSON.

This warrant was originally drawn to Dexter Stetson. Then his name was crossed out and that of Washington H. Johnson substituted. Probably the six or eight or more prime movers for the new town met together and set up the procedure to be followed. If Stetson was slated to be a selectman, to which position he was elected, perhaps it was thought best to have another handle the warrant, and especially the one apparently slated to be town clerk.

There were twenty-eight votes cast. Walter Johnson was chosen moderator, getting nine votes, while William F. Johnson received seven votes. Walter Johnson, son of Joseph Johnson, is best known for his long service as highway surveyor. He owned and occupied the place on Nahant Road, at the corner of Harmony Court, until his death in 1897. This is the place bought, soon after, by Edward Follen and now occupied by his family. William F. Johnson was a son of Caleb Johnson, and father of T. Dexter Johnson, mentioned elsewhere. This first town meeting then chose Washington H. Johnson, town clerk. He received twenty-one votes with no opposition. It was voted to elect three selectmen, and a majority rule was followed. On the first ballot seven men received votes, though only four had more than one each. William F. Johnson led, with twenty-eight. He seems to have been a unanimous choice. Dexter Stetson had twenty-seven, a unanimous choice if he did not vote for himself. Artemus Murdock and Francis Johnson each had thirteen. The first two were declared elected. On the second ballot twenty-seven votes were cast, of which Murdock again received thirteen, while Johnson dropped to nine and John Q. Hammond had five. On the third ballot Murdock had nineteen and was declared elected, while Johnson had one. Welcome W. Johnson was chosen town treasurer, receiving all twenty-eight votes. Walter Johnson, Welcome W. Johnson and John Q. Hammond were chosen school committee, with three other men also candidates. Alonzo Colby was chosen highway surveyor. Five constables were elected and three fence viewers, three surveyors of lumber and three surveyors of wood and bark. There were some duplications, or there might have been difficulty in finding men enough to fill the offices. The first auditing committee was E. G. Partridge, Phineas Drew and Francis Johnson. The important committee to settle financial affairs with Lynn was the selectmen, with John Q. Hammond and Washington H. Johnson. The records of this and other early town meetings are written in the good handwriting of the town clerk of the new town, and start with the act of incorporation, followed by a copy of the warrant.

A week later, on April 16, came the second town meeting, at which appropriations were made, totalling $5,600. The school appropriation was $700 and the highway and bridges was $600. The treasurer was authorized to borrow not over $1,500. A committee was chosen, to bring in by-laws, consisting of John Q. Hammond, Jesse Rice and Joseph Johnson.

The selectmen were authorized to take all legal measures to protect Long and Short Beaches. The library was placed in control of the school committee. This meeting was also at the schoolhouse. The sum of $200 was appropriated to "finish the Town Hall." This meant equipment for this lower room in the school building, which evidently was somewhat unsuitable, for the session adjourned to meet April 23 in the vestry of the Village Church. At this adjourned meeting by-laws were adopted, one of which fixed the annual town meeting at the second Saturday in March. Another, under police regulations, reads that "no disorderly children shall misspend their time in the streets or fields during school hours." This third meeting, or adjourned second meeting, closed with a vote that the selectmen insert an article in the next warrant to "see about a burial place."

The third warrant was for a town meeting on May 4, at which fire wardens and field driver were chosen. The most important business appears to have been the choice of a committee on cemetery, consisting of David Johnson, Dexter Stetson and Walter Johnson.

On June 24, 1853, the assessors returned a list of available militiamen as enrolled by them. There are forty-three names, of which seventeen are Johnsons. Except for these Johnsons only three names have representatives now on Nahant, or owning property here, — Albert Whitney, Alonzo Colby and Charles H. Palmer. Palmer is the father of Nellie M. Palmer, elsewhere mentioned, and of Mrs. Frank G. Phillips, long-time Nahanter. A few others have lived here within the easy recollection of many Nahanters. Henry T. Dunham, Dexter Stetson and Samuel Covell are three — perhaps the latest three.

The fourth warrant was for a town meeting on August 20. The important business was to appropriate money for a cellar under the schoolhouse, and a suitable heating apparatus for the building. A letter from Frederic Tudor was read by which he offered money from the sale of garden products to establish a fund, of which the income should be used to care for trees and to plant new trees. He enclosed a certificate for two shares of Eastern Railroad stock as a beginning of the fund. A vote of thanks was given to Tudor for his "exertions in improving and embellishing the town, and especially for his gift to the town." It was voted that the town accept the Tudor fund and that the selectmen act as trustees of it. Here is the origin of those two shares of railroad stock which have appeared upon the town's published list of assets for so many years that perhaps no one knew how the town happened to have them. The income has not been rigorously applied to the specific purpose, but in most years the town has voted money, in excess of income from any such source, for its foresters and tree warden's department.

On November 14, 1853, came the fifth warrant, for the State election, at which forty-one votes were cast for Governor. On November 28 came the sixth warrant to choose Representatives to the General Court. This was in connection with a part of Lynn, much as is done now, and apparently no Nahant man was a nominee. On February 27, 1854, the committee on a settlement with Lynn rendered a report for record, which was signed by Daniel C. Baker for Lynn and Artemus Murdock for Nahant. The town paid about $2,000 as a balancing of accounts, including a proportion of the city debt and a pro-rating of respective ownerships in public buildings and lands.

Thus the first year of the town saw four town meetings, not including the two State elections, and one of these meetings had an adjourned session. Walter Johnson was moderator at the first two and William F. Johnson at the last two. The latter moved out of town about this time and does not appear later as a town officer. At the second annual meeting, on March 11, 1854, Washington H. Johnson was chosen selectman, with two previous members of the Board, Murdock and Stetson. Artemus Murdock built the house of the present "Edgehill" group which is nearest Nahant Road. This was about 1850. He was related to the Nahant Johnsons through marriage with Clara, daughter of Caleb Johnson. His daughter Mary married the Rev. George S. Noyes, and the Noyes family will be remembered by many people as the owners of the

"Edgehill" property until its sale to the Robinsons in the early 90's, after which it saw frequent extensions until it reached its present size. It was sold again in 1927 to a group of Nahant people who wished to insure its ownership and operation to the benefit of the community. Murdock died in 1882 in his seventy-fifth year. Noyes died in 1875, and his widow and family moved from Nahant in 1891, shortly after selling the property. Mrs. Annie E. Robinson was the chief figure in the upbuilding of the "Edgehill." She was familiar with Nahant before her purchase of this property. At one time she was lessee of the Tudor homestead, before it was taken over by the Nahant Club. After her death in 1918 her family ran it for several seasons, but had other interests and inclinations and so finally sold it.

Washington H. Johnson, who began twenty-three years of service as selectman with his election in 1854, was a son of Joseph Johnson. He was born in 1811 and died in 1892. About 1845 he built the houses on Nahant Road, across from the "Edgehill," now owned by James C. Shaughnessy. He went out of office fifty years ago, so that few remember him as a selectman. As a dignified old man, with white hair and beard, pottering about his front yard garden on a pleasant afternoon, he is a pleasant recollection to a larger number.

Alonzo Colby, Nahant's first highway surveyor, was succeeded in this office by Albert Whitney in 1856. Colby died in 1858 at the age of forty-three. About 1850 he built the house at the corner of Pond and Prospect Streets, later owned by Charles McBurney. McBurney was born near Belfast in Ireland and came to this country as a boy. One of his daughters married Barthold Schlesinger, who built on Prospect Street in 1870, owning about ten acres of land there. Another daughter married Charles Howard, and their children, or most of them, were familiar figures on Nahant. Rose Howard, a daughter, painted several of the old Nahant Houses, which are thereby preserved, and are now in the Nahant Public Library. Two sons, Charles Howard and Philip B. Howard, will be remembered. Schlesinger was born in Hamburg,

Germany, in 1828, and died in 1900. A brother, Sebastian Schlesinger, was a large owner of land near Prides Crossing, farther down the North Shore.

Washington Johnson, the first town clerk, was succeeded in this office by Alfred D. Johnson who served for so long, as related elsewhere. Welcome W. Johnson was town treasurer until 1880, a period of twenty-seven years. The first school committee was Walter Johnson, Welcome W. Johnson and John Q. Hammond. The first two have been mentioned elsewhere. Hammond needs more comment, for he appears to have been one of the far-sighted ones of the time, with a mind able to analyze and develop a situation, and therefore a valuable citizen to the early days of the town. His keenness and ability are shown in his school committee reports, of which he wrote several, and in the special report on beaches and public lands. He was a member of the Legislature in 1853, when Nahant was set up as a separate town. He was born in Maine, in 1821, a descendant of a line of Hammonds reaching back to the beginnings of Kittery. One ancestor, son of the first of the name in this country, was long-time town clerk of Kittery, and his fine handwriting delights researchers into Kittery town records. Hammond came to Boston in 1836, a boy, and had just about money enough left to pay his fare by steamboat to Nahant. He was something of a carpenter and had a mechanical bent, and went to work for Dexter Stetson, later entering into a partnership with him. He had seven children, all born on Nahant but one. The eldest is Charles A. Hammond, born in 1846 and still going strong, with many interesting recollections of old Nahant, where he lived until his father's removal to Lynn in 1866. The partnership with Stetson was dissolved about 1850, when Hammond became owner of the house on Pond Street, known to later days as the Putnam House, taken down a few years ago by Winthrop T. Hodges and replaced by a garage moved there from a few yards southerly on Valley Road. The Putnam house was well known for its peculiar ornamentation of sawed birds and beasts, which seems bad, but which was developed into an artistic and consistent result by John Pickering Putnam, an architect, son of the family. The story is told that Charlie Gove, looking out his window early one murky morning to scan the weather, espied a strange bird on the peak of the Putnam House roof. He grabbed his gun, stalked the bird until within firing distance, and brought down a rare specimen — sawed out of a board. "If it isn't true it ought to be." In Hammond's day the house was a simpler structure in appearance, standing on a range road. Tudor later extended this road, building it in his masterful way, against opposition, to be the present Spring Road. It was once the chief road into town, winding around the hill; but the street up the hill, as now, had been built over to good condition, and Spring Road, until Tudor's work on it, had relapsed to a cart path.

Hammond was a member of the Legislature when Sumner was elected United States Senator, and his was one of the votes which made Sumner a winner by a small majority. In 1861, in the Legislature, he was chairman of the committee on education, and successfully advocated the grant of State land in the new Boston Back Bay reclamation to the newly chartered Massachusetts Institute of Technology. Stephen Oliver, longtime moderator of Lynn town meetings, used to tell that Hammond made a strong speech advocating the purchase of a fire engine for Nahant — long wanted, but not granted to this small wing of the larger town. The result was the purchase of the old "Eagle," with Hammond, so tradition says, made chief engineer with a brass trumpet and fireman's hat.

Hammond was also interested in surveying, and found that the Lewis map of Nahant needed amendment and correction. This led to the new map mentioned elsewhere, a copy of which is in the Nahant Public Library. Hammond did a great deal of building work for Tudor, as well as other house construction on Nahant. During the Civil War he was assistant assessor of internal revenue, located in Lynn, engaged with the heavy sales tax imposed to meet war expenses. He built up a surveying and engineering business and was superintendent of construction on the Lynn City Hall. In 1872 his son, Charles A. Hammond, was taken into the partnership of Hammond & Son, who laid out the Marblehead branch of the Eastern Railroad. Hammond died late in the year 1872, a member of the Lynn City Council and a comparatively young man who might have gone yet farther up the scale of achievement had he been spared; for he started with a struggle for a place in the sun, and no better start is known, if the original metal is of the right temper. And the secret of success is a secretion of the sweat glands.

During the first years of the town several roads were laid out. The first was Pleasant Street from Nahant Road northeast to the beach. Tudor petitioned for this and offered to build it, in the annual meeting for March, 1854. In 1855, at the annual meeting, a road was laid out and accepted by "the Samuel Hammond" place, which is now a part of Nahant Road, while a Samuel Hammond still owns and occupies the same premises. A map drawn by Alonzo Lewis in 1856 shows this road including all land to the waterside. In 1861 Willow Road was laid out from Summer Street to Cliff Street and Wharf Street from the foregoing out to Crystal Beach and Nipper Stage. Note that the old names were used at this time. Coolidge Road is mentioned and appears to be the name of a private way from Cliff Street down the hill, often called Snake Hill, which was made a town way by this new layout of Willow Road. In 1862 a road was laid out covering the present streets of Pond Street from Nahant Road to Prospect Street, along Prospect Street, and back to Nahant Road on High Street. In this same year a dispute between the town and George W. Simmons over land at Little Nahant was settled out of court. Simmons relinquished all claim to the town for land westerly from the main road to Lynn, and to the two triangular pieces near the main road adjacent to the beaches, provided they never should be built upon. In 1863 the Willow Road section between Cliff Street and Summer Street came up again, as a discussion had arisen on its location. Mrs. Jessie B. Fremont offered to build the road from Cliff Street to Summer Street and out to Crystal Beach and Nipper

The "Relay House"
In days when automobiles were mostly open and ladies mostly clothed

Trimountain House, near Bailey's Hill

Stage, where she wished it, and without expense to the town. The town accepted the offer and the road was built as it now runs.

In 1864 the town voted to prevent people from taking sand from the farther end of Long Beach. Apparently there was trouble over the old-time privileges people had, or exercised, of taking sand and seaweed from the beaches. It led to litigation, but the town seems to have established its rights to regulate such matters. In 1853, the first year of the town, it was voted to authorize the selectmen to take all legal measures to protect Long and Short Beaches. Later in the year it was voted that the selectmen have power to prohibit and prosecute all out-of-town persons taking seaweed from the beaches. Then in 1859 came the carefully worded resolution quoted elsewhere. In 1860 it was voted that the selectmen "be instructed to tear down any fence, remove any building, fill up any well, etc., which may be built or dug on Long Beach."

In 1865 came an attempt to anticipate modern garden clubs. The sum of $100 for trees was appropriated, conditional upon the formation of a tree society. The money was spent, according to the auditor's report for 1866, but the tree society seems to have been short-lived. One might hazard a guess that this action was a feeling that something should be done to replace the loss of Tudor, who had given so much attention to this sort of thing. This same year saw Willow Road laid out from Summer Street to Valley Road and Valley Road from Willow Road to Spring Road. This was all called Fremont Street up to 1870 and later. Also came the road on the Lodge estate property, around East Point, as mentioned elsewhere. In 1866 a committee on a new Town Hall building reported recommending a postponement. John Q. Hammond rendered a minority report advocating building at once, but the majority report was accepted. At an adjourned town meeting in April, 1868, the Town Hall committee reported in favor of building, and a building committee of five included the selectmen, Washington H. Johnson, Edward J. Johnson and Thomas P. Whitney, together with Artemus Murdock and Walter Johnson. They were authorized to select a location. The building was begun in 1868 and finished in 1869 at a total expense of $8,400 for the structure and about $600 for furnishings.

Thus passed the first fifteen years of Nahant. Doubtless it was a trying time for those in control, full of criticism and full of blame, for of course mistakes were made. But the leaders of the time seem to have been wise and faithful, and should be remembered as worthy citizens outfitting a new municipality and deserving praise for the results they achieved. There are never enough sensible people in the world, but Nahant seems to have had a large share.

A very interesting paper recently presented to the Public Library by Miss Hattie Lee Johnson, a descendant of the old Nahant Johnsons, was saved by her when the old store was torn down to make room for the new Town Hall. It is a list of the inhabitants of the town in 1847, and was made out by Welcome W. Johnson, as follows:

LIST OF INHABITANTS OF NAHANT IN 1847

Names	Inhabitants	Voters
John Q. Hammond	5	3
Henry Bulfinch	7	1
Washington Johnson	3	1
D. A. Johnson	4	1
Francis Johnson	10	1
Nelson Tarbox	6	1
J. Johnson, Jr.	9	1
Wm. R. Johnson	3	1
Jno. Johnson	6	2
Walter Johnson	4	1
D. W. Johnson	7	1
J. E. Lodge	9	1
Benj. W. Appleton	5	1
Alonzo Colby	6	1
Benj. Hood	6	2
W. W. Johnson	9	2

THE NEW TOWN 267

LIST OF INHABITANTS OF NAHANT IN 1847 — *Concluded*

Names	Inhabitants	Voters
Caleb Johnson	5	2
A. Murdock	4	1
E. A. Johnson	6	1
P. Drew	16	4
Nichaolas Hilbert	4	2
D. Johnson	5	1
J. Rice	4	2
Joseph Johnson	11	6
Mrs. Donham	3	1
Dexter Stetson	4	3
Wm. Johnson	3	1
Eben. Hood	5	1
John H. Gray	8	1
Ed. B. Phillips	3	2
Mr. Clifford	5	1
Samuel Hudson	5	1
A. Whitney	8	3
	197	54

The footing of the first column appears to be 198 and not 197 as this paper gives it. It is interesting to note that in this year there were thirty-three families in town, with a population of one hundred and ninety-eight and with fifty-four voters. There were other families without voters, mostly summer residents. This list would seem to be a summation for use in the application for a new township. Thirteen are Johnsons of the old Johnson family, with a membership of eighty, although this would include hired help, clerks or boarders. David Johnson, the fourteenth Johnson in the list, was not one of this Johnson family. Murdock and Bulfinch married Johnsons, adding two to the list of family affiliations, and making about twenty-three voters in this one family. Nearly all of these people are mentioned elsewhere. Henry Bulfinch built the house, long known as the Bulfinch House, at the corner of Nahant Road and Ocean Streets, later remodelled for William A. Hayes and again more recently for its present owner, Philip Young. Caleb Johnson owned nearly all of the land along the main road from his old homestead, now the Sigourney place, up to Pond Street, and gave each of his children land on which to build their own homes. Without attempting to trace these accurately it is interesting to note the William F. Johnson house, later Oxnard or Archibald, now Williams, at the corner of Summer Street. Across the street is the George L. Johnson house next the Village Church, first given to C. Warren Johnson who died in the Civil War. Then comes Murdock, now Edgehill, and further up is Bulfinch.

In these early days the highway department was small. One man remembers it as Albert Whitney, one man and one horse. Whitney held the office for several years around 1860. This is the Whitney of "Whitney's Hotel." A daughter, Mrs. Alice C. McIntosh, is mentioned elsewhere. A son, William R. Whitney, saw long service on the School Committee and Board of Selectmen. He died in 1922, aged sixty-nine. Another son, Benjamin C. Whitney, was well known to old-timers.

The police department in these early days consisted of small payments to several men for a few days' service each, all included in the selectmen's department of the town report until 1869, when the annual auditor's report set up a police department with an expenditure of $295. This was unexpectedly large, and the money was taken from unappropriated funds, — that convenient way of expressing an overrun. The next year saw an appropriation of $300 for the police department, which had arrived as a separate unit of the town's activities. Even the first year of the new town, however, saw an expenditure for badges and handcuffs.

The fire department, now an important element of town business, seems to have jumped from a trifling expenditure, and less attention, to the position of a town department in 1870. The town report for 1871 records an expenditure of over $3,200 and this is said to be the result of an awakening. The large item is for the purchase of "Dexter No. 1," apparently, though it is hard to see how this could have cost over $1,800. For several years after 1853 the list of the town's assets included fire engine and engine house at around $450, which was later scaled down to $350. This engine house was a shed to hold the old machine, and was located above the old Town Hall in what was later the schoolhouse yard. The old controversies are hard to unravel at this later date, and no town officers made reports in these early days except the school committee. But at a town meeting in 1870 it was voted to sell the old engine house within four days. This curiosity of a vote must have resulted from some discussion now lost, though some old Nahanters may come forward later remembering all about it. After the upbuilding of the fire department by the appropriations of 1870 the apparatus was kept in the basement of the Town Hall, now the old Town Hall.

CHAPTER XIX

NAHANT OF THE FIFTIES

IT is difficult to present a word picture of Nahant as she looked as a new town. On Little Nahant Dr. William R. Lawrence, about 1850, built two cottages. One is still standing, often called the red Simmons cottage, pointed out in much later years as the place occupied by William Dean Howells for one summer. The other stood where now is the Thomas Howe house, and was moved, when the latter was built, in 1880, to the corner of Nahant and Spring Roads. Here it bore a sign "Hotel Tremont," but never met success as a hotel and lay idle for most of the time. Once it was a home for a boys' club, instituted through the interest of George Abbot James, but this also passed. Finally, in rack and ruin, it was torn down, about twenty years ago. Little Nahant perhaps saw pasturage from Lynn later than any other part of the town. Lynn farmers maintained a pen near the foot of Nahant Street, and their cows were driven to it, while one of them furnished a man or a boy to drive the cattle across the beach to Little Nahant. Coming back each farmer got his own cows from the pen. Some Lynn people now tell of this, and how their fathers drove the cattle over the beach, — a service furnished by the farmers in proportion to the number of cows each had in the herd. An old organization of the 1800's was the Proprietors of Nahant Pastures, evidently made up of men still using pasturage there derived from rights under the old division of the town. The sales of land, of course, gradually eliminated this use of the acreage.

Dr. William R. Lawrence was succeeded in his ownership at Little Nahant by George W. Simmons, father of George W. Simmons whom Nahanters mostly remember, and brother of

William A. Simmons who founded Simmons College in Boston. Both men were in the clothing business. Thornton Simmons, another son of George, Sr., will be remembered. The senior Simmons, who died about 1885, built the larger Simmons house, westerly from the little red house, and occupied it. He farmed the land, getting considerable crops, mostly for his own use. He also owned several acres in Great Nahant adjacent to Nahant Road between Pond and High Streets. A small gardener's cottage, in the lower corner of what is now the Howe estate, was moved over to Nahant Road, northerly, on a part of this land, where it now stands in dilapidated condition. These four houses, one later replaced by the Howe house, comprised Little Nahant, even as late as the 90's. In 1896, soon after the death of George W. Simmons, Jr., all the Nahant property was sold at auction. Joseph T. Wilson bought most of the land on Great Nahant, while a group represented by Edward E. Strout took over a majority of Little Nahant, and formed the Little Nahant Land Company to develop it. A considerable section was bought by Carahar Brothers, whose use of it is described elsewhere.

Bass Point, in these early days, was likewise vacant land. The "Old Castle" was still used as a private house, and two others were built by sons of John Phillips. None of these is now standing. There was a stable and stone shack, now gone, on the Relay House property, and the Tudors built a house on the Bass Point House property, about where the office of this resort now stands. The older part was burned in 1893, so that now no part of this outfit is old, unless the removal of the buildings from the Maolis Gardens makes it so. The Trimountain House was originally a small house owned by Tudor. But not so long ago the Old Castle was the only house on Bass Point, and this district was also used for pasturage for cattle from Lynn. Certainly in the 1820's and probably in all the 30's, there was no house on all of Nahant westerly from Summer Street except the Old Castle and the Tudor homestead. Tudor began building cottages, sheds and barns, those mentioned at Bass Point among them. The Old Stone barn on Spring Road, a fruit storage building, dates back to the 50's or earlier, as does the brick house across the street near it, also built by Tudor. This house was occupied for years by Peter Manuel, a gardener for Tudor, who had charge, among other duties, of a greenhouse down near the tall fenced garden between the brick house and Bear Pond. Many Nahanters remember him. An old plan of land around Cliff Street and up to Summer Street, dated 1845, has the whole area westerly of Summer Street labelled "The Great Pasture," while what is now Willow Road from Cliff Street down to Summer Street is labelled "Road leading to the Great Pasture." This plan was loaned for the preparation of these writings through the courtesy of Mr. Joseph Dwight, son of Dr. Thomas Dwight, recent owner and occupant of the house on Cliff Street, formerly the summer home of Charles Amory. There were gates across the roads to keep cattle in the Great Pasture from wandering easterly into the village.

Thus develops the picture of Nahant westerly from Summer Street. For years after 1800, only the Old Castle at Bass Point, and perhaps a herders' shack here and there. Then the Tudor homestead in the 20's and nothing more for another decade or so except what Tudor built, chiefly for farm buildings. Then Lawrence with two houses at Little Nahant and the two Phillips houses at Bass Point. In the 40's this was, as also the Tarbox house near Short Beach; the Bulfinch house at Nahant Road and Ocean Streets, built about 1840; the Tarbox house and stable at Nahant Road and High Street, now two houses; the Hammond house on Pond Street; and the Dunham, Johnson and Colby houses on Prospect Street, all dating around 1850; probably also in this period the Farrell house on Spring Road. All of these houses are identified elsewhere by naming later owners. The Johnson house on Prospect Street was later owned by Thomas P. Whitney and was moved to Pond Street. Whitney was a brother of Worthen Gove's wife, and thereby an uncle of Charles E. Gove. Whitney was at one time agent for the Tudor Ice Company at Cadiz, and

Cartoon showing Two Nahanters, Senator Lodge and Judge Wilson
From "Boston Post," June 19, 1904

From near Tudor Wharf, looking into Dorothy's Cove
Hotel Tudor in center

NAHANT OF THE FIFTIES   273

later was superintendent of the Tudor interests at Nahant. It is said that Mrs. Walter Johnson, coming from Reading to live on Nahant about 1841, told her friends that after leaving the beach, meaning Short Beach, her house was the third on the left-hand side of the road. The two others were the Tudor homestead and the Francis Johnson house now standing close to the street, but below Summer Street, the limit of the area now under consideration.

About 1847 a house was built near Nahant Road and Summer Street, on what is known as the Codman place, now owned by S. G. King. This was occupied by Dr. E. Porter Eastman, the first resident physician of the town. It came to be known as the "Butter Box," and finally Thomas G. Cary moved it down into the "Whiteweed field," where it was modified by one rambling addition after another and occupied by two daughters of Cary, and their husbands. These were Professor Louis Agassiz and Professor Cornelius C. Felton. The latter was president of Harvard University from 1860 until his death in 1862, at the age of fifty-five. For many years, up to 1860, he was Eliot professor of Greek literature at Harvard. Professor Agassiz, born in Switzerland in 1807, came to the United States in 1846, and in 1847 was professor of zoölogy and geology at Harvard. His study of glaciers and glacial drift, explaining many geological phenomena, was an important contribution to geology. It aroused discussion, but after a generation became a fixed part of knowledge in this science. In a journey to Brazil, in 1865, it is stated that he discovered more than eighteen hundred new species of fish. He died in 1873. Mrs. Agassiz, in later years, was president of Radcliffe College. Agassiz, by the many lectures he delivered outside of the classroom, greatly increased the general interest in the subjects of his study. Good stories are told of him and his enthusiasms. One is that on a trip with his wife, she exclaimed, when putting on a shoe in the morning, "Why, here is a little snake in my shoe." The professor's reply was, "What, only one? Where is the other six?" With his boundless ardor the handiest receptacle seems to have served his purpose. The Agassiz house has seen several owners since this time, under some of whom it has been remodelled, but the exterior appearance is much as it was when this famous man lived there. In late years Rufus L. Sewall and Judge Bosson have owned it, and only recently Walter L. Hobbs purchased it for his own use as a summer residence. Judge Albert D. Bosson was of the Chelsea District Court for a generation, until his death in 1926. Near by was the Cary house, elsewhere mentioned.

The 50's saw other houses added to this part of Nahant, but none to Little Nahant, after the two already mentioned, and not much to Bass Point after the two Phillips houses. One of the latter was remodelled in 1868 for C. J. Whittemore, at which time the stable was moved to Spring Road and made into a carpenter shop for Joseph T. Wilson, but that establishment is now enlarged in every direction so that the original building is hard to identify. About 1854 the Codman house on Summer Street was built by Thomas H. Perkins for his daughter Mrs. William F. Cary, but was owned and occupied for many years by Edward W. Codman. Miss Mary Russell once wrote that Colonel Perkins had a sister who lived in a cottage where this house now stands, and that on her death the building was demolished and the present house erected. She also said that Mrs. Cary sold the property because incensed at the insistence of Frederic Tudor that Summer Street be built from the main road northeasterly. This road cut off some fine trees and sheared away the narrow strip across the street from the main portion of the land. Miss Russell, who died in 1918 at the age of ninety, could have given many valuable reminiscences of old Nahant, but so far as is known a few occasional comments are all that is available. Codman was a grandson of Stephen Codman who built the old part of the Lawrence place across Nahant Road from the Public Library building. This latter slight elevation was at one time known as Snake Hill, so relates one old Nahanter, and it is only more recently that the hill around the corner of Willow and Cliff Streets has been called Snake Hill.

A rosebush, now blooming every spring against the rear piazza of the Whitney homestead, was given to Minerva Rice by Stephen Codman over a century ago. Minerva Rice was a daughter of Jesse Rice and married Washington H. Johnson. The "Ned" Codman place is now owned by Samuel G. King, a more recent comer to Nahant, who bought it in 1917.

The "Whiteweed field" was owned by Thomas H. Perkins and included all the land easterly from Summer Street and from the water on the northerly side to a stone wall which extended from the Codman estate to Schoolhouse Lane, marking the line against the Johnson lands, a house-lot's depth away from what is now Central Street, and about as the line now runs back of the Winslow and Rodman places, which were formerly Sears and Snelling ownerships. Mrs. William F. Cary built the house later owned and occupied by Charles Merriam on Summer Street near the water, and recently bought by Richard Harte. Edward Motley built the house and stable now occupied by his grandsons, J. Lothrop and Edward Motley. Motley was a brother of John Lothrop Motley, the historian. David Sears, Jr., soon sold to Lyman Nichols, from whom this place passed to his daughter, Mrs. John S. Wright, and was later sold to its present owner, Dr. Frederic Winslow. The Samuel G. Snelling place was sold in the 80's, and was for years owned and occupied by Miss Emma Rodman and her father. The building of the "Log Cabin" has already been mentioned. Joseph G. Joy, its first owner, was a son of John Joy who lived at the corner of Joy and Beacon Streets in Boston. Another son, Benjamin, had a son John Benjamin and grandson Charles H. Joy, whose widow is a frequent summer resident of Nahant today. She is a daughter of E. R. Mudge of Swampscott. John B. Joy lived on the large Joy place on Ocean Street in Lynn. Joseph G. Joy seems to be remembered as the owner of one of the finest private libraries of his time. The present H. G. Curtis house was built by Mrs. Story, who was the widow of Judge Joseph Story of the United States Supreme Court. This house was first occupied in 1850, as an entry in the "Lynn News" shows. A son of Judge Story was William Wetmore Story, the sculptor, and a daughter was the wife of George W. Curtis, whose writings include many passages about the delights of Nahant. This place later was the home of Alanson Tucker and more recently owned by Horatio G. Curtis who with his two brothers, Louis and Lawrence Curtis, are long-time summer residents, and sons of Thomas Buckminster Curtis, a Nahanter whose house was moved to make room for the Frank Merriam house on Vernon Street, built in 1888, to Willow Road across from Curlew Beach, where it is now owned by Miss Harriett E. Hudson. Horatio Greenough, the sculptor, owned land and planned to build a house about where the Public Library building now stands. Unfinished cellar walls marked the beginning of this project, which was stopped by the owner's death in 1852, only a short time after he had returned from several years in Italy. A sister of Horatio Greenough was the wife of Thomas Buckminster Curtis, and a younger brother was Richard Saltonstall Greenough, who was also a sculptor, and whose best known work is the bronze statue of Franklin in front of the City Hall in Boston. About 1840 E. Augustus Johnson built a house across Pleasant Street, then Schoolhouse Lane, about midway between Nahant Road and Central Street, later known for many years as the Spooner house, and among the buildings torn down when the present Town Hall was erected. About 1850 Charles B. Johnson built his house on the corner of Pleasant and Central Streets. This Johnson was a grandson of Benjamin, the third brother of Caleb and Joseph, who was born on Nahant, but moved away. His wife was Annie E. Johnson, sister of Edward J. Johnson and daughter of Jonathan Johnson. She was gifted with a poetic spirit, publishing many little poems some of which were finally collected into a volume. She died in 1916, at the age of eighty-nine. Charles B. Johnson, often known as Charlie Lamplighter, because of his long-time occupation, died in 1896 at the age of seventy-one. He was for a time agent or supercargo for the Tudor Company in their ice business, and was located abroad. A daughter, Caroline M. Johnson, was a long-time librarian of the Public Library, until her marriage to George D. Foye. She died in 1925, at the age of sixty-six.

The house at the corner of Nahant Road and Summer Street was built about 1845 by William F. Johnson. Later known as the Colby, the Oxnard and Archibald cottage, it is now owned by Wallace D. Williams, a recent comer to Nahant, who owns and occupies the adjoining house on Nahant Road, which was built at a somewhat later date by Caleb H. Johnson, a son of Welcome W. Johnson. Harmony Court, near Summer Street, seems to have been named facetiously by a summer resident, after the line of the Psalm, "Behold how good and how pleasant it is for brethren to dwell together in unity." For here were four brothers, — Francis, Joseph, Walter and Edmund, sons of Joseph. The Joseph Johnson house is now owned by Mrs. William J. McLaughlin.

The Abner Hood house, up Bass Beach Hill, was later owned and occupied by a summer resident, John C. Gray, who sold it and built what was commonly known as the Blanchard house in the early 50's. It was burned in the fire of 1896 and was replaced by the Duncan house, built by the Hon. George Duncan (who married Mrs. Blanchard), and recently bought by Arthur Perry. This is at the corner of Cliff Street and Willow Road. About the same time was built the Longfellow house across the street, also burned in 1896. The cellar walls left standing were developed into a garden pavilion by Arthur Perry, its present owner. Most of the houses around East Point have been named elsewhere. The Inches house, a stone house overlooking Bass Beach, was built by Ebenezer Chadwich in the early 50's, and the James H. Beal house by Chadwick's son, Christopher. A little later came the Samuel H. Russell house, burned in 1896, on the site now occupied by the Herbert F. Otis house. The little Russell house on Vernon Street, known to most Nahanters as the home of Miss Mary Russell, sister of Samuel H. Russell, was owned by their father, Nathaniel P. Russell. It was torn down a few years ago and the space is now vacant. The various houses that Coolidge built are mentioned elsewhere. David Sears, who owned one of them, later Appleton, then Boyden, now Smith, was a Boston merchant, the father of David, Jr., Knyvet W. and Fred R. Sears, who later lived on Nahant. Mrs. K. W. Sears still occupies the house on Swallows Cave Road, built in 1874. The Fred R. Sears house on Cliff Street next to the "Lodge Villa" was built in 1870. None of this family are now in Nahant.

Mrs. K. W. Sears is a daughter of George Peabody. The Peabodys were a Salem and Danvers family, related to the famous George Peabody whom biographical dictionaries tell about. Joseph Peabody and his family came to the old Nahant House prior to 1837. This is the place on Vernon Street built by Coolidge. In 1837 it was sold to Joseph Peabody's sons George and Francis, and in 1847 George became sole owner, and it was this house which he occupied in the summer season until his death in 1892, the long period of fifty-five years. Here came frequently his son-in-law the Hon. William C. Endicott, who was Secretary of War in President Cleveland's Cabinet from 1885 to 1889. In 1892 this house was sold to Dudley Bowditch Fay. Another son of Joseph Peabody was Joseph Augustus Peabody, who died in 1828. In 1866 his widow built the house on Winter Street, now owned by Dr. Morton Prince, and occupied it until her death in 1876. It was sold to Dr. Prince in 1892.

This property on Winter Street was earlier owned by Caleb Johnson. The corner house, commonly known as the Grover House, and later as the Conant House, was built by General Devens. Charles F. Johnson tells that he and his brother dug, and stowed away properly, one hundred bushels of potatoes in one day from this field at the corner of Winter Street and Nahant Road.

The "Lodge Villa" was bought by Henry Cabot. John E. Lodge, coming north in summer from New Orleans, lived at Nahant. After his marriage in 1842 to Anna Cabot he made the town his permanent summer home. The advent of the Civil War added to business cares already pressing too heavily upon him, and he died in 1862, practically burnt out by work. He was a shipping merchant, and amassed a fortune, as did so many others in this business. In 1849, when water freights were so high on account of the gold rush, he had one ship paid for in receipts before she sailed on her maiden trip. In 1853, when sailings from Boston for San Francisco were so numerous as to be bewildering, Lodge had three clipper ships in this service. His two children were Henry Cabot Lodge, distinguished Nahanter of later years, and Elizabeth Cabot Lodge, afterwards wife of George Abbot James. Of Senator Lodge it is not necessary to say much, as he was prominent enough to find place and space in more important writings. Most Nahanters remember him best as riding horseback, his favorite exercise, about town, with a nod and smile for any people he knew; or as town moderator, a position filled whenever he could be present, after advancing years prevented Joseph T. Wilson from any regular attendance at town meetings. From the early 1900's for fifteen or twenty years he thus served the town, in addition to filling the position of public library trustee for the record period of nearly forty-eight years. His last time as moderator was in July, 1921, and the last annual town meeting over which he presided was in 1919. Nahanters well know his careful consideration of many little requests made to him. He was always willing to give his time and energy to help even in small personal matters. It was a privilege, which closer friends enjoyed, to go to his house and talk about things great and small, and his friendship and sympathy were always evident. Nahanters were proud that he was one of them, and all felt a sense of personal loss when he was gone. His first election to the State Legislature was due to his old friend, Joseph T. Wilson, who proposed his name in the party convention at a time when the Lynn districts associated with Nahant were willing a Nahanter should get the nomination because there was no show of winning. It was as one throws a bone to a dog. Nahant was the small end of the district and usually could get no consideration of her possible candidates. The two men were always close friends, and commonly the Senator's morning ride took him by

Wilson's door, where he would stop for a few minutes' chat. The Senator wrote the inscription on the bronze tablet erected to Wilson in the Town Hall in 1915. In 1925 a second tablet, matching the former one, was erected to Lodge's memory, and the two memorials are on either side of the stage. The inscription for the latter was prepared with the assistance of Bishop Lawrence, lifelong friend of Nahant's famous resident. The Senator used to slip into town quietly, in order to get some peace and ease before the politicians found he was home. After a few weeks, when onslaughts of these people were too numerous, he would vanish, perhaps down to Tuckanuck Island with another old friend, Dr. Bigelow, returning again after people found out he was gone. The Senator died in 1924 at the age of seventy-four.

Just before his death John E. Lodge bought the Nahant Hotel property, or most of it, comprising chiefly what is now known as the Lodge and James estates. James built the Lodge house, and then built the house he afterwards occupied. All of this was in the late 60's. The builder was George U. Perkins, who was in business under this name from 1866 until 1888, when his brother James C. Perkins became a partner and the firm name was Perkins Brothers. George Perkins died in 1901 and James in 1916. Before 1866 Perkins was in business with Thomas P. Whitney, and the town report for 1859 names Perkins and Whitney. He came to Nahant some years before that and perhaps worked for Hammond, or for Stetson and Hammond, as it appears that for a time he lived with Hammond in his house on Pond Street. Perkins' first shop was on Nahant Road up the hill from what is now the Whitney homestead; later they had a shop on Curlew Beach, which was in those days more a public beach than it is today; and still later they were in the location, more familiar to present-day Nahanters, on Willow Road near Summer Street. People remember that when the news of Lee's surrender came to town, in 1865, Perkins marshalled together the school children and marched them around town with staves over their shoulders, mostly laths, after which

Hon. Curtis Guild

J. Colby Wilson
Selectman

Albert G. Wilson
Public Library Trustee

Charles W. Stacy
Highway Surveyor

there was a sort of impromptu party at the old Maolis house on Ocean Street. Among the buildings erected by Perkins, besides the two above mentioned, were the old Town Hall, the William F. Cary house on Summer Street, now Richard Harte's, the Longfellow house on Willow Road near Cliff Street, and the Rodman house on Pleasant Street, formerly owned by Samuel G. Snelling. These all reach back to the 60's or earlier.

Other houses around East Point deserve mention because running back through the early years of the town. The Mountford house, located where now stands the house of Mrs. K. W. Sears on Swallows Cave Road, was owned and occupied by Mrs. Mountford's father, Benjamin W. Crowninshield, who was Secretary of the Navy in the Cabinets of Presidents Madison and Monroe, from 1814 to 1818, and Congressman from 1823 to 1831, when he was defeated by Rufus Choate. Elizabeth Crowninshield was a famous beauty and belle of her time. She lived in her father's house after his death, and in 1863 married the Rev. William Mountford. The place was sold to Knyvet W. Sears in 1874. For his son George, Crowninshield built the Warren house on Vernon Street, now occupied by Lawrence Curtis, but remodelled out of any resemblance to the original. This was later owned by Dr. John Mason Warren, whose wife was a daughter of Crowninshield. Dr. Warren was a son of Dr. John Collins Warren and grandson of Dr. John Warren, the latter a brother of General Joseph Warren of Revolutionary fame. Dr. Warren, our Nahanter, is another of the long list of Nahanters whose names are in most dictionaries of biography, as are also his father and grandfather. His daughters married into other Nahant families. One married Samuel Hammond, one Charles H. Gibson and one Thomas Motley, father of present-day Motleys, who are interested and helpful citizens of Nahant. Thomas Motley, also a valuable citizen of Nahant, died in 1909 at the age of sixty-two. He was a son of Edward Motley. The Samuel Hammond house is on land bought from Ebenezer Hood in 1828. The house was built in 1829 by Samuel Hammond, great grandfather of the present owner of the same name, whose father, Samuel Hammond, married Dr. Warren's daughter. The present-day owner is well known for his interest in Nahant and for important work he has done on many town committees. His grandfather, Samuel Hammond, married Susannah, a daughter of Gardiner Greene, thus tying back to the Clarke and Copley ancestry elsewhere mentioned. Then there is the little cottage on the corner of Vernon and Cliff Streets occupied recently by Mrs. George B. Inches. This is an old building, moved there and remodelled into a house, and was the home of Cornelius Coolidge. This occupancy takes it back into the 1840's. Before that it was a barn on the Hood property across from the Whitney homestead. B. C. Clark, enthusiastic yachtsman, is mentioned elsewhere. His house was where Arthur Perry's house now stands, and the property was subsequently owned by Amos A. Lawrence, who bought it in 1864. This point came to be known as Clark's Point, perhaps to avoid the confusion of the use of its old name, Bass Rocks, with Bass Point. Amos A. Lawrence (1814–86), cousin of Abbott Lawrence, who owned the place across Nahant Road from the Public Library building, was the father of Bishop Lawrence, and the latter was much on Nahant as a boy and young man, living here in the summer season, for a short time after his marriage, in the Cunningham house, which was burned in 1896. Amos A. and Abbott Lawrence were sons, respectively, of two brothers, Amos and Abbott Lawrence, of an old firm of Boston merchants. This Clark's Point house has been rebuilt and remodelled so much that it has no resemblance to the original. Perry bought it in 1915 and at once made further extensive changes. Later he bought the Duncan house, and the Dwight house next to it. This latter house was built by Mrs. Thomas Dwight, mother of Dr. Thomas Dwight.

The Abbott Lawrence place, opposite the Public Library building, was owned by Stephen Codman, grandfather of Edward C. Codman, who built the large original building, and built the small cottage close to the corner of Wharf Street for his son. On Codman's death the place was bought by David Eckley, who made many improvements, but died before he used it. Then it was owned by James W. Paige (1792–1868), who was the father of Mrs. Abbott Lawrence. Paige married a daughter of Stephen White of Salem. Daniel Webster's son married another daughter, and Webster was a frequent visitor to Nahant, up to the time of his death in 1852. A third daughter married John B. Joy, elsewhere mentioned. The David Sears house was sold to William Appleton, whose daughter married Amos A. Lawrence. Mrs. David Sears was a sister of Mrs. John Collins Warren. David Sears died in 1871 at the age of eighty-four. Appleton married a daughter of Dr. John Collins Warren. Another daughter was the wife of Thomas Dwight, father of Dr. Thomas Dwight. Appleton was a second cousin of Thomas G. Appleton, whose sister was Mrs. H. W. Longfellow. Another old home is known as the Fremont cottage, built by Edward B. Phillips of the same Phillips family that lived at Bass Point, and later sold to General John C. Fremont, whose wife was Jessie Benton Fremont. The former was known as the Pathfinder, for his explorations in the great West, then comparatively undeveloped. He was born in 1813 and died in 1890, and was an unsuccessful candidate for President in 1856. At that time his home was California. He was on Nahant irregularly, but his wife and daughter were more constant for a few years, and then the estate was sold to Frederic Tudor. This place seems to have included Nipper Stage Point and what is now known as Marjoram Hill. Wharf Street, at this end, was an old range road and was built through to the water in 1863. Marjoram Hill was bought by the town for a public ground or park in 1906, and is one of the improvements attributable to the zeal of George Abbot James, whose services to Nahant are mentioned elsewhere. This area had been used by the town for a few years previous, due to the courtesy of the Nahant Land Company, its owners.

It is interesting to look over these early Nahanters among the summer residents and see how they flocked here and how they were in so many cases closely related through intermarriage. Some of this has been indicated, and here follows a little more of it. One may go back to John Singleton Copley, noted artist, and for whom Copley Square in Boston is named. His house was where the Somerset Club on Beacon Street in Boston now stands, and a bronze tablet affixed thereto tells about this. Copley's father, Richard Copley, came to Boston from England in 1736, and the noted son was born in 1737. The father died in 1737 and later the widow, Mary Singleton Copley, married Peter Pelham. There was a son, Henry Pelham, who was an engraver, now well known in name because of the Pelham Prints. In 1769 Copley married Susannah, daughter of Richard Clarke, and this was the Clarke, agent of the East India Company, to whom was consigned the tea made famous by the Boston Tea Party. Both the Clarkes and the Copleys went to England, but a daughter of Copley, Elizabeth Clarke Copley, born in Boston in 1770, married Gardiner Greene and returned to Boston about 1800, going back to England again about 1840. This Madame Greene, as she was called, lived in the house on Cliff Street lately owned by Dr. Thomas Dwight. A daughter, Mary Copley Greene, married Joseph S. Amory in 1837, and one son was Charles Amory, who owned and occupied this Dwight place for many years. He was well known in Nahant. The Copley name connection was further perpetuated in a son, Copley Amory, while a daughter, Martha Babcock Amory, wrote a life of the famous artist ancestor.

Now consider the Amorys for a moment. Jonathan and John Amory were merchants in Boston. John Amory's daughter married John Lowell, and a son, John Amory Lowell, owned a house where now is the Lovering place on Vernon Street. This Lowell is a grandfather to President Lowell of Harvard University, the father of Mrs. Sprague, wife of Dr. Francis P. Sprague who lived in Nahant so many years, and great-grandfather of Ralph Lowell, a recent occupant of the Sprague house down near Swallows Cave. Another brother of John and Jonathan Amory, Thomas Amory, had sons Jonathan and Thomas Coffin Amory. The former has great-grandchildren known to Nahant. One is Robert Amory, who until recently lived on the corner of Prospect and High Streets, while another is the wife of Dr. Augustus Thorndike, son of Charles Thorndike, who for many years owned and occupied the Moering house on High Street. This descent is through a son, Joseph S. Amory, who married Mary Copley Greene, and Dr. Robert Amory, who married Marianne, a daughter of Amos A. Lawrence. Thomas C. Amory had a daughter Susan who married William H. Prescott the famous historian. Prescott's father, Judge Prescott, came to Nahant and built, in 1828, the house on Swallows Cave Road, later owned by Frederick W. Bradlee, but so enlarged and remodelled that it cannot be considered, today, a historic house. The Prescotts, father and son, lived together until the death of the elder in 1844. The historian's grandfather was Colonel Prescott, who commanded the American forces at the Battle of Bunker Hill. In 1853 this famous Nahanter bought in Lynn and summered there until his death in 1859, at the age of sixty-three. Several things were trying to him at Nahant. The strong light on the ocean affected his weak eyesight, but especially, perhaps, he begrudged the time he was obliged to give while submitting to lionizing. Nahant was at its height as a resort, and the great hotel and the landing wharf were both near by. This was too convenient and he was too gracious.

Then there is the Lawrence family. Besides what has already been written, there is the marriage of Katharine Bigelow Lawrence, sister of Abbott Lawrence and cousin of Amos A. Lawrence, to Augustus Lowell, father of Abbott Lawrence Lowell, President of Harvard University. Amos A. Lawrence, father of Bishop Lawrence, married Sarah, daughter of William Appleton, and it was her brother, William Appleton, who married Emily, a daughter of Dr. John Collins Warren. These Appletons came from Isaac Appleton of Ipswich (1704–94), who had a son Joseph, and three generations named William, the latter being Dr. William Appleton, now a summer resident, and a native of Nahant. It is the latter's father, William Appleton, who married Emily Warren, and they had a daughter who married John S. C. Greene, getting back to the Copley connection again. Old Isaac had another son, Isaac, who was the grandfather of Thomas Gold Appleton and Mrs. H. W. Longfellow.

Then there is the Mifflin house and family. This house was owned by Samuel A. Eliot, father of Charles W. Eliot, long-time President of Harvard. It is said that President Eliot went to school from here to the "old stone schoolhouse." Samuel A. Eliot died in 1862. The house is one of the old ones of the town, reaching back into the 1820's. It was next owned by Dr. Charles Mifflin, who died in 1875, and whose wife was Mary Crowninshield, daughter of Benjamin Crowninshield, elsewhere mentioned. A son, George H. Mifflin of the publishing house of Houghton Mifflin Company, was a later occupant well remembered by Nahanters. He died in 1921. A brother of Samuel A. Eliot was William H. Eliot, who lived on Vernon Street, prior to 1831, in a house early occupied by John Hubbard and later by Charles R. Green, whose wife was a Coolidge, often mentioned as a daughter of Cornelius Coolidge. This house was burned in 1896 and the place is now owned by Mrs. Elisha H. Williams. This Eliot was the promoter of the old Tremont House in Boston, where the Tremont Building now stands, said to be the foundation of the American hotel system. He died in 1832.

This brief consideration of a few of the old Nahant families of summer residents shows how these old Boston families are interrelated. Many other instances could be given, and some others are mentioned elsewhere. The group came mostly from old Boston families who made their money in shipping, at a time when ships from around the world brought novelties or items not in competition with any similar articles produced nearer home. Profits were large, men were able and energetic, far-sightedly capable of seeing possibilities beyond merely local trading. The newspapers of the time advertise the wares these merchants offered, as, for instance, in the "Columbian Centinel" for July 19, 1817:

> Thos. C. Amory and Co. have for sale at No. 38 India Wharf 20 pipes, 46 hhds. and 28 qr. casks old Sicily Madeira wine on board Brig "Brothers" from Madeira: 12 hhds molasses, 7 hhds. sugar per "Shannon:" In store 50 hhds best retailing molasses.

Accumulating fortunes, these people were capable enough to keep them and increase them. The temper of the times was not vain show, nor the symptoms those illustrated by the young man who said he had ten dollars left, what should he spend it for. Means gives leisure and leisure helps to culture, though by no means a sure road to it. Hence these same people looked askance at those whose only claim to recognition was an ability to spend, and therefore came a feeling toward them exemplified by the nickname "Cold Roast Boston," said to have been applied to them by Thomas Gold Appleton, who was considered a wit of his time.

This chapter on old Nahant of the 50's, reaching backward and forward from that decade, may close with a letter of reminiscences written by Miss Emma F. Cary, a few years ago, to Mrs. Fred A. Wilson for the Nahant Woman's Club. Miss Cary was a sister of Mrs. Agassiz and Mrs. Felton. She sets the year 1851 as of the death of Thomas Handasyd Perkins, her grandfather, but this appears to be an error.

> DEAR MRS. WILSON: — My first recollections of Nahant are of the sea, the sky and a hill covered with wild grass, bayberry bushes, and, each in its respective season, the wild rose and the golden rod.
> It must have been in the year 1840, when I was seven years old, that I began to observe critically the charms of Nahant.
> The house I lived in was built about the year 1823, by Thomas Handasyd Perkins, for the pleasure of his children and grandchildren. The blocks of stone were brought from Weymouth in a vessel, where the workmen lived while they built the house; and good workmen they were, if one may judge by the sound condition of the house today. On the cliff above the Spouting Horn was a summer house, a little round temple in form. It was very pretty, but was destroyed by lightning long ago and never rebuilt.

The nearest house to ours, going eastward, was Mr. Samuel Eliot's house, now owned by Mr. George Mifflin. Mr. Eliot parted with it, I think, about the year 1859. The beach we call Forty Steps was then and for many years called Eliot's beach. The Villa, lately occupied by Mr. and Mrs. Ellerton James, was built by Mr. Harry Cabot, who lived there in summer for the rest of his life. He was a man of fine presence and distinguished manners, and his wife was a marvel of beauty and grace. Of the houses that we know today there were already built at the time I am recalling: the Hammond house, the Russell house, the one owned by General Paine, and which was built by Mr. Samuel Cabot, the Inches cottage opposite the Union Church, and the cottage where Dr. Dwight lives. Mrs. Boyden's cottage stands on the ground where her grandfather, Mr. David Sears, lived. On the place where Mr. Dudley Fay lives there was originally a house called "the Nahant House." Ever since I can remember, the charming and hospitable house of Mr. and Mrs. George Peabody stood there, and the Nahant House is only a tradition to me.

Above Swallows Cave, and above the steamboat landing of that day were two houses famed for hospitality, — Judge Prescott's cottage and that of Dr. Edward Robbins.

Judge Prescott and Madam Prescott were the father and mother of the historian, who also lived there for some years. There was told of Madam Prescott a pretty story, showing her perfect tact and good manners. Two strangers mistook the house for an inn, a mistake often made at Nahant in those days. They came on to the piazza and asked for refreshments. The historian's mother ordered all that they asked for and they enjoyed their repast and the fine view in perfect content. When they prepared to pay for the meal their hostess said, "This is Judge Prescott's house and you are entirely welcome to any refreshment it has given you."

Dr. Robbins kept open house, like every one of his race that I have known. He had an only daughter who, after the death of her parents, founded the admirable hospital in Boston, known as the House of the Good Samaritan, and was its guiding spirit while she lived. The Doctor had two lovely wards, afterwards Mrs. William Wharton and Mrs. Edward Perkins. The house was always overflowing with kindness and hospitality in the simple fashion of the day, — abundance without display.

East Point was entirely given up to the guests of Nahant Hotel, a gay throng of Bostonians, southerners, chiefly from the Carolinas and Virginia, and also Canadians, who came often to Nahant in those days. Mr. Chadwick, who afterwards built the stone house

The Old "Eagle"

The "Dexter No. 1"

owned by Mr. Inches, came every summer to the hotel where his delightful family were the life and soul of the place.

The building was very pretty, built of stone with broad piazzas, and big parlors well suited for charades or tableaux or for dancing.

Of the dear old houses in the village I will not write, for there must be many records of these and of their interesting inmates.

Whitney's Hotel and Rice's Hotel were much frequented in those days by families who came for the summer, and by travellers who passed a day at Nahant for the sake of its famous fish dinners.

I remember that one of the joys of my childhood was to be taken by my mother to make visits in the village, to call on Mrs. Nabby Hood and Mrs. Jonathan Johnson, ending, perhaps, with the purchase of a Gibraltar or a Black Jack at Mr. Welcome Johnson's store, the only one that I remember at Nahant. Everything came from Lynn, — provisions of all kinds, medicines and dry goods, except the bountiful variety dispensed by Mr. Welcome Johnson.

Going westward there were not many summer cottages. The Codman family owned the large place now in the possession of Mr. John Lawrence. Mr. Codman cultivated the land successfully with flowers and fruit trees, and the house was substantially the same in appearance as it is today.

Mr. Samuel Perkins had a small cottage near the house where Mr. and Mrs. Edward Codman lately lived. His wife, an invalid, spent her summers there, leading a very retired life. Then came Mr. Tudor's place, now owned by the Nahant Club. It is quite unchanged in appearance except that the beautiful trees of today were then slender saplings, showing how wisely this fine agriculturist planned his work.

I remember nothing beyond the present Club House until we came to "The Castle." This large house had formerly been an inn, but it was already owned by the Phillips family and passed from them to Dr. Reynolds.

I do not remember any names attached to the streets. There was "The Village," East Point, Bayley's Hill, etc., but no names of streets in those days, and naturally enough, because, with few exceptions, everybody lived on the main road.

To Mr. Frederick Tudor Nahant may be said to owe every tree it possesses, except the large willow trees, that justly make its pride.

Mr. Tudor, having succeeded in supplying tropical countries with ice, turned his genius to making strawberries and peaches grow at Nahant. He built garden walls of lattice-work so that the sea wind was filtered through to the delicate plants. He had beautiful fruit and every variety of flower. He planted everywhere the hardy balm of Gilead, and under its motherly shelter planted fruit trees whose shade we enjoy today. The forestry work added to Nahant of late years completed an enterprise begun apparently under insuperable difficulties.

Maolis Garden was a later undertaking of Mr. Tudor's. It gave a pleasant refuge to those who came to Nahant for the day, for it was in a beautiful situation, and all its appointments were well planned.

When I first remember the Union Church it must have been recently built, for I have heard my elders tell of Sunday services in the pretty stone schoolhouse in "the Lane."

The church was quite plain; a parallelogram in form, with pews, a pulpit, and a gallery for the choir. There was no organ; the leader gave the pitch with a tuning fork, and a well-trained quartette sang in excellent taste old-fashioned hymn tunes.

How well I remember the congregation! There was Dr. Robbins, his sturdy figure bent with rheumatism, and the long pew filled with his household and his guests; the ladies in the pretty cottage bonnets then in fashion, and diaphanous summer toilettes.

There was Mr. Tudor in blue frock coat and brass buttons, a striking personality with his aquiline face and silver hair. With him were his beautiful wife and handsome children.

Judge and Madam Prescott were a venerable pair, whom one looked at with deep respect.

But it would be giving a list of the inhabitants of Nahant if I named all the families in the congregation. They were a comely set, and it was a gathering of good friends and neighbors that it is pleasant to recall.

At the death of Thomas Handasyd Perkins in 1851 his estate at Nahant was divided. Thomas Graves Cary, on behalf of his wife, Mary Perkins, kept the stone house by the Spouting Horn, and part of the "ten-acre lot" where he built the house known as the Agassiz cottage. There was a square house in another part of Nahant, popularly known as "the butter box." This house was moved over to the ten-acre lot, and wing after wing was added to it, until it developed into the widespreading bungalow that stands there today. Mr. Cary built it for two of his daughters, Mrs. Cornelius Felton and Mrs. Louis Agassiz. Few houses can have given more happiness than this simple cottage; few can have harbored as many gay, joyous young people, and thoughtful elders.

Agassiz lived much in his laboratory, but he could sit among a throng of boys and girls laughing and talking as completely secluded in his own thoughts as if he were on the glacier of the Aar.

His power of concentration seems to have no limit, but he could come out of this state of absorption and join in the merriment of the young people like a boy free from care and responsibility. The fishermen of Nahant were the Professor's stanch friends and allies, and the pick of their spoils was his, whether taken by net or line. They aided him, too, in dredging for the endless treasures of the deep. Then hour after hour passed uncounted in the laboratory while he examined his treasures with the microscope, delighted if any of the family came to share his enjoyment.

Twenty years Agassiz spent at Nahant, and the world seemed poorer to us all when he left for the last time.

Hoping that these notes may give you part of the information you asked for, I am

Faithfully yours,
(Signed)   Emma Forbes Cary.

CHAPTER XX

TOWN DEPARTMENTS

IT has already been mentioned that the fire department was of little moment until 1870. The machine that John Q. Hammond pleaded for in a Lynn town meeting was undoubtedly the old "Eagle," and its acquisition by Nahant is therefore placed before 1850. Hammond came to Nahant about 1836, but was then only a boy, and doubtless it was in the 40's, and probably late 40's, that the "Eagle" was the Nahant fire department kit. This engine was a tank filled by buckets, with a "walking beam" pump that forced from this tank through the hose. The year 1870 town report records the formation of the Dexter No. 1 Engine Company, so that no doubt the record for that year, of the purchase of a fire engine for $1,800, was for this machine. This Dexter Engine Company seems to have had, or assumed, authority to organize, assess members, choose uniforms, name the engine, and do many other things not now reckoned a part of company procedure. They evidently aimed to be a club, and at one meeting it was voted that each member be assessed one book, to make a library. At other times assessments were laid for a fund, most of which was superseded by the Fireman's Relief Association. At one meeting they voted to call the engine the "Nahanter," but reconsidered the matter. In fact, reconsiderations of actions were very frequent, showing much argument. The uniform was a red shirt, black trousers, and a fireman's hat and belt. This they voted to pay for themselves, but subsequently induced the town to provide reimbursement for hats and belts. These items of the uniform were elaborate, with the name of the engine in raised letters of white leather. Parades and musters seem to have loomed large in their considerations. The "Dexter" was a "walking beam" machine also, but had suction hose to draw water from wells and reservoirs. During the next ten years or so nine reservoirs were built to catch street drainage and provide a water supply for fire purposes. In at least one case, at the foot of Winter Street on Willow Road, a hydrant was placed, connected to the reservoir up on Nahant Road, the down-hill grade giving the necessary service.

In 1869 three extinguishers were bought, of a hand type, and some ladders and buckets. In 1870 the little old engine house was painted and therefore seems to have been still in use. The first Board of Engineers, chosen in 1870, was Edward J. Johnson, Worthen Gove and Welcome Johnson. In 1873 the ladder truck was bought, also more extinguishers. In 1875 the old "Eagle" received minor repairs, showing she was not then relegated to the scrap heap. In 1876 comes the first annual report of the fire engineers, and this tells of the "Dexter No. 1" fire company with fifty men, paid $10 each and $1 additional for each monthly meeting attended; and of the "Relief Hook and Ladder Company" with extinguishers and fourteen men. They recommend the purchase of a large extinguisher, and say that, with two men, it will put out a fire quicker than the Dexter. In 1877 the Babcock extinguisher was bought, and a third company was thus added to the list. There were also two hose carriages, practically hose reels, which carried additional material.

In 1878 the "truck house" was built on town land on Nahant Road near High Street. A hose tower was added to this in 1890 and a wing for a meeting room in 1896. The building was torn down in 1919, when the police station was moved over near its site. The engineer's report for 1880 gives a detailed list of the equipment in charge of each of the three companies, two of which were then in the Town Hall, and the hook and ladder truck was in the "truck house." The engineers in two or three reports stated that the men, all call men, were so accustomed to the bell on the church tower that it did not awaken them when rung for a fire. In 1885 a bell was placed in the cupola of the truck house, and this did valiant service. In this same year the newly installed water system was used by the fire department. This led to a reorganization in 1886. The old Dexter No. 1 was disbanded and two new hose companies were formed, the "Dexter" and the "Alert." A new hose carriage and hose were bought under a special appropriation.

This apparatus was all hand-drawn, although a harness is listed with the equipment of the Dexter hand engine. The use of horses came gradually, until finally all the apparatus was horse-drawn, and $300 a year was paid to near-by horse owners for each horse which was supposed to be kept available for immediate service. On the clang of the bell some one jumped for the horse and hurried to the machine to which he was assigned. The plan was worked out as well as it could be with call men and a couple of bells which might not ring loud enough. Later it became difficult to get horses, and this condition became more acute after the barge lines were given up.

In 1894 the "Nathan Mower Hose Company No. 3" was organized at Bass Point, named for an early Bass Pointer. In 1896 this company was accepted by the town and put on the pay roll of the fire department. This was the fifth fire company. In the former year the Dexter hose reel was placed at Bass Point, and a new hose wagon replaced it in the Town Hall, where another was added in 1895, replacing the second hose reel, which was located a year or two later at Hotel Nahant, near the Lynn line.

The Bass Point engine house was built in 1894 on land which the town report says was leased from the owners, but as it seems to be on a range road, doubtless the rent was nominal, as the town owns sixteen feet of land through to the water. This building has been changed and remodelled several times to reach its present appearance and condition. The year 1897 also saw the first of the fire alarm systems, with five boxes, and striking the town clock bell, the truck house bell, and two large gongs placed outside the Town Hall and the

TOWN DEPARTMENTS 295

engine house at Bass Point. The alarm system was gradually extended until in 1911 there were nineteen boxes well located throughout the town. There are now twenty, another being added in 1922. In 1900 a new combination hose and extinguisher was bought for Bass Point. In 1902 the department was reorganized again, with the system of call horses introduced. Then comes a strong suggestion for a central fire station near Mitchell's corner, probably on town land near Calf Spring. This location is advocated in 1906 because the newly arrived street car lines along Spring Road and the streets down town and toward Bass Point would more likely be passable in winter snowstorms. The difficulty with horses is a principal factor in the recommendation, as it carries the intention to keep horses on the premises, though perhaps using them for near-by town work. A report of the New England Insurance Exchange committee is printed with the 1907 town report to foster this plan. In 1874 the town voted $12,000 to build a fire engine house, so the central fire station idea was not a new one. No one seems to remember what became of this early proposal which was never executed. Very soon, however, the talk of motorized apparatus seemed to displace the central fire station question, and in February, 1910, came the first motor machine, which was at once found to be worthless and was replaced in the fall by another, located at Bass Point. The large fire engine and motor-driven pump was bought in 1918, and was the heaviest expenditure the town ever made for apparatus. This was placed at Bass Point and the one there was moved to the Town Hall. Hose companies 1 and 2 were discontinued. In 1919 the ladder truck was motorized, and in 1923 another piece of kit was made from a police ambulance chassis given up by the police department. In 1925 a new combination engine was purchased. In the meantime permanent men have been employed, with the number increased so that all the needed apparatus can move out as promptly as the alarms ring in, while the call men listen for the box number and report at the fires.

These improvements naturally have meant great increases

in appropriations. In the 70's and 80's the expense stayed under $2,000 a year. In the 1920's the routine cost has averaged over $11,000.

The record of fires has jumped faster than the increased building, and appears to indicate greater carelessness or poorer construction. In the 70's and 80's only twenty-six fires are recorded in fifteen years, averaging less than two a year, with two years in which there were none. Since 1910 the average a year for fifteen years has been over thirty. This period is coincident with the introduction of the fire-alarm system, and after the placing of the twentieth box the fire figures jumped to new heights, reaching seventy-five in 1924. Long arguments claiming logic have been based on no firmer premises than these, but doubtless no one will try to say, the more alarm boxes the more fires, even though it has been true.

Perhaps the three most extensive fires were in 1896, 1897 and 1925. The first was on Great Nahant, when a fire started in the Longfellow house on May 18, while it was being prepared for summer occupancy. It spread from there to the adjacent Cunningham house, to the Blanchard house across the street, the Green house on Vernon Street, and the Russell house on Nahant Road. Other buildings were threatened and a few small blazes started. Attention was given to surrounding property so that much was saved that seemed doomed. Almost at once Miss Mary Russell gave $1,000 as a relief fund, which, with other additions, was set up as a Fireman's Relief Fund No. 1. Then in the next year was a fire at Bass Point, which took out eight houses and damaged five others. They were all small and the engineers' estimate of the total loss was $6,000. Following this a second fireman's relief fund was set up, to which Carahar Brothers were perhaps the first contributors, which is still going and called Fireman's Relief Fund No. 2. In 1925 was the great Bass Point fire, which is mentioned elsewhere.

In all these considerable fires complaint has been made of small water supply. This is also heard in every other place experiencing large fires. Immediately comes pressure for

Breaking Ground for Valley Road Schoolhouse
Joseph T. Wilson with first shovelful; third at his left is Otis A. Johnson

Ellerton James and Senator Lodge
About 1920

more water mains and more fire apparatus. Both are important to a reasonable extent. But the insurance company statistics show clearly that the way to low fire losses and low insurance rates is through adequate building restrictions. Their action in holding rates rather regardless of improvements in fire-fighting capacity is evidence of the statistics. Yet frequently, to meet individual wishes, come efforts to lessen the building restrictions, which, for Nahant, are by no means as rigid as the average for carefully guarded towns. The individual should not succeed in setting aside public welfare, and citizens should view questions from the public viewpoint, and not from sympathy for one person or from any rather natural dislike for restrictions of any kind.

The police department started early, but in a very small way. Little sums were paid to several citizens for duty as police or constables. By 1870, $200 was used, paid out to seven men, none of whom received over $50. In 1871 Charles E. Gove, mentioned elsewhere, received $235 for police duty. In 1874 the appropriation was $1,000, and in 1875 one man served two hundred and fourteen days. The year 1878 was the first that any man was in police service for the entire year, and that man was Frank G. Phillips. He came from Kittery, Maine, in 1874. He stayed on the police force until 1904, was chief of the police for the last twenty years of this period, and retired to accept a position with the Massachusetts Society for the Prevention of Cruelty to Animals. Retiring from that office he is still a well-known citizen of Nahant. The same year (1878) is the first time mention in the town report is made of uniforms, and is the first year of any annual report of the department, which recorded fifteen arrests. In the early 80's the selectmen's report tells of one day man and two night men. For a long time the police station was in the basement of the Town Hall, until in 1888 the extension on the rear of the building allowed better accommodations.

In 1891 a policeman is mentioned for Bass Point and for the Beach Road, the latter "to prevent shooting and racing."

By 1893 the use of a horse and wagon is increasing, a sort of ambulance, and in 1899 the town bought a wagon but still hired a horse. In 1894, in the fall, four extra men were on by night for a time, on account of the presence in town of an incendiary, a fire fiend he is called in the town report. In 1896 a one-story addition was made on the Town Hall, projecting toward the library building, for use as a department office and a court room. In this same year Thomas H. Larkin joined the force, succeeding Chief Phillips in 1904, and still serving in that capacity. Larkin is an old Nahanter, son of Martin Larkin, one of the good old Irishmen whom so many remember. In 1898 Larkin began to ride a bicycle on Long Beach Road. In 1901 the department consisted of the chief and five regular men, with numerous specials. In 1896 the old grammar schoolhouse was remodelled for the department. The basement contained the cells and the main floor was court room and offices. This same year the police were put under classified civil service. In 1915 the town bought a motor ambulance and in 1921 a motor cycle.

This succession of dates is not much of a story of this important branch of the town's activity. But the year-by-year work has been faithful while offering little of special note. The nature of the evidence necessary for court action makes the work difficult and often brings unmerited criticism. People who have evidence too commonly refuse to appear and testify, but expect the police to act when they have no evidence and cannot secure it. Doubtless a hands-off order has sometimes been given them, and they chafe under it, for they are ready to do their part to make a clean town.

The judge of the local court, beginning in 1876, was Joseph T. Wilson, who served until his death in 1914. He was succeeded by Walter H. Southwick, who is not an old Nahanter, though he can reckon almost a generation in town. Wilson was without legal training, but had no appealed case reversed, it is said, and was respected by the legal fraternity as a worthy occupant of such an office. Southwick is a lawyer by training, though devoting much time to business pursuits.

TOWN DEPARTMENTS 299

Around Lynn a good story is told, which is doubtless embellished, but is worth repeating. In the early days of automobiles, when horses were frightened by them, a Lynn man, now a well-known automobile dealer there, was thought to be too careless with his machine, and Larkin, on his bicycle, tried for long to apprehend him. Finally he did so, and the man was fined for driving over fifteen miles an hour, or whatever the old ordinance prescribed. The by-law was not invoked because of the speed on one occasion, but was used only because of alleged carelessness on several occasions. In the fall of the year the police had an outing down the shore somewhere and hired one or two of these new-fangled machines as a novelty for the trip. On the way back, as they neared the Lynn end of the beach, a thunder shower was upon them, and the early motor cars were without tops or other protection against the weather. An attempt to hurry the driver was met with the reply, "I can't do it. My father was fined for driving faster than fifteen miles an hour on this road." He put the car in low gear and the party was drenched. No doubt revenge was sweet, and, again, this story should be true, but is subject to denial.

The use of street lamps began about 1871 with an expenditure of $900 for lamps down through the "village," as it was then, mostly all below Summer Street. In 1872 lamps were put on Long Beach, and more were added through the years until the 80's saw Nahant streets well equipped with them. For a time the Long Beach lamps were used only a part of the year. In 1871 it was voted to use them only in winter, but after a year or two more the beach road was lighted throughout the year, except on moonlight nights. In 1889 appears the first appropriation for lamps at Bass Point, and by the selectmen's report this seems to be the first installation by the town in that section. It seems strange to old Nahanters that any description of these old lamps should be needed or interesting, but many people now here know nothing of them. A few iron lamp-posts may be found about town. They were surmounted by a four-sided lantern of large size, sixteen inches or so square at the largest part. Around the middle was a narrow band of four panes of glass with the street name in red letters. The illuminant was gasolene, or benzine, and the lamplighters went around in the forenoon and filled them, trundling a ten-gallon can of fluid in a cart and filling a small container from it. A short ladder hooked over a crossbar on the lamp-post. Late in the afternoon the circuit was repeated with a gasolene torch, which heated the burner, started vaporization and lighted the lamp. It burned until exhausted, which was usually before daylight. Later on, a horse and wagon were substituted, giving access to the lamp without any ladder. Two or three men were used for this service, and old Nahanters remember Peter Lane, Roger Killilae and Charles B. Johnson going about town for many years. In 1892 electric lights were placed on Long Beach and at Bass Point, and these were gradually extended throughout the town. At first these, and the other lamps, were lighted twenty nights a month, leaving the fair moon to do the illuminating for ten nights. Then the agreements included those nights of the moon when clouds obscured it, and finally they were used throughout the months, as now. Early days did not see all-night service, which is a familiar practice today. The electric lights, and electric service of other sorts about town, were in charge of John R. Killilae until his death a few years ago. He was a familiar figure, always ready to help a householder whose fuses were burned out, and to be found on the beach doctoring his lamps in the worst storms of the winter season. He was a son of Roger Killilae, and his brother, James H. Killilae, joined this same service. John was a member of the Board of Assessors for a time, as the list of town officers shows.

Early house lighting was, of course, kerosene lamps and candles. Some time in these early years of the town a system of gasolene lighting was developed, pumping air out through gasolene in a tank buried outside the house, whence it was forced back impregnated and suitable for use in special burners. Ten or a dozen houses in town used this kind of lighting. Then, when the Public Library building was erected, in the 90's, the trustees persuaded the Lynn Gas and Electric Company, which already had poles on the beach for street lights, to continue into town and furnish house lighting to this building. The town was to pay a part of the cost of installation, but almost at once came other demands for the service which made the venture profitable, while today it would take a long hunt to find houses not equipped with electric lights.

In 1908 gas for cooking and heating was piped to Nahant. In the years before electricity, gas was mostly used for lighting, wherever it was available, but by the time it came to Nahant there was no demand for gas lighting, while other domestic service rapidly increased gas consumption, and pipes were gradually extended in every direction throughout the town.

In the matter of concrete sidewalks, the use of which was bewailed by those who loved the old country paths, very heavy expenditures were made in the first few years. In 1871 $11,600 was spent and nearly $11,000 in 1872. In the first five years, from 1871 to 1876, sidewalks cost Nahant $36,800. The town certainly plunged deeply, and the repeated heavy appropriations indicate an approval of footings as dry and clean to footwear as such things can be. A black tar concrete was adopted from the beginning, and is still used, because it is as little affected by settlement or growing tree roots as any other material. The curbstones were always of rough split granite, until within a few years some cast concrete has appeared.

The highway department started with small expenditures, running $1,200 to $1,500 a year for several years until in 1870 the outlay suddenly jumped to $4,900. These early 70's were the time of increases in town expenditures. People waked up to the possibilities of municipal improvements, and the year 1869 saw an increase in valuations of two million dollars, wholly on personal property. This allowed an increase in expenditures without a change in tax rate. The highways expenditures dropped in the 80's, while the town was economical because of heavy outlays for sewer and water systems, but otherwise has held a rather steady march upward, crossing $10,000 in 1913 and $20,000 in 1924. It would be interesting to enumerate the streets of the town and when they were built, but space will not permit, except for such early or interesting items elsewhere mentioned. Old Nahanters remember Walter Johnson as surveyor of highways, riding about town in his light-covered wagon, getting a little whiter in hair and beard as time went on. Few, if any, remember him also as the moderator of the first Nahant town meeting. Another long-time highway surveyor is Charles W. Stacy, who retired from the office a few years since. Stacy is a son-in-law of Byron Goodell, and Goodell has several descendants now living on Nahant, including a son, Arthur S. Goodell, and a daughter, the widow of Albert G. Wilson.

The first appropriation for any forester's department was in 1881, and it was called "Trees on Highways." Mention has been made of earlier interest in the work so long and well done by Tudor. The first town forester was George Abbot James who served in this office until 1908. The first forester's report was for the year 1895, although James had reported as a committee member in the previous year. In 1892 James was instrumental in getting a town vote to employ Charles Eliot, landscape architect and town planner, to advise on measures to beautify the community. His report is published in the town report for 1893, but he found too much that was bad, and it was impossible to execute his recommendations. A park committee of two years later, in its report written by James, suggests that the Metropolitan Park Commission take over the beaches and a large portion of Bass Point, and speaks of the harbor shore on Castle Road as belonging to the town as far as Black Rock. This appears to be an error, as the area named is now covered with houses. This report also mentions Curlew Beach as one open so long that the public could not be shut off from it. James gave energetically of his time and strength to this department, serving without pay, and deserving much credit for improvements and for maintaining the trees of the town in good condition.

TOWN DEPARTMENTS 303

After twenty-seven years of service he retired, and almost at once Thomas Roland was chosen successor, serving until 1917, when Herbert Coles was elected. The State laws required a forester and a tree warden in late years, and it always has been the custom for the selectmen to appoint to the latter office whoever was elected to the former position. This combines two offices which are bound to interlace under conditions like those at Nahant, and tends toward efficiency and economy.

It is apparent that the early 70's saw a tremendous increase in town expenditures. A look at the schedules and data given elsewhere will show how much. The reason why this jump occurred so abruptly is that 1870 was the tax dodger's year of discovery. Nahant was not blamable for any of this. If people chose to comply with the law and become residents, the town could not prevent it, and there is no indication of any easing of requirements or other encouragement offered to these would-be citizens. They were mostly from Boston, and some are represented in town today by children or grandchildren. The city of Boston sued some of them, with varying success. But all in all, Nahant's total valuation jumped $2,000,000 in one year. The tax rate dropped but gradually worked back as expenditures mounted, and the tax dodgers went away or obtained reductions in their assessment on personal holdings. One prominent man was assessed for $800,000, and then declared it was altogether too high and successfully sought a heavy reduction. A few years later he died leaving many millions, one of the wealthy men of his time. Another honestly stated one year that his assessment was too low, but after tolerating the increase for a short time protested and got a reduction to former figures. On his death he, too, left much more than ever his assessments included. The days of assessing personal holdings locally are over, and it is hoped that the present income tax methods inculcate greater honesty and fairer returns. Perhaps they do. It surely was true, under the old ways, that the workingman, with only a house and lot, was assessed for a far greater proportion of his total wealth than the wealthier residents, most of whose property was not in plain sight of the assessors. All of this was not trouble peculiar to Nahant, of course, but was a general condition provoking comment everywhere.

This chapter can close with an article written by Mason Hammond, published in the "Boston Evening Transcript" for July 5, 1893. On the previous day, the holiday, a group of Russian officers, including a Prince with some long name, were entertained at the Nahant Club, when an alarm of fire was sounded. "Willie Waters," the barge driver mentioned, died many years ago, and is not the present town clerk. The article exaggerates, to make a good story, but the description is accurate enough to be interesting, and witty enough to deserve inclusion here.

> Nahant had a field day on the Fourth of July. There were pool, bowling and tennis tournaments, besides a baseball game, and Admiral Koznakoff, with the officers of the Russian warships, was in town.
>
> But the real sensation of the Fourth, so far as it affected Nahant, was the fire. When there is a fire at Nahant all hands, with one accord, old and young, lame, halt and blind, turn out and rush madly to the scene of action, there to do as much damage as they possibly can in the shortest time. Not that they mean to, but because they can't help it.
>
> When, several years ago, Goodell's stable was burned, which event marks an era in the history of Nahant, the hook and ladder truck, manned by a company of gentlemen in evening dress, came down the hill which leads from the Nahant Road to the water front on the west, at top speed, and never stopped till it reached the water front; and there were scenes equally interesting at the fire in Hervey Johnson's roof on the Fourth of July, 1893.
>
> It was half past five in the afternoon. The house of the Nahant Club was jammed to overflowing. Croquet, tennis, bowling, — all were in progress. The Russian band was playing with all its might and main. The Russian officers were scattered everywhere about the grounds, talking to the ladies, watching the tennis, playing pool and struggling with the English language, when suddenly a loud clanging of bells brought everything to a stop.
>
> At once there was a cry of "Fire!" and in one mad helter-skelter stampede officers, band, ladies, guests and children rushed across the lawn down to the Nahant Road. In this free-for-all, go-as-you-

Home of Senator Lodge

Looking inland, 1879

Town Meeting Cartoon, 1917

please run, Lieutenant Something-or-Other of the Russian fleet won "hands down," and the spectacle was presented of a tall man in scarlet breeches, a long brown coat, a white fur cap, silver belt and silver dagger, leading a motley crew of Russians and Americans down across the lawn of the Nahant Club. Once at the road the crowd paused and wavered, uncertain which way to turn. There was a slight tendency to rush down to what is known as "Irishtown," but suddenly up the Nahant Road came Willie Waters, driving a barge at top speed, and bringing the news that it was "Hervey's" that was on fire. Into this barge climbed all who could, and those who could not fell into the wake, and with Willie Waters and his barge in the lead, the entire company sped as one man to the fire.

But Dexter No. 1, with "Father" Kemp at the end of the hose, was already on the scene. Kemp had manfully fought his way up the stairs of the old Hervey Johnson house and extinguished the small flickering line of fire which extended along the roof. How it caught no one knows. Some said sparks from the chimney were responsible, but as there was no fire in the stove, this seems improbable. Some said firecrackers, but no boy would choose the sloping roof of a two-story house as a place upon which to explode firecrackers; so how the fire started remains a mystery.

But when Willie Waters and his barge, and the Russian officers and band with the Russian lieutenant well in the lead, and the citizens of "Cold Roast Boston" in the rear, reached the scene of action, a great time began. All hands fell upon the house in a body, and rushed upstairs in a solid wedge, carrying all before them, and the old house which Hervey Johnson's great-great-great-grandfather built two hundred years or so ago had the honor of having an officer from the Russian fleet fighting his way up the stairs side by side with little "Buster" Taylor.

The fire department acted with marked energy. It not only put out the fire, but it deluged the whole house and broke many of the windows. After the fire was apparently extinguished Herbert Foster Otis, who is a prominent member of the department and a special policeman of the town of Nahant, appeared astride a ridgepole with an axe, and began to chop a hole in the roof till he was requested to let the old house stand, and threatened with having the hose turned on him if he did not; so he desisted.

Then the hose carriage arrived, and the crowd pulled out the hose and attached it to the engine, not that there was any use for it, but they wanted to do something. After the whole thing was over, and the engine and the hook and ladder truck and the Russians had gone, the police of Nahant arrived at breakneck speed in an express wagon.

CHAPTER XXI

THE SEVENTIES AND EIGHTIES

The second fifteen years of Nahant's life as a separate town is a record of further development as a summer resort, of natural increases in municipal improvements, and of the usual political struggles through which any town passes. The period opens with the sons and grandsons of Joseph and Caleb Johnson holding most of the town offices. There were twenty-three children in these two families and many more grandchildren. Of course, many of them moved away from Nahant. In 1868, of the three selectmen, three school committee, town clerk, town treasurer, highway surveyor and two auditors, eleven in all, nine were Johnsons; and a likewise large majority of town offices were held by them for many years. They were a capable group of year-round residents and naturally could hold their own. But in those days the annual town report was only a list of expenditures, except for the school committee report. Other town departments were not required to make reports and explain their actions. Appropriations were asked for in town meeting with only the hasty explanation and consideration possible during the session. Expenses mounted, as was to be expected, but some of them caused comment. The salary list was moderate enough until the selectmen's salary account jumped in five years from under $400 to over $2,200. There was also the usual unreasonable grumbling that the Johnsons were running things as they liked, and there are always the disgruntled who seize a pretext for complaint. All these things culminated in an auditor's report in the town report for 1876, where comes the first intimation of desire for changed methods. The auditing committee for that year ventured to make some "suggestions, which, if adopted, they think will aid the people in a more intelligent comprehension of their

THE SEVENTIES AND EIGHTIES

municipal affairs." They proceeded to urge annual reports for all departments, with explanations about their work and needs. The proposal was partly followed, for the first time, in the annual town report of 1877. The two boards of auditors for these two years contained three men for the first time. Before that two men were chosen. For 1876 the Board was Alfred D. Johnson, Frederic Tudor and H. C. Lodge, and here appears Senator Lodge's name for the first time as a Nahant town official. This Tudor is, of course, the son of Frederic Tudor who did so much for Nahant. In this latter report reference is made to the "lack of method in making appropriations" and the "inexpediency of making appropriations in town meeting without any previous estimates to judge by." During the two years previous this difficulty was obviated by making small "carry on" appropriations in March, and referring the estimates of appropriations to a committee who reported at a later meeting. The auditors said "the method appears to us clumsy and ineffective," necessitating a second town meeting and leading to confusion and loss of time. Here is apparent the lack of information in town meeting and the efforts to remedy the fault, and it leads up, as years go on, directly to the present-day advisory committee, which exercises exactly the functions found wanting and needed fifty years ago. That Board of Auditors submitted a list of appropriations, and considered them and recommended them to the town in town meeting, and in print in the town report, so that all voters had the suggestion of an independent group to assist them. There can be no question of the need for information. The town departments all have wants, and for them to come into town meeting and ask for money, with only the hasty explanations then possible, means only confusion or political voting, without the balanced consideration necessary for intelligent voting. The budget as a whole gets no thought under such methods. Hence the efforts to improve the system, as evidenced so early in the town's history, and as now culminated in the advisory committee, established in 1922, which is the successor to the warrant committee, established several years earlier.

This group is of non-office holders and therefore is as free from bias and as independent of political influence as seems to be possible. Representatives from all parts of the town are on it. Originally it was instructed to advise the town in writing on all warrant articles requiring appropriations, but in the new by-laws adopted in 1922 the committee can express its opinion upon any matter before the town, and can make suggestions.

The first of these two Boards of Auditors mentioned was Alfred D. Johnson, Edwin W. Johnson and Joseph T. Wilson. Edwin Johnson is mentioned elsewhere, and was until his death a close friend of Joseph T. Wilson, with whom he served in town office for many years. Joseph T. Wilson came to Nahant in March, 1868, to work for the Tudors, and because of his exceptional service in Nahant town offices needs correspondingly exceptional mention. He was born in Kittery, Maine, in 1836, and at the age of nine lost his father and was at once obliged to go to work. There was no compulsory schooling in those days, and Wilson was "bound out" to a farmer. Later he went on various fishing vessels, and this was also hard work, so that his entire boyhood was a part of many years' struggle for a footing in life. As he grew up he was of large stature and great strength, the strong man of the town, until finally he injured himself, and for several years, in the 60's was somewhat out of condition. In his teens he learned the cabinet maker's trade, working in Beverly and Boston, and finally returning to Kittery, where he set up in business as a building contractor. During this period he had studied by himself as well as he could, and finally taught school several seasons. School was then open only in the winters and did not interfere with the other occupations by which he was struggling upward. Then, with a foothold, came the Civil War, in which he could not participate, and its resulting rapid rise in prices brought him face to face with ruin. Fending off, he left Kittery and landed in Nahant because of the job with the Tudors that he found there. But before the end of 1868 he again started building,

THE SEVENTIES AND EIGHTIES 309

and in succeeding years did a majority of the building on Nahant and a larger amount out of town. In 1869 Wilson fell from the Schlesinger House on Prospect Street and was picked up not expected to live, and with his chest crushed. His great constitution saved him, but while he was in the midst of this trouble the heavy September gale of 1869 blew down the Schlesinger House, which he was then building. If struggle builds character, as surely it does, here was struggle. From nine to thirty-three years of age knowing only work, whatever work he could get, — farmer's boy, fisherman, plowman, haymaker, cabinet maker, school teacher, — and fitting one job into another in a strenuous effort to win. Then came rebuffs, even when a step upward was reached, throwing him down so that only his sturdy spirit was left, and he might have repeated the Henley line, had it been written, "My head is bloody but unbowed." But in these uncommonly difficult years he had met men and experiences which gave him character, and on Nahant he made some fast friends almost at once, among them E. Francis Parker, Amos A. Lawrence and Dr. J. Nelson Borland. In 1870 he was elected to the school committee and served until 1897, and was chairman for most of the time. In 1871 he was elected to the library committee, later becoming library trustee, and served until 1897. In 1876 he was elected selectman, serving until 1906, and was chairman for twenty-eight years. He was appointed trial justice in 1876, and held that position until his death in 1914 in his seventy-ninth year. He was moderator at sixty-eight town meetings. This means that he was elected by the people of Nahant for well over a hundred times to various town offices, and his retirement in every instance was voluntary and due to advancing years. The quarter century ending in 1900 saw this one man with very exceptional authority in the town of Nahant, and standing like a rock in his position, but, after all, only holding his place because the people voted for him and had confidence in him. In 1915 a bronze tablet was erected to his memory in the Town Hall, which, after recounting his various services, contains these lines by Senator Lodge: "An able, upright and fearless public servant. A high-minded, public-spirited citizen." Then follows this quotation:

> A friend to truth, of soul sincere,
> In action faithful and in honor clear,
> Who broke no promise, served no private end;
> Who gained no title and who lost no friend.

The summer residents of Nahant supported Wilson in his early undertakings in town. Soon came trouble over the purchase of the gravel pit lot, near where the J. T. Wilson schoolhouse now stands, at the corner of Nahant Road and High Street. The town records for two or three years carry votes of appointment and discharge of committees of investigation, and at one time two or three committees were at work on the question, if ill had been done for the town or if it were only a case of indiscretion leading to suspicion. There is an old adage, "Do not stoop to tie your shoes in your neighbor's melon patch," which should have applied. This gravel pit was described as containing a "sufficient amount of gravel for all coming time." Two of the selectmen had bought this lot from previous owners, claiming they were serving the town's interests because it would have been sold for other uses or beyond the town's recovery. During one of the fiery meetings over the question, the crew of the "Lizzie Phillips," a fishing schooner owned by the Gove family, poured into the town meeting in sea boots and oilskins, just off the vessel, and their timely arrival turned one vote on the subject upside down. During the stir over this purchase the town voted to increase the Board of Selectmen to five members, and the two added in 1876 were Edwin W. Johnson and Joseph T. Wilson. In 1877 Washington H. Johnson went off the Board and William Luscomb was elected in his place. This terminated twenty-three years of service, and a unanimous vote of thanks was given to the retiring officer for his long term as chairman of the selectmen and assessors. The March meeting of 1876 was the first one at which Wilson was moderator, continuing in this position for all but three or four meetings, when he was not present, until 1908, when Senator Lodge began to serve when Wilson was absent. After the first few years Wilson was always re-elected by large majorities, despite the fact that he never catered for votes either with patronage or other political favors. Soon after he came to Nahant he was joined by other members of the family, including Captain Albert Wilson, who died in 1896 and whom many will remember. He was a retired sea captain and held a commission in the United States Navy during the Civil War. With him came his family, which included Albert G. and Frank H. Wilson. All of these were with Joseph T. Wilson in his business. These were distant cousins of J. T. Wilson, but became more nearly related by his marriage with Sophila A. Wilson, a daughter of Captain Albert Wilson. Another daughter, Ellen M. Wilson, married J. Colby Wilson, a brother of J. T. Wilson, and it was Colby, as he was familiarly called, who knew everybody in town and was popular with all. He went on the Board of Selectmen in 1882 and retired in 1906 with his brother. He died in 1917 at the age of seventy-four.

A few notes from the town records for this period are interesting. In 1869 it was voted to "restrain neat cattle" from running at large. Before that cattle were driven westerly beyond Summer Street to what was called the Great Pasture, and allowed to wander at will. By that year there were several residents in the westerly part of great Nahant who objected. There was much discussion, as the "down towners," who had always done this, did not care to lose the privilege. In 1871 it was found necessary to pass another vote "to enforce the state law against cattle running at large." In 1871 came the appropriation of $8,000 for edgestones and concrete sidewalks, with Welcome W. Johnson, George U. Perkins and Henry T. Dunham a committee to expend it. Here was the first extensive installation of the sidewalks now so familiar in town. E. J. Johnson in his history of the 80's, bewails this innovation, saying "so that at the present time these long, black, cheerless walks extend through nearly every street and lane throughout the town. Perhaps in the future the footpaths and green grass may be restored, for then there was beauty and life, even to the grasshopper that flew away under our feet." But the grasshopper may be a burden, as even the Bible reminds us, and sidewalks seem to be an accepted feature of town life everywhere.

In 1872 the town appropriated $500 for a flagpole at the "head of Cliff Street," and old Nahanters remember this tall pole in the little plot, now planted, where Cliff Street meets Nahant Road. Apparently it replaced the old staff erected at the beginning of the Civil War, and it was itself removed in 1882, when it became unsafe. This same year there was an appropriation of $4,000 for a public bathing place at the southwest end of Summer Street, but it was reconsidered and left with the selectmen with full powers. The plan was dropped, although some agitation over it continued for a time. This year also saw the purchase of a gun which was given in charge of the engine company. This appears to have been located on Cannon Hill, above High Street, but the name of the hill seems to antedate this purchase. What finally became of it is the subject of several stories. It was used for Independence Day celebrations well into the memory of Nahanters not very old. Some say it was thrown overboard by some people who were annoyed by it when boys had carried it "down town," and some say it was lost overboard from a boat to which it had been "toted" for the celebration. Others remember it as stored in the old town barn on Spring Road. In 1873 the town bought the road roller that many people remember slowly operating under the power of a pair of horses. This year saw the beginning of a squabble over the road by Bass Beach and Castle Rock. A motion to spend town money to preserve the shore east of this road was not accepted, and in 1875 it was voted to discontinue a "part of Washington Street" against the estate of James H. Beal. In 1874 the town voted to pay Julius A. Palmer, Jr., $5,000 for

B. Frank ("Tony") Taylor and Capt. William H. ("Cap'n Bill") Kemp
Tudor Wharf in background, Nahant Dory Clubhouse at left. From a cartoon by J. Harleston Parker

President Roosevelt introduced by Joseph T. Wilson
At Chairman Wilson's left, G. A. Gove, C. D. Vary, H. C. Wilson, J. C. Wilson. At President Roosevelt's right, W. J. Johnson, R. L. Cochran

rights at Bass Beach. Palmer had built a house on the steep bank near where the steps now go down to the beach, and this was the only building on the water side of the road from Bass Beach to East Point, excepting a small building used for a blacksmith shop and burned prior to 1860, nearly costing the lives of two men then living in it. This was across the road from the Samuel Hammond place. The Palmer house was bought by George W. Simmons and moved up to Pond Street, where in a much altered condition it is the home of James C. Shaughnessy. Palmer was a character in town meeting because a witty and forceful speaker. He was the writer of "Julie and I" letters which many will remember in the "Boston Transcript." Later he left Nahant and passed out of its history.

This period of the 70's was perhaps the time of most talk about tax dodgers from Boston. The Nahant tax rate was low and Boston authorities were sometimes alert. The allegation was wrongly applied to most of the summer residents, for they and their fathers before them were such long-time Nahanters that their intentions were obviously not the dodging of taxes. A good story comes from one instance, however. A wealthy Boston man hired the house owned by Washington H. Johnson, chairman of the selectmen and assessors, — the house on Nahant Road now owned by J. C. Shaughnessy. Boston sued this man for taxes, and in court tried to prove collusion between Johnson and his tenant, whereby if the latter hired Johnson's house his assessments would be light. It seems to have been only the sort of lawyer's littleness which is too often seen. Johnson on the witness stand was asked how much of a house it was that he had let for $1,500, and not seeing the drift of the question he replied lightly, "Oh, it is a little more than a cottage." In his summing up the lawyer for Boston bore heavily on the fact that the chairman of the Nahant assessors had admitted that the house he let for $1,500 was only a little more than a cottage. Therefore the implication that a low assessment was a part of the bargain for the house.

In 1874 Henry W. Longfellow, Alfred D. Johnson and

Joseph T. Wilson were chosen a committee to name the streets of the town, with one name on each cross street from shore to shore. This same meeting voted $30,000 to build a schoolhouse and buy a lot, and it was voted to buy the lot at the corner of Washington Street and Maolis Road. Few could say today where this is, but Washington Street is now Nahant Road and Maolis Road is Ocean Street from Nahant Road northeasterly. At the same time, $12,000 was appropriated for a fire engine house. Neither of these buildings was erected under these votes. The question of annexation to Lynn had arisen, and this same meeting voted that the committee of the Legislature considering an act allowing this be informed that the town of Nahant was against it. Rising valuations had made the town look more attractive to Lynn than when the city avoided all responsibility for the beach road by placing the town line as far against the mainland as it could go. In 1876 it was voted that each town department make a detailed annual report according to the recommendation of the auditors. The previous committee on naming streets appears not to have proceeded far, for in 1879 another committee was chosen consisting of the selectmen, George A. James, Alfred D. Johnson and William Tudor. The latter was a son of Frederic Tudor, Sr. This committee reported in the same year, and the report was accepted, giving street names as they are used today. The town report for 1886 lists the streets of Nahant, giving a brief location of each. It is interesting as showing what they were at that date, and is as follows, except that the locations are not given, as they remain the same today: Nahant Road, and by this time there is no question about its running between Castle Rock and the adjoining estates; Castle Road, Willow Road, Spring Road, Marginal Road, Valley Road, Flash Road, Swallows Cave Road and Bass Point Road. The roads are mostly lengthwise of the town and the streets crosswise, as follows: Cliff, Vernon, Wharf, Pleasant, Summer, Winter, Ocean, Pond, High, Prospect and Emerald. The latest of these was Wharf Street, which was intended to run on the range line which would have placed it as a continuation of

THE SEVENTIES AND EIGHTIES 315

Pleasant Street. In 1884 it was changed to curve around the Abbott Lawrence estate and built as it now runs. Emerald Street was laid out in 1881, but not all built at one time; from Pond Street to Ocean Street it was constructed several years later.

Closing this period under consideration came the discussion of sewers and water supply. The water supply was chiefly from wells, though many houses had tight cisterns catching rain water from the roofs because it was softer for laundry purposes. The few bathrooms were supplied from a large tank in the attic, and this was kept filled by hand pumps. Most year-round houses had only the kitchen sink with a pump over it, and nearly every house had its cesspool and outdoor privy. This method of drainage is not inherently bad, indeed most country towns use it today, but Nahant is ledgy, and it was impossible to know just what underground slopes and pitches were doing to the water supply. When trouble came, perhaps brought in from out of town, one well, for example, near where the post office block now stands, was found badly contaminated. It was so serious that strong chemicals applied to disinfect the drainage gave the water a flavor in a half hour. This well was used by the neighborhood because of its fine water, and children on their way to school drank freely of it. In 1881 a committee consisting of E. W. Codman, Walter Johnson and E. Francis Parker was chosen to investigate the sewage and drainage of the town. Later the same year it was voted to hire experts, to buy special apparatus for cleaning and disinfecting, to instruct the Board of Health to take extreme measures to protect the water against the drainage and to close all wells condemned by the experts. Dr. Thomas Dwight and Dr. Edward P. Reynolds had the water analyzed, and Ernest W. Bowditch was called into conference as a sanitary engineer. The outbreak of typhoid fever had come and there were forty-eight cases between July and October. The possibility foreseen by the town in its appointment of a committee at the spring meeting developed into an actual condition, and of course was full of harm to a place famous as a healthy summer resort. High-speed measures were adopted, however, and a report was given to all citizens just prior to a special town meeting in February, 1882. At this meeting it was proposed to expend $40,000 for a sewerage system, and the unprecedented sum shocked nearly every one. E. F. Parker, of the committee of investigation, said in his bluff manner, which those who knew him will appreciate, "Wilson, you will ruin us, but I'm going to vote for it." The motion to spend this "enormous" sum was made by H. C. Lodge and carried by a large majority.

The work of insuring the town against further trouble, and of assuring people that nothing of the sort was likely to repeat its unwelcome visit, had to go farther. There always would be some ground drainage in places hard to reach by a sewerage system, and the selectmen promptly went to work on the water question. There were many springs in town, and most wells gave un unfailing supply. For years the town maintained large tanks on Flash Road near Spring Road, near or westerly from the Flynn house at Mitchell's Corner. These were used for street watering, and were set up on posts so that the watering carts could drive under and fill quickly, while two or three men operated hand pumps that supplied these tanks. The outfit was in charge of the highway department which operated three or four of these carts, all painted a light blue, and used until other methods kept down dust or made dustless roads. This water came chiefly from the ditches in the Great Marsh, but partly from springs. The town authorities prospected for a water supply, driving wells in likely places. The possible supply from these was estimated and found to be inadequate, but the town went on, and in December, 1883, authorized the selectmen to obtain estimates of the cost of piping the town for water according to plans made by E. W. Bowditch, who had so capably done the engineering work for the sewerage system. In February, 1884, $20,000 was appropriated for water piping to be installed under the direction of a committee consisting of H. C. Lodge, E. F. Parker and J. T. Wilson.

THE SEVENTIES AND EIGHTIES 317

In the hunt for an out-of-town supply of water the town naturally turned first to Lynn, and the response was favorable, but no action followed. Finally the selectmen negotiated with the Marblehead Water Company, who had driven wells and set up a pumping station in Swampscott. This was a private corporation. In July, 1885, the town authorized the contract with this company, and they supplied the town with water until 1899. When this arrangement was made, but before it was public or ratified by the town, Wilson happened to meet, one day, some prominent Lynn men lunching together in Boston. They asked where Nahant was to get water, and if Lynn would not be the natural supply. Wilson's reply was that Lynn was the first place considered, and that the mayor had received the suggestion cordially and said that Lynn could do it, and the only question would be of price. Wilson said he then supposed the mayor meant the price of the water, but after so much delay and no action he felt uncertain about it. He went on to say that Nahant's water supply would come down Ocean Street, Lynn's principal residential street, which would be ditched for the purpose. These men all exclaimed against this and said that it was impossible, but this impossible happening came to pass, and Nahant was able to get what it wanted when it wanted it.

In 1899 the Marblehead Water Company did not desire to go on with the service, and the selectmen applied to the Metropolitan Water Board for a supply. Nahant and Swampscott had been included in the district intended to be served by this State undertaking, but it involved a new water main laid out to these towns for several miles, and their entry was supposed to be together. Swampscott was not ready to enter, whereupon Nahant proposed to pay the entrance fee of $20,000 for herself, and to pay interest on Swampscott's sum until that town chose to apply for admission. The suggestion was approved, but Nahant never paid this $800 interest, as Swampscott entered the system a few months later.

In the year 1881 there was a public meeting in the Town Hall at which resolutions were passed on the death of President Garfield, and in 1885 a memorial service was held after the death of General Grant. At the latter meeting H. C. Lodge was the principal speaker. The year 1878 saw the first selectmen's report, signed by Artemus Murdock, chairman. Up to about that time information about the activities of the several town departments had been lacking and voters had to be content with sidewalk gossip or with what was told in town meeting. The policy of letting citizens know as much as possible about town affairs had begun, however, and continues to the present day, as it should. Probably the wind of suspicion, which whined and whistled occasionally, would have been quieted had there been opportunity for citizens to appreciate and consider thoroughly what was going on.

This period of the 70's and 80's saw continued prosperity as a summer resort. The list of houses and dates of buildings given elsewhere indicates when many people called Nahant their permanent summer home, but a little further comment is needed. The poet Longfellow is a man many Nahanters remember, although he died in 1882. Apparently his first year in what came to be known as the Longfellow house was 1858. Subsequently he bought it and occupied it regularly. This house was earlier known as the Wetmore cottage. Longfellow came to Nahant first about 1850, for an entire season, though he writes of earlier visits. This first summer he lived at the Jonathan Johnson house, which stood on Nahant Road where now is the post office block, and which was moved, enlarged and remodelled into the Rockledge Hotel at Willow Road and Wharf Street. This Johnson was a son of Joseph Johnson and the father of Edward J. Johnson and Annie E. Johnson. Here he wrote "The Golden Fleece" and a part of "Hiawatha." From here he writes of seeing the cows going over the beach at sunset from the cow rights of Nahant to the cow sheds of Lynn, saying it was one of the prettiest pictures of Nahant. He speaks of it in "The Bells of Lynn," written fifteen years later, the original manuscript of which was presented to the Nahant Public Library by his daughter, Miss

Alice Longfellow. He mentions famous men and their coming here, speaking of meeting Agassiz and Sumner at the steamboat wharf. Emerson was often here, dining with Longfellow and walking the beach towards home. After five years here, the poet spent the season of 1855 at Newport, but returned to Nahant in 1856, to the Mountford cottage, elsewhere mentioned, on Swallows Cave Road. Then he boarded at the Hood house, directly opposite the Whitney homestead. He speaks of being with R. C. Winthrop, Lord Napier and Mrs. Kemble, the famous actress, all at Nahant.

From his own house Longfellow overlooked the fleet of boats and yachts anchored, as always, around Nipper Stage Point. This he enjoyed; indeed, the activities of the sea interest nearly every one. Here he wrote —

> Four by the clock! and yet not day;
> But the great world rolls and wheels away,
> With its cities on land, and its ships at sea,
> Into the dawn that is to be!
>
> Only the lamp in the anchored bark
> Sends its glimmer across the dark,
> And the heavy breathing of the sea
> Is the only sound that comes to me.

One of the fleet under his eyes was the yacht "Alice," which many remember. A photograph of her is in the Nahant Public Library, as also of the poet's brother-in-law, T. G. Appleton, surrounded by the crew of the yacht. Appleton owned the "Alice," although Longfellow's son Charles was a prominent spirit in it, and sailed in it across to Europe. The poem "Three Friends of Mine" is the poet's appreciation of Agassiz, Felton and Sumner. The first two lived on Nahant in summer time, and Sumner was a frequent visitor to several homes and to the Nahant Hotel. George Abbot James had a room in his house called the Senator's room, from its frequent occupancy by this guest.

Daniel Webster also visited at Nahant, often with his relative James W. Paige. In 1852, when Webster failed of the nomination for the presidency, a reception to him was given by Paige, to which all Nahant citizens were invited. Again in this same year he was back, much enfeebled, only a short time before his death.

John Lothrop Motley on Nahant reaches back to an earlier period, also. It has already been related how he went to school in the old stone schoolhouse. Apparently he came here, in summer time, whenever he returned from Europe, where he spent so much of his life. At least a part of the "Rise of the Dutch Republic" was written while he was staying at the old Hood house, across from the Whitney homestead. In 1875, the last summer he was in America, he was the guest of Mrs. John E. Lodge, Senator Lodge's mother, at her home on Cliff Street, called for a long time the "Lodge Villa." Motley's correspondence, edited by George William Curtis, contains many letters written from Nahant. One speaks of staying at his brother Edward's and dropping in on Agassiz. These two places were adjoining, and though altered, are more or less unchanged in general appearance from those early days. N. P. Willis is another writer who came to Nahant, usually stopping at the hotel on East Point. George William Curtis is already mentioned. Both these men write of the delights of the town. Then come Sarah Orne Jewett, Frances Hodgson Burnett and Elizabeth Stuart Phelps Ward. Mrs. Ward lived at Little Nahant and Mrs. Burnett in the Tudor Homestead, now the Nahant Club. Many remember the latter as an enthusiastic horsewoman, riding about town. James T. Fields, a brother-in-law of Mrs. James H. Beal, was frequently here. William Dean Howells was at Little Nahant for a season. Cyrus W. Field, who laid the first Atlantic cable against many disappointments, lived at the Tudor homestead when it was a hotel. In 1881 he lived in the house now owned by Alexander Lincoln on Pond Street, since remodelled. Some of these names come down to later years, but few into the present century. Whittier

Harry C. Wilson

Selectman and Assessor

Thomas Roland

Charles Cabot Johnson

Town Treasurer

Otis A. Johnson

School Committee

was here, as well as Hawthorne. Both wrote about Nahant.
Whittier's lines are familiar:

> But fairer shores and brighter waters
> Gazed on by purer, lovelier daughters,
> Beneath the light of kindlier skies,
> The wanderer to the farthest bound
> Of peopled earth hath never found
> Than thine — New England's Paradise.

The early 70's saw Oliver Wendell Holmes coming here sometimes as a visitor, and in 1873 occupying the "Charles Amory house," now known as the Dr. Dwight house. In 1876 he was with his daughter, Mrs. Sargent, in the Welcome Johnson house, just above the old post office and store. He also wrote stanzas in praise of the town. Then there was Harriet Beecher Stowe, spending her later years with her daughter, Mrs. Henry F. Allen, first in the Washington Johnson house, now Shaughnessy, across from the Edgehill, and later in the Dr. Haven house, at the corner of Nahant Road and Pond Street. Her grandson, Dr. Freeman Allen, is now a summer resident, owning a house at Summer and Cary Streets. Robert C. Winthrop may be mentioned, mostly remembered as an old man occupying the Winthrop house on the corner of Nahant Road and Winter Street. He succeeded Daniel Webster as United States Senator, but served only one year, and was an unsuccessful candidate for Governor of Massachusetts in 1851.

Many people remember the annual encampment of the First Corps of Cadets of Boston, changed over during the World War to the Two Hundred and Eleventh Coast Artillery. Cadet week was a lively time, with its flock of tents, fine band concerts, brilliant uniforms and Governor's Day. Many of the men were from the families of summer residents, or related to them, and much entertainment seemed to reach a climax during this period of four or five days. Cadet week was always in July, except in 1870. In 1869, July 13 to 17, the camp was near Mrs. Moering's house on Pond Street, later owned and occupied by Charles Thorndike. This was Cannon Hill, and perhaps earlier called Lindsey's Hill. This house was built in the winter of 1867–68, and the development of the grounds and planting seems to have made its use for a camp ground inconvenient, for in 1870 the camp was in the large field back of the Schlesinger house on Prospect Street, between Pond and High Streets. The Schlesinger house was near, and its owner leased this field from the Tudor heirs, afterwards buying it. This year the encampment was from August 9 to 13. The further dates follow:

1871	.	.	. July 25 to 29	1876	.	.	. July 17 to 22
1872	.	.	. July 23 to 27	1877	.	.	. July 16 to 21
1873	.	.	. July 22 to 26	1878	.	.	. July 8 to 13
1874	.	.	. July 21 to 25	1879	.	.	. July 14 to 19
1875	.	.	. July 19 to 24	1880	.	.	. July 12 to 17

Thus over a period of twelve seasons this event was an annual occurrence of much interest to Nahant. Children lined the adjoining streets and watched the doings, for at least there were always sentries pacing their routes, and when the Governor of the Commonwealth came, and a review was held, the martial music sounded from a band that was always a good one, and the attraction was complete. This field was known for years as the Cadet Field, but one must have been a Nahanter for nearly fifty years to have personal knowledge why it was so called, and many good Nahanters of today would not know what was meant by it. After 1880, for a season or two, the summer residents arranged among themselves to have band concerts (were they once a month?) at several estates offered for the purpose; but this plan languished and band concerts as a regular and expected event were not again known until they were an activity of the Nahant Club, mentioned elsewhere. There is evidence of earlier encampments at Nahant, but the records of this organization, as now available, do not support it.

Another item of interest to Nahant relates to tennis playing. Dr. Haven, who built his house at Nahant Road and

Pond Street in 1882–83, maintained a first-quality gravel court in the rear, close to Pond Street. Here were held annual tournaments for several seasons around the late 80's. They were invitation tournaments and not a part of the National Championship layout, but here played many experts. James Dwight, Richard D. Sears, Philip S. Sears and Herbert M. Sears were all Nahanters. The first two were National Champions, in succession, and the three Sears brothers are sons of Frederic R. Sears and grandsons of David Sears who owned the early Coolidge-built house on Swallows Cave Road. To Dr. Haven's came also Larned, Beekman, Wrenn and Hovey, together with many others. The grounds were private, but proximity to the street provided a vantage ground offering a good view of fine playing.

Not so very many years earlier the first lawn tennis game in America apparently was played at Nahant. In August, 1874, J. Arthur Beebe, a son-in-law of Mrs. William Appleton, brought over a set from England, and it was at once set up by James Dwight on the Appleton place, formerly David Sears, on Swallows Cave Road, in the part of the lawn easterly from the house. The house and this lawn now occupy the same positions and present a similar appearance, though there has been some remodelling and planting. A Newport man imported a set the same season, but it was not set up until the following year, and in the spring of 1875 E. H. Outerbridge of New York brought in a set which was used at the Staten Island Cricket Club. This appears to have been the first of lawn tennis on any club grounds. In the summer of 1875 two more sets arrived at Newport. Bishop Lawrence, in his "Memories of a Happy Life," writes: "Later, in 1874, I played upon the first lawn tennis court in the country, with a tennis set which had been brought from England and set out on the lawn of my Aunt Emily Appleton. When in the Brookline Country Club a short time ago, my attention was called to a very old-fashioned racquet to which was attached this inscription: 'Racquet used by Bishop Lawrence in the first lawn tennis game in this country.'" Bishop Lawrence adds the statement of another who saw the game played on the grounds of the Germantown Cricket Club in September, 1875. James Dwight, later national champion, who laid out this tennis court in 1874, is a brother of the late Dr. Thomas Dwight. Richard D. Sears, also one time national champion, gives much of this information, and adds that there was an informal Nahant Tennis Club which held a handicap tournament first in 1876. Some of the members were James Dwight, F. R. Sears, Jr., Horatio Curtis, Robert Grant, Lawrence Curtis, Louis Curtis, W. C. Otis, Jr., H. G. Otis, S. E. Guild, Frank Merriam, Morgan Post, C. A. Prince, M. H. Prince, R. S. Greenough, William Lawrence, Senator Lodge, Samuel Hinckley, W. C. Otis, Sr., and Henry R. Grant. This list is from memory and may not include all of the original players. Several of these will be recognized as Nahanters of much later years. For several seasons Richard D. Sears occupied the Dr. Haven house, but later moved elsewhere, as did his brothers, so that the only ones of the name now coming to Nahant are Mrs. K. W. Sears and her daughter, Clara Endicott Sears, who is the author of an interesting volume on Bronson Alcott's "Fruitlands," and another entitled "Gleanings from Old Shaker Journals."

CHAPTER XXII

BASS POINT

BASS POINT was the name given to the point of land now the Bass Point House property. In later years the name came to be associated with a far larger area, until it would be rash to venture establishing its nominal limits. Certainly it is everything as far as the marshes in a northeasterly direction; and while Fox Hill and Castle Road may seem outside of Bass Point, very many people understand it to include everything beyond the marshes southwesterly or westerly. It would seem that this district, including these wider limits, had no permanent residents or permanent buildings prior to 1800. Earlier mention is made of men of whom no record remains affecting Nahant. The 1706 division of the town mentions Taylor, Jacobs and Hudson, as if they were living there, but they may only have been the men to whom land was allotted in this division of Lynn's common land. All who have dealt with the question seem to agree that the "Old Castle," built shortly after 1800, as is described elsewhere, was the first permanent building on Bass Point. The old roads were Flash Road and Castle Road, with Castle Road connecting through in crooked fashion to the first range road easterly. They were only cart paths, and in the easy fashion of the times, with land fairly inaccessible and of little value, their location was not too definite, though doubtless old deeds and their accompanying records would show how far they were laid out. The old roads within present-day memories are Flash Road and Castle Road as now, with Willow Road running by Bear Pond and up the hill and down again to the Bass Point engine house, with another branching off near Bear Pond to run over by the foot of

Bailey's Hill and along the shore, returning to Willow Road through what has come to be known as the "Midway." This name was applied to this section of the road after the Chicago Fair of 1893, with its Midway of varied amusement enterprises. Many other streets have been built, all to accommodate the breaking up of the land into house lots.

Nathan Mower started his career on Nahant by bringing parties over from Lynn, making chowders and frying fish over near the North Spring in the early days of the Maolis Gardens, and perhaps before that. This was wholly on Great Nahant. Soon he bought the property at Bass Point, now known as the Relay House. There were two buildings on it, one a pavilion on the ledges near the present dance hall, and one a barn which Mower changed into a kitchen, near which were rough tables at which dinners were served. In 1862 Mower built the oldest part of the hotel, leaving the kitchen as it was. Some of this construction can still be recognized among the many changes which have since been made. He ran this house for twelve years, till his death in 1874. In 1873 he enlarged the house. He was succeeded by his son, John D. Mower, who managed the hotel for seven years. It was then let to Mack & Searle for two years, George Batchelder for two years, and Searle, formerly of Mack & Searle, for seven years more. In 1892 Eugene H. Brann leased the property and has operated it until 1927, buying the entire estate in 1907. Brann has made many changes and additions, developing the place to considerable size. Of late years it has been open all the year, claiming to be the first hostelry in town open in the winter. Among houses of any size this is undoubtedly true. It is also claimed that the many ways of cooking lobster originated here, with Mower, before which time lobsters were only boiled, or were boiled first and fried or broiled afterwards. Mower or his successors thus contest for a share in the development of the lobster industry, and certainly the food sprung into greater general favor and use during these times.

The Trimountain House, at the foot of Bailey's Hill, was a

small house on land owned by the Tudors. An early proprietor was John Granger of Lynn, but the place is indissolubly associated with Sylvester Brown. Brown was born in Lynn at the corner of Nahant and Ocean Streets, but was a familiar figure on Nahant in the 70's. He kept this house open from 1874 until the United States government bought the property in 1901, and he lived on it afterwards until his death in 1919, at the age of eighty-five. He was known to the town as "Vess" Brown, and he used to tell of his descent from a Brown who was one of the first settlers of Lynn. He was one of "Master King's schoolboys," a group that once went to school together under this teacher in Lynn. For many years an annual outing was held at the Trimountain House, where one might see dignified men playing leapfrog, marbles, and other reminders of days perhaps sixty years gone. This house was enlarged by Brown, and another built near by for further accommodations. The older building was torn down in 1922, and now nothing remains of this place famous for its fish dinners.

The first Bass Point House was built by Mrs. Tudor, after her husband's death in 1864 and probably before 1868. In 1870 it was opened by Thomas Demster, who previously was the proprietor of the Bay View House at Summer Street and Willow Road in Great Nahant. After Demster came Batchelder & Howard, and in 1891 Anderson. In 1892 Andrew G. Fuller and J. A. Flanders leased the property from the Tudor heirs for five years. In 1894 the Bass Point Hotel Company was formed. Members of the Clyde Steamship Company, then furnishing steamboat service to Nahant, were in this company, and later the entire assets were taken over by Fuller and members of his family. The oldest part of the house built by Mrs. Tudor was burned in 1894, and was at once rebuilt, a complete plastered house, in the record time of eighteen days.

A later hotel was the "Bay Side Inn," built in 1907 by Walter H. Southwick, who for a time was proprietor with a manager. Afterward he leased it, and finally it was sold.

Then there was the "Brenton," built in 1909 and opened in 1910 by Frank Keezer who was for a time owner and manager. Later it was sold to other parties. Keezer opened another place, but finally moved away from Nahant, to which he had come several years before, interesting himself in Bass Point enterprises. Southwick, also not a native, has lived here so many years he has earned the title of Nahanter. In 1915, after the death of Joseph T. Wilson, he was appointed judge of the local court, a position he has held since that time. Brann, of the "Relay House," like most of his predecessors, has not been active in general town affairs, but always interested and always helpful, and when the hat is passed around for some organization or needy individual he is a subscriber. Neither he, a Maine man, nor the Fullers of the "Bass Point House" were natives of Nahant.

Besides these larger houses Bass Point has had many smaller ones, crowding thick upon each other as is usual in amusement resorts. Before the days of prohibition Nahant was a license town, and most of the larger places on Bass Point supported barrooms with bars of considerable length. There were also many places selling illegally, and there were other things, also common accompaniments of such places. In short, Bass Point as an amusement resort was something of a problem for a town otherwise sedate and orderly. It was no worse than other similar places. In fact, at any time a respectable family could go all about the district, get a good dinner, enjoy good music, and return home without seeing any outward semblance of things not quite as they should be. It was a peculiar condition. Many people were interested in these activities, legal and illegal, proper and improper. Many others came there to enjoy them or did not object to them.

Many more, who would have complained under other circumstances, held silent because of unpleasantness that might result from neighbors. Complaints were made and withdrawn when the complainants were told they must appear in court as witnesses. Evidence was hard to get. Spotters were quickly spotted. Plain-clothes men from out of town could

The Old Town Hall and High School

Town Meeting in Old Town Hall
Senator Lodge, moderator; D. G. Finnerty Beyond
Foreground, standing, C. D. Vary, F. A. Wilson

not help much. Convictions were few, though the district often needed cleaning up. Those uninformed wondered at it. Sometimes a minister in the village church would fulminate against the town officers on account of it. But as Judge Wilson often explained it, he knew Boston hotels sold liquor. They had a right to do so, and he was positive they did. But his testimony to it on the witness stand would not be accepted because it was an assumption and not personal knowledge.

In the summer of 1914 came one of the times when a minister fulminated against Bass Point conditions, but made an initial mistake by antagonizing many who would have been his ready helpers in any clean-up campaign. His accusations, based on insufficient or erroneous information, made the usual few days' stir, but no results followed. To "muddle along somehow" can get to be a tiresome policy. At that time the "Lynn Item" gave several columns to the question, and in the issue of August 20 stated that "every fair-minded person that ever visited Bass Point recognizes the fact that existing conditions are a menace to the morals of the young." Whether this condition yet persists let those say who know of drunkenness, for one instance, among boys of school ages who visit this section.

Then came 1916, with no steamboat service to Boston, and soon 1920, which stopped all legal liquor selling. Bootlegging started. Nahant is a coast town and liquor was landed in it. Men formerly in the Bass Point enterprises became bootleggers, with others not so connected. Some bars were opened, and are still doing business. Soon some of the hotels, struggling for a living, yielded to the stress of finance and re-entered the game of selling liquor. Another section of the community, that around Short Beach, sells more or less, also, and there are other scattered sore spots. The shadow of impropriety rests upon the town from the efforts of men to do business yielding large profits because illegal and a little risky. A larger price may always be charged for goods sold thus. As Dr. William J. Mayo once expressed it, the doctrine of moral obligation may become ingrained, but with too many people "the Oriental point of view more or less prevails that no obligation exists which is not enforcible." He also named another group with a similar point of view. Again, the evidence against them is hard to get, although it would seem to be rather nonsense that in so small a town official activity may not lead to rapid discouragement.

In the meantime some attempt to spread the amusement resort section to other parts of the town is made. Short Beach village would like it, and none too scrupulous attempts, assisted by lawyers who are ready to circumvent a law or regulation, would lead to more of this character of town in this vicinity. By wide-awake measures it will fail. Farther out along Short Beach is another effort to develop in this way. The entire main road to Nahant might be kept clear of such things, if the maximum attractiveness as a residential town is to be maintained.

The Bass Point amusement district is one of the most beautiful parts of the town. Bass Point itself and all the adjacent shores, and Colby Hill, with its wonderful outlook, were jammed with cottages, mostly small, and many of them so flimsily built that they were practically summer camps. In fact, forty years ago or so a large section of this district was a tent colony, and from tents came shanties, from shanties, camps, and from camps some cottages of good appearance. Colby Hill was mostly owned by Miss L. Hortense Colby, a daughter of Alonzo Colby, an old Nahanter who built the McBurney house on the corner of Pond and Prospect Streets. Back of the amusement district, westerly, was the property formerly of Phillips, elsewhere mentioned, and a few good houses with ample land around them. These were broken up into smaller lots, with streets made to serve them, and the place was developed to the pleasant residential district now in evidence. Still later, land by Castle Road to the north, and Fox Hill near by, were laid out into house lots and are now well covered with houses. The last twenty-five years have seen all of this. Flash Road on either side was residential, mostly owned by people of Irish nativity or descent.

Thus it may be seen that the amusement section or shore resort district, at Bass Point, is restricted to one part, where it always has been and where it developed gradually from small beginnings. The householders in other parts seem to desire none of it extended further, or near them. Thus is the usual experience repeated. Everybody goes more or less to such places of amusement, but nearly everybody would rather not live too near them. Even the good people who come to the midst of it for a summer month, and accept sardine can conditions for a while, would not choose it for a permanent home. Yet many homes are near to it and good houses are along some of the near-by streets. For these the hustle and hurly-burly of a few months in summer become familiar and unnoticed, and there are also those who like it, and who are none the worse for it in nerves or disposition. Every one to his taste. The general statement seems to be correct, however, that amusement resort conditions are more or less antagonistic to home-making conditions, exceptions notwithstanding.

More recently Bass Point appears to have suffered a decline as an amusement resort. There are those who say much of the district will change over to houses, with the hotels more like summer hotels elsewhere, instead of places chiefly known for dinners and dancing. What the future holds for Bass Point may be hard to prophesy, but to be a proud part of the town it must further interest itself in community beauty and welfare, so that it may be a district exciting admiration for its good looks in houses and grounds and general cleanliness.

On June 11, 1925, a disastrous fire swept over a large part of Bass Point, starting in a house back of the Relay House property and running easterly over Colby Hill nearly to the water. About sixty houses were burned, including some of the best and some of the poorest in the district, and not so much affecting the part most given over to shore resort business. Many people were heavy losers. Insurance rates were high, as they usually are in a closely packed area of wooden houses not adequately guarded by building laws against a fire menace. The building ordinances of the town are not now sufficient to reduce a conflagration hazard, but they are far superior to those in effect when most of these structures were built. In spite of the perils already exemplified by the fire, efforts have been made several times to modify the building laws, even since this lesson was taught in such a terrible way. These regulations, like all other rules and laws, are restrictive and often cause an increased expenditure. It is the old story over again. When people live together in communities they lose more or less independence of action, and must in many ways do what is best for the whole group. The only way to get what is best for all is by means of rules and laws, and frequently, in specific cases, these seem too restrictive and arbitrary. The fire hazard at Bass Point is still tremendous, as is evidenced by the insurance rates which remain very high. These rates are not guesswork, but are the result of careful analysis of experiences. Better building laws will reduce them as will nothing else. Adequate water supply and fire-fighting apparatus help a little, but appear not to be the chief factors reducing a conflagration hazard. The insurance rate certainly may be considered a comparative measure of the danger of fire.

During the Spanish American War the United States government maintained a range-finding station on Bailey's Hill, which was soon after developed into a permanent fixture. Almost at once came the proposal to build a fort on one of the hills, the one westerly from Bailey's Hill, and the government bought all the land from Bailey's Hill to Flash Road and from Bear Pond and Pond Beach to Castle and Trimountain Roads. In 1900 and 1901 the transfers were made of the many pieces of property, which included one hotel, the Trimountain House, and thirty-three houses. The hill was full of small houses, mostly for summer use, and out toward Flash Road were others, the latter owned by year-round residents. The former owners were allowed to stay on for a while, but finally all the remaining buildings were sold at auction. The fall of 1903 saw many houses moving at once, chiefly across Flash Road to land bordering on it or on the newly made Fox Hill Road. One building mover towed one house behind another, three at once. Some house owners were lulled to security by this occupancy after they had sold, and paid no attention to the auction or to preparations for houses in a new place. Thus they lost their homes and bought them back again from the shrewd purchaser, who made a large profit while not taking too great an advantage of the losers.

Then for several years this tract of nearly two million square feet of land lay idle and filling up with wild growth as does all uncared-for land. Soon most signs of any habitation were gone, while the houses moved over across Flash Road lost all the appearance of travellers and seemed permanent fixtures. In most cases they were improved, as the whole gamut of transactions, with the government paying fair prices, resulted in some money available for betterments. Finally plans for the fort were completed and construction began. The hill was undermined with passages, magazines, barracks, and whatever pertains to such an establishment. Two great guns were brought on scows and landed on Pond Beach, to be dragged laboriously up slopes left or made for the purpose, and mounted ready for use. One went up the old Willow Road and along a nearly level cut to its position; and one around to Trimountain Road and thence up the hill to a similar runway, left to give access for such a heavy weight, to the masonry platform whereon it was mounted. Soon after the World War was over this addition to the defences of Boston Harbor was completed, and stands today in such condition that readiness for effective service would mean only a short time. This fort was named Fort Gardner for the Hon. Augustus P. Gardner, a Congressman from Essex County and son-in-law of Senator Lodge, who died in service during the World War.

A familiar place dismantled by this government purchase was the homestead of Robert Coles, an Englishman and well-known figure about town until his death in 1913 at the age of eighty-two. He left a large family of children many of whom are now Nahanters. A son, Robert, has been chief engineer of the fire department; Herbert is town forester and tree warden; and James A. is sewer commissioner. This home place was westerly from Willow Road and up a hundred yards or so from Bear Pond.

This acquisition by the government meant the discontinuance of Willow and Bass Point Roads where crossing this land. The former now comes to a dead end westerly just beyond Bear Pond, and the latter runs along easterly as far as Trimountain Road. The government has permitted the use of the abandoned portion, but with no maintenance they are in bad condition. This land, bordering Bear Pond and a part of the marsh adjacent, cuts Bass Point off from the rest of the town so that there is no public access to it except by Flash and Castle Roads. These seem ample for all needs, though sometimes less convenient than was Willow Road.

Further speculation on the development of Nahant is rather idle. The influx of visitors on wheels is a nuisance to Nahanters, who can thank their lucky stars that the Beach Road is a town road over which they have full control, or can speedily get it, even in front of the State Bath House up to the Lynn line. One can, however, imagine Nahant increasingly infested by automobiles, with its present shore resort district altered to serve this newer sort of temporary crowd, and with other sections also given over to it. Perhaps the State might step in and turn the whole town into a State reservation. The State inundates towns for a water supply, why not condemn them for a breathing area? It already places the State's rights, or imagined rights, above the town's sovereignty. As an example, consider the Little Nahant sewerage construction, well under way in the fall of 1927. Permission to enter the sea through any near-by outfall was refused. It was too near the State-owned beaches, and the town was compelled to expend a few thousands more to reach another location near a town-owned beach. The fact is immaterial, as pollution from these outfalls on Nahant is wholly negligible; but the principal remains. The State's interests, through its park system, are deemed superior to the town's interests. How much further this will go, who can tell? Already there is a spoiled Short Beach, and recently an important town road was used for parking, for bathhouse, eating place and rest room, regardless of the real traffic conditions for which the road was built. Lately the State authorities have increased available parking areas outside the road limits along Long Beach. These are most used at night, and are a paradise of a petting place, as well as a haven of refuge for those who would evade the true-name law at hotels. There are also a few who use it appropriately. A part of the training of the modern miss appears to be the reverse of reserved, while of course the callow youth takes what he can get. All this, with such splendid opportunities afforded, contributes to the terror and sometimes humiliation of parents, and thus becomes an important factor in adult education by the young.

Most Nahanters want Nahant a pleasant residential town, with citizens interested in town welfare, living, therefore, in houses that are not merely summer camps, and not so crowded together that no one looks at them with pleasure. Good people herd this way. That is not the point. Nahant as a fine place in which to live will not grow that way. Houses may be small or large, but they must aid community beauty, and their owners must strive for Nahant welfare as a residential town, or else the place will cease to be such. If one does not want a public dance hall, a whiskey still, a blatant band or a half dozen shacks on the next lot to his own home he must assist in keeping them away from other homes, for most Nahanters do not want these things next door. Such have their place and are sought by many people once in a while. It is the old question put yet again. What do Nahanters want their town to become? The things which are indicated are not matters depending upon money. In England or France the smallest cottager's house fits and enhances the landscape, usually, while in America too often it does not. Great corporations try for results by carefully planning and building, and careful communities have planning boards and zoning committees, both of which are on the way to help Nahant. The important related question of valuations, taxation and expenditures is considered elsewhere.

But the crux of the matter now considered is that citizens cannot watch the town drift, doing or allowing one action or another, and see the community reach a condition they may desire. The better way is to look ahead, if possible, and set a standard they think should be attained, and measure contemporary activities by it. This seventy-fifth birthday year is a good time to halt for a while and look backward and forward, planning what may come and what is wanted and work accordingly.

The Nahant Town Hall

The Nahant Public Library

CHAPTER XXIII

THE NINETIES AND LATER

THE period of the 1890's is often called the glorious 90's. Events were not moving too fast for general appreciation. People were not puzzled by new incidents of life and living, as they have been in this last decade. Prices were low. Wages were low, also, though it is often questioned if the wages of that time did not buy more of the so-called needs and luxuries than the wages of today can buy of the greatly increased "needs" of this period. It is often claimed that the 90's were a far more comfortable time in which to live than has been any decade since.

On Nahant a transition was occurring. Bass Point was growing. Opposing political forces were gaining in strength, and the number of men increased who could get their will in town meeting, and get election to town offices on account of a following of their own which their activity and aggressiveness had built up. Among these was James A. Carahar, a Bass Pointer, who served on the Board of Selectmen three years. He was a candidate for the Board of Selectmen for several years, but had consistently opposed the opinions and policies of Joseph T. Wilson and J. Colby Wilson, so that he was not successful until their retirement at the end of 1905. The annual town meeting in 1906 saw the greatest change most voters ever knew in town officers. The older Wilsons were gone and the Board of Selectmen was Charles D. Vary, Harry C. Wilson and James A. Carahar. Vary had been on the Board for some time and was therefore experienced. He was almost an old Nahanter, coming here a score of years earlier, and marrying a daughter of C. Hervey Johnson. He retired from the Board of Selectmen in 1915, on account of ill health, and died in 1917. Wilson, son of J. Colby Wilson, had completed a term on the school committee and retired from that office. He also is linked with the old Johnson family of Nahant through his marriage to a daughter of H. Shepard Johnson. The town meeting item for which Carahar is best remembered is his advocacy of the purchase of a stone crusher. This he brought forward many times, but never successfully, and it was some years later, in 1915, that the town made the purchase. For several years this was operated under the control of the highway department. The counterclaim always was that crushed rock could be bought cheaper than the town could make it. Apparently this claim was justified, for although no accurate account of production was kept, rough measurements and calculations occasionally made seemed to show a high cost. During the last few years the plant has not been used and is now out of condition. Charles D. Vary is among the men rising to public notice during this time and serving first on the school committee and then as selectman, and later as chairman of the Board. Harry C. Wilson, coming to town office first as school committeeman in 1897, went over to the Board of Selectmen, where he has now seen nearly a quarter century of service. Charles Cabot Johnson is another who gathered a constituency of his own, serving the town first as town clerk and then as town treasurer, a position he now holds with over a score of year's service behind him. Johnson has also been a member of the Legislature and of the Senate of Massachusetts, — positions which, of course, meant a following beyond the limits of Nahant. Walter H. Southwick is another, not holding town office, except the Governor's appointment as trial justice, but frequently bringing new ideas and proposals to town meetings. The beginning of this decade finds Joseph W. Hammond and Samuel H. Hudson on the school committee, as will be seen in the lists of town officers. Hammond is a son of John Q. Hammond, an early school committee member who is mentioned elsewhere. Soon after this he moved out of town and does not appear in Nahant affairs.

THE NINETIES AND LATER 339

Hudson is a son of Samuel Hudson who lived on Pleasant Street, owning the house now owned and occupied by William F. Waters. He was librarian of the Public Library for several years. He resigned from the school committee before completing his three-year term of office. Soon he ceased to be a Nahant resident, and he is today a prominent lawyer of Boston.

Another man of this period was Dr. William Donison Hodges. He was for many years a resident of Nahant and interested heartily in the welfare of the town. He served as town physician for four years, disinterestedly, and in 1892 was elected to the school committee. In this same year he was a member of the State Legislature from the district which included Nahant. He was born in 1854, a son of Dr. R. M. Hodges, well known in his profession in Boston, who built the house at the corner of Pond Street and Nahant Road in 1872. This house is now owned and occupied by another son, Winthrop T. Hodges, also a well-known Nahanter, interested in all Nahant affairs and Nahant people, and giving frequent service on various town committees. In 1927 he was elected to the Board of Public Library Trustees, succeeding Albert G. Wilson. Dr. W. D. Hodges, who died in 1893, is remembered by many for his cordial friendliness which endeared him to all who knew him. He practiced his profession in Nahant, making long seasons here, latterly in the Welcome W. Johnson house next to the old general store and post office, and even those who only met him professionally felt a pleasure in his geniality. He was an amateur enthusiast in the weather, and for several years some of his records were published with the town report.

Dr. Hodges was succeeded on the school committee by Jonathan E. Johnson, who served for one year and then resigned to accept an out-of-town pastorate in the Episcopal ministry for which he had studied at Harvard and elsewhere. Johnson's successor was Otis A. Johnson, another native Nahanter, who served on the Board for twenty-one years and was chairman for a good part of the time, until his death in

1915. He was a son of J. Bishop Johnson, who lived on Nahant most of his life, but who was not related to the larger Johnson family of the town, although his first wife was a sister of Edward J. and Annie E. Johnson. Bishop Johnson and a crew operated a fishing vessel, when fishing was an industry here, and he also conducted a retail business, continued by his son, in a building lately remodelled into a house and located at the corner of Willow and Valley Roads. J. Bishop Johnson was a selectman in the early days of the town. He died in 1896. Daniel G. Finnerty soon loomed as a political factor, serving as selectman and as assessor. He was always a well-known old Nahanter, reckoning many years of life in the town until his death in 1928, and often called the "most good-natured man in town." And there are others, of a later period, who will not be specifically mentioned because contemporary. Many of those mentioned have come through to the present time, but it is not intended to discuss individuals or their policies of within fifteen or twenty years, except for unattached general statements. An exception may be made of William F. Waters, who does not go back to the 90's. He was first elected town clerk in 1904, and has held the position ever since, and so acceptably that he has no opposition, proving himself careful, accurate and impartial in his conduct of his office. These various elements, more in number, perhaps, than previous years had shown, meant political conflict and some turmoil. This extends to the present time. Usually the various aims are for the town's welfare, but sometimes the individual, group or sectional need is placed ahead of the town as a whole. There is much honest difference of opinion, much that is mere politics of good and bad kinds, and much that is only intolerance, for tolerance, like the measles, is always more or less unpopular.

The turmoil sometimes occurring in the Board of Selectmen is often confused by the election of the whole Board each year. With a board of three, two are a control and choose a chairman. Hence there is a concentration on two candidates, many people voting for two and not for a whole Board. The ardent supporters of any one candidate vote "bullets" for him, casting two blanks. Thus there are always, nowadays, many blank votes cast for this important office. People who would like to vote for a full list of three often dare not, fearing the third (or even second and third) vote may put another candidate up to defeat the one who has their first preference. The cure is easy, and was proposed in town meeting by Fred A. Wilson a score of years ago. Elect this Board one a year for three-year terms. Then the candidates will be squarely opposed to one another and the issue will be direct and not confused. This proposal has been rejected in two town meetings, but it is hard to see why any should oppose it excepting those who want to continue this less direct method, trusting sometimes to its chances to slip into office, and fearing a direct single-headed opposition vote. The wishes of the people would, however, then be executed, and every elected member would receive a clear endorsement which present conditions do not allow. If the vote were for one candidate he would be rather certain to receive a majority of the votes cast. Under present conditions often no one gets any such vote, and the blanks mean that a political or personal following has preferred one or two candidates, regardless of a proper consideration of the three best among those running, which is what the town has a right to expect for its highest welfare.

In a town report of the late 80's Joseph T. Wilson, looking forward, advised the speedy payment of the debt for water and sewer systems in order that other expenditures might be made as they were found necessary. The building to house the Public Library is of this period of the 90's. This was followed by the Valley Road schoolhouse, the Town Hall building, the Long Beach Road, and the J. T. Wilson schoolhouse, besides many other expenditures of considerable size, though smaller than those mentioned.

A prominent figure among the summer residents appearing during this time was Curtis Guild. He never was a legal resident of Nahant, but spent the greater part of each summer here except when away on government service.

In 1892 he married Charlotte, daughter of Edward C. Johnson, a long-time summer resident living on the shore at the northeast end of Pleasant Street, which runs through to the water between this estate and the Agassiz place. Guild went to the Spanish War in 1898. He was Lieutenant-Governor of Massachusetts from 1903 to 1905, and Governor from 1906 to 1908, inclusive. In 1910 he went to Mexico for the Federal government, and in 1911 began two years' service as Ambassador to Russia. He died in 1915. Because of his official position Nahant saw some famous people whom he entertained. Other sources of information easily reached make it unnecessary to write in more detail about this distinguished man. His hearty cordiality will be remembered by all who knew him, and his high qualities as a public speaker are known to a far larger number. Perhaps Nahanters remember best his appearance with Senator Lodge in the old Town Hall during the free silver campaign of the 90's; and again these two men, whom Nahanters were so fortunate to have among them, were together on the platform as speakers at the semi-centennial celebration in 1903.

It would be difficult to name all the bright lights among people who came to Nahant for a season or two. Such a list is sure to be far from complete. A little recollection would result in a few authors of note, or others high in their profession, such as De Forest Brush, who lived in the Edmund Johnson house on Central Street in the 90's, while he was painting his "Mother and Child," now in the Boston Art Museum. Fortunately this avenue of investigation is not important. Nahant attracted many such people who, because of their short stay, were little identified with any town activity or influence.

This period of the 90's saw many and familiar summer residents growing older and going to a final reward. In some cases the splitting up of estates among several children found none of them able to carry on here. Another factor was the trend toward greater acreage, even to farm-size places, than is possible in Nahant. These things led to the sale into other hands of fine estates that had been identified with one family for a generation or more. The town has been mostly fortunate in these transfers, for usually the new owners have bought for single occupancy and have continued the places as they were. The breaking up into small lots with small houses, if carried to too great an extent, would be unfortunate for the town, considered municipally. It is pointed out elsewhere that houses paying taxes of under a hundred dollars do not pay their share, and if the town were filled with such, increasing taxes and heavy retrenchments in expenditures would become necessary. The greater costs of maintenance of houses and grounds, which since 1914 have mounted like everything else, have borne heavily upon people living on incomes from investments. They were justified in spending about all of it, and this class of income has increased only slightly. The result is a necessary economy which shows, in some cases, in less well kept places. While still handsome and still a valuable asset to community beauty, they may lack that last spick-and-span touch of perfection which was possible when money bought more.

The town report dated 1897 contains an exhaustive report by a special committee on underground wiring and municipal electric light plant. The committee was Fred A. Wilson, George E. Poland and Ellerton James. To get poles and wires out of sight is always desirable, and had been discussed in town for several years. This report set out the cost of such an undertaking, which was so great that the town never went further with the project. This was the period when municipal ownership of public service plants was much in mind, and the committee report was in sufficient detail to show clearly that no advantage would accrue to Nahant from any such undertaking. The committee had the assistance in their investigations of expert service from the well-known firm of Stone & Webster of Boston.

The year 1897 saw the retirement of Joseph T. Wilson from the public library trustees and the school committee, after a generation of service on both boards. It was particularly hard for him to leave the latter, especially after a large petition from the school children urged him to continue.

At the annual town meeting for 1894 the town voted to adopt the so-called Australian ballot system of voting, now so familiar everywhere, but then fairly novel. Previously voting was by ballots prepared by the candidates, some of whom furnished sheets containing an entire slate for all offices. Two or three of these were obtainable outside the polls, while "stickers" for use over any printed name were widely circulated. A voter usually took every ballot and sticker that was offered to him, and then more or less surreptitiously crumpled what he did not use into his pocket, and folded up one and voted it. Of course, it was not such a secret ballot as the present system, which was, according to law, used for State elections for a short time before its adoption for local voting. The "new" method is now such a fixed part of election practice that anything else would seem strange, and indeed a person must be past middle age to remember these old ways. One curious feature of town elections is the repeated attempts of candidates strong enough to be sure of their own election to carry one or more others into office. Instances of this are spread over the last thirty years or more, since more and more men have built up a personal following. The efforts seem almost uniformly unsuccessful. It would appear that it is one thing to secure a personal vote at the polls, and quite a different and far more difficult matter to get that same following to vote for another.

In 1908 Fred A. Wilson proposed that salaries for the school committee be abolished, and this met the hearty approval of Otis A. Johnson of the Board, who was instrumental in making the change. The question had also been raised if it was legal to pay salaries to the school committee. It had been felt for several years that too many men ran for this office merely because of the salary attached to it. It seemed to be a Board which, like the Public Library Trustees, who were never on the salary list, might find its membership among people willing to serve and be sufficiently

The Nahant Church
Built 1868

Village Church
Built 1851

St. Thomas Roman Catholic
Church
Built 1872

remunerated by the honor of this service. Men fit for public positions are rarely those attracted only by the pay. The principle may hardly be extended to other town offices, however, for they require more time than is allowed by spare time opportunity. The enthusiastic student of either of the educational branches of the town's efforts does worth-while work regardless of pay. The other branches of the town's work are more like business positions, for which pay is expected, even though there is great opportunity for energy expended beyond usual limits or any thought of money compensation. This is the same as in any occupation of life.

It was in 1909, while serving on a committee for better fire protection, that Thomas Motley died. His fellow members on this committee were Walter H. Southwick and Joseph T. Wilson. Several special committees on fire protection and the fire department have their work spread through the years, and their reports published with the town report, and each has contributed to the efficiency and good condition of this arm of the town's service.

In 1908, following the death of Frederick R. Sears, the State Tax Commissioner directed the assessors of Nahant to assess his estate for a large sum discovered by the executor's returns, under which it appeared further taxes could be collected for certain years. The details of this wrangle are not now important. The town was dragged into it, though the final court decisions made it appear that the claims against this estate were justified. Action in various courts occupied several years, until finally the town emerged victorious, though with such large legal fees to pay that for a time it seemed hard to say which lost most, the victor or the vanquished. This is a usual concomitant of every sort of war, even of our recent World War. With the dust finally cleared away, however, after a half dozen years of trouble, the town had money to pay off the balance of a heavy debt incurred by building the new Town Hall and the road over the beaches to the Lynn line. These undertakings found the town at one time owing $85,000.

In 1908 a change in State laws made a separation of the Boards of Selectmen and Assessors, and provided that the latter be elected one-third each year for a term of three years. The same men could still hold both offices, and for a time this was done, but in late years the personnel of the two boards has been different. There never has been a time, as it happened, without at least one member of the Board of Selectmen serving on the Board of Assessors. Another change, by State law, requiring a separate Board of Registrars where the number of voters exceeds 300, came in 1907. The registrars are now appointed by the selectmen under certain restrictions imposed by the law. One of these is that no registrar shall hold any elective town office. For one of this new board the selectmen promptly chose Joseph T. Wilson, who had lately retired from the last elective office he held, but was of long years' experience in the registration of voters. Wilson remained in this service until his death in 1914.

In 1903 came the fiftieth anniversary of the town, and a celebration extending over three days honored the event. The March town meeting authorized a committee and made an appropriation for expenses. The following committee was chosen, the first two afterwards elected chairman and secretary, respectively: Fred A. Wilson, Albert G. Wilson, Lawrence F. Cusick, Charles B. Goodell, George A. Gove, Samuel Hammond, Winthrop T. Hodges, Arthur S. Johnson, Charles Cabot Johnson, James C. Shaughnessy and Harry C. Wilson. Incidentally it seems unusual to note that the first death among these eleven men was of Albert G. Wilson, twenty-four years later, and almost on the eve of the seventy-fifth anniversary of the town. Two other members, G. A. Gove and C. B. Goodell, have since removed from town, while eight are yet residents of Nahant, with five holding elective town offices. The celebration came on July 12, 13 and 14, the first day being Sunday, when special services were held in the three Nahant churches. Monday forenoon was given to land sports and the afternoon to water sports. Tuesday forenoon saw the parade, and the afternoon was devoted to speeches from a stand erected on the Nahant Club grounds near the corner of Ocean Street and Nahant Road. Band concerts were interspersed, to the number of seven, throughout these two latter days. Through the efforts of Senator Lodge a fleet of eight warships lay south of the town, open for inspection. There was a band concert one day from the squadron, and they participated in the water sports, while a large shore party joined in the parade on Tuesday. Samuel Hammond of the committee was chief marshal of the parade, with Thomas S. Bradlee as chief of staff with a corps of fourteen horsemen, a few of whom, horsed for the first time, ended with a declaration that it would be the last. Nothing of this showed outwardly, however, and the grand parade was an impressive scene, moving on time and without a hitch past the reviewing stand on Nahant Road midway of the Nahant Club grounds. On this stand were the notables, town officers, Governor Bates and his staff, Lieutenant-Governor Guild, Senator Lodge, officers from the warships, and some of the town celebration committee, together with officials from neighboring towns and cities. The parade included two battalions and bands from the fleet, the Governor and other guests, the Nahant Life Saving Station crew and exhibit, the Massachusetts Humane Society boat and crew and the band, several floats and exhibits of a half dozen town departments, and floats or exhibits of various trades in town. After covering the town for three miles or so the line of march ended down Nahant Road easterly beyond Winter Street. The officials alighted at the reviewing stand and saw the rest pass by. Tuesday afternoon was given to speaking exercises. Senator Lodge delivered the principal address, which was later printed by the town in a little monograph done by the Merrymount Press, and therefore a fine piece of bookmaking. Governor Bates and Lieutenant-Governor Guild also spoke. Joseph T. Wilson, as chairman of the selectmen, was presiding officer. Then in the evening came a fine display of fireworks and the last concert. This was in the field, then wholly open, bounded by Nahant Road, Pond Street and Spring Road, the streets affording ample opportunity for spectators.

The Hotel Tudor was open throughout Tuesday to invited guests from out of town. The entertainment available there was in part of a sort to lure some kinds of people away from the parade, the speaking and the concerts. In fact, some quite worthy visiting officials stuck close to the hotel for most of the day. So far as was known, however, they were able to return to their respective abodes and constituencies without moral damage to their reputations. How sweet are the uses of opportunity!

Tuesday evening also saw a fine illumination. A majority of the houses in town had been decorated with bunting and flags, and strings of electric lights were everywhere. The searchlights from the fleet played over all, and the last evening of the celebration was an event to be remembered. The day went out in a blaze of glory that was veritable as well as proverbial. The whole town was awakened, enthusiastic and helpful. The various beforehand preparations incited even those who had been slow or careless. Participation was general. A two-day holiday was declared in all town departments, except for the police, which was overworked, as is usual with celebrations and holidays. The total expense to the town was over $4,000, a sum which probably would not be spent in these days when it would add a dollar to the tax rate. But in making good community feeling and a worthwhile town spirit it was reckoned money and energy well used. The committee worked hard. It was divided into subcommittees of three, each handling a feature of the events, and getting together often for a general discussion and general approval of subcommittee suggestions. By working through to the end with careful attention to all details, everything appears to have gone smoothly. For the seventy-fifth anniversary the town is more restricted by law in its expenditures, but it may be hoped that 1928 will see some notable recognition which may reawaken a town spirit which will strain forward for best things as a municipality, and not rest content, as too many do, to muddle along and condone. The best is not too good as an aim in town welfare, for that way lies progress toward it. Everywhere too many people are saying something should be done, and doing nothing. No town is so good it may not be improved, and indifference means backwardness. Prayer and perspiration are both necessary to good results.

CHAPTER XXIV

ORGANIZATIONS

It is an impossible task to trace very much of the organized groups Nahant has had. Doubtless early days, back of the recollections of any now living, had their groups; and even the clubs of recent years, with people now living who were a part of them, have so quickly faded into the haze of the past that accurate data are not available. The churches have always had their assisting societies, active under enthusiastic leadership, or waning when the push of a few was lacking. This is true in any sort of group, even a small temporary committee. Give it an active worker and results follow.

Connected with the schools came, in later years, the Parent Teachers Association. This also seemed to flourish for a while, and then interests changed and apathy followed. Some stirring personalities may push it along again, when doubtless it may become the good influence it is intended to be. Of recent origin is the Crocker Chapter, Firemen's Relief Association Auxiliary, named for Francis B. Crocker, so long chief engineer of the Nahant Fire Department. This is a more or less social body aiming to be of value within the circle of the fire department members. There are Boy Scouts and Girl Scouts, the latter not now strong. There was a Patriotic Forum that functioned in Nahant in 1918 and an organized group was desired to assist the community singing. Miss Olive R. Grover at once started mustering in a group of girls, and it was discovered that a Girl Scouts Council was starting in Boston. Hence Nahant was in at the beginning of Girl Scout work in Massachusetts, organizing in February, 1919. Mrs. Abby May Roland was commissioner, Miss Bertha L. Johnson was secretary-treasurer, Miss Olive R. Grover was captain of the Girl Scout Troop and Miss Emma L. Poland was captain of the Brownie Troop. The Boy Scouts depend upon voluntary aid, but if filling a gap in public education, might well be a part of the public school system. The Girls' Community Club, a purely social group, was started in 1923, and kept going for two or three years, apparently filling a need.

All these days have seen others. In the 80's, when roller skating was a fad, five young men were a group who once a week turned the old Town Hall into a skating rink, where all could enjoy or watch. It was well patronized. These men were, if memory serves, Fred Taylor, John Cole, Everett Covell, Otis Johnson and Frank Wilson, all now deceased. Taylor and Cole were drowned when returning from Boston to Nahant in their catboat, the "Zantho," in 1885. It is supposed that the mast slipped out of its step and broke through the side of the boat. Everett Covell was a son of Samuel Covell. These five adopted the initials, printed on the admission tickets, "B. U. F.," the meaning of which was not divulged, but the boys of the time, now mostly gray headed but remembering this, derisively called it "Bust Up Friday" or "Five United Bums." Friday was roller skating night.

Then there was the "Friday Night Club," the "Peninsular Club" and others which met around at the houses of members and read papers or had some other form of entertainment once a fortnight. These were gone before the 90's were over. The "Nahant Magazine Club" circulated magazines, just as is done in other places today. The need for this ceased when the Public Library moved into its new building in the early 90's, and opened its reading rooms with plenty of magazines. Later comes the "Dickens Circle," where a group of Dickensians read Dickens, acted Dickens, or, on occasion, dressed to portray his characters. The activities of this group over a decade or so included a float in the parade held July 4, 1919, to celebrate the homecoming of Nahant soldiers from the World War. Only recently has this club seemed also to languish, not because of a lessened interest, but because changing times bring other demands for time and energy, and the driving force is directed elsewhere.

Among the men's clubs maintaining club rooms came the "Crescent Club" down on Summer Street, where much whist was played, much tobacco burnt, and stories, grinds and jokes held sway. As is usual in club rooms a few were to be found there almost nightly, while others visited once or twice a week, and some infrequently. Then the Canary Club, down on Willow Road, in the store building owned by D. G. Finnerty, and of which Finnerty was called the patron saint. This was an enthusiastic group, mostly of Finnerty political admirers, and therefore assumed to be a political club. On more than one occasion they marched in celebration of his victories on town meeting day. This club flourished to a zenith coming, perhaps, about 1912, and now for many years has been forgotten. In 1912 came the formation of the "Maolis Club," the most pretentious of them all because it at once raised money and built a club house, containing all the usual appurtenances of a neighborhood club on a scale suited to the town and its needs. Built near the center of Nahant's present-day population it aimed from the start to be a social center. But again it has fallen short, part of the time, of those marks which were set for it. The World War hurt by diverting much energy into more important channels. Rising prices gave a more difficult road to travel than it had before. Yet it yields, as it always has, an opportunity for a community center such as any town needs and should develop. As in other groups the active, driving leadership is a first requisite, but any work of club officers or committees is much lightened if the response is hearty, and members get what seems to be only a habit, — a habit of participation. Even an electric button has to be pushed. The movie theatre has been a growing distraction, and the automobile has extended the radius of social activities. Both of these factors have yet to prove their value as elements of human welfare.

The 90's saw a vigorous "Village Improvement Society." It was founded in 1897 and had as its object the preserva-

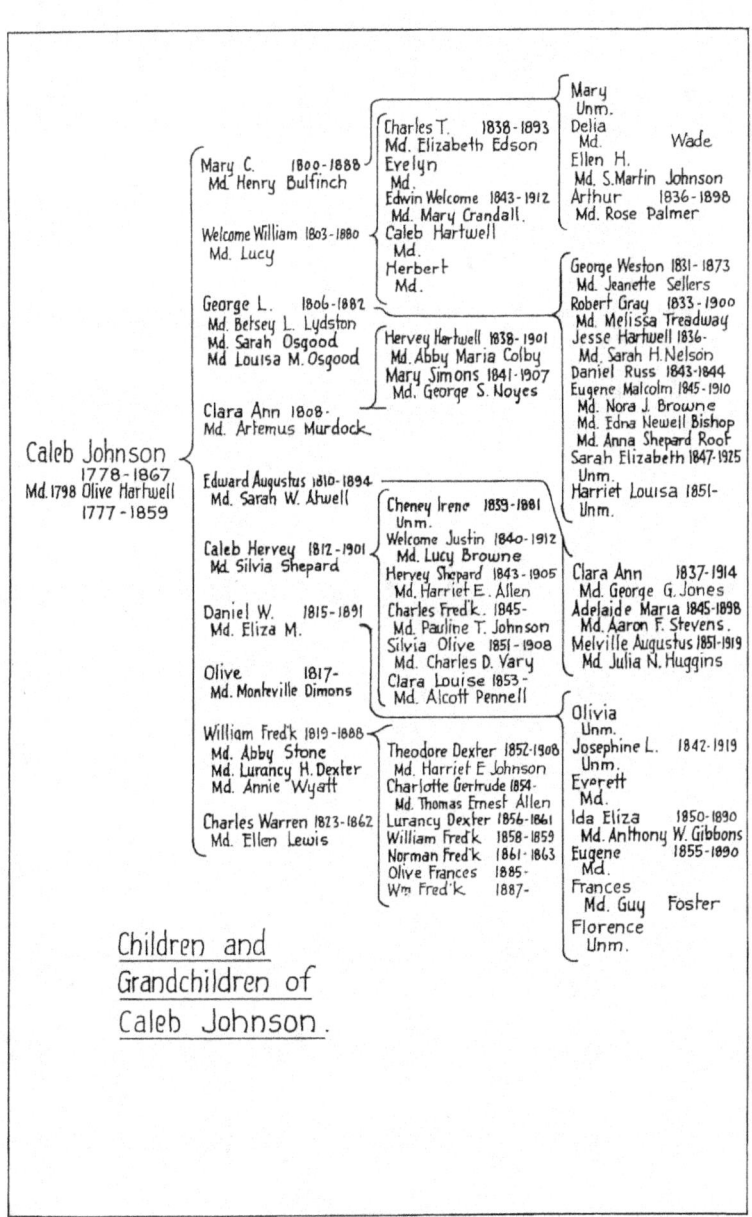

Children and Grandchildren of Caleb Johnson.

Family of Caleb Johnson

tion of the natural beauties of the town and the improvement in welfare of the people. It met once a month in summertime, and its first officers were George Abbot James as president and Miss Abby E. Wilson as secretary-treasurer. The latter is a daughter of Joseph T. Wilson. James was succeeded as president by Horatio G. Curtis, and Miss Wilson, on her marriage to David Demarest and removal from Nahant, was succeeded by Mrs. Samuel Hammond. Various committees pursued their work and good results followed. One year the society sponsored a course of lectures in the winter at the Town Hall, a reminder of the old-time lecture courses mentioned elsewhere. This group was also partly responsible for the purchase by the town of Marjoram Hill for a public park.

The meetings, with reports of committees, were sometimes curious. Conflicting ideas were thrashed out, but as usual in such groups, trifles sometimes caused most trouble. They strained at a gnat and swallowed a camel. Then on one occasion was a discussion about rubbish barrels for the beaches. One dignified summer resident arose, and with an accent tempered by a recent visit to England, said, "And do you think the trippers would know for what they are?" The last four words were spoken with a rush that carried James, the president, into realms of not understanding, although he was partial to the English pronunciation of certain words. The question was repeated, and given a third tryout, before many knew what was being said. This organization, like so many others everywhere, finally waned from lack of enthusiasm. The clock ran down and there was no one to rewind it.

The Nahant Women's Club is another instance of an organization which has lived through the counterforces of war, movie, automobile or what else. These groups seem to be an American institution, not sprung from the seeds of English or European custom, as have so many of our ways and means. They represent a more or less spontaneous movement grown in forty years to a membership over the country of over three millions. Perhaps no equally large grouping can be cited, anywhere in the world, which is devoted to mental self-improvement. Women may take up golf, or they may continue trying to learn something, or they may more and more get swept into the maelstrom of business; but the women's clubs have for a generation been a torch of learning doing a good part in an important development.

The Nahant Women's Club was founded in 1895, and apparently the idea emanated from Mrs. Pauline T. Johnson, wife of Charles F. Johnson. Mrs. Johnson is another example of how Johnsons flocked to Nahant, for she was born a Johnson, not related to the old Nahant Johnson family. Her father was Joseph Johnson, a brother of Charles T. Johnson, who will be remembered as keeping a fish market down on Nahant Road near what is now the corner of Wharf Street. A sister of these men was the wife of Captain William H. Kemp. Mrs. Pauline Johnson's mother was also a Johnson, whose two sisters married Jesse R. and S. Martin Johnson, brothers, and grandsons of Joseph Johnson of the old Nahant Johnsons. This newly mentioned Johnson family came to Nahant from Harpswell, Maine, and were distant cousins of J. Bishop Johnson, who was himself a nephew of "Uncle" William Johnson, and therefore cousin of David Johnson. Mrs. Pauline T. Johnson taught school on Nahant, and in later years served on the school committee. She discussed this matter of the women's club with several others, and after some informal meetings of a small group, a call was issued for an organization meeting. Most of the first officers were of the preliminary group. Mrs. Sophila A. Wilson, wife of Joseph T. Wilson, was an enthusiastic worker for it, and was chosen its first president, a position she held for several years. The first vice-president was Mrs. Pauline T. Johnson. The first secretary was Mrs. Lu C. Johnson, wife of Otis A. Johnson. The first treasurer was Miss Mary Johnson, a daughter of H. Shepard Johnson. The first board of directors included those officers and Mrs. Emma O. Whitney and Miss Florence A. Johnson, the former the wife of William R. Whitney, and the latter mentioned elsewhere. The husbands named are nearly all mentioned elsewhere and have been men of importance in town, but are only second fiddles, recalled for identification purposes, in this Women's Club movement. None of these women, however, are of the advanced type of non-malleable independents who object to being called by the names of their husbands, with a "Mrs." prefix. The club has increased the social welfare of the town and has broadened the lives of many of its members. Its early meetings were held in the old Public Library room in the old Town Hall. The town improved this room for such purposes, and it was named "Wood Hall" in honor of William Wood, the founder of the library. Latterly the club has met mostly at the Maolis Club House.

The Nahant Golf Club dates back to the early 90's. This was laid out on the "Great Marsh," starting from Emerald Street and continuing toward Bear Pond and westerly to Mitchell's Corner. After a few years the course was extended across Spring Road and up the hill west of the Maolis Club House. This was before this latter land was developed into house lots with the roads built as they now run. Still later, perhaps around 1910, this newer part was given up and the course continued for a while as it was originally. It was always a short course, and devoid of interest compared with any first-class golf links. But it was an early effort to provide this game for Nahant enthusiasts, before days when the automobile could whisk people ten or fifteen miles away to courses greater in area and more diverting in variety. The club had only a locker building on the course. Perhaps people recall Edward C. Johnson as one of the latest players, persistently pursuing this exercise with a regularity which gave suspicion that it was done for exercise only.

It was on this golf links, on June 24, 1911, that Harry Atwood, an early airman of this vicinity, first brought an airplane to land at Nahant. He carried Edward E. Strout as a passenger. The landing was about a hundred yards inward both from Emerald and Pond Streets. It was a real event, and whistles blew in Lynn as he flew in from Atlantic, over on the South Shore. Strout carried a letter from Senator Lodge to Joseph T. Wilson, as follows:

MY DEAR MR. WILSON: — I gladly avail myself of the first opportunity to send you a letter by way of the air, which is offered to me by my friend Mr. Strout. I trust that he and the letter will arrive at Nahant in perfect safety, and I hope it will find you well and everything going well with you. I am coming home for Commencement at Cambridge, and I hope that I shall be able to see you next week.

       Very truly yours,

         HENRY CABOT LODGE.

There were also letters from Mayor Connery of Lynn to Judge Wilson and to Charles D. Vary, chairman of the selectmen. It seemed an accomplishment, this safe ride and safe landing, in 1911.

The Nahant Book Club is an old organization which is still active. It circulates worth-while books, mostly non-fiction, among the summer residents. It was started about 1880 by Mrs. Edward Motley and her neighbor, Miss Nancy Cary. Since the former's death in 1898 Mrs. Thomas Motley has interested herself in its management. At present three books are circulated weekly throughout the summer.

A later Nahant organization is the Mortimer G. Robbins Post 215 of the American Legion. It was named for the first Nahant boy killed in the World War. Robbins enlisted in the Canadian Forces and met death on the battlefield in the fall of 1917. News of the event reached Nahant about the middle of November. He was a son of Mrs. Dana A. Sanborn. Sanborn, not a native of Nahant, is one of a considerable group of present-day good citizens who were enabled to take up residence here after transportation facilities were improved by the electric railroad and the automobile. He has served on the Board of Selectmen and on several committees. The first meeting of Nahant veterans for the purpose or organizing was held at the Maolis Club House on September 23, 1919. About ten days later, at another meeting, officers were elected, and a charter was obtained from the American Legion dated August 1, 1920. The membership increased from an original fifteen to a roster of seventy-five on August 1, 1924. On Armistice Day, November 11, 1920, a set of flags was presented to them: the national colors, by the Nahant Auxiliary of the American Red Cross; the Post colors, by Mrs. Dana A. Sanborn; the State colors, by the Nahant Public Safety Committee; and the Navy colors, by the Crocker Chapter, Firemen's Relief Association Auxiliary. The Post has been active and has endeavored to fill a gap in town life. In 1924 the town voted to give over the old Town Hall for its purposes, and appropriated a part of the money needed to remodel the building and put it in condition for Post uses. Here it was proposed to encourage games, and assist the Boy Scouts and the Girl Scouts and do other appropriate things. Before this building was used the Post occupied two rooms in the new Town Hall, which were large enough for its own purposes, but not suited for the greater place it was planned to fill in Nahant activities. Annual carnivals have been held, yielding each year money sufficient for the execution of these plans. The Post, however, is finding the financial load rather burdensome, through no fault or lack of its own, but because people now have to pay so much for the bare necessaries of life, such as automobiles, radios and silk stockings, that just naturally their support of churches, clubs and institutional work of all kinds must lag. Moreover, the wage-earning class, which has seen its income enlarge more than others, has not yet acquired the habit of giving to these things. Other people, with proportionately less income than fifteen years ago, are urged to give more, but are less able to give as much. As a result, whole pages of newspaper and daily mail appeals frantically plead for money institutional work should have, for these factors of life are important, and their expenses have increased as much as any. Thus all Nahant organizations, like those elsewhere, have felt a pinch of poverty, and should not. At the same time, it should be remembered that the town is small, and the total sum, by optimistic count, that may be raised here for churches, clubs and charities, may be less than expected, and far less than enthusiastic planners of all these activities would like to see.

Then there is the Nahant Auxiliary of the Lynn Chapter of the American Red Cross. This group was organized, in 1917, to work for the World War. Mrs. Alice C. Wilson was chosen chairman at the first meeting, a position to which she has been re-elected annually to the present writing. She is Mrs. Fred A. Wilson. The first secretary-treasurer was Miss L. Ernestine Whiton, now removed from town, and the next, who now holds the office, was Miss Agnes Follen, a daughter of Edward Follen. The first meeting was of delegates chosen from other Nahant organizations. Several of the members took courses of instructions in making surgical dressings. Those certified to be monitors in Red Cross workrooms wore a blue veil, and for greater proficiency a red veil could be worn. At the first work meeting in the Town Hall eighty-one women were present, with a teacher from out of town, as at first no blue veil women were among the local membership. Mrs. Carrie E. Bruce, wife of Frank E. Bruce, had charge of sewing during the war period; and Mrs. Elizabeth H. Sherman, wife of Lawrence F. Sherman, had charge of knitting. On her removal from town Mrs. Lucy R. Sanborn, wife of Dana A. Sanborn, conducted this branch of the work. Bruce is another comparatively new Nahanter who has given good service for several years on the school committee and on special town committees.

The organization has continued in service to the present time, answering calls for help in peace-time disasters. The great local trouble where it played a part was the Bass Point fire, in 1925, where promptly doctors, ambulances, trucks and food were on hand. Fortunately the two former were not needed. Again it met the lack of money to give and the lack of habit of giving, which hampers other groups. Any one who spends a few dollars a year for gasolene should feel a real personal urge to pay a dollar a year for Red Cross membership. Yet people have to be pursued, corralled and cajoled, and, in ways strange to those who appreciate the need for institutional work, will avoid what should be an obligation. It takes a lot of coercion to secure free-will offerings.

ORGANIZATIONS 359

Another group is the Little Nahant Improvement Association, organized in 1914. The first officers were E. F. Fiedler, president, G. H. Green, treasurer, and George A. Wood, secretary, and these, with Arthur H. Wilson and Frank C. Stuart, made up the executive committee. The aim was to promote social intercourse and to meet to discuss local problems of general interest and act to promote the welfare of the town and of the Little Nahant section. During the World War this group also went dormant because of so much to do in other ways. In 1925 it was brought to liveliness again, and George F. Hogan was chosen president, with Fred Kaulback, vice-president, C. C. Whittemore, treasurer, and George A. Wood, secretary. Hogan continues in his office to the present time. All of these people are what old Nahanters call newcomers. As is stated elsewhere, Little Nahant had no colony of residents until so lately that it is the newest section of the town. Yet some of them, going back over fifteen years, no doubt feel almost Simon pure, and certainly many of them are interested citizens of the town.

The Nahant Dory Club seems to be a crystallization of amateur boat racing, with temporary committees and enthusiastic participants, reaching back over many years, even to the regattas of old Nahant Hotel days, and including all sorts and conditions of boats. The club started about 1894, with Mason W. Hammond, commodore, and Kenneth Horton, secretary. Hammond was a brother of Samuel Hammond and wrote the two newspaper articles elsewhere quoted. Soon he moved to New York and was succeeded as commodore by Francis S. Parker, son of E. Francis Parker. In 1896 Winthrop T. Hodges became secretary. For a few years the club flourished, and then the War with Spain in 1898 took away many leading spirits, decidedly killing its activities. The inertia continued until some more enthusiasts aroused it, about the time the first "bugboats" were built. In these later years Arthur S. Johnson looms as a prominent figure, as well as a decided fan on small boat sailing. His earlier yachting experience was on the "Breeze," owned by his father, although he had made a trip to Australia in the ship "Big Bonanza."

The club house at the wharf was built by permission of the town in 1906. The summer Saturday afternoon races, familiar for many years, are a feature of Nahant life. To overcome the difficulties of proper handicaps, clubs everywhere began many years ago to separate racing boats into classes. This did not stop inadequacies, alleged or real, and it began to be the custom, within ten or fifteen years, for a group of enthusiasts to order boats all of one model from one builder. By this means all handicaps were avoided, and it would seem that skill in handling played the whole part and determined the winners. But still questions arise. The boats of a group may be as nearly alike as skill can build them, but can hardly be exactly alike. Slight variations come in the hulls and the rigging, and the set of a suit of sails cannot be exactly the same. Summer breezes are "streaky," and often the distances between the boats on the course is the luck of the wind. All of this is the gamble of the game, and zest is added, perhaps, when a little chance is thrown in. Winners may strut, but losers can congratulate themselves on their skill with luck against them. They do not have to seek "that proud misery's peace no victor ever knows." It is the same in all games, even that bane of womankind, auction bridge. In 1927 the town recognized this sport as an asset to life here, and made appropriations to repair the wharf and landings. This summer boating is an attraction and should be maintained, with suitable encouragement from the town when needed. The sea around Nahant is ideal for pleasure sailing, and always there will be many people interested in it. For over eighty years this has been evident. To maintain the wharf and approaches in suitable condition for this sport is a desirable and important piece of the town's activities.

Another organization familiar to all Nahanters is the Nahant Club, a club devoted to summer residents and open only in the summer months. In 1888 Francis Peabody, Jr., a son-in-law of Abbott Lawrence, was the chief figure in a

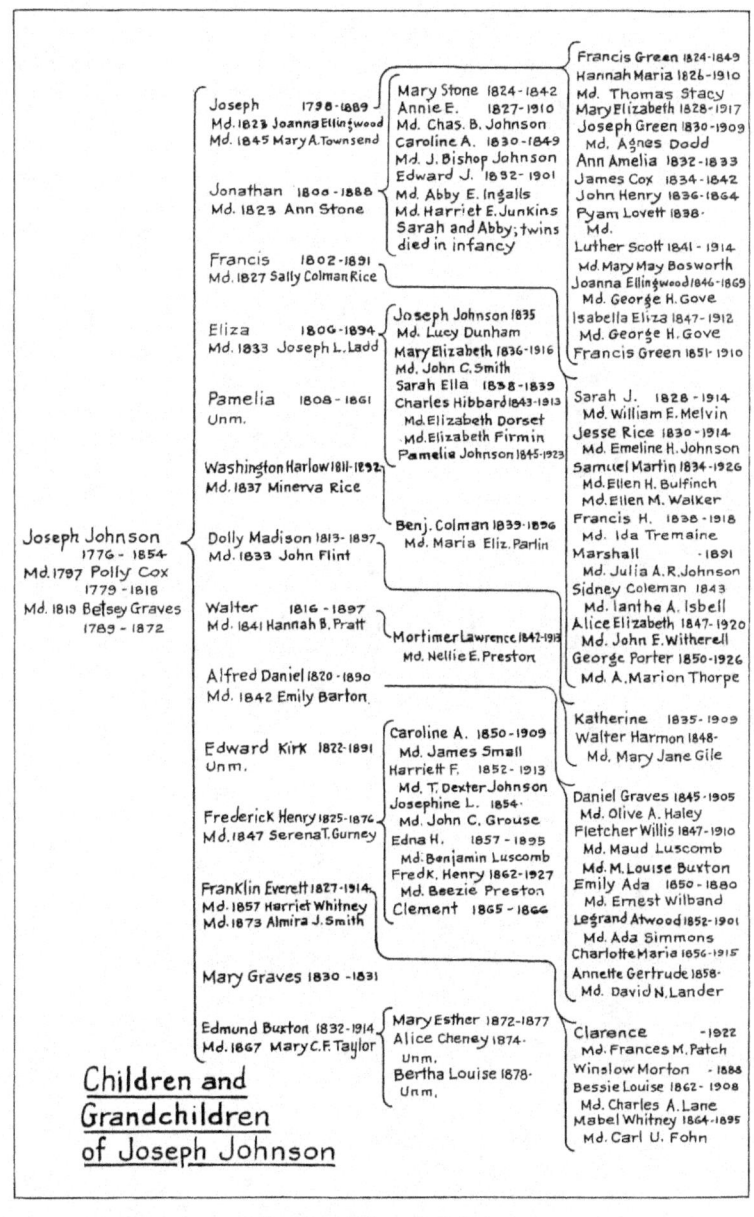

Family of Joseph Johnson

group that hired the field in front of the old Tudor homestead, and constructed there several tennis courts and a baseball diamond, the latter with the catcher's position backed up to what is still the corner of Ocean Street and the driveway to the club house. The homestead had been let for several years, partly as a hotel or boarding house. In 1889 Thomas Motley and others leased the entire place, buildings and land, for a club. The Nahant Club was formed in March, 1889, and was formally incorporated in 1895. The incorporators were George P. Upham, Charles Merriam, Laurence Curtis, Frank Merriam, Philip V. R. Ely, C. P. Curtis, Jr., Francis Peabody, Jr., Herbert M. Sears, Thomas S. Bradley and Dudley B. Fay. The first president, or chairman of the executive committee, was Abbott Lawrence, who served for five years. His successors have been Edward W. Codman, George P. Upham, Frank Merriam, W. P. Lyman, Thomas S. Bradlee, John A. Blanchard, Thomas Motley, Harold Blanchard and Warren Motley. Of the above, the record service was of Frank Merriam, who held this office for six years. Thomas Motley and Warren Motley are sons of Thomas Motley, elsewhere mentioned, and grandsons of Edward Motley. Dudley B. Fay was well known for an interest in birds, and their comings and goings on Nahant.

The club bought its property in 1892 and extensively remodelled and enlarged it in 1895. Tennis courts have been increased in number, now almost filling the field on Nahant Road, and there are courts on Ocean Street in the area which old Nahanters will remember was one of Tudor's orchards, — a peach orchard enclosed by a high windbreak and boy-proof fence.

For years the club flourished and was the center of social activity among the summer colony. Outdoor band concerts were a feature well remembered, for the strains of the fine old Salem Cadet Band were not restrained by the club lot lines, and half the town could enjoy them.

In these early days of the club there were weekly baseball games between a club nine and a Nahant nine made up of year-round residents. For the latter, Joseph H. Gove and Harry C. Wilson were usually pitcher and catcher, respectively. Gove, a son of George H. Gove and nephew of Charles E. Gove, is not now a Nahanter, though a familiar figure here, for his well-known band in Lynn is often summoned for Nahant celebrations or other occasions. Sometimes these nines worked in "ringers." Once or more the club nine had a famous Harvard Varsity nine player, and the Nahant nine would retaliate by finding some crackerjack from another source. They were good games, as amateur games, enthusiastically played, are always good to play and to watch. Wilson still carries a crumpled finger as evidence of one of Gove's swift balls.

The Nahant Club at once played an important rôle in Nahant, providing another attraction for summer residents; and it is people of means who are needed, as ever, if the town is to remain a comfortable country town with city conveniences, rather than a closely packed suburb with mounting taxes. This doctrine has been preached for a generation, and by some denied for as long. Under the State income tax law the town does not get as much from summer residents as formerly, but still it may be shown that the larger places are the best for the financial interests of the town. The Nahant Club is a needed Nahant element, an aid to keeping the town a prosperous community.

Mention is made of the use of the so-called "Hotel Tremont," at the corner of Nahant and Spring Roads, for a boys' club. This building, after its removal from Little Nahant, received practically no repairs, and at last became disreputable and dangerous, when steps were taken to condemn it as a public nuisance. In the early 90's George Abbot James sponsored its use for a boys' club, with the idea of keeping boys off the streets and out of mischief and temptation. The need existed, but the plan failed of its full usefulness, and operation was given up after a couple of years or so. A committee of Nahanters managed it, of which H. Shepard Johnson was chairman and Winthrop T. Hodges secretary. Money was spent for equipment, and Patrick H. Larkin, soon after removed from town, was chosen superintendent.

The usefulness of women as workers with men's organizations is recognized by many attendant groups disporting under various names. For the American Legion there is the American Legion Auxiliary, and the Nahant organization is attached to the Nahant Post of the Legion. Membership is restricted to near relatives of participants in the World War, and to women directly engaged in the struggle. It was organized in the fall of 1924, with Mrs. Lucy Robbins Sanborn as president. In 1912 the charter membership list was closed, with forty members enrolled. The purpose is to assist the Legion itself in its various efforts for community welfare, and especially in the work for disabled veterans and their families. This brings the families of veterans into direct contact and interest with the Legion aims, and leads to greater interest.

The Nahant Mutual Benefit Association was an assessment organization, with each member paying $2 on the death of a fellow member, plus a small fee to cover expenses. This gave a sum assisting a bereaved family, of a size depending upon the number of members. As the years passed, from the 90's onward, not enough attention was given to new members, until young men grew skeptical of it, visualizing many payments made to a group full of oldsters. For many years, until his death in 1920 at the age of eighty-two, Charles E. Gove was treasurer and kept the association alive. A benefit payment in 1918 amounted to about $40, thus accounting for twenty or more members who were keeping up their interest.

The Nahant Firemen's Relief Association was started in 1879 by the men of the three fire companies of the time, — the "Dexter No. 1," the "Babcock Extinguisher" and the "Relief Hook and Ladder." The first president was William R. Whitney. The last meeting was in 1887, when it was voted to disband. Any member of the fire department was eligible to this association and paid an admission fee and annual dues. Several annual firemen's balls were held, intended to yield further revenue. There was a sick benefit of $2 a week, later raised to $3, and apparently not confined to incapacity resulting from duty as firemen. For a year or two this group held together and then members began to drop out. The same causes entered as have been cited for so many other groups. The strong push of either self-interest or desire to help general welfare must obtain and continue. It is as important to provide for a sustained interest, after the natural enthusiasm over a new thing disappears, as it is to start in strength. The importance of a new idea makes it shine, and its originator with it, but the importance of the plodders who keep the ball rolling is too often overlooked. Each factor is of value, but even a nightingale would take no prize in a poultry show.

CHAPTER XXV

LATER YEARS

THE period since 1900 contains some events well worth recording while memory is fresh. Much already treated covers through to the present time, but scattered events of the last quarter century need mention. President Roosevelt visited Senator Lodge in 1902, and as no President can ever travel as a private citizen he was received with acclaim everywhere, and made public appearances which were the delight of the people. He arrived in Lynn on Sunday, August 24, and was welcomed by Mayor William Shepard. This was the first appearance of a President in Lynn since Lynn became a city. The route from the station to Senator Lodge's home was lined with people welcoming the distinguished visitor. Joseph T. Wilson, chairman of the Nahant selectmen, gave him the town's welcome. The special escort for the President was Troop F, cavalry, M. V. M., from North Chelmsford. They arrived in Lynn Sunday morning and went at once to Nahant and pitched camp in the open field between Nahant Road, Pond Street and Spring Roads, using mostly the upper part, against the westerly end. Valley Road did not then run across this field. Special police precautions were taken, and the Nahant police were assisted by a squad from the Metropolitan Park Police. Of course, secret service men were also on hand. The ride to Nahant, and other rides to and fro, were in Senator Lodge's victoria, for, it seems strange to say, automobiles were not then the common means of conveyance.

Nahant was well decorated for the occasion, flags and bunting appearing everywhere. Especial mention was made by the newspapers of the display of color at the Life Saving

Station, since named the Coast Guard Station. On Monday there was a reception at the Public Library building, and speaking exercises from a platform erected at the street's edge and over and around the front entrance path to the building. Photographs show several notables, George B. Cortelyou, Henry Cabot Lodge, William H. Moody and Curtis Guild among them. The platform also held town officers, G. A. R. men and other special guests. The street in front was closed to carriages, and quickly filled with people anxious for sight and hearing of this interesting man and principal officer of the country. The President delivered another address on the City Hall grounds in Lynn that same afternoon, and then was rushed away to Boston, where he spoke in Symphony Hall in the evening. The visit to Nahant was short, but the little peninsula was gratified. To see, hear or shake hands with a President is not so very uncommon, yet most who do it often recall it and speak of it with pleasure and mild pride. Especially does the world love a sincere, hearty and outspoken leader, even in those times when it may not agree with him.

There were other details on this occasion. Even a one-day visit is full of complications to be worked out, and the selectmen had much to arrange. The visiting party included clerks, newspaper men and others, who were put up by them at the Whitney Homestead, the Rockledge and Hotel Tudor. The extra police were accommodated at the Relay House. And there was a band, for band music sets up an outdoor affair of the celebrative sort as does nothing else. It was a busy time for some, as well as a great pleasure to the whole town and her many visitors. Shortly after this visit Senator Lodge obtained for the Public Library the autographed portrait of President Roosevelt which is now displayed in the building.

It was in 1909 that the town accepted Valley Road as a new street, between Spring Road and Nahant Road, cutting the field used for this visit, and in 1903 for a part of the anniversary celebration, into two parts. Today other buildings upon it leave it no longer the "large open field" it was once described to be. This part of Valley Road is the most used piece of road the town has accepted in many years. Most new streets are for the development of a tract of land into house lots, but this short section carries traffic to and from all parts of the town.

The year 1904 saw the death of Samuel Covell at the age of seventy-three. He was a well-known Nahanter, and at the time of the fiftieth anniversary celebration in 1903 he was the only man still living in town who voted at the first town election in 1853. His house at the corner of Valley Road and Pond Street is now owned by Frank R. Killilae. It was specially marked, during the celebration, as the home of an 1853 voter.

This recent period now under consideration seems to have seen two other changes in town government methods. In 1922 the school committee was increased from three to six members, which has been its number ever since. There appears to have been no real need for this change, nor has any apparent gain developed from it. It was a purely political move, carried out at a special town meeting in the summer of 1921 and intended to curb or change a balance of power on the committee.

The other change was with the adoption of revised town by-laws at the annual meeting in March, 1922, whereby the moderator was elected annually. Before that he was chosen at each meeting, and with the opening hour early, as it had been in later years, few were present and often a half dozen or so made the choice. It was obviously fairer to give all voters a chance to share in this election, as with other town officers, and now the office is filled at the ballot box. Because of Senator Lodge's less frequent attendance at recent town meetings he seemed not the logical candidate, and Fred A. Wilson was chosen, and has been re-elected annually ever since. Had Senator Lodge appeared at any meeting, there is no doubt Wilson would have been absent long enough for an election from the floor to occur, for the people wanted Lodge when they could have him.

The Spanish-American War saw several men gone from Nahant. George Cabot Lodge entered the Navy as a cadet and came out an ensign. He was a son of Senator Lodge, well known and popular on Nahant, where he always spent his summers, growing up with the nickname "Bay" Lodge, a hold-over from baby days. He was a poet by avocation, with some published work to his credit. He died in 1909 at the age of thirty-six. Two other men in this scrap were sons of E. Francis Parker, an old Nahanter. They were not legal residents, though well known in town. Francis S. Parker was on the second Brigade staff up to 1898, and was then mustered in as second lieutenant, fifty-fourth Regiment, U. S. V., serving at Jacksonville as aid-de-camp, on the staff of the second Brigade, second Division, seventh Army Corps. Frederick Parker, who is still a familiar figure among Nahant summer people, was a lieutenant in the Navy on the U. S. S. "Peoria." Samuel Hammond was an ensign in the Navy in 1898, on the "Justin" and the "Caesar." D. G. Finnerty, Jr., son of D. G. Finnerty, elsewhere mentioned, enlisted as a private in the first Heavy Artillery, stationed at Fort Warren, Fort Pickering and at Framingham. This Battery expected to go to Cuba but did not. Finnerty has also been nineteen years in the National Guard. He was in Nahant only in summer time, but has since become a year-round resident. Major William Hennessy is another non-resident but familiar figure, from many summers in town. He was an officer in the ninth Massachusetts Infantry. There were others, more or less known on Nahant, but no complete list is at hand, and this much detail is given because there is no local group organized or equipped to yield even such meagre information.

It was at the annual town meeting in 1910 that the growing agitation for a better and larger Town Hall took the form of a warrant article asking for the appointment of a special committee to prepare plans and estimates and report on remodelling the old Town Hall building. This committee was Charles D. Vary, then chairman of the selectmen, Samuel Hammond and Fred A. Wilson. The committee soon found that it was not desirable to try to remodel the old building, and devoted their energies to preparing sketches for a new building, calling into consultation Mr. Robert D. Andrews, a prominent Boston

Edward J. Johnson
1832–1901

Albert Whitney
1810–1892

One of Dr. Piper's Drawings
Looking toward Bailey's Hill. The number of trees seems exaggerated

architect. All town officials felt the need of economy in any large appropriation. The solons at the State House were toying with schemes which would take away taxable property from Nahant and increase state taxes heavily. Much of this has since materialized, bringing increased taxes to Nahant. The committee therefore recommended the least that could be provided and be worthy, and also recommended the purchase of the property now occupied by the "new" Town Hall. This was carried into the town meeting warrant for March, 1911, in seven articles.

In the meantime Daniel G. Finnerty went to work on his own initiative, using another Boston architect, and had plans drawn for a pretentious Town Hall building which it was proposed to erect on the George Johnson lot at the corner of Summer Street and Nahant Road. He presented plans and estimates involving an expenditure of $80,000 in total, and petitioned the matter into the same town meeting warrant in three articles. Thus was precipitated one of the hottest of many town meeting fights.

The original committee were long getting over their surprise that the town would consider spending so much money, or that Finnerty, better known as a stickler for economy, should advocate such an expense. Doubtless he believed the best was none too good, and stood among those willing to spend freely to get a result the town deserved. The committee was further alarmed by their belief that the building Finnerty proposed was underestimated, and the resulting cost would be many thousands higher. There never was any question that the absolutely fire-resistive building would be best, provided the town could afford it, but there was a belief that a practically safe building would cost much less and be adequate for all purposes.

After a hard-fought battle the town decided to put Finnerty's proposed building upon the lot at the corner of Pleasant Street, where the Town Hall now stands. Then, getting somewhat alarmed at the cost, the town voted that the sums proposed should not be exceeded. This latter vote brought the matter back to the town for further consideration, for the building committee soon found that the cost was underestimated. At this later town meeting — a special meeting held August 8, 1911 — Senator Lodge presided. His house guest, Senator William Warner of Missouri, sat on the platform by courtesy of the meeting and witnessed as hot a contest as ever his political experience had opened to his wondering eyes and ears. Finnerty had used maximum means to develop enthusiasm for his plans and the needed additional money. An editorial of the next day called it the "Battle of Nahant," and spoke of the torchlight procession of the night before election, arranged by General Finnerty. It says the opposing forces were led by General W. K. Richardson, and the latter until recently was an active participant in town meetings. The newspaper continues: "And in spite of the Finnerty torchlight parade, the cheers and speeches and varied hullabaloo, the Richardson forces won. The Finnerty plans provided for an *omnium gatherum* of community activities, a fireproof structure with a hall on the second floor which would seat one thousand, and under this administrative offices, — a gymnasium, a police courtroom, a lock-up and a fire station. Had there been any space remaining it might have been utilized for a roof garden, a shooting gallery and a moving picture show. By a vote of 156 to 76 Mr. Finnerty's committee was discharged, the $75,000 appropriation was renewed, and Moderator Lodge was authorized to appoint a new committee. We question whether Mr. Finnerty and public-spirited citizens who sided with him will wholly regret this action after they have taken time to review the situation. It would be superfluous and absurd for a small town, even though a wealthy one, to exceed so generous a sum as $75,000 in erecting a municipal building." These sentences are from a Boston newspaper, which gives a ten-inch space on its editorial page. Such was the fuss that Finnerty fighting could force.

The town then changed over from Finnerty's architect to the one the committee had used in their investigation. The

LATER YEARS 371

building was modified to be as nearly fire-resistive as the appropriation would allow, and the result was the structure now in evidence. It seems a notable building, and one which no participant in the fierce wrangle of 1911 regrets. But the expense was nearly $92,000. The building committee was Samuel Hammond, chairman, Ellerton James, secretary, J. Lothrop Motley, Winthrop T. Hodges, Walter H. Southwick, Edward E. Strout, and Francis H. Johnson. The new Town Hall was dedicated on November 9, 1912, with the exercises usual on such occasions. The principal address was by Senator Lodge.

Very soon the Sears tax suits, elsewhere discussed, were settled in favor of Nahant, and the money received cleared off this heavy debt more quickly than anticipated, and the burden of it was hardly felt by the town.

As to location, there seems no question that the public buildings should be nearer the geographical center of the town. The Town Hall and Public Library buildings are almost at one edge of the winter population, and sometimes in winter the travelling bothers most. It was no great gain, however, to put one building up by Summer Street, while there is much to be said in favor of keeping them together. They both should be a half mile westward. The mistake was with the location of the Public Library building a generation ago.

The selectmen, in their report for 1912, published in February, 1913, congratulated the building committee on their work, and stated that the hall provided would be ample for the needs of the town for many years. But all at once, a few years later, women became voters and the number of voting citizens was almost doubled. "Votes for Women!" was a cry abroad in the land, and in other lands, but seems not to have been a serious factor in determining town hall capacity and provision for future growth of the voting population. Fortunately, up to the present, the accommodations have proven sufficient, and it seems likely that all who wish to attend the business sessions of town meetings may do so for several years without undue crowding. At about the same time women became "emancipated" they became emaciated, also, so that more can be stowed in each square yard of area. Many towns have been obliged to adopt some sort of a delegate system to prevent overcrowding, but it is to be hoped this may not become necessary for Nahant.

The work of Nahant during the World War was guided and encouraged throughout the year and a half by a Public Safety Committee of about forty chosen by the Board of Selectmen. All three selectmen were on this committee, and the chairman of the Board, Harry C. Wilson, was chairman of the committee. The committee was organized on April 7, 1917, and divided into eight subcommittees. These were Home Guard, Finance, Children's Work, Conservation, Publicity, Red Cross, Recruiting and Food Production. Winthrop T. Hodges was general secretary. The general chairman, general secretary, and eight subchairmen were an emergency committee empowered to act when time was too short for summons to a general meeting.

The Home Guard was found popular and desirable in many towns, and drill was started on Nahant early in May with about forty men participating. The interest waned, however, and after continuing as long as possible this branch of the committee activity was abandoned. George E. Hanson, not now a Nahanter, was subchairman, and the drill master was a sergeant of the United States Regular Army.

The Finance Committee was led by Charles H. Richardson, since removed to California, where he died in 1926. They raised for 1917 about $2,600 of which over $1,000 was expended in plowing and other garden work. A further campaign for 1918 yielded a similar sum.

The Children's Work Committee was headed by Fred A. Pirie, and was more or less combined with the Food Production Committee of which J. C. Shaughnessy was subchairman. In food production lay the greatest work and expense of the Public Safety Committee. The wisdom of encouraging amateur efforts has been questioned because it used materials which would have yielded better results in the expert hands of the farmers. On the whole, this criticism seems ill founded. To foster an interest in gardening is desirable, and at least there was saved some strain on overloaded transportation systems which have to carry food not raised locally.

The Conservation Committee was headed by Ellerton James, and their work reached into food saving, waste curbing, and the use of materials not on the list important for war purposes.

The Recruiting Committee was led by George A. Wood, but the adoption of the forced draft registration and subsequent calling by quotas made this work of less importance.

The Red Cross Committee co-operated with the Red Cross Auxiliary, which was quickly formed and which is mentioned elsewhere. Some financial aid was given by the Public Safety Committee, but the Auxiliary went out and raised most of its own money. A drive for membership late in 1917 yielded four hundred and twenty from the year-round residents.

The Publicity Committee chairman was Fred A. Wilson, and the many circulars of information pouring in from the State Public Safety Committee and from numerous other sources were edited, rewritten and republished from Nahant. Over fifty circulars were issued and much other material distributed, especially with the four Liberty Loan drives. For these and for the Red Cross drive of 1918 quotas were set for each community and proper results were expected. The quota habit was then new, but has persisted since and in drives where it should not. Slogans were used everywhere. A poster collection of the time, and the air was full of posters, will show how slogans loomed large in the pressure brought to get work and enthusiasm for what was proposed. In those days to rouse a nation or sell a notion meant a slogan. They are still used, now chiefly in advertising, but they have been overused and misused, as are stories about the Ford car, so that they all seem trite. A fresh look at the war period needs the reminder that then slogans were new and were undoubtedly effective. There was also exaggeration, and the Nahant Committee circulars kept the pace but did not set the pace. To stir the very apathetic and slow or muddy-minded meant efforts and methods hardly applicable to others, who might find the meat served up too strong for their appreciation. All in all, the activities of the Nahant Committee were commended by the State Committee, and were in some cases the envy of other committees, which were not getting such good results from their own work. A scrapbook in the Public Library contains all the printed matter issued by the Nahant Public Safety Committee.

Other subcommittees were formed as they were needed. In the Town Hall were many lectures, exhibitions and demonstrations. A garden exhibition was held on September 13 and 14, 1917, and on September 9 and 10, 1918. They were of the usual type, with prizes and ribbons and cups to encourage Nahant gardens. The material shown was of surprisingly fine quality. In 1918 the proceeds from the show all went to the Nahant Auxiliary of the Red Cross. One of the well-remembered demonstrations was by an old negress called Aunt Jemima, who showed how to cook corn in various ways. This was at a time when America's allies needed wheat, and people in this country were urged and trained to use more of other cereals. Then there were meat and sugar shortages, and the gasolene-saving day, when all people were urged to refrain from automobiling. How empty were the streets! One could really walk about in comfort, except for those to whom walking was a lost art.

The draft registration on June 5, 1917, included all men who had reached their twenty-first but not their thirty-first birthdays, except for those already in military service. On Decoration Day, 1917, there was a flag raising at the Town Hall, with appropriate exercises. A feature was singing by Mrs. Leonora Robertson Calef, since deceased, a daughter of R. H. Robertson and a Nahanter until her marriage. Her voice was frequently given to Nahant for worthy causes. One song, "The Unfurling of the Flag, 1917," was written by Miss Clara Endicott Sears, daughter of Knyvet W. Sears.

A special police force of about fifty was established and commissioned by the selectmen. It was an emergency group, and their services were not much required, though individual alertness and influence proved useful. And there were parades. Nahant joined with Lynn in a great war chest parade held in that city, where one contribution was divided among a half dozen war services. And Nahant had at least one that was conspicuous, for the Third Liberty Loan. On one occasion Calvin Coolidge came to town and joined in the demonstration.

There was some shortage of coal in 1917 or early 1918, and people were told how to conserve fuel. In the fall of 1918 the condition was more acute. Allotments were made by the Government Fuel Administration, and that for Massachusetts was a tight fit. Transportation facilities were needed for war service, and other uses for them were cut to a minimum. Lawrence F. Sherman was chairman of the sub-committee on fuel during this period. During the second year of service of the Public Safety Committee the subcommittees were different. L. F. Sherman was sub-chairman of the Transportation Committee and of the Fuel Committee; C. H. Richardson, Drive Committee; H. C. Wilson, Protection Committee; F. A. Pirie, Food Production Committee; F. A. Wilson, Publicity Committee and Conservation Committee; D. A. Sanborn, Service Emblem and War Savings Committee; G. M. Clark, Soldiers Information Committee; D. G. Finnerty, Red Cross; and there was an associate thrift committee of women headed by Miss Mildred G. Cochran, who is now Mrs. Olaf A. Olsson.

So much of what happened is so recent that it seems superfluous to recount even what has been said, and the aim is to name some of the items which may pass out of recollection or record after a score more years. During the influenza epidemic in 1918 a circular told people how to guard against it as well as possible. An interesting feature of the War Savings Stamps campaign was the offer by Ellerton James of $200 worth as prizes to children in the public schools who would learn and recite to their teachers short poems. Nearly the full amount was awarded in this way. The poems were selected and grouped by Fred A. Wilson, who made the original suggestion, and the school department co-operated to rouse enthusiasm and make the plan successful. Many children learned poems they should know, of a quality not above their appreciation, even as very unripe students.

To look back only a decade is hardly far enough to get a good perspective and make any accurate conclusions. Yet it would seem that the Nahant Public Safety Committee was unusually alert, and contained many men who kept on tiptoe for results and strove with might and main. Of course, in any committee workers are important. Too often people accept appointments to such, and then do nothing and suggest nothing.

The story of men who went to the World War from Nahant cannot be told adequately except by a special investigation, preferably by the Nahant Post of the American Legion. The organization of the Post is described elsewhere. The men went off in several groups, escorted, with more or less of a real send-off, to their trains at Lynn. Many were individual enlistments in one or another part of the service. In the fall of 1917 the Public Safety Committee sent out seventy-one letters to men, or their families, known or even rumored to be in active war service. Doubtless some rumors were incorrect and to some letters no replies came. The town report published in March, 1918, lists fifty-one, and gives for most of them the branch of service entered. Eighteen were in the National Army, that new great army formed from the selective draft. Thirteen were in the United States Naval Reserve Force, on shipping board vessels, or in the Naval Reserve. Three or four were driving ambulances in France. Others were scattered about in other positions. Still more were not legal residents though perhaps long-time dwellers in town for a part of the year.

The town report for the next year records eighty-one in military service and sixteen in other branches, yielding a total well over any quota assessed against the town. This also does not include non-residents. It includes three Coast Guard men and several Shipping Board men. One of the latter is Captain Charles F. Kemp, whose experience qualified him to be senior fleet captain with all the gold braid a cap could carry. Mayland P. Lewis, coming back from service a lieutenant, brought a German machine gun which he presented to the town, and which was put in the custody of the Public Library, where it has been on exhibition most of the time. Of course, many souvenirs came to town with returning veterans, while those not so fortunate as to get to France were envious, but had done what the country asked of them.

The men came back irregularly, but on July 4, 1919, they were nearly all returned, and the town had a welcome home celebration, using a small town appropriation and a larger sum raised by private subscription. On July 3 a banquet was given them in the Town Hall, which was filled to capacity. The speakers were Lieutenant-Colonel Harold Blanchard, Lieutenant Henry R. Guild and Dr. Morton Prince. The roll of honor published in the program for this occasion contains just one hundred names, and is subject to additions and changes, as are those formerly mentioned, to make it complete or make it contain only legal residents. Special honor medals were presented by the town, through Harry C. Wilson, chairman of the selectmen, to all of these men.

On July 4 the morning was devoted to band concerts and games. The afternoon saw another band concert. Then came a parade of the best the town contained, — the Army, Navy, Shipping Board, Coast Guard, G. A. R. and Spanish War Veterans, town officers, Red Cross, Junior Red Cross, Boy Scouts, Girl Scouts, several small groups, decorated automobiles, a float section, and the fire department. John A. Blanchard was chief marshal, and the committee in charge included the selectmen, Harry C. Wilson, Dana A. Sanborn and Charles A. Phillips, with Winthrop T. Hodges, Robert Cushman, Jr., Dr. Lawrence F. Cusick, Joseph D. Lydon, Edgar Levinstein, John A. Blanchard, Joshua B. Holden, John H. Foster and Ralph G. Calef. Some of these will be recognized as old reliables for committee work, always ready to do a part for Nahant. Others are less known as Nahanters, or in town for a shorter period, but all worked to make this welcome home celebration noteworthy.

In 1920 a great boulder was laboriously dragged from the shore and set up in the cemetery. A bronze tablet was mounted on it bearing the names of four Nahanters who died in service, and an inscription which was written by Senator Lodge. Formal dedication by the Legion Post was in 1921. During this same year (1921) the town, through an appropriation at its March meeting, erected a large bronze tablet in the Town Hall in commemoration of ninety-nine names, intended to be a complete list of all who were legal residents of Nahant. The town committee in charge of this was Thomas Roland, chairman, Harry C. Wilson, Dana A. Sanborn, Warren Motley and Mayland P. Lewis. The two latter were Commander and Vice-Commander of the Post. Lewis later succeeded to the chief office. This tablet, so appropriately placed, is in marked contrast to many which may be seen on the edges of lawns in front of public buildings or parks. Usually at their best they resemble bill boards, fit to contain some temporary information or misinformation, and even when well designed are ill set, and seem to obtrude the information "I served." This is farthest from the aim of the Legion, and should be farthest from the act of any one. The American Legion is capable of being a valuable force in the United States. But it may not be too obtrusive, or it will lose its influence. Nor may it be too meek, for the meek never get far. If the meek should "inherit the earth," say during the last fifteen years, wouldn't they have held a hot iron? As in so many ways of life a firm, steady progress comes in the midstream between two extremes.

In 1911, after Senator Lodge's re-election by the State Legislature, his last election by this body, a celebration was started on Nahant in the afternoon, and in the evening a full-fledged parade marched over the town with the ever-present band and plenty of red fire. This was on January 18. It was almost spontaneous, worked up and executed in a few hours. A more pretentious celebration to this distinguished citizen was on the afternoon of September 5, 1922. A welcome home was extended to him, with exercises on the grounds of the Town Hall. Charles A. Phillips, chairman of the selectmen, presided and introduced Fred A. Wilson, who, in a ten-minute introductory, presented Senator Lodge. Wilson mentioned the long friendship of his father, Joseph T. Wilson, with the guest of the occasion, and in responding the Senator eulogized his old friend, in the course of which he said: "He might have gone far in the State or national politics, but he never seemed to have the least desire to go beyond the work which he did for thirty years as chairman of the Board of Selectmen." Continuing, he spoke with evident feeling of his love for Nahant, where so much of his life had been spent, and of his appreciation of the reception accorded him. The formal exercises closed with the presentation by Dr. Lawrence F. Cusick of a piece of silver plate, suitably inscribed, which had been provided by contributions from many Nahant friends. It was the Senator's last appearance before most Nahanters, and in a little over two years more, on November 9, 1924, he was gone forever. He was a great Nahanter, and to the little town, which had felt his presence and his influence for so many years, came an appreciation of the poet's words, applied to a greater man. There was a lonesome place against the sky.

CHAPTER XXVI

TAXES, VALUATIONS AND EXPENDITURES

THERE is always discussion in any town over valuation and taxation. Yet it would seem that a few things among those often debated might be set down as axiomatic. The important question for a taxpayer is the taxes he pays, and these depend upon town expenditures. The taxes of each payer are a product of the valuation and the tax rate. If the valuation is low the tax rate is high, and *vice versa*. Three times two is the same as two times three, and the same tax comes from a rate of $20 per thousand on a $3,000 valuation, as from a $30 rate on a $2,000 valuation. There are those who want valuations raised to keep the tax rate down. But this is illusory. If done to encourage newcomers it is deceptive. The shrewd ones will not be content to know the rate, but will also want to know the valuation, and will want to analyze the possibilities of increase or decrease in total valuations and in town expenditures. A difficult matter, but the tax rate has little to do but vary according to the other factors of greater importance. To cite a tax rate is telling very little.

The valuations have always been low, or so rated, ever since the town was founded. There are frequent efforts to get them raised, because certain State assessments are proportionate to the valuation, and the higher this is the more the town pays. Indeed, this might well be a subterfuge to avoid this form of assessment. But the town's consistency in the matter, reaching back before the time of this sort of assessment, stops any allegation of this kind from becoming a real argument. Recently people from the State House brought down a list of mortgages, held in some cases by leading Boston banks, in an effort to prove Nahant appraisals for valuation were too low.

They were badly discomfited. In one case a bank had $9,000 on a property offered for sale a few years ago for under $3,000 which had about $3,000 spent on it afterward. And this is only a sample of what banks do with their wrong appraisals, or methods of appraisal. Frequently some of the larger places on Nahant have changed hands at less than the assessor's valuations. It is yet to be proven that valuations in town are at all out of reason, though admitted to be low.

The important factor in the case is that valuations be uniform, for of course there is a grievance if one place is rated higher than another similar one. With valuations even and comparable, the taxes any owner pays are the same, so long as appropriations remain the same, and valuations are then fair, whether high or low, because the total tax does not thereby vary.

In the question of equable valuations, however, lies much trouble, especially since the rapid rise in costs which doubled the price of a building. Assume two houses, alike in accommodations, appearance, location and amount of land. One was built in 1915 at a cost of $5,000 plus $1,000 for land, and has been kept in first-class condition. The other was built in 1920 at a cost of $10,000 plus $1,000 for land. They are the same except in cost. What should be the valuation of each? Assume a house and land costing $10,000 in 1914 and well kept. If desirable it is worth more in 1925 because replacement costs have mounted. A man offers $20,000 to the owner, who occupies it. The owner refuses because he likes it and wants to live there, but is tempted to sell at $25,000. For what should the place be valued by the assessors?

There is a fairly simple method of appraisal which sets up a market value and escapes the confusion of some of these elements of changing costs, sentimental values, and such things. If it may be assumed that suitable gross rental for a well-built place, thus not carrying too heavy depreciation and maintenance costs, is $12\frac{1}{2}$ per cent, or one-eighth the value, then a market value is eight times the rent which may be obtained. It is usually fairly easy to determine for how much a place will rent. If an owner occupies his house he should still be considered, for this purpose, as paying that rental. It may well happen that he would not sell for such a price as the valuation thus obtained, but why should he pay more taxes on that account? The affirmative answer is that he should be taxed on the money invested, and that this money is the amount he refused for the place; for had he taken it he would have the money in hand, and accordingly it must be considered, in effect, as invested in the place.

W. B. Munro says, in "Invisible Government," that every sensible person knows the doctrine of equality has often been carried too far. Experts are too much unconsidered, and yet all persons are not equally competent. But this principle of parity is not carried into the field of taxation. Men are not considered equal in their capacity to bear the burden of government. Tax laws adopt quite the reverse of any levelling principle. There is a point at which interest in the principles of Rousseau and Jefferson cease. A selected few are conceded to be superior whenever sacrifice is involved.

There is, however, a strong feeling that taxes should be collected mostly on money that is earning and not on money that is idle; that if a man has a picture in his house worth $500 he should not be obliged to pay $15 a year for the privilege of looking at it, even though this valuation is an actual market value. In the same way, a man who for sentimental reasons refuses a fancy price for his house has no active money in his place above its market value established at eight times the rent, a price at which any investor might make a purchase without any sentimental reasons. The income taxes, State and Federal, are upon money that earns, — active money, — and never upon idle money. The money a man spends on a house up to eight times the rent it would bring is active money, for it is earning for him the rent he would pay if he did not own it. But any sum above this market value is for further factors affording pleasure and satisfaction to the owner, but yielding no income, as a picture yields no income. A man may plant several acres with trees and shrubs. Nursery stock costs very little, and when full grown has a low market value because hard to transplant. This statement does not mean trees with a timber value. The place so developed adds greatly to community beauty, but is not even a permanent asset. Without continual care and expense it would revert to field conditions in a year or two. A well-kept lawn means little original outlay, but much annual effort. Under these conditions how can a so-called beautiful estate be valued for its land at much more than its worth when only wild land.

These are some of the arguments on assessors' valuations. The counter claim, which may affect these, relates to the procedure, now a fairly general practice, which makes the rich man pay more taxes than the poor man. Income taxes are about all on this basis, State and Federal. Before the days of income taxes the fact was different. Property other than real estate was easily hidden or hard to appraise, so that most rich men did not pay taxes on all of it. At the same time, the poorer man, with all of his property more visible, perhaps in a house and land, paid taxes on a full valuation. If valuations on Nahant are three-quarters, many a small house owner paid for years on three-quarters of all he had, while many a rich man paid only on one-quarter. The income taxes changed all that, if returns are honestly made, and local taxation is only on real estate and on personal belongings. The latter are mostly in the class of property which does not earn, and which, according to many thinkers, should accordingly be taxed lightly if at all.

Large houses have a lower market value than small ones, for a man able to afford a large place usually wants to build it himself according to his own ideas, and is less willing to buy any that comes upon the market. Rentals also are comparatively low, for similar reasons. Eight times the rent obtainable would usually give a low valuation, and yet why not a fair one?

A compromise on valuations by assessors is suggested whereby, after establishing a market value by way of the rent obtainable, as suggested, a further sum be added to the valuation, based on a percentage of the expenditure less an allowance for deterioration. On this principle, if a man built a house for $10,000 which would rent for $600, his market value would be in round numbers, $5,000. On the remaining $5,000 his house value might be set at one-third or one-half, making a total valuation of around $7,000, in which case he would be paying taxes on $2,000 of non-earning money. The depreciation is a more confused condition. If the $10,000 represents a well-built house, it might have been poorly built for $7,500, and the depreciation would be far more rapid. The $2,500 additional money does not represent more of a house, but is only in lieu of heavy depreciation and upkeep expenses. The depreciation should then be figured as more on the lesser expenditure, while any method of direct percentage figuring accounts it more on the greater expenditure. There is no easy road for assessors through this part of the tangle, but it does seem a good start toward fair valuations to base a market price on the rent, and then use common sense, comparisons and good judgment to establish whatever sum is added to this basic appraisal. More space than is allowed here would explain this situation further, but enough has been shown to enable any one to see that the problems of assessors are not simple, especially after a doubling of building costs over a short period of years. Certainly it would appear, however, that to have assessors' valuations run proportionate to real market values would yield a fair result appealing to every one as just, at least for a basis. Then the argument on additional money invested, money not earning and not reflected in a market value based on rental, might or might not vary any appraisal from this basis so established. Thus assessors' values might be higher or lower than market values. So long as they were proportionate the proper end would be served, for the taxes paid would be the same in any case. The amount of taxes depends on expenditures only, after valuations are established as fair, one with another, and do not vary much from year to year.

The valuation of Nahant about sixty years ago was around $1,000,000 for taxation purposes. Then, and until 1917, personal property was included. This meant stocks, bonds, mort-

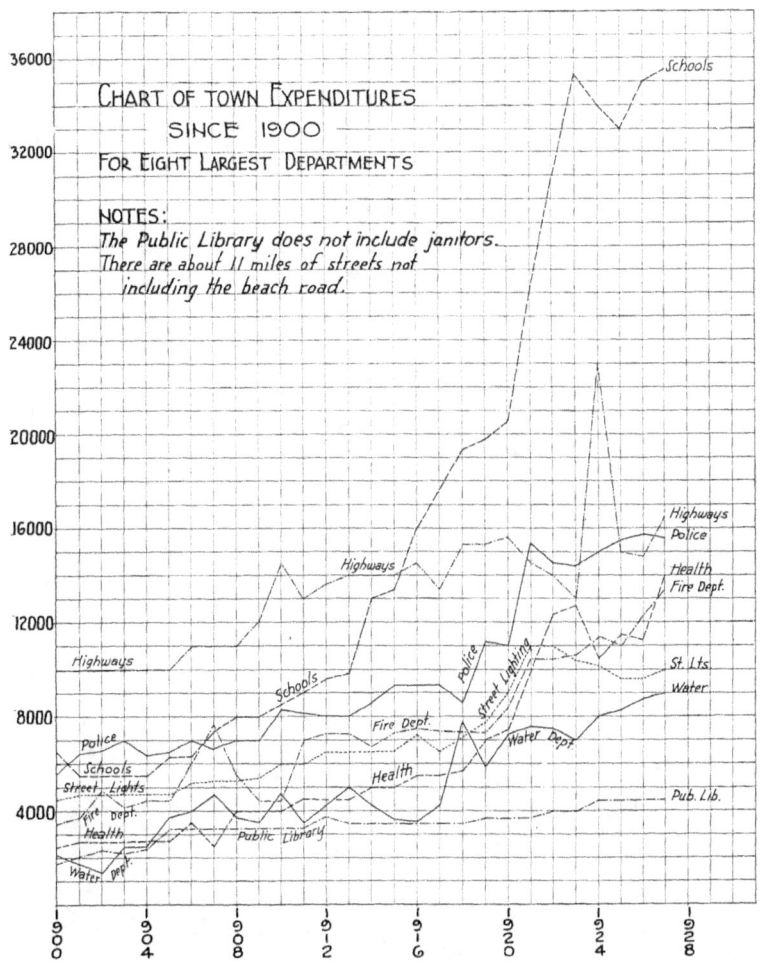

Town Expenditures

TAXES, VALUATIONS AND EXPENDITURES 385

gages, etc. The State has always taxed corporations within the State, and distributed the money so collected among the towns where the various stockholders resided. This is the money, commonly called bank and corporation taxes, which the many town reports of these years enter as received from the Commonwealth. If a man owned stock in a corporation outside of Massachusetts its value was supposed to be returned to the local assessors, and was included in the personal property valuation.

In 1869 the Nahant tax rate was $4.50 on a valuation of $2,900,000. In 1870 the valuation jumped to $5,100,000, reached over $6,000,000 in 1872, where it remained for five years. Then it dropped into the fives again and went under $5,000,000 in 1879. The tax rate in 1870 and 1871 dropped to $2.50, but the town quickly learned how to spend money and the rate gradually rose to $6.50 in 1877. Then it dropped, reaching $4.50 in 1881, rising again to $6 in 1887, thence to $6.50 in 1889, where it remained until 1896, when it went to $7.50. It reached $8 in 1898 and stopped there until 1905, when it was $9. From 1908 to 1917 the tax rate fluctuated widely between $8 and $12. In 1917 it began its upward march toward present-day figures, reaching $33 in 1926.

Valuations remained fairly steady, between $4,500,000 and $5,000,000, for the period of 1879 to 1899. Then they increased again, gradually, except for a spurt which is not significant, on account of the Sears estate. In 1917 came the State income tax, which removed all personal property from local assessment, leaving only real estate and so-called intangibles, meaning clothes, furniture, etc., much of which means a yearly expenditure for replacement. It does not go so far as to tax food, which is also on hand in every house, though subject to replacement at more frequent intervals. Automobiles are included in the present personal property taxed locally, and again comes a difficulty of assessments. A person who buys a new car at the end of March is likely to pay $20 or $30 more taxes on it for the current year than if he waited ten days and was found on April 1 with his old car; for by the time another year swings around his new car will become old and be so assessed. Assessors try to be fair, but their problems are often troublesome. Then there is double taxation. A house owner pays on the assessed value of his house. If it is mortgaged for two-thirds of that value the holder of the mortgage may pay an income tax on the interest he receives. This is reflected in the interest rate, and the owner thus may pay two taxes on what may be two-thirds of his property. This is not a local matter, however, but a question of laws made by State or Nation. Tax money has to be raised by some means, but double taxation on mortgage money presses heavily on those who have least.

There is a very common disregard for the community expense of small places. In a city of Essex County, some years ago, strenuous efforts were made to locate a prominent industry there, employing thousands of men. At once came three-flatters, — that ugliest and most economical of dwellings. These could be assessed, in those days, for not over $9,000 each, yielding $60 per family at a $20 tax rate. But these apartments averaged to send nearly one child per family to the public schools, and this at once used all the taxes paid, though the school expenses were only about a third of all municipal expenses involved. Furthermore, school expenses per pupil, as commonly given, do not include capital expense or money interest, and this city, as cited, at once was obliged to build more schoolhouses. Other communities show similar figures.

On Nahant the figures are in the same class; for example, the town revenue for 1925 is listed at $177,000, of which $34,000 was spent for schools. About one hundred and sixty-four houses on Bass Point, including Fox Hill and Castle Road, sent one hundred and thirty-five children to the schools. The total school attendance was about two hundred and ninety-three, or an expenditure of about $118 per pupil. For the Bass Point children this makes a total expenditure of about $16,000. On the official list of valuations for 1926, as published by the Nahant assessors, there are forty-seven houses listed on Castle Road, with a total valuation of about $129,000, or an average of under $2,800. This, at the 1926 rate of $33, makes these houses pay about $93 taxes each, or a total for the forty-seven on Castle Road of about $4,300. If these forty-seven houses sent the average for this section to the schools there would be thirty-eight pupils, and at the cost of $118 each the expenditure would be nearly $4,500. This is more than the taxes received, and this is only for one item, though the largest one, of the town's expenditures. According to this same assessors' list there are about eight hundred houses in Nahant, and if they averaged to pay $93 each in taxes the total revenue would be less than one-half of the town's expenditures. Many of these outlays are proportional to the population. Certainly the cost of schools, fire, police, health, water and sewer departments may be nearly so; while for highways, public library, and several smaller appropriations there would be an increase as the population increased, though not proportional. The Bass Point illustration is only typical. It was used, with Castle Road selected especially, because this section and this short street are illustrations of divisions into fairly small lots, containing houses variable in size and cost, yet averaging to what a closely built-up town might expect to become.

Now assume an increase in Nahant from the present eight hundred houses to twenty-four hundred, with as many not used in winter and a proportionate school population. The schools would then also triple in size and expenditure, — an added cost of $69,000 in 1925 figures. If protection to persons and property, together with health and sanitation, also tripled, this would add $100,000. Then add for new schoolhouses, some increase in other appropriations, of which the largest non-proportional one is for highways. The total would probably exceed $200,000. But at $93 each, the average payment from the street used for illustration, the sixteen hundred added houses would contribute in taxes only $149,000, and this would not be an added sum, because the land newly built upon already pays taxes. The Castle Road houses cited use an average of less than an eighth of an acre each. At this rate the sixteen hundred new houses being considered would use about 184 acres, now yielding over $30,000 in taxes. The increase in revenue to the town, therefore, from the addition of sixteen hundred houses of the sizes chosen for this illustration, would be less than $120,000. The increase in expenditures, though somewhat hard to determine, would obviously run heavily in excess of this sum.

The expenditure on Nahant per family is over $200, and each family benefits as much from any town expenditure as any other. Even in cities the same implication may be made. Somerville is able to spend about $30 per inhabitant per year, while Lynn, Lowell, Salem and most others can spend $40 with similar tax rates. Revere, another city notably a suburb of Boston, or chiefly so, only spends around $40 per inhabitant by using a $40 tax rate. The question presented is not of desirability of one group or another. It is merely the matter of income and expense to the town. Small houses on otherwise vacant land increase expenses faster than income. Vacant land does not use schools, and demands little from police, fire or highway departments.

These figures should impress those who want low tax rates to lure people to town. They should influence opinions on real estate development into small lots, some of which has been done and more attempted. It is just the difference between a poor town and a rich town. Nahant's four hundred acres, filled with three-flatters, ten to the acre, would give room for twelve thousand families, an increase to fifteen times the present eight hundred families. They could hardly be assessed for over $3,000 a family, or yield a tax of over $100 a family, while the present eight hundred families yield a tax of more than twice as much, and this with a considerable number giving half as much.

Look at the matter another way. The two-acre place occupied by a summer resident may be assessed for $20,000, yielding a tax of $650, and not use the schools at all. Suppose it were cut up into small lots and resulted in ten year-round

TAXES, VALUATIONS AND EXPENDITURES

houses assessed for a total of $100,000 and yielding $3,300 in taxes, — an addition of $2,700 or less. The ten houses would send, at present figures, eight children to school at an expense of nearly $900 as expenses now run. This leaves these houses carrying their town charges or nearly so. But if instead of ten houses twenty are built, averaging the same as for Castle Road, only $1,900 in taxes, at $93 each, would be turned in to the town, but sixteen school children, the average for twenty year-round houses now, would use all of this revenue. This leaves no chance for an increase in any other department.

The conclusion is that a town full of small houses is a poor town, and must economize as well as expect a mounting tax rate, and that if a little vacant lot is supplied with a house no one need gloat over the additional taxable property, for maybe the house contains a child or two and is paying under a hundred dollars taxes. Figures are subject to dispute as to where increases would come and how much. For that reason rather evident factors have been considered, leaving others by merely stating that they would increase and showing enough to cause a thought for these conclusions. Of course it would be foolish to claim that three hundred and one children in the schools would cost much more than three hundred. No argument here used depends upon such an assumption. But a continuing growth, however slight, each year, leads to figures to which these statements do apply. Of course all of these figures, as related to those who pay a poll tax only, include taxes paid by the owner on rented property. A poll taxpayer uses property yielding taxes to the town, and he pays these taxes through his rent.

An analysis of the expenditures per inhabitant is interesting and likewise open to a discussion of how expenditures increase as population increases. In 1925 there were one hundred and fifty-four towns in Massachusetts with a census population of between one thousand and five thousand. Five of these towns had a revenue of over $100 per inhabitant, and four others were over $80. The average for all was around $40, with a dozen or so under $30. Nahant was among these high five. All of the high ones are towns with many summer residents, as Nahant has. This gives an increase in population not all counted in the census, paying high taxes, and not using the schools. The schools are almost invariably the largest expenditure in any town, and the one naturally running most closely proportional to the population. Thus the summer residents are a double municipal benefit, by not contributing to the expense of this department while heavily participating in its support. All but one of these eight towns had tax rates, in 1925, close to the Nahant tax rate. To take a look at them might be helpful in determining if the public service rendered by Nahant is what it should be in efficiency. The seven towns thus cited are Dover, Falmouth, Hull, Marion, Marshfield, Oak Bluffs and Scituate.

The income of various towns, of course, runs lowest for the smallest towns. In 1925 nine towns had a population under two hundred and an annual revenue under $15,000. Thirty-five towns have under four hundred population and under $25,000 revenue. Eighty-three towns with under $65,000 revenue had under one thousand residents. Out of two hundred and twenty towns of under four thousand population, ninety-seven were over fifteen hundred population, and their revenues varied between $100,000 and $200,000, with a half dozen exceptions.

Of the twenty towns nearest to Nahant in population, Nahant had, in 1925, the largest income, with Marshfield second, and with only six town incomes of over $100,000. Nahant's was $177,000. The average tax rate was $26.90, and eight were over $30, with Nahant at $31.

The twenty towns nearest to Nahant in valuation, running between four million and five million four hundred thousand, had an average tax rate in 1925 of $27.70. There were eight over $31, with one at $38.

The twenty towns of over $135,000 revenue, and the smallest populations reaching up to this expenditure, had average

TAXES, VALUATIONS AND EXPENDITURES 391

revenues of $160,750, with a low of $135,000 and a high of $193,000. These towns averaged to spend 5 per cent of their revenues for protection to life and property, 15 per cent for highways, and 33 per cent for schools. Nahant spent, respectively, 19, 17 and 19 per cent. It is strange to Nahanters to note so many towns spending comparatively little for protection, meaning chiefly police and fire departments. Thirteen of these towns spent less than $10,000 for these factors. The other large Nahant expenditures, for schools and highways, run about the same as the average for the other towns in this class. The smaller appropriations are more variable and less vital to these figures. The water and health departments are next largest, and vary more widely among comparable towns. The water expenditure on Nahant is mostly counterbalanced by the income from charges for water. The Public Library expenditures are also too variable for comparisons, because so many of these are supported wholly or in part by gifts and other outside incomes. The Nahant Library has had about the average income for towns of similar valuations yielding the sole support of these institutions.

On the basis of efficiency the Public Library stands very high among Massachusetts libraries. The labor efficiency in town departments using most labor has been brought in question, unfortunately, by the labor itself. Two or three times motions in town meetings for committees to investigate efficiency have been defeated by the votes of the labor men. They have been emphatic in disapproval, which, of course, leads people to ask of what they are afraid. When a department is questioned it should be the loudest in welcoming an investigation unless it is fearful that allegations will be proven and does not want its conditions aired. But free air and publicity are the best things to establish confidence in any department. Town meeting killing of suggestions to open up and ventilate only leads to further suspicion. The proper course for town labor is to foster, even to initiate, movements of this sort.

Some people of the town want lower taxes at any cost. Others want efficiency, continually increasing values in its public service, and are willing to pay what it costs. Such would rather see the town one of the best appointed of residential towns rather than one with the lowest taxes. The two factors do not work together, but the third one, efficiency, may help both of the other aims. Both higher taxes and less public service through decreased expenditures will come if the town grows poorer. Several elements may contribute to this increasing poverty, of which only one least considered and most important has been presented, but there are no significant indications at present of important changes in financial condition. The State income tax law was a blow impossible to meet without rising tax rates, for other accompanying laws reduced the amount from this income tax which reverted to the towns. More important than this is the fact that the State income tax does not run over three or four dollars a thousand, a maximum of 6 per cent of the income, while local taxation collected more than that even when applied to partially hidden property returns. The total amount spent by the State itself has increased many fold during a span of twenty-five years. It is said that the longest endurance test is to be a taxpayer, but when taxpayers get superior municipal service and obviously snappy and efficient results, they are able to compare their standing with other towns, find it favorable, and cease to grumble.

LIST OF TOWN OFFICERS

LIST OF TOWN OFFICERS

Moderators

1853	. . Walter Johnson	
	William F. Johnson	
1854	. . Walter Johnson	
1855	. . Walter Johnson	
	John Q. Hammond	
1856	. . Walter Johnson	
1857	. . Walter Johnson	
	Luther Dame	
	William E. Melvin	
1858	. . Edward J. Johnson	
	Walter Johnson	
1859–60	. . Luther Dame	
1861	. . Luther Dame	
	Harrison Barnes	
1862	. . David Johnson	
1863	. . Walter Johnson	
1864	. . David Johnson	
1865	. . David Johnson	
	Walter Johnson	
1866	. . David Johnson	
	George L. Johnson	
1867	. . David Johnson	
	Walter Johnson	
1868–75	. . David Johnson	
1876	. . David Johnson	
	Joseph T. Wilson	

1877–98	. . Joseph T. Wilson	
1899	. . Joseph T. Wilson	
	Francis B. Crocker	
1900–07	. . Joseph T. Wilson	
1908	. . Joseph T. Wilson	
	Henry Cabot Lodge	
1909	. . Joseph T. Wilson	
	Henry Cabot Lodge	
	William F. Waters	
1910	. . Joseph T. Wilson	
	Henry Cabot Lodge	
1911	. . Henry Cabot Lodge	
1912	. . Joseph T. Wilson	
	Henry Cabot Lodge	
1913–14	. . Henry Cabot Lodge	
1915	. . Henry Cabot Lodge	
	Harry C. Wilson	
1916	. . Henry Cabot Lodge	
	Fred A. Wilson	
1917	. . Fred A. Wilson	
1918–21	. . Henry Cabot Lodge	
	Fred A. Wilson	
1922–27	. . Fred A. Wilson	

Town Clerks

1853–56 . . . Washington H. Johnson	1891–97 . . Fletcher W. Johnson
1857–90 . . Alfred D. Johnson	1898–1903 . . Charles Cabot Johnson
1890 . . Alfred D. Johnson	1904–27 . . William F. Waters
Fletcher W. Johnson	

Town Treasurers

1853–79 . . Welcome W. Johnson	1899–1903 . . George A. Gove
1880–98 . . Edmund B. Johnson	1903–27 . . Charles Cabot Johnson

Selectmen

Year			Year		
1853	.	. William F. Johnson Dexter Stetson Artemus Murdock	1868	.	. Washington H. Johnson Edward J. Johnson Thomas P. Whitney
1854	.	. Washington H. Johnson Dexter Stetson Artemus Murdock	1869	.	. Washington H. Johnson Edward J. Johnson Joseph Johnson
1855	.	. Washington H. Johnson J. Bishop Johnson Jesse Rice	1870	.	. Washington H. Johnson Edward J. Johnson Artemus Murdock
1856	.	. Washington H. Johnson J. Bishop Johnson Jesse Rice	1871	.	. Washington H. Johnson Edward J. Johnson Artemus Murdock
1857	.	. Washington H. Johnson J. Bishop Johnson Artemus Murdock	1872	.	. Washington H. Johnson Edward J. Johnson Artemus Murdock
1858	.	. Washington H. Johnson J. Bishop Johnson Walter Johnson	1873	.	. Washington H. Johnson Edward J. Johnson Artemus Murdock
1859	.	. Washington H. Johnson J. Bishop Johnson Artemus Murdock	1874	.	. Washington H. Johnson Edward J. Johnson Artemus Murdock
1860	.	. Washington H. Johnson J. Bishop Johnson Artemus Murdock	1875	.	. Washington H. Johnson Edward J. Johnson Artemus Murdock
1861	.	. Washington H. Johnson Walter Johnson Artemus Murdock	1876	.	. Washington H. Johnson Joseph T. Wilson Edward J. Johnson Edwin W. Johnson Artemus Murdock
1862	.	. Washington H. Johnson Dexter Stetson Artemus Murdock	1877	.	. Joseph T. Wilson William Luscomb Edwin W. Johnson Edward J. Johnson Artemus Murdock
1863	.	. Washington H. Johnson Albert Wyer Artemus Murdock			
1864	.	. Washington H. Johnson Albert Wyer Edmund B. Johnson	1878	.	. Joseph T. Wilson William Luscomb Edwin W. Johnson C. Hervey Johnson Artemus Murdock
1865	.	. Washington H. Johnson Albert Wyer Edmund B. Johnson			
1866	.	. Washington H. Johnson C. Hervey Johnson Edmund B. Johnson	1879	.	. Joseph T. Wilson Edwin W. Johnson Edward J. Johnson
1867	.	. Washington H. Johnson Edward J. Johnson Thomas P. Whitney	1880	.	. Joseph T. Wilson Edwin W. Johnson Edward J. Johnson

LIST OF TOWN OFFICERS

1881	. Joseph T. Wilson	
	Edwin W. Johnson	
	Edward J. Johnson	
1882	. Joseph T. Wilson	
	Edwin W. Johnson	
	J. Colby Wilson	
1883	. Joseph T. Wilson	
	Edwin W. Johnson	
	J. Colby Wilson	
1884	. Joseph T. Wilson	
	Edwin W. Johnson	
	J. Colby Wilson	
1885	. Joseph T. Wilson	
	Edwin W. Johnson	
	J. Colby Wilson	
1886	. Joseph T. Wilson	
	William R. Whitney	
	J. Colby Wilson	
1887	. Joseph T. Wilson	
	William R. Whitney	
	J. Colby Wilson	
1888	. Joseph T. Wilson	
	William R. Whitney	
	J. Colby Wilson	
1889	. Joseph T. Wilson	
	William R. Whitney	
	J. Colby Wilson	
1890	. Joseph T. Wilson	
	William R. Whitney	
	J. Colby Wilson	
1891	. Joseph T. Wilson	
	William R. Whitney	
	J. Colby Wilson	
1892	. Joseph T. Wilson	
	William R. Whitney	
	J. Colby Wilson	
1893	. Joseph T. Wilson	
	William R. Whitney	
	J. Colby Wilson	
1894	. Joseph T. Wilson	
	William R. Whitney	
	J. Colby Wilson	
1895	. Joseph T. Wilson	
	William R. Whitney	
	J. Colby Wilson	
1896	. Joseph T. Wilson	
	William R. Whitney	
	J. Colby Wilson	
1897	. Joseph T. Wilson	
	T. Dexter Johnson	
	J. Colby Wilson	
1898	. Joseph T. Wilson	
	T. Dexter Johnson	
	J. Colby Wilson	
1899	. Joseph T. Wilson	
	T. Dexter Johnson	
	J. Colby Wilson	
1900	. Joseph T. Wilson	
	Charles D. Vary	
	J. Colby Wilson	
1901	. Joseph T. Wilson	
	Charles D. Vary	
	J. Colby Wilson	
1902	. Joseph T. Wilson	
	Charles D. Vary	
	J. Colby Wilson	
1903	. Joseph T. Wilson	
	Charles D. Vary	
	J. Colby Wilson	
1904	. Joseph T. Wilson	
	Charles D. Vary	
	J. Colby Wilson	
1905	. Joseph T. Wilson	
	Charles D. Vary	
	J. Colby Wilson	
1906	. Harry C. Wilson	
	Charles D. Vary	
	James A. Carahar	
1907	. Harry C. Wilson	
	Charles D. Vary	
	James A. Carahar	
1908	. Harry C. Wilson	
	Charles D. Vary	
	James A. Carahar	
1909	. Harry C. Wilson	
	Charles D. Vary	
	James C. Shaughnessy	
1910	. Harry C. Wilson	
	Charles D. Vary	
	James C. Shaughnessy	
1911	. Harry C. Wilson	
	Charles D. Vary	
	James C. Shaughnessy	
1912	. Harry C. Wilson	
	Charles D. Vary	
	James C. Shaughnessy	

1913	. . Harry C. Wilson Charles D. Vary James C. Shaughnessy		1921	. . Harry C. Wilson Dana A. Sanborn Charles A. Phillips
1914	. . Harry C. Wilson Bernard F. Carahar James C. Shaughnessy		1922	. . Harry C. Wilson Leon M. Delano Charles A. Phillips
1915	. . Harry C. Wilson Dana A. Sanborn James C. Shaughnessy		1923	. . Harry C. Wilson Leon M. Delano Charles A. Phillips
1916	. . Harry C. Wilson Dana A. Sanborn James C. Shaughnessy		1924	. . Harry C. Wilson Leon M. Delano John A. Blanchard
1917	. . Harry C. Wilson Dana A. Sanborn James C. Shaughnessy		1925	. . Harry C. Wilson Leon M. Delano Charles A. Phillips
1918	. . Harry C. Wilson Dana A. Sanborn Charles A. Phillips		1926	. . Harry C. Wilson Leon M. Delano Charles A. Phillips
1919	. . Harry C. Wilson Dana A. Sanborn Charles A. Phillips		1927	. . Harry C. Wilson Leon M. Delano Charles A. Phillips
1920	. . Harry C. Wilson Daniel G. Finnerty Charles A. Phillips			

ASSESSORS

Prior to 1908 the selectmen were also the assessors

1908	. . Charles D. Vary Harry C. Wilson James A. Carahar		1914	. . James C. Shaughnessy Harry C. Wilson Daniel G. Finnerty
1909	. . Charles D. Vary Harry C. Wilson James C. Shaughnessy		1915	. . Arthur E. Richardson Harry C. Wilson Daniel G. Finnerty
1910	. . Charles D. Vary Harry C. Wilson James C. Shaughnessy		1916	. . Arthur E. Richardson Harry C. Wilson Rinaldo D. Potter
1911	. . Charles D. Vary Harry C. Wilson James C. Shaughnessy		1917	. . Arthur E. Richardson Harry C. Wilson Rinaldo D. Potter
1912	. . Charles D. Vary Harry C. Wilson Daniel G. Finnerty		1918	. . Daniel G. Finnerty Harry C. Wilson Rinaldo D. Potter
1913	. . Charles D. Vary Harry C. Wilson Daniel G. Finnerty		1919	. . Daniel G. Finnerty Harry C. Wilson John R. Killilae

LIST OF TOWN OFFICERS

1920	. . Daniel G. Finnerty Harry C. Wilson John R. Killilae	1924 . . James C. Shaughnessy Harry C. Wilson Daniel G. Finnerty
1921	. . James J. Deveney Harry C. Wilson John R. Killilae	1925 . . James C. Shaughnessy Harry C. Wilson Daniel G. Finnerty
1922	. . James J. Deveney Harry C. Wilson Ralph W. Johnson	1926 . . James C. Shaughnessy Harry C. Wilson Daniel G. Finnerty
1923	. . James J. Deveney Harry C. Wilson Ralph W. Johnson	1927 . . James C. Shaughnessy Harry C. Wilson Daniel G. Finnerty

SCHOOL COMMITTEES

1853	. . John Q. Hammond Walter Johnson Welcome W. Johnson	1864 . . John Q. Hammond Franklin E. Johnson Walter Johnson
1854	. . John Q. Hammond Walter Johnson Francis Johnson	1865 . . John Q. Hammond Franklin E. Johnson Alfred D. Johnson
1855	. . John Q. Hammond Alfred D. Johnson Thomas E. Colby	1866 . . John Q. Hammond John E. Whitney Franklin E. Johnson
1856	. . John Q. Hammond Alfred D. Johnson Jesse R. Johnson	Walter Johnson 1867 . . John E. Whitney Franklin E. Johnson
1857	. . John Q. Hammond Alfred D. Johnson Harrison Barnes	Walter Johnson 1868 . . Samuel Hudson Franklin E. Johnson
1858	. . John Q. Hammond Alfred D. Johnson Harrison Barnes	Edmund B. Johnson 1869 . . Samuel Hudson Franklin E. Johnson
1859	. . John Q. Hammond Alfred D. Johnson Harrison Barnes	Edmund B. Johnson 1870 . . Joseph T. Wilson Franklin E. Johnson
1860	. . John Q. Hammond Alfred D. Johnson Harrison Barnes	Edmund B. Johnson 1871 . . Joseph T. Wilson Franklin E. Johnson
1861	. . John Q. Hammond Alfred D. Johnson Harrison Barnes	Edmund B. Johnson 1872 . . Joseph T. Wilson Franklin E. Johnson
1862	. . John Q. Hammond Alfred D. Johnson Walter Johnson	Edmund B. Johnson 1873 . . Joseph T. Wilson Franklin E. Johnson
1863	. . John Q. Hammond Henry Colman Walter Johnson	Edmund B. Johnson 1874 . . Joseph T. Wilson Franklin E. Johnson Edmund B. Johnson

1875	. . Joseph T. Wilson Franklin E. Johnson Edmund B. Johnson		1891	. . Joseph T. Wilson T. Dexter Johnson Charles D. Vary
1876	. Joseph T. Wilson Franklin E. Johnson Edmund B. Johnson		1892	. . Joseph T. Wilson T. Dexter Johnson William D. Hodges
1877	. . Joseph T. Wilson Franklin E. Johnson Edmund B. Johnson		1893	. . Joseph T. Wilson Jonathan E. Johnson Charles D. Vary
1878	. . Joseph T. Wilson Franklin E. Johnson Edmund B. Johnson		1894	. . Joseph T. Wilson Jonathan E. Johnson Otis A. Johnson
1879	. . Joseph T. Wilson Franklin E. Johnson Edmund B. Johnson		1895	Charles D. Vary . . Joseph T. Wilson Otis A. Johnson
1880	. Joseph T. Wilson Franklin E. Johnson Edmund B. Johnson		1896	Charles D. Vary . . Joseph T. Wilson Otis A. Johnson
1881	. . Joseph T. Wilson Joseph A. Crandall Edmund B. Johnson		1897	Pauline T. Johnson . . H. Shepard Johnson Otis A. Johnson
1882	. Joseph T. Wilson William R. Whitney Edmund B. Johnson		1898	Pauline T. Johnson . . H. Shepard Johnson Otis A. Johnson
1883	. Joseph T. Wilson William R. Whitney Edmund B. Johnson		1899	Pauline T. Johnson . . H. Shepard Johnson Otis A. Johnson
1884	. Joseph T. Wilson William R. Whitney Edmund B. Johnson		1900	Charles B. Goodell . Frank M. Coakley Otis A. Johnson
1885	. . Joseph T. Wilson William R. Whitney Edmund B. Johnson		1901	Charles B. Goodell . Frank M. Coakley Otis A. Johnson
1886	. Joseph T. Wilson William R. Whitney Joseph W. Hammond		1902	Charles B. Goodell . Peter H. Lane Otis A. Johnson
1887	. Joseph T. Wilson Samuel H. Hudson Joseph W. Hammond		1903	Harry C. Wilson . Peter H. Lane Otis A. Johnson
1888	. Joseph T. Wilson Samuel H. Hudson Joseph W. Hammond		1904	Harry C. Wilson . Solomon Alley Otis A. Johnson
1889	. Joseph T. Wilson Samuel H. Hudson Charles D. Vary		1905	Harry C. Wilson . Solomon Alley Otis A. Johnson
1890	. Joseph T. Wilson T. Dexter Johnson Charles D. Vary		1906	Harry C. Wilson . Solomon Alley Otis A. Johnson James J. Deveney

LIST OF TOWN OFFICERS

1907	. .	. Francis B. Crocker, Jr. Solomon Alley James J. Deveney
1908	. .	. Francis B. Crocker, Jr. Otis A. Johnson James J. Deveney
1909	. .	. Francis B. Crocker, Jr. Otis A. Johnson James J. Deveney
1910	. .	. Francis B. Crocker, Jr. Otis A. Johnson James J. Deveney
1911	. .	. Francis B. Crocker, Jr. Otis A. Johnson James J. Deveney
1912	. .	. Frank H. Wilson, Jr. Otis A. Johnson Charles B. Goodell
1913	. .	. Frank H. Wilson, Jr. Otis A. Johnson Charles B. Goodell
1914	. .	. Frank H. Wilson, Jr. Otis A. Johnson Charles B. Goodell
1915	. .	. Frank E. Bruce Otis A. Johnson Charles B. Goodell
1916	. .	. Frank E. Bruce Fred A. Pirie Georgiana Wilson
1917	. .	. Frank E. Bruce Fred A. Pirie Georgiana Wilson
1918	. .	. Frank E. Bruce Fred A. Pirie Georgiana Wilson
1919	. .	. Frank E. Bruce Fred A. Pirie Georgiana Wilson
1920	. .	. Frank E. Bruce Fred A. Pirie John S. Tombeno
1921	. .	. Mary T. Cusick Fred A. Pirie John S. Tombeno
1922	. .	. Mary T. Cusick Arthur H. Wilson Abby M. Roland Harry R. Cummings John S. Tombeno Georgiana Wilson
1923	. .	. Mary T. Cusick Arthur H. Wilson Abby M. Roland Harry R. Cummings John S. Tombeno Georgiana Wilson
1924	. .	. Susan M. Crocker Harriet E. Ham Abby M. Roland Harry R. Cummings John S. Tombeno Georgiana Wilson
1925	. .	. Frank E. Roberts Harriet E. Ham Abby M. Roland Thomas A. Finn George W. Nixon Georgiana Wilson
1926	. .	. Frank E. Roberts Harriet E. Ham Abby M. Roland Thomas A. Finn George W. Nixon Georgiana Wilson
1927	. .	. Frank E. Roberts Harriet E. Ham Abby M. Roland Thomas A. Finn George W. Nixon Georgiana Wilson

Public Library Committees and Trustees

1871	Joseph T. Wilson Alfred D. Johnson Edward J. Johnson	1883–88	Henry Cabot Lodge Joseph T. Wilson William S. Otis
1872–76	Joseph T. Wilson Edward J. Johnson Alfred D. Johnson J. Nelson Borland	1889–96	Henry Cabot Lodge Joseph T. Wilson Albert G. Wilson
1877	Joseph T. Wilson Henry Cabot Lodge Alfred D. Johnson Edward J. Johnson	1897–1924	Henry Cabot Lodge Fred A. Wilson Albert G. Wilson
		1925–26	Isabella H. Williams Fred A. Wilson Albert G. Wilson
1878	Joseph T. Wilson Henry Cabot Lodge Alfred D. Johnson H. Shepard Johnson	1927	Isabella H. Williams Fred A. Wilson Winthrop T. Hodges
1879–82	Henry Cabot Lodge Joseph T. Wilson H. Shepard Johnson		

Highway Surveyors

1853–56	Alonzo Colby	1886–88	Henry T. Dunham
1857–61	Albert Whitney	1889–1905	Charles W. Stacy
1862	Albert Wyer	1906–07	George W. Kibbey
1863	Dexter Stetson	1908–19	Charles W. Stacy
1864–85	Walter Johnson	1920–27	Patrick J. O'Connor

Index

INDEX

Advisory committee 307
Agassiz, Elizabeth Cary 52
Agassiz, Prof. Louis 52 83 161 273 290 291 320
"Alice," the 114 319
Allen, Dr. Freeman 321
Allen, Rev. Henry F. 321
Alley, Hugh 37 38 39 40 41 46 47
"America," the 114
American Legion Auxiliary 363
American Legion monument 378
American Legion tablet 378
Amory, Charles 67 106 133 215 284 321
Amory, John 284
Amory, Robert 227 285
Amory, Thomas C. 285 287
Annexation to Lynn 314
Appleton, Thomas G. 114 283 286 319
Appleton, William 56 106 215 283 285 323
Appropriation shortcomings 307
Archibald, William B. 111
Assessor's appraisals 381 382
Assessors, Board of 346
Australian ballot system 344
Aviation, Harry Atwood 355

Bailey's Hill 201 326 332
Baker, Daniel C. 154 260
Balloting methods 344
Barges 81 228 229 230
Baseball 361
Bass Beach 197 312
Bass Point 142 156 201 271 325
Bass Point fire 331
Bass Point House 185 271 327
Bass Point Wharf 195
Bassett, Deliverance 42
Bassett, William 42
Bath house 312
Bay View House 76
Beaches, ownership of 205
Beal, James H. 224 312
Bear Pond 24 201 202
Beginnings of New England 3
Bird Collection 177
Black Mine 198
Black Rock 201 302
Black Rock Wharf 195
Blackstone 5
Blackstone, William 8
Blagden, Rev. George W. 50
Blanchard, Lieut.-Col. Harold 377

Blanchard, John A. 215 277 361
Boat House Beach 51 196
Bolger's Beach 196
Bootlegging 329
Borland, Dr. J. Nelson 172 309
Bosson, Judge Albert D. 274
Boston, Nahant and Pines Steamboat Company 156
Boyden, Mrs. C. C. 288
Boys' Club 270 362
Boy Scouts 350
Bradbury, Charles 46 106
Bradford, William 12
Bradlee, Frederick W. 285
Brann, Eugene H. 235 326 328
Breed, Allen 17 21 41
Breed, George Herbert 43 117
Breed, Jabez 42 43
Breed, Nehemiah 42 50
Breed, Samuel 40 41 42 43 44 50 73
Breed, William 42 96 170
"Bridal of Pennacook" 14
Brown, Sylvester 327
Bruce, Frank E. 358
Bryant, John F. 56 116
Bulfinch, Henry 75 268
Bull fight 96
Burchsted, Dr. John H. 37 40 41 43
Burnett, Frances Hodgson 320
"Butter Box" 273

Cabot, Henry 278 288
Cabot, Samuel 162 288
Cadet encampment 321 322
Calden, Capt. A. W. 155 181 194
Calf Spring 30, 31 51 63 202
Canary Club 352
Cannon Hill 201
Cannon owned by town 312
Canoe Beach 197
Carahar, Bernard F. 228
Carahar Brothers 149 228 229 271
Carahar, James A. 228 233 235 337
Cary, Emma F. 52 287 290
Cary, Thomas G. 52 106 273
Cary, Mrs. William F. 75 274 325
Castle Road 52
Castle Rock 197 312
Celebration for Senator Lodge 378
Cemetery 223
Cemetery gates 224

Central Wharf 192
Chadwick, Ebenezer and Christopher 277 288
"Chesapeake" and "Shannon" 96
Churches 213
    Independent Methodist 215 216 217 218 219
    Nahant 56 106 214 215 216 290
    Old Stone Schoolhouse 214
    Pastors 219 220
    Roman Catholic 219 220 221
    Y. M. C. A. 219
Civil War 103
Civil War list 104
Clark, Capt. Arthur H. 110 114
Clark, Benjamin C. 56 106 109 110 226 282
Clark, George M. 375
Clark, Col. Robert F. 110
Clark's Point 197 282
Coaches 81 99 196 197
Coakley, Thomas F. 46
Coast Guard Station 196 199 365
Cochran, Mildred G. 375
Cochran, Robert L. 105
Codman, Edward W. 274 289 315
Codman, Stephen 59 106 274 282 289
Colby, Alonzo 205 225 259 261 330
Colby Hill 330
Coles, Herbert 303 334
Coles, James A. 48 334
Coles, Robert 333
Conant, Roger 8
Coolidge, Hon. Calvin 375
Coolidge, Cornelius 55 73 106 191 192 216 286
Coolidge's Wharf 191
Copley, John Singleton 264
Covell, Samuel 117 259 367
Crescent Club 352
Crocker Chapter, F. R. A. A. 350
Crocker, Francis B. 117 238 350
Crocker, Richard H. 117
Crowninshield, Benjamin 131 281 286
Crystal Beach 134 190
Cummings, Harry R. 131
Curlew Beach 134 196
Curran, Martin 227
Curtis, George W. 276 320
Curtis, Horatio G. 275 276 353
Curtis, Louis and Lawrence 276 281 361
Curtis, Thomas B. 106 276
Cusick, Dr. Lawrence F. 130 379
Cusick, Mary T. 131
Cusick, Thomas J. 105 130

Dame, Luther 103
Decoration Day 224
Denier, John 197
Deveney, James J. 222
Dexter, Thomas 14 18 21 22 26 27
Dicken's Circle 351
Dixey, William 20 23
Donham, Michael 221

Dorchester Adventurers 8
Dorothy's Cove 189 196 201
Dory racing 116
Drew, Phineas 78 147
Drowning accident, Cole and Taylor 351
"Dr. Robbin's" Wharf 192
Duncan, Hon. George 277
Dunham, Capt. Henry 101 103 227
Dunham, Henry T. 101 227 259 311
Dwight, Dr. Thomas 133 220 282 288 315 321
Dwight, Thomas 282 283

Early houses 23 40
Early landing place 190 191
Eastern Railroad stock 259
Eastman, Dr. E. Porter 273
East Point and path 197 209
Eckley, David 106 283
"Edge hill" 261
Egg Rock 22 183 203
Eliot, Charles W. 241 286
Eliot, Samuel A. 106 109 215 241 286 288
Eliot, William H. 106 214 286
Ellingwood Chapel 224
Emerson, Ralph Waldo 319
Endicott, John 8 21
Estates broken up 342
Expenditures compared 389 390 391
Expenditures per family 387 388 389
Expenditures per inhabitant 389

Farming 136
Farrell, John 221 272
Fay, Dudley B. 74 192 278 361
Felton, Prof. Cornelius C. 53 273 290 319
Fferne, Susanna 37 38
Field, Cyrus W. 320
Fields, James T. 320
Fiftieth anniversary celebration 346 347 348
Finnerty, Daniel G. 130 340 352 368 369
Fire Department 268
    Babcock extinguisher 293
    Bass Point engine house 294
    "Dexter No. 1" 268 292 293 294
    "Eagle" 263 292 293
    Engine house 269 290 314
    Extinguishers 293
    Fire alarm system 294
    Fire records 296 297
    First Board of Engineers 293
    Hose companies 294
    Humorous account of fire 304 305
    Motorized apparatus 295
    Nathan Mower Company 294
    Relief Hook and Ladder Company 293
    "Truck house" 293
    Use of horses 294
    Water supply 296
Fishing 24 131 190
Flagpole at Bass Beach 312 325

INDEX

Flash Road 30 52
Flora of Nahant 211
Flynn, John 221
Follen, Agnes 302
Forester's department 302 303
Fort Gardner 333
Fox Hill 31
Foye, Caroline M. 180 325
Franklin, Benjamin 92 168
Fremont, John C. 134 196 264 283
Friday Night Club 351
Fuller, Andrew G. 327

Garden Club 265
Garden exhibitions 374
Geology of Nahant 87 212
Gibson, Charles H. 281
Girl Scouts 350
Girls' Community Club 351
Goodell, Arthur S. 302
Goodell, Byron 228 302
Gorges, Sir Ferdinando 7 8 9
Gosnold, Bartholomew 4 13
Gove, Anna H. 117
Gove, Charles E. 116 120 220 263 297 310 363
Gove, Edith H. 43 117
Gove, George A. 116
Gove, Joseph H. 117 362
Gove, Worthen 134 220
Government purchase of land 332
Grant, Patrick 54
Grant, Judge Robert 54
Gravel pit 310
Graves, Thomas 37 40
Gray, Jeremiah 43 46 47
Gray, John C. 46 277
Great and Little Furnace 200
Great Marsh 63
Great Pasture 272 311
Green, Charles R. 56 215
Green, George H. 359
Greene, Gardiner 106 282 284
Greenlawn Cemetery 223
Greenough, Horatio 276
Greenough, Richard Saltonstall 276
Grover, Olive R. 350
Guild, Hon. Curtis 341 347 366
Guild, Lieut. Henry R. 377
Guild, Samuel E. 54
Gurney, Capt. William 101

Hammond, Caroline V. 181 244
Hammond, Charles A. 13 180 186 187 248 262 264
Hammond, John Q. 67 180 205 217 225 244 258 262 280 292 338
Hammond Joseph W. 338
Hammond, Mason W. 116 359
Hammond, Samuel 32 106 111 116 281 288 359 368 371
Harmony Court 277

Harte, Richard 275 281
Haven, Dr. Henry C. 321 322
Hay, Allan 148
Hennessy, Maj. William 368
Higgins, Morris 221
Highest part of Nahant 201
Highway department 268 301
  Beginnings 301
Hobbs, Walter L. 274
Hodges, Dr. Richard M. 339
Hodges, Dr. William D. 339
Hodges, Winthrop T. 173 262 339 359 362 371
Hogan, George F. 359
Holmes, Oliver Wendell 321
Home Guard 70 103 134
Hood, Abby May 45 124
Hood, Abner 43 44 45 46 50 55 169 277
Hood, Ann Amelia 45 196
Hood, Ann Maria 45
Hood, Annie 41 46
Hood Benjamin 45 46 169
Hood, Ebenezer 45 46 169
Hood Elbridge 45 46
Hood, Elbridge Gerry 45 105
Hood, Julia Pond 45 196
Hood. Louisa Phillips 45
Hood, Rebecca 41 46
Hood, Richard 43 44 45 46 50 51 74 169 240
Hood, Theodate 43 45 46
Hotels:
  Bayside Inn 327
  Bay View House 76 327
  Brenton 328 362
  Edgehill 261
  Nahant 53 76 226 289
  Nahant House 73 192
  "Old Castle" 72
  Rice 44 73 289
  Tudor 75 189
  Whitney 37 40 42 43 44 61 74 190 226 289
"Hotel Tremont" 270
Hotel Tudor 75 366
Houses, dates of construction 124
Howard, Charles, and family 261
Howe, Thomas 270
Howells, William Dean 270 320
Hudson, Miss Harriett E. 276
Hudson, Samuel H. 175 338
Hutchinson, E. J. 75
Hyde, Edward J. 221

Inches, George B. 282 289
Indian collection 177
Indian encampment 197
Indians 11
Industries 123
Ingalls, Edmund and Francis 20
Ingersoll, Capt. Joseph B. 155
Inhabitants, early 266
Insurance rates 331

INDEX

Irene's Grotto 197
Irish 221
Iron Mine 198
Iron Works, Saugus 26 198

Jackson, James 172
James, Ellerton 57 191 210 233 288 343 371 373 375
James, George Abbot 53 209 278 280 283 302 314 353 362
Jewett, Sarah Orne 320
John's Peril 199
Johnson, Alfred D. 68 101 133 172 227 238 262 307 308 313
Johnson, Annie E. 181 276 313 314 340
Johnson, Arthur S. 100 359
Johnson, Benjamin 47 276
Johnson, Caleb 47 48 50 96 128 131 132 133 147 169 172 217 278 306
Johnson, Caleb H. 129
Johnson, Caroline M. 276
Johnson, Charles B. 181 276 300
Johnson, Charles Cabot 235 338
Johnson, Charles F. 123 216 278 354
Johnson, Rev. Charles T. 354
Johnson, C. Hervey 48 75 172 337
Johnson, C. Warren 268
Johnson, David 223 259 354
Johnson, E. Augustus 131 276
Johnson, Edmund B. 50 74 228 240 277
Johnson, Edward 47 100
Johnson, Edward C. 100 342 355
Johnson, Edward J. 136 172 175 176 244 313 340
Johnson, Edward Kirke 101 102
Johnson, Edwin W. 129 130 308 310
Johnson, F. Henry 102 220
Johnson, Florence A. 136 244 354
Johnson, Francis 75 135 154 196 205 217 277
Johnson, Francis H. 135 196 224 371
Johnson, Frank E. 196
Johnson, Franklin E. 101 231
Johnson, George L. 128 268 369
Johnson Homestead 43 47 48 72 190
Johnson, H. Shepard 172 175 196 338 362
Johnson, J. Bishop 100 120 135 340 354
Johnson, Jesse R. 238
Johnson, Jonathan 43 46 47 50 100 101 181
Johnson, Jonathan 75 134 136 181 276 313
Johnson, Jonathan E. 136 175 339
Johnson, Joseph 47 48 51 74 101 132 133 136 168 169 181 217 241 277 306 354
Johnson, Capt. Joseph 50 51 72 201
Johnson Joseph 277 354
Johnson, Luther S. 105 224
Johnson, Mary 354
Johnson, Admiral Mortimer L. 104 105
Johnson, Otis A. 339 344 351 354
Johnson, Samuel 100 114
Johnson, S. Martin 227 354
Johnson, T. Dexter 129 130 253

Johnson, Walter 105 217 223 258 259 260 262 273 277 302 315
Johnson, Washington H. 223 256 258 260 261 310 313 321
Johnson, Welcome J. 48 200
Johnson, Welcome W. 128 129 130 216 221 256 257 262 289 311 339
Johnson, William 354
Johnson, William F. 61 129 216 258 260 268 277
Johnson, William R. 216
Johnson's Express 101 238
Joseph's Beach 197
Joy, Charles H. 275
Joy, Joseph G. 99 275

Keezer, Frank 328
Kemp, Capt. Charles F. 117 376
Kemp, Capt. Joseph H. 117
Kemp, Capt. William H. 114 117 194 354
Kibbey, George W. 46 228
Killilae, James H. 300
Killilae, John R. 300
Killilae, Roger 184 300
King, Samuel G. 273

Labor efficiency 391 392
Labor used by the town 138
Lane, Peter 221 300
Larkin, Thomas H. 298
Lawn tennis and its players 322 323 324
Lawrence, Abbott 104 106 282 360
Lawrence, Amos 162 217
Lawrence, Amos A. 110 282 285 309
Lawrence, Katharine Bigelow 285
Lawrence, Rt. Rev. William 282 323
Lawrence, Dr. William R. 217 270
Leavitt, Charles F. 202
Lecture courses 249 353
Lewis, Alonzo 63 210 221
Lewis Beach 201
Lewis, Mayland P. 377
Libbey, Fred B. 46
Lighthouses 141 203 204 205
Lighting:
   Electric 300
   Gas 301
   Gasoline 300
   Municipal plant 343
   Street 299 300 301
   Underground wiring 343
Lincoln, Alexander 320
Lindsey, Christopher 22 40
Linehan, Patrick 105
Linn, named 25
Little Bridge 210
Little Nahant 147 200 270 271
Little Nahant Improvement Association 359
Little Nahant Land Company 271
Lobstering 133
Location of public buildings 371

INDEX

Lodge, George Cabot 367
Lodge, Henry Cabot 53 80 162 172 175 203 238 278 279 280 307 310 311 316 318 342 347 365 366 367 370 371 378
Lodge, John E. 103 106 209 215 278 280 320
"Lodge Villa" 37 39 56 278 320
"Log Cabin" 99 196 275
London Company 3 5 7
Long Beach and its road 141 142 143 144 147 200 259 265 345
Long Beach breakwater 21 145 147 148
Longfellow Beach 51 196
Longfellow, Charles A. 114 319
Longfellow, Henry W. 85 277 283 286 313 318 319
Lovering, J. S. and C. T. 216 284
Lowell, A. Lawrence 284 285
Lowell, Augustus 285
Lowell, John Amory 106 110 284
Lowell, Ralph 54 284
Lund, Capt. Thomas W. 156
Luscomb, William 221 310
Lynn, incorporated 23
Lynn Harbor flats 200
Lynn Steamboat Company 158

Maolis Club 64 352 355
Maolis Gardens 68 138 180 192 326
Maolis House 186
Maolis Pool and Spring 180 182
Map of Nahant 263
Marblehead Water Company 317
Marginal Road 68 185
Marjoram Hill 189 209 283 353
Marram grass 146
Mary's Grotto 200
Massachusetts Indians 11
Master King's schoolboys 327
Mather, Rev. Cotton 12
Maverick, Samuel 8
May, Rev. Samuel J. 214 241
McBurney, Charles 261
McIntosh, Mrs. Alice C. 43 44 175 268
McLaughlin, William J. 277
Melvin, Mrs. Sarah J. 75 135
Merriam, Frank 216 276 361
Metropolitan water supply 317
Miantonomo 38
Mifflin, Dr. Charles 241 286
Mifflin, George H. 241 286 288
Mills, James 30 39 40 41 189
Moderator 367
Moering, Mrs. A. L. 285 321
Montowampote 12 13
Mortimer G. Robbins Post 215, A. L. 356
Morton, Thomas 8
Motley, Edward 275 356
Motley, J. Lothrop 241 275 320 371
Motley, Thomas 234 281 345 356 361
Mountford, Rev. William 281

Mower, John D. 326
Mower, Nathan 326
Murdock, Artemus 75 223 258 260 318

Na-an 13
Nahanta 13
Nahant, a residential town 334 335
Nahant Auxiliary of Lynn Chapter, A. R. C. 358 373
Nahant Book Club 356
Nahant Club 61 65 360
Nahant divided 28
Nahant Dory Club 194 359
Nahant Firemen's Relief Association 363
Nahant, first town warrant 256
Nahant Golf Club 355
Nahant Hotel 53 76 226 288
Nahant House 73 192
Nahantiana 177
Nahant in 1800 50
Nahant incorporated 147 254
Nahant laid out 27 28 36
Nahant Land Company 71 288
Nahant Magazine Club 351
Nahant Mutual Benefit Association 363
Nahant, old roads 27 30 31
Nahant ranges 28 29 30
Nahant Road 30 51
Nahant Street 36 42
Nahant titles 35
Nahant Women's Club 353 354
Nanapashemet 12 17
Newhall, Benjamin F. 164
New Town Hall 368 369 370 371
Nichols, Lyman 275
Nineties, the glorious 337
Nipper Stage 134 191 194 283 319
North Spring 180 326
Noyes, Rev. George S. 260

O'Connor, P. J. 221
O'Connor, Thomas P. 225
"Old Castle" 50 72 235 271 289 325
Old Stone barn 64 272
Old Stone Schoolhouse 170 214 241
Old store 128
Old Wharf 191
Olmstead, Frederick Law 148
O'Shaughnessy, Patrick 221
Otis, Herbert Foster 116 173 177 277
Otis, William S. 173
Oxnard, George D. 111

Paige, James W. 103 216 217 283 320
Paine, Gen. Charles J. 111 115 288
Paine, Frank C. 111
Paine, William 26 53 76
Palmer, Charles H. 46 259
Palmer, Julius A., Jr. 312
Parent Teachers Association 252 350

Parker, E. Francis 155 227 309 315 316
Parker, Francis S. 359 368
Parker, Frederick 368
Passaconaway 13 14
Pasturage on Nahant 22 26 27 270
Peabody, George 73 192 278 288
Peabody, Joseph A. 106 278
Pea Island 197
Peninsular Club 351
Perkins, George U. and James C. 280 281 311
Perkins, Samuel 75 106 289
Perkins, Thomas Handasyd 52 59 61 78 106 109 162 215 223 274 287 290
Perry, Arthur 56 57 110 277 282
Petticoat Beach 197
Phillips, Charles A. 379
Phillips, Edward B. 283
Phillips, E. D. 106
Phillips, Frank G. 259 297
Phillips, George W. 50
Phillips, John 50
Phillips, Rev. John C. 50
Phillips, Wendell 50
Pilgrim Society 5
Piper, Dr. R. U. 68
"Piper Guards" 70 103
Pirie, Fred A. 372
Playground 209
Plymouth 5 18
Plymouth Company 3 4 6
Point of Pines 157
Poland, Emma L. 351
Poland, George E. 129 130 343
Police department 268 297
    Early days 297
    Police station 298
Pond Beach 201
Popham, Sir John 4
Poquanum 13 14 17 18
Post Office 130 227
Prescott, Judge William 106 215 285 288 290
Prescott, William H. 85 106 285
Prince, James 162 163
Prince, Dr. Morton 278 377
Progress of steam 158
Proprietors of Nahant Pastures 270
Public Library 54 168
Public Library building 175
Public Safety Committee 372
Puritan exodus 9
Putnam, Mrs. J. P. 61 262

Quakers 36

Racing on Long Beach 97
Railroad 98 147 230
Ram Pasture 29 30 53 55 76
Range finding station 332
Range roads and ranges 29
Reed Cove 201

Regattas 111 113
Registrars, Board of 346
Relay House 158 186 271 326
Relay House Wharf 195
Revere Beach 156
Reynolds, Dr. Edward 50
Reynolds, Edward P. 315
Reynolds, Dr. John P. 50
Rice, Henry G. 54 106
Rice House 46 73 81 289
Rice, Jesse 43 44 55 74 81 170 217 226 258
Richards, Albert J. 177
Richards, George L. 186
Richardson, Charles H. 372
Richardson, W. K. 370
Riley, Patrick 221
Road by Castle Rock 312
Roads 264 265
    Castle 52
    Flash 52
    List of, in 1885 314
    Long Beach 143 144 147 200 345
    Marginal 183 198
    Nahant 51 52
    Naming of 313 314
    Old 30 31 51
    Road by Castle Rock 313 314
    Watering 316
    Willow 189
Robbins, Dr. Edward H. 53 56 78 106 288 290
Robbins, Mortimer G. 356
Robertson, David 46
Robertson, R. H. 117
Robinson, Mrs. A. E. 75 261
Robinson, Harold W. 178
Rodman, Miss Emma 275
Roland, Thomas 45 46 123 170 219 225 303
Roller skating 351
Roosevelt, Theodore 365
Rouillard, Frederick 75 128
Russell, Miss Mary 274 277
Russell, Nathaniel P. 56 106 277
Russell, Samuel H. 32 178 215 216 277 288

Sagamore Hill 12 13 15 93
Sanborn, Dana A. 356 357 358
Sand Point 200
Saunders Ledge 198
Savage Rock 15
Schlesinger, Barthold 228 261 322
Schools 240
    Art committee 251
    Carrie V. Hammond 243
    Committee changed to six 252 367
    Early list of pupils 240 241
    Exhibitions 248
    Expenses 250
    First "School Room" 240
    First school superintendent 248
    Florence A. Johnson 244

INDEX

Schools — *Con.*
  Grammar schoolhouse 243
  High 242
  J. T. Wilson schoolhouse 243
  Junior high school 247
  Lecture courses 249 353
  Lists of teachers 243
  Medals 252
  Nellie M. Palmer 245
  Old Stone 170 241 251
  Pleasant Street building 241
  Pupils to Lynn 247
  School books 242
  Schoolhouse 314
  School physician 251
  Summer Street primary schoolroom 242
  Valley Road schoolhouse 243
Sea clams 161
Sea serpent 160 187
Sea sleds 159
Sears, Miss Clara Endicott 324 374
Sears, David 56 106 215 275 277 283 288
Sears, Frederick R. 37 39 216 278 345 371
Sears, Knyvet W. 131 278 281
Separation from Lynn 147
Seventy-fifth anniversary celebration 348
Sewerage system 315 316 334
Shaughnessy, James C. 80 221 261 313 372
Sherman, Lawrence F. 156 358 375
Shipwrecks 25 140
Shoemaking 137
Short Beach 196 199 264
Sidewalks 301 311
Sigourney, Henry 49 240
Silsbee, Nathan 50 72
Simmons, George W. 264 270 271 313
Simpson, John 105
Small houses 386 387 388
Smallpox 93
Smith, Capt. John 4 5 7
Snake Hill 274
Snelling, Samuel G. 275 281
Soldiers in World War 376 377
Soldiers' monuments 225
Soule & Son 149
South Garden 65
Southwick, Walter H. 235 298 327 328 338 345 371
Spanish-American War 332 367
Spouting Horn 198
Spouting Horn path 208
Sprague, Dr. Francis P. 54 284
Spring Road Well 202
Stacy, Charles W. 302
State reservation 149 334
Steamboat landing 191
Steamboat service 151 329
Steamboat subsidy 155
Stetson, Dexter 45 46 75 99 196 217 223 257 258 259 260

Stetson, Helen 45 196
Stevens, Paran 79 80
Stone barn 64
Stone crusher 338
Stone Lions 187
Stone Reservoir 202
Stony Beach 198
Storms 140 141 145
Story, Judge Joseph 275
Story, William Wetmore 276
Stowe, Harriet Beecher 321
Street lighting 299 300 301
Strout, Edward E. 50 73 235 271 355
Summer hotel resort 81 82 83
Summer residents, list 106
Sumner, Charles 319
Sunset Hill 31
Swallows Cave 18 191 197

Tarbox, Samuel and Nelson 221
Taxation 380 382
Tax dodgers 303 304 313
Tax rates 385
Taylor, B. Frank 117 194
Taylor, Eben 117
Taylor, Fred 117
Taylor, George B. 117 120
Taylor, George W. 117 194
Thacher, Anthony 25
Thorndike, Albert 227
Thorndike, Dr. Augustus 285
Thorndike, Charles 285, 322
Thorwald 16
Tightrope performer 197
Timmins, Fred L. 101, 227
Town Hall 128 131 242 265 368
Town Land at Little Nahant 264
Town officers lists 393
Town reports 307, 318
Transatlantic yacht racing 114
Tree cutting 27, 51
Tree planting 169
Trees on Long Beach 150
Trimountain House 271 322 326
Tudor anecdotes 68
Tudor, Mrs. Fenno 65 70 130 185 192 219
Tudor, Frederick 43 57 75 104 106 109 147 180 188 195 215 227 259 265 274 283 289 290 307 361
Tudor Gardens 63
Tudor Orchard 64
Tudor Wharf 134 193
Tudor, William 314
Typhoid epidemic 315

Upham, George P. 208, 361

Valuations 380 381 382 384 385
Vary, Charles D. 337 356 368
Village Improvement Society 352
Village store 128, 289

Walker, Nathaniel 104
Ward, Mrs. Elizabeth Stuart Phelps 320
Warren, Dr. John Collins 281 285
Warren, Dr. John Mason 281
Washington Street 28
Watering carts 316
Water supply 315 316 317
Waters, William F. 241 339 340
Webster, Daniel 68 283 320 321
Weetamoo 14
Welcome home celebration 377
"Welcome home" for Senator Lodge 378
Wenepoykin 13 14
Wenuchus 18
West Cliff 201
Weston, Thomas 7
Weymouth, George 4 7
Wharves:
    Bass Point 156 195
    Black Rock 158 195
    Central 186 192
    Coolidge 191
    "Dr. Robbins" 192
    Early landings 190 191
    Nipper Stage 134 189 192
    Old 191
    Relay House 195
    Tudor 134 156 186 189 193
White, James C. 46
"Whiteweed Fields" 273 275
Whiting, Rev. Samuel 25 213
Whitney, Albert 43 44 74 259 261 268
Whitney, Benjamin C. 268
Whitney Homestead. See Whitney's Hotel.
Whitney's Hotel 37 40 42 43 44 61 74 226 289 366

Whitney, Thomas P. 183 272 280
Whitney, William R. 268 363
Whittemore, C. J. 274
Whittier, John Greenleaf 320
Williams, Mrs. Elisha H. 286
Williams, Wallace D. 111 129 173 277
Willis, Nathaniel P. 320
Willow Beach 189 196
Willow Road 189
Wilson, Capt. Albert 311
Wilson, Albert G. 128 173 302 311 339
Wilson, Frank H. 311 351
Wilson, Fred A. 124 156 173 176 233 234 341 343 344 358 367 368 373 379
Wilson, Harry C. 337 362 372 377
Wilson, J. Colby 128 311 337
Wilson, Joseph T. 124 155 172 202 231 233 245 271 274 279 298 308 309 310 311 314 317 328 337 341 343 345 346 354 365
Winn, Patrick H. 69
Winslow, Dr. Frederic 275
Winthrop, John 9 21
Winthrop, Robert C. 321
Witch House 186 187
Wollaston, Captain 8
Wonohaquham 12
Wood, George A. 359 373
Wood Hall 355
Wood, William 14 16 17
Wood, William 54 61 168 169 241 355
World War 376
Wright, Mrs. John S. 275

Yachting 109
Young, Philip 75

www.ingramcontent.com/pod-product-compliance
Lightning Source LLC
Chambersburg PA
CBHW071220290426
44108CB00013B/1234